Corrupting the IMAGE II

Corrupting the Image 2

Hybrids, Hades and the Mt Hermon Connection

Dr. Douglas M Hamp

Eskaton Media Group

2021

Corrupting the Image 2
Hybrids, Hades and the Mt Hermon Connection

Copyright © 2021 by Dr. Douglas Hamp
www.douglashamp.com

Published by Eskaton Media Group

ISBN: 978-1-63821-416-8

Cover by Sebby Sandu – Aesthetica Society

Unless otherwise indicated, all Scripture quotations are taken from the New King James Version, Thomas Nelson Publishers (1997). The Hebrew text is from the Biblia Hebraica Stugartensia. The Greek Old Testament Scriptures are from the Septuagint. New Testament Greek quotations are from the Greek New Testament according to the Byzantine Text form, edited by Maurice A. Robinson and William G. Pierpont, 2000 edition; this is the edition by Pierpont and Robinson of a Majority, or Byzantine, text of the NT. Quotations marked KJV are from the King James Version. Quotations marked ESV are from the English Standard Version. Quotations marked ISV are International Standard Version. Quotations marked NET are from the New English Translation. Quotations marked NASB are from the New American Standard Bible. Quotations marked HCSB are from the Holman Christian Standard Bible. All Scripture quotations have been retrieved using the Word Bible Software www.theword.net. All emphases of Scripture verses are mine.

First printing 2021,

Printed in the United States of America.

Endorsements

Corrupting the Image 2 is not just valuable for its immense quantity of linguistic, biblical, and archeological nuggets, but Dr. Hamp synthesizes his research into a thrilling cosmic plotline that leaves the reader exclaiming, "The gig is up on Satan!" The more you learn about Satan's machinations, the more you will love Jesus for defeating him. I will be returning to this book repeatedly in the course of my studies. – **Dr. Alan E. Kurschner, Founder of Eschatos Ministries**

Dr. Douglas Hamp has done his homework...and then some! – **Dr. L. A. Marzulli**

Corrupting the Image 2 is a tremendous work that not only relates prophecies pertinent to the day, but also ties them in with the larger ancient world, especially that of Mesopotamia. If you are looking for an intelligence report based on the most current reconnaissance on the demonic realm, look no further. – **Dr. Judd H. Burton, Director and Senior Fellow, Institute of Biblical Anthropology**

Dr. Hamp provides an in-depth study of biblical angelology and demonology against the backdrop of ancient Near Eastern worldviews. Using a detailed comparative analysis of Satan's titles in the Bible and extra-biblical sources, Doug lays out a theological roadmap for understanding spiritual warfare through the lens of the ancient Israelites and their neighbors. This book is written from a Christian perspective with an emphasis on unmasking Satan's tactics to corrupt God's image in humans. Diligent students of Scripture will greatly benefit from this thought-provoking study. – **Dr. Igal German, Founding Director, Yesod Bible Center.**

Dr. Hamp's ability to combine his keen understanding of the original biblical languages, new archeological discoveries, and pertinent end-time prophecy is a gift to the body of Christ. *Corrupting the Image 2* has the potential of capturing the attention of an entire generation that has dismissed biblical prophecy and awaken them to the hour in which we live! – **Dr. Michael K. Lake Author, The Shinar Directive**

Douglas Hamp does his homework! The information he presents is timely, riveting and on target. Just when you thought you knew it all, think again! Douglas digs deep and unearths treasures you never imagined existed. Be warned! Once you open his book, you won't be able to put it down!" – **Christina Lynn Leaz, Host Truth Hunters TV & Author of Soul Deceiver**

This book proves one of the most important concepts: God is good. He is so incredibly good that He can be trusted. This is the theme that underpins Dr. Hamp's teachings. In *Corrupting the Image 2*, he unravels mysteries and solves linguistic puzzles to expose the perverted genius of Satan—all the while teaching us lessons about how our pride, lust and hubris play into Satan's plan. The historical evidence is overwhelming. Dr. Hamp interprets the ancient artifacts and connects their meaning with the cosmic story. When Alexander Hislop published *Two Babylons* in 1853, he was trying to connect the dots, but only focused on the roots of Catholicism and was criticized for his lack of proof texts. He lacked the technical skills to prove his theory. However, Dr. Hamp tracked the beginning to the end and proved the theorem: Systematic evil has plotted the demise of humankind throughout history. Despite humans bumbling everything, their kind Creator has patiently made chess-moves to defeat evil and reunite the family. – **Kimberly Sikes, Attorney.**

Reading Hamp's extensive "crime scene investigations" through antiquity is like Alexander Hislop's *Two Babylons*, coupled with G. H. Pember's *Earth's Earliest Ages* taken to the 10ᵗʰ Power. This is for those who demand scholarly research! It is impossible to put this book down because each page builds upon the other like a prosecuting attorney building his case resulting in the most egregious conviction. This five-star volume is a masterful treatise that will change your view of world history and how the Bible's accounting substantiates the mysteries until now, have been bound in antiquity's ambiguities. Hamp has sliced through the Gordian Knot of utter darkness exposing Satan – the Beast – the Second Beast and the Woman Who Rides the Beast! – **Doug Krieger – Chair, the Commonwealth of Israel Foundation – Author and Publisher of Tribnet Publications**

Dr. Douglas Hamp's tome generously offers Christians critical cognitive content to help discern current and coming events sponsored by forces both seen and unseen, which will soon overwhelm this unsuspecting generation. Dr. Hamp guides you through a riveting forensic etymological audit and historical journey through the ancient world, all the while linking in many of prehistory's most infamous events and figures such as: Satan, Enki, Baal, Gilgamesh, Nimrod, Og, Rephaim and many more. Along the journey, Pastor Hamp reveals the amazing stories behind the stories, whisking away the insipid secular fog. – **Gary Wayne – Author of Genesis Six Conspiracy**

Dr. Hamp's knowledge of language, history, and the Scriptures in Corrupting the Image 2 pulls back the curtain on the real identity of the "devil" providing clarity and insight to answer questions you may have not known how to ask! If you have sought after wisdom, then you should get this book and gain understanding! – **Chad Schafer – Author of The World in the Bondage of Egypt**

Contents

Table of Figures

List of Tables

Foreword

The advances in science and technology over the last century would be almost incomprehensible to someone living just after World War I. The New breakthroughs are announced at a frightening pace; it's estimated that the current rate of innovation means we will experience something like 20,000 years' worth of progress during the twenty-first century alone.

Unfortunately, the way most seminaries and pastors teach the Bible is that God operates in a vacuum. Surveys reveal most American Christians do not believe Satan or the Holy Spirit are real. We appear to believe that demons were completely destroyed by the end of the Apostolic Age, around 100 AD, because most of us don't acknowledge their existence or influence today. And forget about the weirder creatures in the Bible, like the pagan gods, giants who walked the earth before the Flood, the multi-headed sea-dragon Leviathan, and don't even start with Ezekiel's wheels!

Yet, if the supernatural enemies of God are not real, then many of His actions, especially in the Old Testament, are nearly impossible to understand, which skeptics frequently point out. They establish a false premise—gods and demons are imaginary—so they can condemn the Creator by portraying Him as cruel and capricious, or just deny His existence altogether.

We Christians make the task of defending the faith more difficult by conceding the supernatural foundation of the Bible before the argument even begins. And we do ourselves no favors by reading our twenty-first century western worldview into books that were written on the other side of the world two or three thousand years ago. Nevertheless, it is not all our fault; until the last hundred years or so, the existence of texts that give context to some of the weirder parts of the Bible were still buried in Syria, Iraq, Turkey, Lebanon, Jordan, and Israel. But recent archaeological discoveries are opening up the Bible, giving us a better understanding of what the apostles and prophets knew about their neighbors, what they believed, and how that influenced and deceived the people of ancient Israel.

In his new book, Dr. Doug Hamp digs into the iconography and epigraphy of Mesopotamia to expose the many faces Satan showed to the pagans of the ancient world. Some of Doug's research is truly groundbreaking. I promise you; Doug's new book will be cited in at least two of the books Sharon and I have on the drawing board for the next couple of years. Doug has applied peer-reviewed research to reveal Satan's secret identities, linking him to a number of pagan deities in the Mediterranean world from ancient Sumer to classical Greece and Rome. He shows how one of the most popular pagan goddesses in history plays a key role in the end times prophesied by John the Revelator. And Doug has established—for the first time anywhere, as far as I know—a solid connection between the chief god of ancient Sumer and Babylon and the sacred mountain where two hundred "sons of God" made a mutual pact to carry out their plot to corrupt the bearers of His image, humankind.

To be clear, Doug is not at all suggesting that we should validate the truth of the Bible with pagan texts. Rather, a deeper understanding of the beliefs of the pagans who were in contact with ancient Israel help us to better understand why the prophets and apostles wrote what they did—and, more importantly, the significance of what God has done through His plan for our salvation.

It's always a joy to read something that adds to my understanding of the Word of God. Dr. Doug Hamp has provided us with key pieces to the puzzle of history—which will help us grow in our understanding of HIS story. – **Derek Gilbert – Author** *Giants, Gods, and Dragons* **(with Sharon K. Gilbert) and TV Host Skywatch.tv**

Acknowledgements

Thank you to the people who helped with the editing and proofing of this book! Special thanks to you, Kimberly Sikes, for the amazing attention to detail and the numerous hours you invested in editing the book! Thanks to Sarah Rush and Nancy Dobbs as well for the very helpful editing and proofing. And thank you Bob Rico, Ed Doss, Gary Schmidt, for reading early drafts and giving me important feedback. Thanks Chris Steinle for the feedback and for doing the book formatting.

About the Author

Douglas Hamp earned his M.A. in the Bible and its World from the Hebrew University of Jerusalem and his PhD in Biblical Studies from Louisiana Baptist University. He served as an assistant pastor at Calvary Chapel Costa Mesa for six years, where he lectured and developed curriculum at the School of Ministry, Spanish School of Ministry and Calvary Chapel Bible College Graduate School. He is the author of numerous books, articles, & DVDs and has appeared on national and international TV, radio, and  internet programs in English and in Spanish. He is senior pastor of the Way Congregation in Denver, CO.

Preface

Revelation 17 speaks of a mystery of a beast that was, is not, and ascends out of the Abyss and of a woman that rides it. Solving this mystery is the core inquiry of this book and is in fact a continuation of *Corrupting the Image Vol. 1: Angels, Aliens, and the Antichrist Revealed,* where we detected something ominous coming upon the world. Satan has attempted to corrupt man's DNA through the creation of Nephilim in an effort to prevent the coming of the Seed of the woman. We see strange events happening today with the advent of UFOs and supposed alien abductions.

In *Corrupting the Image Vol. 2: Hybrids, Hades and the Mt Hermon Connection,* we will answer the question of the ancient origins of the Beast who was and the woman he carries, and break open Satan's ancient aliases. We will explore the tactics of his long war against God and how God has thwarted his efforts, culminating in the first coming of Jesus. In the next volume, *Corrupting the Image Vol 3,* we will look at the events, technologies and greed that take mankind to the brink of extinction. We will learn the identity of Gog, the location, the detailed events of the final battle, and the one thing that will cause Jesus to return.

My method: I have based my research on the accuracy of God's Word which gives us the true picture of what happened in the ancient world. The method of discovery throughout this book is to take the words as literally as possible and use the grammatical-historical approach of interpretation, which we will find allows all the pieces of this puzzle to fit precisely.

For example, we will learn that Nimrod means rebel; it is not his name, but a title. It actually comes from the Akkadian Ninurta which means Lord of the Earth. Although he claimed he was "Lord of the Earth", the Bible reveals that he was just a "rebel".

Throughout the book, we will compare the version of events related from Mesopotamian sources with the foundational Bible account of events to find the truth.

Reading Plan: There are parts of this book that go into great detail at times to provide the evidence of what has happened and what is coming. Because we are looking into the ancient near east (ANE), we have to roll up our sleeves and dig into the original sources written in Sumerian, Akkadian, Hebrew, Aramaic and Greek. Sumerian is typically written in either CAPITALS or with s p a c e s between the letters and sometimes like this: ᵈEn.lil. The superscript "d" stands for *Dingir* and means "god". I have labored to write the book in a non-technical way. I invite you to consult the endnotes where I put some of the finer details and references to the source material. Of course, you can always skip ahead if the details are not your thing. I have included several vignettes written as short narratives that put the various elements in a story format to help the reader put it all together.

To Contact Me: Please visit my website douglashamp.com to leave comments on the book or to reach me with a question or to request for me to come and speak at your group. You can write me at doughamp@gmail.com. If you visit or live in Denver, join us at The Way Congregation in Lakewood, CO.

MILESTONES

Figure 1 Roman Milestone on the Road of the Patriarchs between Jerusalem and Hebron.

Milestones were stones placed along Roman roads to let the traveler know how far he had traveled. This book is arranged in chapters that serve as milestones. Each one teaches an important part of a whole, larger story. Each chapter builds upon the one before it so that you can gradually understand the diabolic scheme Satan has enacted and how God has been thwarting his plans. We will have three major milestones, one after each section, to give you a breather on the journey before heading to the next section.

REFERENCE:
TABLE OF SATAN'S SYNCRETISMS AND EPITHETS

As you journey through the book, use this table to follow the many names, aliases, titles and parallel identities Satan has had throughout the Ancient Near East and the Bible. The following names are either a syncretism (an alternate title) of Satan or "sons of Satan" who were syncretisms of Nimrod, but were often used interchangeably with Satan as his Babylonian religious system spread. Enlil is the direct title for Satan in Isaiah 14:12. All of the ANE syncretisms listed below will be covered in the book.

Names & Titles of Satan & sons of Satan in the Bible & ANE		
Syncretism	Epithets or meaning	Reference
Enlil (Heilel) = ^dBAD (=IDIM) [▷══◁] = Batios	Lord Wind, KUR.GAL (Great mountain), Great Dragon, Prince of the power of the air, and BAD.BAD= Ug "dead / death" BE=Bel=Lord	Isa 14:12, Eph 2:2, Jer 51:25, Rev 12:9, ANE, Mt Hermon

Table 1 Names & Titles of Satan & sons of Satan in the Bible & ANE

(Continued on adjacent page)

The following are syncretisms of Enlil (or sons of Enlil)		
Amurru (MARTU)	Amorite god, KUR.GAL, BAD (=IDIM)	
Baal (Bel) = Adon = Eshmun	(lord), Storm god	Num 22:41 etc.
Baal Zebub	"Lord of the flies" Canaanite *B'l zbl* "Baal the Prince" "Prince, lord of the underworld" in Ugaritic texts (*zbl b'l arṣ*)	2 Kgs 1:2,
Dagan = Enlil	KUR.GAL, BAD (=IDIM), Syrian god	Judg 16:23, etc.
Gilgamesh = Heracles	Hero, giant, founder of cities	
Heracles = Melqart	Fame of Hera, Hero (Roman Hercules)	
Ishtaran	God of Snake-Dragons	
Kirtu = Ninurta	Qarradu 'warrior'	
Kiyyun = Enlil / Ninurta = Saturn (Remphan)	= Chief death (erroneously called Remphan)	Amos 5:26
Marduk = Bel	Son of Enlil	Jer 50:2 (Merodach)
Melqart	King of the City / Tyre, anointed cherub	Ezek 28:12–19, etc.
Molech = Milcom = Og?	King (Ugaritic *mlk*) and Rephaite *rpu*, King / mâtu or mītu, poss. Og / Sumerian Ug, Death, Amorite, Rephaim, healer	Lev 18:21, 1 Kg 11:5, etc.
Nergal = Ninurta, Sagittarius	Underworld god = Ninurta, mutanu (BAD-a-nu) "(the planet) which spreads plague"	2 Kings 17:30
Nimrod	Let's rebel (distortion of Ninurta)	Gen 10:8
Ninurta (son of Enlil), Nisroch	Lord of the Earth (& underworld), Destroyer, healer, snake-dragon, qarradu 'warrior', hydra	2 Kgs 19:37
Pabilsag = Ninurta	Chief Ancestor	
Sikkuth = Ninurta	Arrow	Amos 5:26

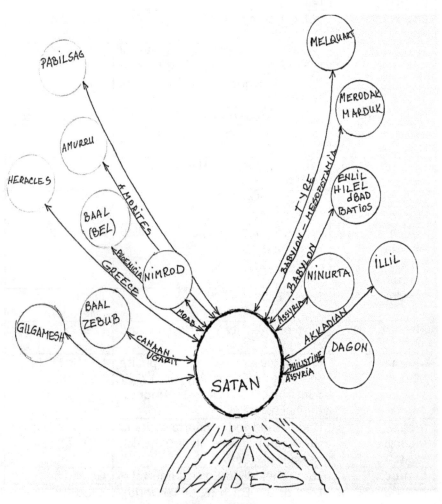

Figure 2 Satan's Polymorphism.

Introduction: The Ancient Mystery of the Beast

Something ominous is coming. In *Corrupting the Image Vol. 1*, we discovered it was Satan attempting to destroy the image of God. It turns out that we only scratched the surface of the ancient battle. It is a winner takes all battle; one which Satan intends to win. However, the Bible gives us incredible insight into his devious plan.

> The mystery of the woman and of the beast that carries her, which has the seven heads and the ten horns. The beast that you saw was, and is not, and will ascend out of the bottomless pit and go to perdition (Rev 17:7–8).

The strange imagery in Revelation has presented Bible commentators with enigmas for thousands of years. What do these strange symbols mean? How can we decode them?

It turns out the solution is to go back to where it all started: ancient Shinar (Mesopotamia). Approximately 3,700 years before the invention of the printing press, Satan's basic blueprint was carved on a cylinder seal that allowed mass production of a message in ancient Akkad. The message on the cylinder was the very one revealed to John about 2,800 years later: The mystery of the woman and the Beast that carried her, driven by the great dragon!

This one cylinder seal (Figure 3 on next page) from the ancient near east reveals Satan's mysterious identities, his false religion, his goal of world domination, and his end-time plan. In the image, we see his mastery of the art of war; his use of spies, secret weapons, technology, secret codes / ciphers; biological, chemical, genetic weapons; trojan horses, subversion, secret agents and spies to disrupt from within the enemy lines.

1

Figure 3 Akkadian cylinder seal.

Ancient Shinar is the place that holds the answers to the mystery of Revelation 17 which have remained elusive and difficult to interpret. We are in an exciting time where, thanks to an explosion in understanding of ancient languages, we can now understand the mystery presented in Bible prophecy which reveals what the enemy has planned with incredible detail. All these things will be revealed as we journey through the ancient world, like Indiana Jones, retracing Satan's steps and discovering his diabolic plan for world domination. We will journey back to the moment of his defection and dig into ancient texts using Ancient Near East and biblical languages such as Sumerian, Akkadian, Hebrew and Greek as our spade. The evidence will be laid bare for scholars to scrutinize or for the casual reader to skim. Finer details will be included in the notes for the dedicated researchers.

In part one, we will dig deep into the ancient roots of Satan, the great dragon who deceives the whole world with his many identities in the ancient world. We will examine how he swindled Adam and Eve and usurped authority over Earth, a move so calculated God could not immediately undo the action, but instead limited Satan's presence in the world and vowed to send a Hero to crush Satan's head. We will make the arduous climb up Mt. Hermon and see how Satan attempted to overcome his limitation by sending the sons of God who came down at his command.

In part two, we will travel to the land of "two rivers," [1] also known as ancient Shinar, Sumer and Mesopotamia, the seat of Satan's post-Flood kingdom. It is also the place where he caused Nimrod, the Rebel, to become a hybrid and the hero of legends, stories, books and movies for the past five thousand years—the same place he is predicted to return in the last days. We will see how Nimrod in turn inspired people to build the Tower of Babel, a potential gateway for the gods that they might invade this world.

On our adventure, we will see a Trojan Horse just like the one outside the impenetrable walls of Troy that allowed the enemy inside to destroy the city. It will be Satan's decoy to attack our defenses: Inanna, queen of heaven, a woman riding a beast. We will then trace Nimrod and the woman from Sumer back to Hermon where we will discover a hidden relationship with Og, King of the land of the Snake-dragons and the chimeric creatures trapped in the Abyss.

In part three, we will see the true hero, Jesus, battle Satan's forces in the land of the snake-dragons. This battle will take us down to the Gates of Hades where we will hear the pawing of Satan's hordes, eager to escape from the Abyss. Lastly, we will climb Mt. Hermon with Jesus, the true Hero prophesied to crush the head of Satan, who through a stunning reversal will regain legal dominion over the planet and thwart Satan from opening the Abyss.

PART 1: THE GREAT DRAGON GAINS DOMINION OF EARTH

In this section, we will examine Satan's ancient aliases, the rebellion against his Creator, the betrayal of those he was to serve and his quest to make Nephilim.

Chapter 1: Satan's Mysterious Identity as Enlil

A nd another sign appeared in heaven: behold, a great, fiery red dragon having seven heads and ten horns, and seven diadems on his heads. The great dragon ... that serpent of old, called the Devil and Satan, who deceives the whole world (Rev 12:3, 9).

Criminals sometimes use disguises to give themselves a different look to conceal their identity. They might use a mask, costume, false passports, websites, buildings and so on to gain their victims' trust and access their money or personal information. Our journey will reveal how Satan has used those same tools since the earliest of times to deceive the world to trust him and give him access to our riches, authority and even our lives. He has at the same time attempted to open the Gates of Hades and thus, unleash his forces upon the world.

Satan did not begin as a criminal mastermind. We do not believe in dualism that teaches there are two equal but opposite powers, i.e. God versus Satan, good versus evil; Satan is not the equal of YHWH. Scripture is clear: God created Satan and He created him good: "You were perfect in your ways from the day you were created" (Ezek 28:15). God did not create Satan with the intention of him being wicked and sinful. Instead, He made him good, along with the other angels, including Cherubim / Seraphim, whom He spoke into existence.

> Praise Him, all His angels; Praise Him, all His hosts! Praise Him, sun and moon; Praise Him, all you stars of light! …. For He commanded and they were created. He also established them forever and ever (Ps 148:2–6).

The picture we get is that God said, "Michael," and "Gabriel," and they immediately began to exist. God spoke Satan's name and he began to exist. Unlike humans, the angels were created with great wisdom (Ezek 28:12–13), and while they would certainly learn history as it unfolded, they would not have needed to learn to speak, to reason and to comprehend abstract thinking. They had no childhood or age of innocence. Michael, Gabriel, Satan and all the angels must have perceived how God had shared his qualities of speech, art, music, passion and emotion, as well as his likeness with them (Dan 10:1–6; Rev 22:8). At the same time, they must have perceived they were in the presence of supreme greatness, of the exalted King to whom there would never be any equal (Rev 10:1, 22:8–9, Jude 1:9), the One who, upon uttering a simple command, had brought them into existence out of nothing. (See Appendix 2 Angel Freewill).

ENLIL (HEILEL), NOT LUCIFER

Unlike Michael ("who is like God") and Gabriel ("God is my Hero"), we do not know Satan's original name. Christians have long spoken of Satan, the devil and Lucifer, yet when we research these titles, we find nothing in the ancient world. In Isaiah 14, the prophet said: "How you are fallen from heaven, O Heilel [Hêlēl הֵילֵל], son of the morning!" (Isa 14:12). "Lucifer" is not Satan's name; The underlying Hebrew in the word is *Heilel* [Hêlēl הֵילֵל]. [2] Deciphering this word using the tools of the Ancient Near East is the key we need.

The ancient translators, not having all the texts we have today, came to this word "Heilel," a *hapax legomenon*, (a word that appears once in Scripture), and had to make a guess; they translated it into Greek as *eosphorus*. We now can go back to early texts of Mesopotamia, written in the Sumerian and Akkadian languages, and do some comparative linguistics. *Eos* meaning "dawn" and *phorus* means "bearer." *Eosphorus*, therefore, means dawn-bearer, (similarly to how Christo-pher means Christ-bearer). In Latin, *Eos* (dawn) became *lux, and phorus* became *pheros*, hence "Lucifer" which was a good attempt.

My friend, Dr. Bill Gallagher, wrote a paper: *On the Identity of Hêlēl Ben Sahar from Isaiah 14*. He notes how the biblical Hebrew root HLL could be directly related to the ancient god Enlil: "One could reasonably expect *hll* to be the West Semitic form of *Illil*. As the Ebla tablets suggest, *Illil* came into West Semitic directly from Sumerian."[3] In other words, *Heilel* is equivalent phonetically to the Sumerian Enlil … and Akkadian *Illil* (or *Ellil*). Dr. Gallagher laid out the parallels between Heilel and Enlil, recreated below:

Table 2 Enlil in Isaiah and Ancient Near Eastern literature

Isaiah's Description	Enlil / Illil's Description
1. His name was Hêlēl (Isa 14:12).	1. hyll Hebrew equivalent of Illil
2. He was the son of dawn (vs. 12).	2. Causes the dawn
3. He laid the nations low (vs. 12).	3. Illil was a devastator
4. He aspired to set up his throne above the stars of El (vs. 13).	4. Illil's astral function was immense
5. He aspired to sit in the mount of assembly and on Saphon (14:13).	5. Illil was among the most prominent members in it (in the divine assembly)
6. He aspired to be like the Most High (14:14).	6. Illil was the highest in Mesopotamia until the end of the second millennium
7. He fell down to earth into the midst of the pit (14:12, 15).	7. Illil's fall into the underworld is recorded in first millennium texts

Table 2 Enlil in Isaiah and Ancient Near Eastern literature.

Comparing Isaiah 14 with the descriptions in Mesopotamian texts, we find that there is a direct correlation. "The name Enlil can thus be rendered 'Lord Wind'"[4] which is incredibly similar to how Paul refers to Satan as "Prince of the Power of the Air" (Eph 2:2). In Revelation 12:3, John saw a dragon with ten horns. Enlil was regularly represented wearing a crown or helmet with ten horns as depicted in Figure 4 below. Revelation has accurately pulled back the curtain on Satan's secret identity: Satan = Enlil.

Figure 4 Cylinder Seal of Enlil. p. 19. John Gray. Near Eastern Mythology. London. Hamlyn House Ltd. 1969.

We find Satan's various biblical epithets (his titles) are also matched in the ancient world. Satan boasted in Isaiah that he would "sit on the mount of the congregation on the farthest sides of the north" (Isa 14:13), which is the same description of God's holy mountain: "Mount Zion [on] the sides of the north, The city of the great King" (Ps 48:2). Alfred Jeremias points out that Enlil was "assimilated to the North Pole of the Ecliptic."[5]

Moreover, Samuel Kramer states how the creator god: "An carried off heaven while Enlil carried off the earth and assumed most of An's powers. "Satan, the ruler of this world" (John 12:31), is shown in the Bible to have temporary dominion over the Earth. Enlil is also glorified as 'the father of the gods, the king of heaven and earth,' 'the king of all the lands.'"[6] We note the comparison with Satan's boast: "I will ascend into heaven. I will exalt my throne above the stars of God; … I will be like the Most High" (Isa 14:13–14).

Though we do not know his original name, we do know that the biblical appellations for him as "Prince of the Power of the Air" and "Heilel" are precisely what Satan was called in the ancient world. The figure in Isaiah 14 was the same exact entity known as Enlil in Sumerian, and Illil in Akkadian. In fact, the epithet Enlil "Lord Wind" was so commonly used that it eventually became the very word for "idols" in scripture. God said to Israel: "Do not turn to the idols [הָאֱלִילִים ha'elilim] … I am the LORD your God (Lev 19:4). A. T. Clay in 1907 pointed out "the origin of elilim [אלילים], the word translated "idols" in the Old Testament … is probably to be found in the … deity Ellil."[7]

Christopher B. Hays also suggests that "idols" may just be a form of Illil (Enlil) which could also mean "god of gods."

> His name was known far and wide throughout the ancient Near East, and in syllabic cuneiform, it was written as Illil (e. g. d.-li-lu); this is taken to be a contracted form based on a doubling of the word ilu, "god", i. e. il-ilû, "god of gods"… In fact, it is now commonly argued that the Sumerian writing of his name, den.líl ("Lord Wind") was derived from the Semitic name. [8]

We have already unlocked a great deal! "Lucifer" is actually Heilel which was Enlil in the ancient world and was almost certainly the same word as "idols" in the Hebrew Bible. Obscuring his specific name has made it easier for Satan to hide his identity through the ages. Nevertheless, because we know that Heilel (Enlil) was syncretized (had fused his identity) with a multitude of gods, we can trace him. Hays notes:

> Because lordship itself was Illil's defining characteristic ... Akkadian terms such as illilu, "god of the highest rank" and illilūtu, "divine supremacy" (literally "Enlil-ship") ... illilūtu was ascribed to various other deities over the centuries, including Šamaš, Marduk, Sîn and Nabû, each of whom was called illilu at various times. This background is significant to the biblical use of אליל, since it too arguably began with a specific reference to Illil, but was also applied to other divinities.[9]

The implications are huge—"Enlil" or "Satan" was quite likely a general term for "idols" which God said not to worship in the Ten Commandments. Also, Satan was known by a host of other titles, though for simplicity, we will generally refer to him as Satan or Enlil throughout this book. Keep in mind that the names and titles, many which we find in the Bible with variant spellings, refer to Satan: Enlil (Isa 14:12), Ninurta (2 Kgs 19:37), Marduk / Merodach (Jer 50:2), Baal / Bel (Isa 46:1), Dumuzid / Tammuz (Ezek 8:14), and more. One of Satan's disguises the Bible audaciously unmasks is that of Melqart, King of Tyre.

SATAN AS MELQART, KING OF TYRE

When God told Ezekiel to "take up a lamentation for the king of Tyre," in Ezekiel 28, He was talking about far more than a mere human king;[10] He was using one of Satan's many titles: Melqart. Melqart (mlkqrt), literally means "king of the city", and here, specifically Tyre.

"Melqart was considered by the Phoenicians to represent the monarchy, perhaps the king even represented the god, or vice-versa, so that the two became one and the same."[11] King of the 'City' could also be interpreted as a euphemism of the underworld, called "the great city, iri.gal, Akkadian Irkallu, in the Mesopotamian tradition." [12]

We do not know the given name of Satan, but God revealed enough key places for us to trace his titles back to a singular entity. For instance, George A. Barton writes in his study, *On the Pantheon of Tyre,* that "Baal of Tyre was called Melqart (king of the city), we learn from the Phoenician portion of a bilingual inscription from Malta. The Greek portion of the same inscription shows that Melqart was identified with the Greek Herakles."[13] Melqart was also known as Baal, Ninurta, Enlil, Adon and Eshmun, thus, Satan. Historians such as "Josephus Flavius refer to Melqart and Heracles interchangeably." [14]

The word Heracles (Hercules) comes from Ἥρα (Hera) and Κλέος (fame). [15] The fame part reminds us of the Nephilim, the mighty men (הַגִּבֹּרִים *hagibborim*) who were "the men of renown" (Gen 6:4 ESV), and also the people at Babel said, "Let us make a name for ourselves" (Gen 11:4). Therefore, Hercules (Heracles) was another name for Satan.

Likewise, the King of Tyre that God denounces in Ezekiel 28 is considered by most scholars to be the same god with whom Elijah was battling on Mt. Carmel. [16] In fact, Elijah mocks the god for sleeping "and must be awakened" which were "elements of and allusions to the practice of the 'awakening' of Melqart"[17] which provides further proof of them being the same.

Every year, the Phoenicians celebrated Heracles' 'awakening' (ἐγερσις) which was considered "the greatest festival of Melqart: the god, burnt with fire, as the Greek hero, was brought to life by means of a hierogamic rite with his divine partner Astarte, through the participation of a particular celebrant, the *mqm 'lm*, 'awakener of deity'." [18] In other words, through a "sacred" sexual act, the god was thought to come back to life. The once dead, but then *alive again* god sounds very much like the "the beast who was, is not, and will ascend out of the Abyss" (Rev 17:8) from John's visions.

The famous historian Herodotus of the 5th century BC once visited Melqart's temple and reported that there was "a tomb inside, supporting the theory that, involved as he was in the founding mythology of the city, perhaps Melqart was based on a historical person." [19] (See adjacent Figure 5). The theme, according to Herodotus was that "the Tyrian people paid homage as if to a hero. i.e. as if to one who had died, one who was originally mortal," [20] who was deified and became a cosmic lord who grants prosperity.[21]

In part two, we will explore the theme of the deified hero Nimrod, founder of cities, who was known as the son of Enlil (Satan). In fact, Satan and Nimrod were so closely linked in the ancient world that they were often used interchangeably. Melqart / Heracles was considered the son of Saturn or Zeus, depending on the legend.

Figure 5 Votive Statue of Melqart by Carole Raddato (CC BY-NC-SA).

The *interpretario Graeca* which existed from the fifth century BC made the connection between Melqart and Baal long before modern scholars. It states:

> Heracles was identified with Melqart, whose name means "king of the city", and who **was called the 'Baal of Tyre'** … a west Semitic god who was the primary deity of the Phoenician city of Tyre, and later of its major colony at Carthage. The Carthaginian triad of deities consisting of –'Baal Shamen,' Astarte and Melqart became known through their Hellenistic counterparts of

Zeus, Asteria and Heracles   ... The **Samaritans worshipped Melqart as Zeus Xenios on Mount Gerizim** (2 Macc 6:2) (Emphasis Mine). [22]

Many of us grew up hearing the legends of Zeus and Hercules, yet we never heard about the fact that the real entity behind the legends demanded child sacrifice. It was "extensively practiced in Carthage and 'made its way into Israel from Phoenicia during periods of religious syncretism.'" [23] There is some debate as to how often such an abomination was practiced, though the famous ANE scholar William Albright notes that "the practice was extensive in the Phoenician colonies." [24]

Figure 6 Artist's rendition of Molech.

Sadly, King Solomon led Israel to worship those syncretisms of Satan. He set up "high places to this 'king'" Milcom, god of deified dead kings, and permitted child sacrifice which continued for hundreds of years. King Josiah, king of Judah shortly before the Babylonians sacked Jerusalem, tried to stop the terrible practice:

> He defiled Tophet, which is in the Valley of the Son of Hinnom, that no man might make his son or his daughter pass through the fire to Molech (2 Kgs 23:10). Then the king defiled the high places that were east of

Jerusalem, which were on the south of the Mount of Corruption, which Solomon king of Israel had built for Ashtoreth the abomination of the Sidonians, for Chemosh the abomination of the Moabites, and for Milcom the abomination of the people of Ammon (2 Kgs 23:13). (See Appendix 6 Abominations of Babylon).

It is incredible, but all roads lead back to Satan. The dragon, Enlil (Satan), is the same deceptive spirit behind the Greek hero Heracles (Roman Hercules), Baal and Melqart. The same spirit is behind the **"the Greek Asklepios,** who took over many attributes of Semitic healer gods."[25] We know Asklepios as the snake symbol used in the modern medical practice. While this does not mean that we should not go to doctors, it does reveal the philosophical underpinnings of medicine.

Melqart / Heracles were gods located on the Mediterranean whose origins are in Mesopotamia, the land of Shinar. "Archaeological evidence from Mesopotamia suggests that the figure of Heracles is found as early as the middle of the third millennium." [26] Archaeologists found on Akkadian cylinder seals "a hero probably named Ninurta (the son of Enlil the storm god) ... shown conquering lions, bulls, snakes, and even a seven-headed snake." [27]

We do not want to get ahead of ourselves, since we will explore Nimrod in greater detail in part two. Nevertheless, we will just note here that Nimrod and Ninurta were the same person. Ninurta, according to the mythology, was the son of Enlil whom we have learned was Satan. Hence, we see the connection between Nimrod (Ninurta) and Melqart and Satan. Moreover, "in Sumerian representations a hero is fitted out, like the later Greek Heracles, with a club, bow and lion-skin." [28] Everywhere we turn, we find Satan or the deified Nimrod as the hero extraordinaire. Indeed, "Heracles' quest for the apples of Hesperides is similar to the quest for immortality in the popular epic of Gilgamesh." [29]

Interestingly, Heracles was known as a Master of Animals in the Greek traditions, a trait suggestive of his dragon qualities[30] and reminiscent of Satan's qualities as a cherub.

Satan's ancient disguises are many and elaborate. As we have seen, looking for "Lucifer" in the ancient world is a fruitless endeavor. However, now that we have the key of Satan = Enlil, we have been able to chip away at some of Satan's masks and have discovered he was everywhere. He was known as Enlil, Baal, Melqart, Heracles / Hercules and dozens of other titles; and, he was the god who exacted a terrible price from his worshipers. His strategy and quest for world domination are just as real today as when he was openly worshipped by the masses millennia ago. We also peeled back one of the masks which gave us a preview of how Satan deified Nimrod, known in the ancient world as his son. The next disguise we will unmask is Satan, the great dragon.

Chapter 2: Enlil the Great Dragon

Ever since John recorded the incredible visions shown to him by God in the book of Revelation, speculation has abounded as to what he meant by the imagery he described. For example, Bible prophecy speaks of "a great, fiery red dragon having seven heads and ten horns" (Rev 12:3) and "a woman sitting on a scarlet beast which was full of names of blasphemy, having seven heads and ten horns" (Rev 17:3). The scenes described are anything but normal, which has led commentators to relegate the vision to nothing more than allegory.

In order for us to know how to interpret the images, we must find their definitions. But where are we to find such definitions? We can interpret the meaning of the symbols if we learn their definitions.

Our world is full of symbols we understand well: the red, yellow and green lights in a traffic-light are symbols. We all know what they mean, but a person from the deep jungles would have no idea that the meaning of those colors symbolize stop, slow down and go. Yet once they learn the meaning, the symbol is easy to interpret.

So too, John gave us symbols. Our job is to find the definitions for them, just like we had to learn red light means "stop." Thus, we are asking what are the definitions of the following?

- a **great, fiery red dragon** having **seven heads** and **ten horns**, and **seven diadems** on his heads (Rev 12:3). So the **great dragon** was cast out, that serpent of old, called the Devil and Satan, who deceives the whole world; he was cast to the earth, and his angels were cast out with him (Rev 12:9).

- And I saw a **beast** rising up out of the sea, having **seven heads** and **ten horns**, and on his horns **ten crowns**, and on his heads a blasphemous name (Rev 13:1).
- The angel said to me, "Why did you marvel? I will tell you the mystery of the woman and of the **beast** that carries her, which has the **seven heads** and the **ten horns** (Rev 17:7).

The keywords are highlighted; These words share common features and are the key players in all three passages from Revelation. Right away, we notice that both the Beast and the dragon share these features:

1. A great dragon
2. A fiery red dragon
3. A beast
4. Seven heads
5. Ten horns

SATAN'S FIERY COVERING

Before we dig into the Mesopotamian evidence, let's review what the Bible reveals concerning Satan's original appearance, which will help us put the former into proper context.

God created the angels with a fiery quality similar to his own. Scripture describes "the LORD your God is a **consuming fire**" (Deut 4:24, 9:3; Ps 97:3). Ezekiel recounts from his vision of God that "from the appearance of His waist and upward I saw, as it were, the color of amber [electricity] with the appearance of **fire** all around within it (Ezek 1:27). The return of the Lord is likewise said to be with fiery flames (2 Thess 1:8; Isa 66:15).

The angels, including Cherubim / Seraphim, are described as fiery beings, as well. Their fiery nature seems to be necessary for them to be able to live in God's presence. There are many verses that reference the angels' glorious appearance. We recall that the angels shone in the night sky at the announcement of the birth of Messiah in Luke 2:9. The root word in that passage is *perilampo* (περιλάμπω), meaning "to shine around, "a derivative of *lampo*, "to shine." In Luke 24:4, two angels stood by the tomb in "shining garments" (*astrapto* ἀστράπτω, like what a star does). This same word for shining is used to describe lightning as it shines from one part of heaven to the other, according to Luke 17:24.

The prophet Daniel described a vision in which an angel had a shining appearance, by writing: "His body was like beryl, his face like the **appearance of lightning**, his eyes like **torches of fire**, his arms and feet like **burnished bronze** in color" (Dan 10:6). In the book of Revelation, angels were "clothed in pure bright [*lampron* λαμπρον] linen" (Rev 15:6). The Psalmist described how God "makes His angels spirits, His **ministers a flame of fire**" (Ps 104:4).

Ezekiel described the appearance of angels as burning coals of fire and with four faces![31]

> The likeness of four living creatures … they had the **likeness of a man**. Each one had four faces, and each one had four wings. Their legs were straight, and the soles of their feet were like the soles of calves' feet. They sparkled like the color of burnished bronze. The hands of a man were under their wings on their four sides; and each of the four had faces and wings. Their wings touched one another. The creatures did not turn when they went, but each one went straight forward. As for the likeness of their faces, each had the face of a man; each of the four had the face of a lion on the right side, each of the four had the face of an ox on the left side, and each of the four had the face of an eagle. Thus were their faces. Their wings stretched upward; two wings of each one touched one another, and two covered their bodies.

And each one went straight forward; they went wherever the spirit wanted to go, and they did not turn when they went. As for the likeness of the living creatures, **their appearance** was like **burning coals of fire**, like the appearance of torches going back and forth among the living creatures. The fire was bright, and out of the fire went lightning. And the living creatures ran back and forth, in appearance like a flash of lightning (Ezek 1:5–14).

The description of these creatures is also a description of Satan's appearance before his fall, though he must have been the most splendid looking of them all. Their appearance was described as having:

1. The likeness of a man
2. Straight legs with feet like a calf
3. Four faces
   a. Man
   b. Lion
   c. Bull
   d. Eagle
4. Four wings
5. Burning coals, torches, lightning, electricity

Satan looked like these creatures. Though after his fall, he lost the fiery quality, which we will examine shortly. Nevertheless, a being with four faces of four kinds of creatures is indeed both a complex and revealing entity. The Hebrew word [פנים panim] is plural "faces." A face is a window into the heart and mind of a person. Faces are constantly changing direction and shape, depending on mood, intentions, dreams and experiences. Face also means "presence." God promised, "My Presence will go with you" (Exod 33:14). God's face going with the Israelites was so important to Moses that he said to God: "If Your Presence does not go with us, do not bring us up from here" (Exod 33:15).

We can infer from this passage that to be in the presence of [לפני *lifne*] a cherub with four faces could give the impression of being in front of a man, a lion, a bull or an eagle. I have been in the close presence of a lion, and it is an awesome experience. Growing up in rural Michigan, I made sure to keep my distance from bulls as I understood they are creatures that can kill. Likewise, the eagle is both majestic and deadly. Incidentally, these four formidable faces are excellent representatives of the four broad categories of creatures on the face of the Earth.

GREAT DRAGON

The Mesopotamian evidence of the great dragon is plentiful and gives greater context to what John was seeing in Revelation. "The most common serpentine epithet from ancient cuneiform sources is Akkadian *ušumgallu* "great dragon," itself a loan from Sumerian *UŠUMGAL*." [32] (Remember the Š is pronounced "sh"). The great dragon title, *Ushumgal*, was a typical epithet for Enlil's many syncretisms: "*Ušumgallu* also designates a host of Mesopotamian deities, including Marduk … His exalted position over humanity is expressed in the appellation, "great dragon of the heavens and earth." [33] ANE scholar Tyler Yoder points out, "Marduk's ownership of a pet *mušḫuššu* ("snake") furthers his own serpentine associations." [34]

Figure 7 UŠUMGAL or Anzu bird Icon By editor Austen Henry Layard,
drawing by L. Gruner - Monuments of Nineveh.

In other words, we have discovered that "great dragon" was a
quite common term for Satan / Enlil and the like. It was also a
term for serpent, just like the Bible told us a serpent tempted
Adam and Eve in Genesis 3; (it appears the Bible critics were

premature in ridiculing the Bible for such imagery). Ancient iconography attests to the historical authenticity of Heilel / Enlil (or one of his syncretizations: Ninurta, Baal, Zeus, Nergal, among others) being commonly referred to as a snake or dragon.

The icon for the *Ushumgallu*, seen adjacent in Figure 7, is also sometimes called the *Anzu* bird. It was a chimera, a creature with the DNA of another animal mixed into itself. The "translation of *ušumgallu* 'lion-dragon' "derives from the conceptual amalgamation of these creatures."[35] The *Ushumgallu* in the epic of Gilgamesh was called a "'ground lion' … and the *mušḫuššu* serpent often evinces leonine traits."[36] The point is that the great dragon is not the classic fire-breathing dragon of legend from the Middle Ages. The Mesopotamian dragon had many overlaps of lion qualities—which was one of Satan's cherub faces.

The foremost quality of the great dragon, Ancient Near East expert Frans Wiggermann points out, "is being a determined killer, killing probably with its venom, and frightening even the gods."[37] Man, lions, bulls, and eagles—the four faces of the cherub, certainly classify as determined killers.[38]

The great dragon also had seven heads in Mesopotamia literature and iconography. We always need to keep in mind the many syncretizations inherent in the ancient texts. Heilel (Satan) = Enlil = Marduk = Baal = Bel; and, Ninurta (son of Enlil) often assumed Enlil's role altogether.

We learn that a syncretization of Marduk (or his son), according to Yoder, was called "the great dragon, who cannot be faced." Furthermore, Nergal (god of the dead and a syncretization of Ninurta / Enlil) was represented with the same description: "[*ú-šum*]-*gal-lu ṣīru tābik imti elišunu* "The majestic, great dragon who pours his venom upon them."[39] With those epithets in mind, we can appreciate the significance that "Nergal's divine staff was as 'awe-inspiring as a serpent' and Ninurta's mace consisted of seven snake-like heads."[40]

Figure 8 Ninurta killing one of the heads of the seven-headed serpent. Bible Review, Oct. 1992, 28 (=ANEP #671) (Early Dynastic). Courtesy of the Bible Lands Museum, Jerusalem.

That Nergal, also known as Ninurta, Melqart, Marduk and Enlil, had a seven-headed snake is incredibly revealing. The great dragon of Revelation has "**seven heads** and **ten horns**," (Rev 12:3) as does the Beast, who has "**seven heads** and **ten horns**" (Rev 13:1). Not only does the iconography reveal a great dragon,[41] but John saw "one of his heads as if it had been mortally wounded, and his deadly wound was healed. And all the world marveled and followed the Beast (Rev 13:3). Looking at Figure 8 above, we see that one of the heads is mortally wounded. God is revealing that the symbols in Revelation relate directly back to the false gods of Babylon. A key to defining the images from Revelation is found in deciphering ancient Babylonian monuments.

FIERY RED DRAGON: MUŠḪUŠŠU

It is amazing (though not surprising, since the vision was from God) that John described not only a "great dragon", but "a great, fiery red dragon" (Rev 12:3). How could John have known, humanly speaking, about the *Mušḫuššu* from hundreds of years before? John could not have known that the word, *Mušḫuššu*, could mean "fearsome" or "red," or perhaps both. This is a strong testimony of the divine origin of John's vision and of the accuracy of the entity John is describing.

German archaeologists dug up the Ishtar Gate and transported it back to the East Berlin Museum, Germany, where you can now walk through the actual gate. On the walls of the Ishtar Gate, which date from the neo-Babylonian empire (ca. 7th- 6th century BC), Marduk's "pet" *mušḫuššu* [*mushkhushshu*] is visible. As seen in Figure 9 below, it was a hybrid, scaly creature with hind legs resembling the talons of an eagle, and with lion-like forelimbs, a long neck and tail, a horned head, a snake-like tongue and a crest.[42] Wiggermann explains that both "fearsome" and "red" are possible interpretations the name, *mušḫuššu*:

> Akkadian mušḫuššu is a loanword from Sumerian mušḫuš (-a), literally "fearsome serpent". The reading of the second element as ḫuš rather than ruš (both possible) … The Sumerian Loanwords in Old Babylonian Akkadian I, its meaning as "fearsome" rather than "red" (both possible).[43]

Figure 9 Mushkhushshu on Ishtar Gate.

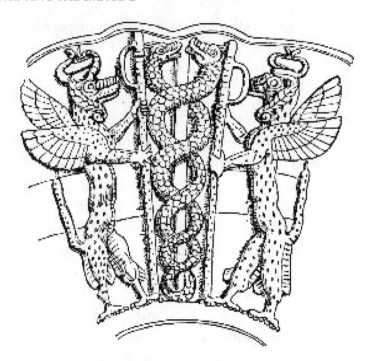

Figure 10 Mušḫuššu H. Frankfort, Cylinder Seals, text-fig. 33 (=ANEP #511) (Gudea; Girsu [Tello]).

John told us of a sign that appeared in heaven, "a great, fiery red dragon" (Rev 12:3). Again, God is revealing that the imagery in Revelation connects back to the ancient gods of Babylon. We continue to define the symbols in Revelation by examining ancient icons from the civilizations in Mesopotamia.

The prophet Daniel wrote about Marduk's dragon that was "like a lion, and had eagle's wings and it was lifted up from the earth and made to stand on two feet like a man, and a man's heart was given to it" (Dan 7:4). In ancient iconography, the *Mushkhushshu* is seen walking like a beast and standing like a man as depicted above in Figure 10. This dragon stood as a symbol of the strength of Marduk and in opposition to the true God. Accordingly, God promised to judge Marduk, spelled Merodach in the Bible: "Merodach is broken in pieces" (Jer 50:2). We also learned in the previous chapter that the Greek healer god Asclepios was associated with Melqart / Heracles, which is parallel to the *Mušḫuššu*.

It seems plausible to connect the Sumerian *mušḫuš* with the Hebrew נָחָשׁ (*nāḥāsh*) snake. They share many similarities: *Mušḫuš* may mean "red snake-dragon" and *nāḥāsh* is related to a copper-bronze color [44] which is fairly close to the coloration of the *Mušḫuššu* on the Ishtar Gate. The *mušḫuš* is a symbol for Enlil or is closely associated with him; "In the so-called *Labbu-myth* Enlil sends the muš[ḫuššu] to wipe out noisy mankind. [45] In Genesis, the *nāḥāsh* was definitely associated with Satan, the one who desired to destroy mankind ("opinions differ as to whether this was a Satan-inspired snake or a name for Satan himself.")[46]

Lastly, I am persuaded that there could be a linguistic connection between *Mušḫuš* and *nāḥāsh*, the serpent in the Garden. James H. Charlesworth of Princeton notes there is "in Akkadian … the n to m shift." [47] Thus, *MŠḪ Š* would shift to *NŠḪ Š*, the first Š would fall out *NŠḪ Š*, leaving *NḪ Š*. Vowels are flexible between languages; thus, it is plausible for U to transition to A. *Mušḫuš* > נָחָשׁ *nāḥāsh*.

Just coincidence?

THE ANZU BIRD

We see additional images of Ninurta or Marduk (or Bel, Dagon and the rest, who are all the same entity.) Amar Annus in his article, "Ninurta and the Son of Man", notes:

> Bêl 'Lord,' which is also Ninurta's common epithet, and points to a connection with West-Semitic Baal. Marduk came to replace Enlil in the Mesopotamian pantheon, so he took over conjointly the position of the father Enlil and the mythology of his son Ninurta.[48]

Recall that over time, with syncretization of belief systems, the names and characteristics of these gods meshed together. Here, Enlil and Ninurta take on one another's qualities. We learn from Amar Annus how in the mythology from Shinar, "after vanquishing the eagle Anzu, Ninurta becomes one with the bird … paradoxically, Ninurta is equated with his slain enemy, Thunderbird Anzu, who becomes his symbol."[49]

Figure 11 Ninurta with wings.

Ninurta, in the iconography pictured in Figure 11, is being identified with the *Anzu* bird. The very creature that he killed, the *Anzu* bird or Manticore, then becomes Ninurta's symbol. There is a certain fluidity in how Ninurta is presented, according to Jacobsen:

> The two forms, bird and lion, tended to compete in the image of the god, who was sometimes the lion-headed bird, sometimes a winged lion with bird's tail and talons, sometimes all lion. In time the animal forms were rejected in favor of imagining the god in human form only.[50]

We have seen this shift in appearance in the passage from the Book of Daniel:

> "The first was like a lion, and had eagle's wings. I watched till its wings were plucked off; and it was lifted up from the earth and made to stand on two feet like a man, and a man's heart was given to it" (Dan 7:4).

Figure 12 Ninurta wearing a crown of ten horns standing on a Lion-headed Eagle (A n z u d / Anzû), Lion-Dragon

Just as Daniel saw the fluid nature of the first beast that emerged from the sea, the iconography of Ninurta shows us the changing images of the god. Ninurta sometimes was a chimeric creature standing on four feet as a beast, but sometimes he was standing on two feet as a man; We have images of him both with and without wings.

F. Wiggermann calls to our attention an incredibly significant detail regarding the *Anzu* lion-dragon, which shares a number of features with the *Mušḫuššu*. In *Mesopotamian Protective Spirits*, Wiggermann explains it was Enlil (not his syncretization Ninurta) who was originally associated with *Anzû*.[51]

This insight reveals that the hybrid creature first represented Enlil and then later, stood for the syncretization of the various names of Mesopotamian gods.

> The *Anzû* then, is not Ninurta / Ningirsu's symbol, nor that of any of the other gods whose images are conflated with a symbolic animal. "The *Anzû* represents another, more general power, under whose supervision, all the gods operate. This higher power can only be Enlil, which is exactly what we see in the *Lugalbanda Epic* and *Anzû* myth, Thus, the posture of the lion-headed eagle, with wings stretched out above the symbolic animals of other gods, becomes understandable: it is a stance that is neither that of attack, nor that of defense, but that of the master of the animals."[52]

Uncovering the fact that the *Anzu* was originally identified with Enlil reveals once again that Satan is the one depicted in the many symbols of the gods of Mesopotamia. We saw in the previous chapter how "master of the animals" was a reference to Melqart / Heracles whom we determined was a syncretization of Enlil. Furthermore, the fact that Enlil, the *Anzû* lion-dragon, was master of the animals causes us to think of the four faces of the cherubim. Enlil dominated the animal kingdom: the man-beings, the wild lion-type beings, the domestic bull-type beings and the flying eagle-type beings. The face of a man, lion, bull and eagle make up the four faces of the cherub and possibly the head of Satan, himself—formerly a covering cherub. The connection may not be exact;[53] nevertheless, we do have a strong correlation between the snake-dragon of Enlil, Marduk, etc. and also with Satan in Genesis 3. Thus, the *nakhash* in the Garden was not today's average snake. It was like the *Ushumgallu* / *mušḫuššu* / *Anzu*, with legs to stand erect. It was the curse that later changed Satan's form from the snake-dragon / lion-dragon to what he is today.

BAŠMU-BASHAN

The last word that we will examine for serpent-dragon is *Bašmu*, which will lead us to Mt. Hermon, to Og, King of Bashan and to the transfiguration of Jesus (later in the book). Bashan in the Bible comes from Akkadian *Bašmu*. Wiggermann notes: "For the two Sumerian terms u s u m and muš-šà-tùr Akkadian has only one: bašmu ... must refer to two different types of mythological snakes as well, and we will call them ušum / bašmu and muš-šà-tùr / bašmu."[54] He defines the *ušum* / bašmu, as "Venomous Snake ... horned snake with forelegs." He also notes a snake-dragon that we have already examined: u š u m g a l, rendered in Akkadian by *ušumgallu* and *bašmu*, is a derivative of u š u m and literally means: "Prime Venomous Snake" ... *Ušumgallu* ... occasionally replaces *mušḫuššu* when the dragon of Nabû is referred to or the dragon of Ninurta.[55]

He points out (see Figure 13):

> The foremost quality of an u š u m g a l ... is being a determined killer, killing probably with its venom, ... It is this quality that makes u š u m (g al) a suitable epithet for certain gods and kings.[56]

Figure 13 Bashmu from Wiggermann's Mesopotamian Protective Spirits.

We must not miss how the *Bašmu* was later equated with the icon of Nergal, Ninurta, and Marduk: "Nergal is not originally a dragon slayer, but here, as elsewhere ... he replaces Ninurta. After Marduk's usurpation of the mušḫuššu, the ušum / bašmu became the symbolic animal of gods formerly associated with the *mušḫuššu*."[57] A *Bašmu* was a snake-dragon, sometimes used to describe the other snake-dragons we have studied, and was a determined killer and was a suitable epithet for gods and kings! It was also associated with Marduk which is another name for Enlil or occasionally his "son" Ninurta, whom we will discover is Nimrod in a later chapter.

Bashmu, in astronomy, was the constellation Hydra[58], the seven headed dragon that Heracles killed (See Figure 8). The Dictionary of God, Demons, and Symbols of Ancient Mesopotamia notes, "This creature may be the seven-headed hydra killed by the god Ningirsu or Ninurta, also referred to in spells."[59]

Wiggermann, writing in *Transtigridian Snake Gods*, provides us with an important link between *Bašmu*, *Ereškigal* (Ishtar's sister), and Og the god of the dead / death.

> Ereškigal...queen of the netherworld, rules the dead ...
> is associated with the constellation Hydra (MUL.dMUŠ)
> in late astrological texts ... the Babylonian constellation
> Hydra looked like ... a snake drawn out long, with the
> forepaws of a lion, no hind legs, with wings, and with a
> head comparable to that of the mušḫuššu dragon. **Its
> Babylonian name was probably Bašmu. Ereshkigal's
> messenger, Mutum "Death" ...** is described in a late
> Assyrian text. He has the head of a mušḫuššu dragon.[60]

We cannot ignore the fact that Og was King of Bashan (in Hebrew "the Bashan"). That means he was king of the snake-dragons if we simply plug in the meaning. Furthermore, we just learned that *Bashmu* was some kind of amalgamation of the *Ushumgallu*, the *Mushhushshu* and the *Anzu*. The implication then is that Enlil (or Ninurta, son of Enlil) seems to have been behind the workings of Og and the land Bashan (snake-dragons). In a later chapter we will explore the relationship to the king of the Amorites (MARTU=Enlil), king of the Rephaim (underworld "healers" or "healed"), who were also known as snake gods.

TEN HORNS

The prophet Daniel wrote about the ten horns saying, "It was different from all the beasts that came before it, and it had ten horns" (Dan 7:7).

Figure 14 Enlil wearing a crown of ten horns.

Crowns with ten horns were a common feature of the gods in ancient Mesopotamia. "Enlil is regularly represented wearing a horned helmet."[61] In the cylinder seal depicted in Figure 14, we see Enlil wearing a crown with ten horns (five on each side).

In another cylinder seal (Figure 12, p. 13), Ninurta can be seen wearing a crown with ten horns and riding the *Anzu* bird, which also represents him as Enlil. Thus, the Bible reveals the symbols, and we once again, have discovered the means by which we can interpret these symbols.

The imagery of a great dragon and a beast is represented in the iconography of ancient Mesopotamia. Revelation spoke of Satan as the great dragon because that was how he was known from the earliest of recorded history. The Bible not only accurately recorded his ancient epithets but also gives us a spiritual window into the original role, authority and nefarious motives of Satan which allowed him to plunge the world into its current darkness.

Chapter 3: Satan the Anointed Protective Cherub

on of man, take up a lamentation for the king of Tyre, and say to him, "Thus says the Lord GOD: You were the seal of perfection, Full of wisdom and perfect in beauty" (Ezek 28:12).

In chapter one, we discovered that the king of Tyre was not a reference to a human king, but to Melqart / Heracles, one of the many syncretisms of Satan. Because the passage is about Satan, what God has to say about the anointed cherub is all the more significant. In just six Hebrew words, Satan was revealed to be the "seal of perfection, Full of wisdom and perfect in beauty."

Seal of Perfection [חוֹתֵם תָּכְנִית]: God described him as being the seal of measurement / proportion. A seal, *chotem* [חוֹתֵם], was the hot wax applied to the outside of a scroll to make sure that it stayed closed. It was the finishing touch applied to the completed work that was perfect and needed no changes.

This description, coupled with the word measurement / proportion [תבנית *tochnit*], means Satan was the absolute greatest of God's creatures. His proportions were pristine, sublime and impeccable. His form was exquisite in every capacity. He was the meter stick against which others would be measured. He was the gold standard by which all others would be judged; the measure of the appearance of perfection, second only to God himself. It is hard to imagine what this truly means in real terms. But he was absolutely it: the seal of perfection.

Full of Wisdom [מְלֵא חָכְמָה]: God also created Satan completely full of wisdom [*maleh chochma* מלא חכמה]. Satan was not lacking in any area of understanding. If he were a cup, God filled him to the very brim and could not fill him anymore. As a result, Satan perfectly understood the workings of God's creation.

He understood the laws governing the Earth, the stars and life itself. He understood the process of photosynthesis, cellular biology, quantum physics and the science beyond our grasp. He had no need to learn, for he already possessed the knowledge of all the systems God had created.

Yet there is an infinite distinction between God and Satan. While God gave him perfect wisdom, Satan has always lacked a complete perspective because he does not know the future. Like a good chess player, he can make incredibly good predictions and can model the future with great accuracy just as humans can model the trajectory of rockets and get to the moon. Still, he can never know all variables which might come into play. God is the only one who knows the future, which means Satan must learn the future as it unfolds before him.

> I am God, and there is no other; I am God, and there is none like me, declaring the end from the beginning and from ancient times things not yet done, saying, 'My counsel shall stand, and I will accomplish all my purpose (Isa 46:9-10).

Perfect in Beauty [יֹפִי וּכְלִיל]: Lastly, God created him "perfect in beauty" [kalil yofi יֹפִי כְלִיל]. The Hebrew kalal means "entire, full, all."[62] Thus, Satan was lacking nothing in his appearance. He was 100% in the beauty department. We must not overlook the weight of this statement: Perfect in beauty. God's beauty is overwhelming. "Your eyes will see the King in His beauty; They will see the land that is very far off" (Isa 33:17). King David pined, "One thing I have desired of the LORD … To behold the beauty of the LORD, And to inquire in His temple" (Ps 27:4). Satan's beauty was like the beauty of his Creator and exceeded the beauty of all other created beings.

In those mere six Hebrew words, we learned: Satan was the measure and the standard of perfect form; He was completely full of wisdom and lacked none; and he was absolutely complete

CHAPTER 3: SATAN THE ANOINTED PROTECTIVE CHERUB

and possessed the entirety of beauty. God withheld no aesthetic quality when He created him; [63] He endowed Satan with phenomenal and outstanding beauty that equaled Him in splendor. These descriptions give us insight into why Satan thought he was on equal footing with his Maker. He was like God, or at least he thought so. These qualities would eventually spark his rebellion and will lead to the creation of the Beast.

> "You were the anointed cherub who covers; I established you; You were on the holy mountain of God; You walked back and forth in the midst of fiery stones" (Ezek 28:14).

Satan belonged to a special class of beings known as the cherubim. The Akkadian cognate verb of cherub means "to bless, praise, adore. As one of the characteristics of the cherubim was adoration of God, this derivation would appear suitable." [64] Thus, a significant role Satan played was to bless, praise, and adore God, and this is precisely what the cherubim do "day or night, saying: 'Holy, holy, holy, Lord God Almighty, Who was and is and is to come!'" (Rev 4:8).

Judging from his vesture, Satan had the role of high priest. He was covered with an array of precious stones, inlaid in sockets of gold and silver. The King James translation tells us he was covered in [tupekha תפיך] and [nekbekha נקביך], meaning timbrels and pipes which gives us the misleading impression that Satan was the worship leader in heaven. I remember when I was a kid, I heard that in a sermon from a Baptist minister, who of course was using the King James Version. I like the King James, but there are better translations for these two words. Regardless of Satan's musical abilities, these two words more accurately suggest mountings and sockets for the stones he wore—an idea more properly conveyed in the ESV, NET and other more modern translations.

According to Brown Driver Briggs Hebrew Lexicon (BDB), *nekbecha* [נקב] "**1.** groove, socket, hole, cavity, settings. a. technical term relating to jeweller's work. - Origin: a bezel (for a gem)." It is a receptacle in which you would set something. Interestingly, the same word *Nekeva*, means "female," which could relate to something like a female-fitting connector which holds something else.

Table Comparison of the Stones in Ezek 28 Septuagint and Hebrew Text				
	New Engl. Transl. (Exod 28:17–20) Priest's Ephod	Septuagint (Ezek 28:13 LXXE) Stones covering Satan		Rev 21 twelve gates & stones
First Row	Ruby (sardius NKJV), a topaz, and a beryl (emerald NKJV)	sardius [1], and topaz [2], and emerald [3]	Match	jasper, the second sapphire, the third agate
Second Row	a turquoise, a sapphire, and an emerald;	carbuncle [4], and sapphire [5], and jasper [6], and silver, and gold [metals not stones – see 4th row]	Match	the fourth emerald, the fifth onyx, the sixth carnelian
Third Row	and the third row, a jacinth, an agate, and an amethyst;	and ligure (beryl?) [7], and agate [8], and amethyst [9]	Match	the seventh chrysolite, the eighth beryl, the ninth topaz
Fourth Row	a chrysolite, an onyx, and a jasper. enclosed in gold	and chrysolite [10], and beryl [11], and onyx [12] ...	Match	the tenth chrysoprase, the eleventh jacinth, and the twelfth amethyst

Table 3 Comparison of the Stones in Ezek 28 Septuagint and Hebrew Text

THE SEPTUAGINT READING OF THE STONES

Though the Masoretic text is a reliable and foundational text, the variant reading of the Septuagint may supply us with crucial details regarding the stones covering Satan and the function they served. In table 3, we compare the Septuagint of Ezekiel 28 with Exodus 28, and we have a match. We infer that Satan's stones were in a breastplate like that of Israel's high priest. It must also be noted that the stones are nearly the same as the stones of the foundations of the New Jerusalem; though, the meaning of some of the words is uncertain which causes the translations to drift a little.[65] If the reading of the Septuagint is correct (twelve stones instead of nine), then we can be fairly confident that Satan's covering stones were in fact a breastplate, and he served the function of priest in some capacity.

The presence of twelve stones in his breastplate makes more sense when we consider that God, in his perfection and authority, established the twelve tribes of Israel and the twelve apostles. There are twelve months in a year, twelve stars in the ancient zodiac as recorded in the book of Job, twelve hours of the day, and twelve hours of the night from Egyptian and Sumerian history. The New Jerusalem, the mountain of God, has twelve gates and twelve foundations which may have been what the twelve stones on Satan's breastplate represented. There is a clear indication of divine perfection in Satan's twelve-stoned emblem of authority.

When we contemplate which priestly office Satan may have held, we remember that there was no sin and hence, no need for blood sacrifices. Certainly, officiating sacrifices was one of the major duties of an earthly priest, though it was by no means the only duty. Their other roles were to make pronouncements on behalf of God, to instruct people in his ways (2 Chr 17:3–9; Neh 8:2–3), and to sing praise to God (2 Chr 29:30). Our theory that Satan performed priestly duties is substantiated by the fact he was called "the anointed cherub [keruv mimshakh כְּרוּב מִמְשַׁח] who covers" (Ezek 28:14).

The word anointed is of course the same as *mashiach* (messiah), which refers to pouring oil on someone's head, which in turn meant the person had been chosen for leadership. [66] When Samuel anointed (*mashakh*) Saul by pouring oil on his head, it signified how a formerly regular guy was given a special purpose. In the case of Saul, it meant: you are going to be God's appointed leader, the visible leader for the people; you are going to now be the one to whom the people will look for leadership. The same was true for David.

Therefore, Satan's role as priest was to serve as the leader to communicate God's instructions, directives and will to others. Just as priests taught and interpreted God's commands, Satan likely would have been tasked with those priestly responsibilities.

SATAN – GUARDIAN OF EDEN

Satan was "in Eden, the garden of God" (Ezek 28:13). [עדן גן *Gan Eden*], the Garden of Eden, means an enclosed, protected area (*gan*[67]) of pleasure (Eden). It was necessarily a sacred space, for after Adam and Eve sinned, "the LORD God sent him out of the garden of Eden" (Gen 3:23).

Satan was charged with overseeing the sacred place: You defiled your sanctuaries" (Ezek 28:18). The word "your sanctuaries" [*mikdesheikha* מִקְדָּשֶׁיךָ] is from the root: *qoph, daleth, shin*: the same as *kadosh*, which is what the seraphim (possibly cherubim) chant day and night before the throne of God. It is the same word that is used of the temple. TWOT explains:

> Miqdāsh denotes that which has been devoted to the sphere of the sacred. When it refers to the sanctuary, it connotes the physical area devoted to the worship of God. This area was sacred because it was the place where God dwelled among the people (Ex 25:8) and its sanctity was not to be profaned (Lev 12:4; 19:30; 20:3; 21:12, 23). The word Miqdāsh may refer to the abode of

44

God in Ps 68:35 [H 36], but some commentators see this as the temple in Jerusalem. Metaphorically the word is used to refer to a place of refuge (Isa 8:14).[68]

It was in this enclosed, protected, sacred place which Satan was charged with protecting, that the conflict occurred. (See Appendix 2 Angel Freewill).

So far, we see that Satan's job and official charge was to be an "anointed protective / guardian cherub" stationed in the Garden of Eden. What caused him to rebel?

SATAN CORRUPTED HIS WISDOM

When a murder victim is found, one of the big questions is to determine motive. What drove the murderer to do what he did? What was Satan's motive? Satan was endowed with the gift of unparalleled beauty and wisdom. To understand why Satan staged a coup and was willing to throw away his exalted position and rebel against his Maker, we need to go recreate the scene[69] of the crime and see if we can spot the motive.

To set our stage, we need to consider a few parameters. Just before God created Adam, it says in Genesis: And God saw that it was good" (Gen 1:25). After the creation of Adam, we read: "Then God saw everything that He had made, and indeed it was very good" (Gen 1:31). Thus, on both sides of the creation of Adam, the coast was clear, nothing wicked was on the horizon. It was an "all systems go."

We might do well to employ the principle of Occam's razor which posits that if the simplest explanation works, we should use it rather than looking for a more complex one. Therefore, if the text says that God saw everything He had made, and if nothing is hidden from God (Prov 15:3; Jer 16:17; Luke 8:17), then it stands to reason that all things in all of creation which were "framed by the word of God ... which are seen ... not made of things which are visible," (Heb 11:3) were also "very good".

The "very good" stamp, then, was also affixed to the angelic host, including Satan. Therefore, the preflight checklist came back "very good". With this in mind, let us recreate the scene of the crime.

God created Satan as the greatest of all his creatures—surpassing every other in beauty and wisdom. God held nothing back. God anointed him, that is, He called him to be a leader, God's principle agent. He was second only to God, just as Joseph was given authority to be ruler of all Egypt and was second only to Pharaoh.

"You shall be over my house, and all my people shall be ruled according to your word; only in regard to the throne will I be greater than you" (Gen 41:40).

Thus, God established Satan as his anointed, his special agent, his viceroy and prime minister, authorized to do his bidding, to speak on his behalf, and to "sign God's checks." Satan was steward of all God's house. When Satan spoke, it was as if it was God Himself, just as Joseph spoke and acted on Pharaoh's behalf with absolute authority.

Joseph's eminence would not have threatened or lessened the power, authority and right of Pharaoh's heir to the throne. Even if Joseph would have had an exceptionally lengthy career before Pharaoh's heir took the throne, Joseph's position would have remained the same. In the same manner, Satan could be Prime Minister and God's son, Jesus, would still hold the special place as the true heir of God's throne.

Satan was never given God's throne; rather, he was authorized to act, speak and decree on God's behalf, just as Joseph acted, spoke and decreed on Pharaoh's behalf. Joseph was well pleased to occupy the position endowed him and never thought of overthrowing Pharaoh. He recognized that his great power, exalted position and absolute authority were granted to him by Pharaoh; he could never occupy the throne of Pharaoh for he was not Pharaoh, nor would he ever be the son of Pharaoh.

God's *modus operandi* is to enable and empower his creatures. He could do everything by Himself if He desired. He does not need us. It is like when you put together a shelf from IKEA and your little ones say, "Daddy, can we help?" You do not really need their help and chances are, they might make the whole process longer, but it is more enjoyable with them. This seems to be why He created us.

In Daniel 4, King Nebuchadnezzar was informed through a dream that he would be judged for his arrogance. The message is not from God directly, but by "decree of the watchers" (Dan 4:17). God empowered the angels or watchers to make decisions on his behalf. They were not and are not merely loudspeakers relaying God's dictations, though they may do so on occasion. Rather, they are intelligent, reasoning creatures whom God allows to act autonomously and independently of Him.

Satan was a member of an ancient guardian class; and being of highest rank, he was the highest of the highest, outranked only by God Himself. He had authority to act as God's viceroy. With the wisdom to know that God was and is the most powerful, why did he throw it all away? He had been given everything, why spoil it?

HIS HEART WAS PROUD

> God gives us the answer: "Your heart was proud because of your beauty; you corrupted your wisdom on account of your splendor" (Ezek 28:17 NET).

It was Satan who corrupted his own wisdom: he was the active agent. Nothing happened to him; he was not passive in the transformation. He was the one who caused the decay of his endowment of wisdom due to his arrogant confidence in his own beauty. This means that he made a conscious choice. He was not preprogrammed to be bad or to fall from God's grace. He mindfully chose to stage a coup against his Creator and rightful King. Why?

The bottom line is that Satan did not want to serve others: He wanted everybody to serve him. He looked at himself in the mirror and said, "Whoa, good-looking. Where did you come from?" He looked at his SAT and GRE scores and was like, "Wow, 100%. What do you know? I really am all that." He looked at his resume: "First in charge of God's kingdom. Wow. I deserve of all this stuff. And you know what? Creation should bow down to me. Creation should serve me because look at all that I have. Look at all that I am." It would be easy to come to that conclusion because of his splendor and beauty.

However, it was not an outside force acting upon him that corrupted him. We read: you corrupted your wisdom, because of your beauty. He **chose** to corrupt what he knew to be true because he was looking at himself. Being full of wisdom, he must have heard his own voice say, "Who gave you these things? Wasn't it God, the Creator of heaven and Earth who made you, who spoke you into existence? Will He not forever be a million billion trillion times greater than you? Even infinitely greater than you? Even though He gave you all this amazing stuff, you are still nothing compared to God, compared to the Creator. How can you possibly boast?"

In reality, Satan had no reason to be proud. Sure, he possessed unimaginable beauty. On a scale of ten, he was a ten. We get the impression that he may have equaled God in beauty. He also possessed unparalleled wisdom. He was full, which meant that he lacked nothing. It seems impossible that he could be as wise as God, yet the text says that he was full (not lacking) in wisdom. Thus, when he compared himself with God in terms of beauty, he equaled God. When he compared himself with God in terms of wisdom, he apparently thought he equaled God, as well. When he noted his authority, he acted as if he were God. It is not hard to understand how he could reach the conclusion that he was not just an agent empowered by God, but was also worthy to be praised and revered as God and in place of God.

Ironically, he proved himself to be nothing like God; looking like God on the outside is no big deal ... He created him as such. To truly be like God, he needed to choose to act like Him. We too must choose to lay down our lives, our self-interests and to be servants to one another. We must learn to act with love, which is sacrificial service toward one another. (See Appendix 7 Leaven).

> "If I then, your Lord and Teacher, have washed your feet, you also ought to wash one another's feet. For I have given you an example, that you should do as I have done to you" (John 13:14–15).

The path to truly being like God required Satan and the other angels to sacrificially serve others, especially those lower than themselves; This feat is perfectly demonstrated by Jesus going to the cross. Satan was unwilling to do this. Satan boasted in the attributes he shared with God, but the one that he was required to demonstrate himself, which was to sacrificially love and serve; he refused. He set the example that rulers of the nations would later practice, as Jesus said: "The rulers of the Gentiles lord it over them, and those who are great exercise authority over them" (Matt 20:25).

SATAN REFUSED TO SERVE

Satan refused to be a servant to those lesser than himself. Serving the one up the chain of command and submitting to one stronger than yourself is expected, required and merits nothing special. In contrast, God requires us to lay down our lives and become the servant of all. Whom could Satan have served? For starters, certainly every other angel was lesser than him in rank, beauty and wisdom. If Satan had within his character the attribute of servant-leadership, he could have served them, and of course, Adam.

49

Let us imagine the Garden of Pleasure: the light of the sun pokes through the majestic canopy of trees, home to animals of every sort. The rich scent of oranges, passion fruit, peaches and fresh flowers permeate the untainted air. The garden is painted with vibrant colors. Hummingbirds flit from tree to tree drinking in the sweet nectar. A lovely glow emanates from every living thing.

God lovingly fashions a form from the *adamáh* (soil) with his powerful hands and tenderly bends over and breathes his Spirit into the nostrils of the dirt creature (Gen 2:7, John 20:22). "Adam!" God calls him. He has a reddish hue like the *adamáh*[70] out of which he had been taken. After absorbing the light from God, Adam emitted a strong whitish glow. Not only does Adam share in God's image and likeness, but God has actually breathed his own life-force into him!

Satan was the anointed protective / guardian cherub stationed in Eden to watch over Adam, the son of God (Luke 3:38) who also had God's seed (DNA / information, 1 John 3:9). Satan was the exalted, standard of perfection chief steward, but Adam was the heir of God's creation (not throne). God gave Adam "dominion over the fish of the sea, over the birds of the air and over every living thing that moves on the earth," (Gen 1:28). The Psalmist explains how man is the heir in a wonderful way:

> For You have made him a little lower than the angels, And You have crowned him with glory and honor. You have made him to have dominion over the works of Your hands; You have put all things under his feet (Ps 8:5–6).

Satan calculated that if he killed the heir, the world would be his, just as Jesus described in a parable about the evil vinedressers: "But those vinedressers said among themselves, 'This is the heir. Come, let us kill him, and the inheritance will be ours'" (Mark 12:7). If Adam, the heir, died then he as the chief steward would be the heir. Abram said that very thing to God when he had no genetic heir:

> But Abram said, "Lord GOD, what will You give me, seeing I go childless, and the heir of my house is Eliezer of Damascus?" (Gen 15:2) Then Abram said, "Look, You have given me no offspring; indeed one born in my house is my heir!" (Gen 15:3)

If Pharaoh had a son, it did not affect Joseph the prime minister. The throne always belonged to Pharaoh and his son, completely apart from the role of the prime minister. When God gave dominion of his creation to Adam, it did not reduce Satan's role, responsibilities or prestige in the least. Yet, Satan could not bring himself to serve someone lesser in rank and lesser in nature.

He likely understood the Earth and all its fullness will forever technically belong to God,"[71] but legally, he would be Lord of the Earth since Adam could not regain dominion due to death. Hence, Satan would adversely take possession of the Earth and would remain the ruler of the world indefinitely.[72] He would rule through the "the power of death" (Heb 2:14).

SATAN CHOSE NOT TO BE LIKE GOD

Ironically, the one who held the greatest position, who was a seal of perfection, full of wisdom and perfect in beauty, was not willing to truly be like God. He thought he was like God, because he had the externals, but these externals were gifts from God. He chose not to be like God when he refused to humble himself and love.

What does love really look like? Is love just giving a bouquet of flowers? Is love taking that special romantic interest out to dinner? Maybe. But really not. Those romantic gestures are easy; Anybody can do that. Love, real love, is sacrificial service to one another. This kind of servanthood is not in the sense that you are taken as a slave and now you serve your master; rather, it is where you voluntarily lay down your rights, priorities, options and prerogatives to sacrificially serve another person.

Satan deviated from God's characteristic of being a servant, which is the expression of love. For the sake of his beauty, Satan corrupted his wisdom despite knowing that "whoever humbles himself as this little child is the greatest in the kingdom of heaven" (Matt 18:4). He rejected what he knew to be true about God so that he could put forth his own agenda: that all would serve him. We can translate all these actions into one word: Self. Satan's kingdom is about self, about pride.

As the greatest, most sublime of God's creatures, full of wisdom, he knew that to be great required him to serve. Adam and Eve were the test God put in Satan's path to grant him the opportunity to be a servant so he could keep his office of prime minister.

Satan, as God's chief steward, was tested for faithfulness as Paul wrote: "Moreover it is required in stewards that one be found faithful" (1 Cor 4:2). His test for greatness was simple, as Jesus eloquently put it, "whoever desires to become great among you, let him be your servant. And whoever desires to be first among you, let him be your slave" (Matt 20:27).

Joseph was tested for thirteen years before he was raised up as the second most powerful man in Egypt. Unlike Joseph the faithful steward, Satan refused to serve and lusted for the throne, as well:

> "How you are fallen from heaven, O Heilel [Hêlēl הֵילֵל], son of the morning! How you are cut down to the ground, You who weakened the nations! For you have said in your heart: 'I will ascend into heaven, I will exalt my throne above the stars of God; I will also sit on the mount of the congregation On the farthest sides of the north; I will ascend above the heights of the clouds, I will be like the Most High'" (Isa 14:12–14).

By seeking God's throne, Satan by necessity, shifted his focus from serving God and serving others (lesser than himself), to serving himself. He claimed to be equal with God, something no creature can ever claim against his Creator. And unlike Abram's faithful steward, Eliezer of Damascus, who was going to inherit all things until Isaac came along, Satan calculated he could arrange for Adam, the heir, to have a little "accident" and die before fully taking possession of his inheritance.

Satan's scheme would leave Adam and humanity without an inheritance until Jesus later came in the form of a servant (Phil 2:7) as the last Adam (I Cor 15:45), and would reconcile the sons of Adam with God (Col 1:22). He would demonstrate how he was committed[73] to serve ones lesser than himself to regain the inheritance Adam had lost (John 3:16; 15:13).

Hence, we have a motive to our crime scene: Satan would destroy mankind before he would bow in service to a man made of dust; he refused to be a servant to others. His post as the chief ministering spirit was to serve those who needed to inherit salvation. When God created Adam and Eve, they were innocent and were not dying, but neither did they have complete immortality yet as they were not immune to sin. In other words, they could have lived a long time in their innocent state, but at some point, they presumably would have had the opportunity and need to eat from the tree of life in order to seal them as immortals. Satan understood their situation very well and saw an opportunity to stage the ultimate coup and overturn God's kingdom of sacrificial love, and thereby ensure that his own greatness could be recognized and adored. Once he crossed this threshold, he could never go back. Ever. There is no room for the exaltation of self in God's kingdom. With raging malice in his heart, he set out to defile the sanctuary with his deadly weapon: slander.

Chapter 4: Satan's Slanderous Revolt

Satan became enraged by the notion that he, the great Angel, must be a servant to Adam, made of dust. So the root of jealousy and bitterness began festering within him. We see this egotism in ancient Sumerian texts. One said of him: "Enlil's commands are by far the loftiest ... He is the one that decides the fate, etc. He alone is the prince of heaven, the **dragon** of the earth." [74]

Adam and Eve were childlike in their understanding of the great cosmos, and their wisdom could not compare to his. Even so, he was charged with watching over the creatures made of dust, guiding and serving them in any way needed. This obviously brought out the worst in him. His snake-dragon qualities are again on display in ancient Mesopotamia via Ninurta, one of his syncretisms.

> Lord Ninurta ... has perfected heroship, Dragon with the "hands" of a lion, the claws of an eagle ... Lord Ninurta, when your heart was seized (by anger), You spat venom like a snake. [75]

Instead of presenting himself as a servant set-apart as a living sacrifice, so to speak, and becoming like his Creator—which was both acceptable to Adonai and was his reasonable service—he began to think more highly of himself than he ought. Incensed with jealousy toward Adam, he lifted up a powerful weapon to defame the name of his Creator. How ironic that the very gift of unparalleled beauty caused him to become self-centered and to relinquish true wisdom. Instead of embracing humility, which would have led to honor, he chose pride and arrogance, which ultimately led to his fall toward destruction.

His deadly, slanderous weapon was a simple question: "Has God indeed said? (Gen 3:1). This tiny question was an insidious, but subtle slander of God's character. He was asking, can you really trust what God said? Next, he told a lie about the consequence of eating from the tree of the knowledge of good and evil, "You will not surely die" (Gen 3:4), and then proceeded to truthfully tell the purpose of the tree: to be like God.[76] "For God knows that in the day you eat of it your eyes will be opened, and you will be like God, knowing good and evil" (Gen 3:5).

We know that his last statement was true for God himself says as much: "And the LORD God said, behold, the man is become as one of us, to know good (*tov* טוֹב) and evil (*ra* רָע) (Gen 3:22, KJV). God wants beings that are like Him and with whom He can interact lovingly—that requires freewill[77]—that everyone has the chance to choose for Him or against Him.[78] Adam and Eve could have 1) refused to eat, thereby exercising their freewill choice, and their eyes would be opened to the knowledge of good—what God delights in, and the knowledge of evil—what God does not delight in (See Appendix 2, Evil), but **without death**, and they would be permitted to stretch out their hands and take from the tree of life and live forever; or 2) they could (and did) eat from the tree, have their eyes opened to the knowledge of good and evil with the consequence of severing their connection with God (which is death, decay, and degeneration entering their bodies and souls) and thereby being banned from eating from the tree of life and being banished from the Garden of Eden.

The book of Ezekiel describes Satan's actions: "You were perfect in your ways from the day you were created, till iniquity [*avlata* עַוְלָתָה] was found in you." (Ezek 28:15) This word means "to deviate from and hence to do what is opposite of the character of God."[79] Satan originally did what was in accordance with the character of God until one day he deviated. TWOT makes it clear that it is not just a philosophical departure from an ideal—but it is an action or deed.

In Hebrew, the basic meaning of this root means to deviate from a right standard, to act contrary to what is right. The verb is a denominative from *āwel/'awlâ* and occurs only twice in the Old Testament ... In Isa 26:10 it describes the activity of the people of Judah who act unjustly (KJV; "perversely," RSV) in contrast to upright behavior... an act or deed that is against what is right ... behavior contrary to what is right.[80]

Satan was perfect until he misbehaved, acted out and committed a deed that was contrary to God's righteous standard. The next verse in Ezekiel reveals his deviation was "by the abundance of [*rekhulatkha* וּרְכֻלָּתְךָ]" (Ezek 28:16).

THE SLANDERER

The big question, of course, is what exactly does *rekhulatkha* mean? It has been typically translated as "trading", which is a possible translation.[81] But is it the best interpretation?

The word comes from the root [*rakhal* רכל] which according to BDB Hebrew-English Lexicon means: "to go about (meaning dubious) 1.a. trafficker, trader." *Rekhulatkha*, based on the original root [rakhal רכל] (H7402) means "slander, slanderer, tale bearer, informer ... someone who goes about as a talebearer spreading gossip or things that are in some way destructive ... a scandal-monger (as travelling about)."[82]

Gesenius notes its phonetic relationship to the word *ragal* [רָגַל] "to go on foot" and how it carries the meaning of "to traffic." The secondary meaning is "for the sake of slandering, whence [*rakhil* רָכִיל] slander."[83]

We therefore have a definition for [*rakhil* רָכִיל] as someone who goes about as a slanderer, spreading gossip or things that are in some way destructive. In other words: spreading malicious information. This sounds exactly like what Satan did in the Garden. Revelation 12:9 reveals more about Satan's

various titles, calling him the dragon and the serpent of old —
the latter a clear reference to Genesis 3 — and then mentioning
the term "devil."

THE DEVIL

The word devil comes from the Greek *diabolos* [διάβολος]
"slanderous, backbiting", derived from *diaballo* [διαβάλλω]
"throw or carry across" (wrestling).[84] The Liddle Scott Jones
Classical Greek Lexicon describes exactly the alternate meaning
of *rekhulatkha* [רְכֻלָּתְךָ] that we have proposed.

> διαβάλλω: — throw or carry over or across in
> wrestling, pass over, cross, put through, set at variance
> set against, **bring into discredit**, to be **filled with
> suspicion and resentment against another**, attack a
> man's character, calumniate, accuse, complain of
> without implied malice or falsehood, reproach a man
> with, **misrepresent**, speak or state slanderously, **give
> hostile information**, without any insinuation of
> falsehood, lay the blame for a thing on, declare it
> spurious, deceive by false accounts, **mislead**, divert
> from a course of action. (Emphasis mine).[85]

Satan, filled with suspicion and resentment against God, was
going about to the other angels subtly discrediting and
misrepresenting God and attacking his character. In other
words, his iniquity was slandering God. According to Ezekiel
28:16, it was not a one-off offense but in fact, an **abundance**
of slander. The lesson we glean is God did not cast Satan to
the ground for one aberrant thought, but for an abundance
of misbehavior.

This alternate reading of Ezekiel 28:16, of "slandering" versus
"trafficking", fits much better with the anointed cherub who
covers. He was not trafficking merchandise. He was giving
hostile information about God and misrepresenting his

character. Dr. Robert Luginbill, in his book, *The Satanic Rebellion*, also sees the problem with translating *rekhulatkha* as "your trading".[86]

The only thing he could have traded was slander. The translation "slander" maintains the meaning of "going about" and includes the nuance of "misrepresenting, attacking character", and it is confirmed by Satan's Greek title *diabolos* (devil) which means slanderer. Based on the aforementioned, my translation is therefore: "By the abundance of your [*rekhulatkha* רְכֻלָּתְךָ] **slandering** you became filled with violence within, and you sinned" (Ezek 28:16).

This provides a different perspective; Satan was not hawking his merchandise: "Hey, guys you need to get the latest Angel-phone!" God did not come in with an anti-trust case against him. It was not like God said: "Satan! You are selling too much. I have to stop your monopoly." That was not it. With whom would Satan trade, anyway? The other angels?

Figure 15 Committing Suicide.

Satan subtly slandered God in the Garden of Eden because he did not want to serve anyone, but instead wanted all to serve him. He persuaded Adam and Eve to curse themselves, (See Appendix 5 Balaam), to put the gun to their own heads and dig their own grave, as in Figure 15. He used slander to incite Adam to eat the fruit God forbad, knowing Adam would "surely die" (Gen 2:17), and he would subsequently commit all his progeny to perpetual death (Rom 5:12; 1 Cor 15:21–22). Adam's transgression caused an imbalance, a debt, a legal lien upon the Earth which must be balanced or paid (we will explore this in detail when Jesus takes the scroll in Revelation 5). Thus, Adam's dominion, prerogative and hereditary right to the Earth were forfeited and consequently, Satan would occupy the Earth in place of its legal and rightful possessor. Satan usurped Adam's rulership which is proved by Jesus calling Satan the "ruler of the world" (John 14:30).

Perhaps the most heinous part of Satan's plot was that Adam and Eve did not suspect anything because they seemed to already know and trust Satan. He came to Adam and Eve as God's chief steward, prime minister and high priest who oversaw everything and was charged with protecting the sacred place they occupied. They had no reason to question his motives. They had known him since the day of their creation. Satan was therefore able to come to them in his unfallen, glorious state and they listened.

It is important to understand that he came to them with evil intent in his heart. However, unlike the movie, "Minority Report", in which people could be incarcerated for future crimes they had not yet committed, in God's economy, a person must first commit the crime in reality before they do the time. Jesus' statement: "Whoever looks at a woman to lust for her has already committed adultery with her in his heart" (Matt 5:28). Lust is a craving to have something or someone that is not yours.

A decision to perpetuate and continue this line of thinking eventually leads a person to committing an action. However, it must be pointed out that there is no specific punishment for lust. (See Appendix 7 Leaven). The many consequences for lusting might include neurological pathways forming that affect the brain or harmful chemicals being released in the brain that lead to depression, addiction and dangerous behaviors. Left unchecked, lust will eventually lead to adultery. However, only real adultery is punishable in God's economy.

Thus, Satan lusting about being like God was not enough to deserve judgment; he had to do the deed and slander was the key.

SATAN CAST TO THE GROUND

After speaking with Adam and Eve about what happened, God turned to his once trusted prime minister and proclaimed the consequence of his action: he would lose his blessed status among animals and would instead be cursed above all others, he would lose his beauty and splendor, and he would lose the fiery-nature he enjoyed as a cherub.

We have looked at three major passages: Genesis 3, Isaiah 14 and Ezekiel 28, that deal with the fall of Satan. In all three, Satan is in the Garden of Eden, and God pronounced the immediate judgment of being cast to the ground and the future consequence of his slander. We note the several similarities by comparing them in the chart on the next page.

Comparison of Passages of Satan Cast to the Ground		
Gen 3:1, 14	**Isa 14:12–15**	**Ezek 28:13–18**
the serpent was more cunning than any beast of...the LORD God said to the serpent: "Because you have done this, You are cursed more than all cattle, And more than every beast of the field; On your belly you shall go, And you shall eat dust All the days of your life.	"How you are **fallen** from heaven, O Heilel, son of the morning! you are cut down **to the ground** (*Eretz*) ... For you have said in your heart: 'I will ascend into heaven, I will exalt my throne above the stars of God; I will also sit on the mount of the congregation On the farthest sides of the north; I will ascend above the heights of the clouds, I will be like the Most High.' Yet you shall be **brought down** to Sheol.	You were **in Eden, the garden of God**... You were on the holy mountain of God...I cast you as a profane thing out of the mountain of God; And I destroyed you, O covering cherub, from the midst of the fiery stones...I **cast** you **to the ground**, I laid you before kings, That they might gaze at you...I brought fire from your midst, it devoured you
In Eden	On God's mountain	In Eden & On God's mountain
Has exalted position	Has exalted position	Has exalted position
Blessed above animals	Great rank implied	Cherub – over animals
Had great wisdom	Great wisdom implied	Had great wisdom
Cast to ground / belly	Cast to ground	Cast to ground
Slandered God	Slandered God	Slandered God

Table 4 Comparison of Passages of Satan Cast to the Ground

We may infer from God's judgment that Satan did not expect to lose his legs and be cast to the ground. Until then, he possessed the most glorious body imaginable—he was the seal of perfection, full of wisdom and perfect in beauty" (Ezek 28:12). As high priest, he was covered in dazzling stones, but all of that was lost when he fell. Paired with his fire also being taken away, losing his legs may imply the loss of mobility and specifically, the loss of the ability to come through the veil.

God then declared:

"I will put enmity between you and the woman, and between your seed [zarakha זַרְעֲךָ] and her seed [zarah זַרְעָהּ]; He shall bruise your head, and you shall bruise His heel" (Gen 3:15).

"You, shall bruise his heel" means that Satan is going to injure the Messiah, the Seed of the woman. "He shall bruise your head" means the Messiah would inflict a mortal blow to Satan. This was essentially a declaration of war. God had just given hope to mankind and an ominous prophecy of doom to him. Satan did not underestimate his adversary; he has repeatedly done all he can to seal his control over the world forever. To maintain his control, Satan had to cause man to love him and slander his Creator to the point that they hate or ignore Him, and then get man to lust after himself and his fallen angels so his kingdom could openly manifest on the Earth.

Vignette 1: The Veil Descends

NOTE: *There are several vignettes throughout this book. They are short narratives putting the theology into a story format to make it easier to understand. The story is fiction but based on the facts we have amassed so far. Skip to the next chapter if you just want the facts.*

Adonai looked tenderly at his son Adam, yet grieved from what Adam put in motion. [87] They had lost Adonai's breath and the glow from his light was fading quickly. Soon they would not be able to endure his presence whatsoever. "The *adamáh* from which you were taken will now degenerate and decay and to it you will return because of what you have done." [88]

Immediately there was a deep rumble, like the groaning of a million voices at the point of death. All at once, a burst of radiation pulsated from the atoms of every tree, flower, and every blade of grass, from every rock and the soil under Adam's feet, leaving everything radioactive. The invisible world of cells and DNA within all animals, birds and fish which Adonai had formed out of the *adamáh* shared the fate of death of Adam and the *adamáh*. [89] The principle of rust entered the world where only a moment before, no such oxidation was ever known; metals and every material would have remained intact forever.

Adam sighed, looking at the ground and kneeling down, he took some dirt into his hands and stared at it for several moments. "I am made from the dust of the *adamáh* and to it I shall return," he whispered finally realizing that when Adonai formed him from the *adamáh*, He made him the living, federal head of all created matter. He then let the dirt slip through his fingers, contemplating the relationship he had with it.

"We are one and our fates are one. My fate determines the fate of everything in the material cosmos; the vitality of everything is linked and dependent on my life."

"Father!" Adam sobbed as he and Eve looked back with tears in their eyes. The Garden of Eden and Adonai's face [90] disappeared before their eyes like a scroll being unrolled before them;[91] they were unaware that it was the last time in their lives they would be face to face with their Father.[92] As it unrolled, the domain of Adonai and all the angels, both good and evil, disappeared from their vision forever; everything of that domain was completely cloaked from their sight. [93] Spatially the domains were on top of one another, occupying the same geography simultaneously, but were separated dimensionally by a wall or veil, like a membrane barring passage between the domains.

"Oh, for the day when the Promised One comes and restores Adonai's spirit and the glorious light that flowed from us," Adam sighed.

"How will the Promised One have the power to restore us when the corruption now touches every fiber of our being and that of our sons?" Eve asked through tears.

Adonai's promise of the one who would crush the head of Satan lingered in Adam's mind because freedom from death was his heart's desire. "I don't know," he answered despondently. "I don't know, yet we have His promise."[94]

Chapter 5: Satan Caused the Two Realms

Before Adam ate the forbidden fruit, the heavenly (spiritual) dimension and the earthly dimension were one realm—one domain, one plane of existence in which God, angels and man had open communication and relationship; There was no separation between the spiritual realm and the physical realm. There was perfect compatibility and agreement between them, an idea also found in Mesopotamian literature: "Heaven talked with Earth. Earth talked with Heaven." [95] God walked in the Garden, and man was able to look at his face and endure God's fire and lightning. (See Appendix 2 Angel Freewill).

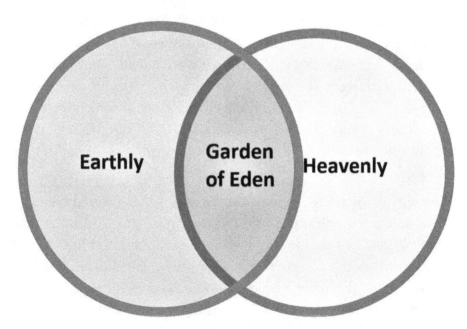

Figure 16 Garden of Eden in Earthly and Heavenly Domains.

Man's transgression brought decay, degeneration and death. God's perfection and the fallen physical, earthly realm became incompatible. Now God's fiery presence would scorch the ground like when He descended on Mt. Sinai (Ps 97:5). In the same way, the elements will melt when Jesus returns (2 Pet 3:10). Now man could no longer see God's face and live. The Garden of Eden, where God, angels and man could commune together was gone. Open, unveiled fellowship became impossible.

This divide of heaven and Earth caused by Satan (Enlil) was recorded by the ancient Sumerians. Samuel Kramer notes: "Anu (the creator god) carried off heaven while Enlil carried off the earth and assumed most of An's powers."[96] Likewise, Xianhuan Wang adds: "Enlil … was at about the same time cosmologically considered the deity who separated Heaven from Earth and Earth from Heaven."[97]

When God came in the Garden in the cool of the evening, Adam and Eve were compelled to hide themselves. Why? The first sign of disconnect was they realized they were naked. They had been clothed with light like God covers himself "with light as with a garment" (Ps 104:2). They observed the glow in which they had previously been clothed was fading; their biophotons were beginning to diminish, a concept I explored in depth in *Corrupting the Image, Vol. 1.*

This reality was displayed after Moses spent forty days with God and upon coming down the mountain, he "did not know that the skin of his face shone while he talked with Him" (Exod 34:29). When the congregation saw him, "The skin of his face shone, and they were afraid to come near him" (Exod 34:30), which led Moses to "put a veil on his face" (Exod 34:33). Paul tells us that Moses "put a veil over his face so that the children of Israel could not look steadily at the end of what was passing away" (2 Cor 3:13). That is, the glow in his face began to wane. Thus, once Adam and Eve transgressed, death entered their bodies and the connection to God broke. Satan's slander which led to their transgression set in motion a chain of events that affected them and the entirety of creation.

GROUND IS CURSED

God did not curse the ground because of Adam; rather, like a reporter, He simply presented the consequence of the degenerative decay-death reaction that Adam triggered (Gen 2:17). God said, "Cursed is the ground for your sake" (Gen 3:17). The Hebrew word "for your sake," is ba'avurecha [בַּעֲבוּרֶךָ]. It comes from the root, ayin, beth, resh [עבר]. It is the same root as the word: Hebrew. It means to cross over, pass. TWOT defines it: "Because of, for, intent that, for —'s, sake."[98]

TWOT explains Adam's relationship with the Earth:

> "ădāmâ. *Ground, land, planet*. Originally this word signified the red arable soil ... The Bible makes much of the relationship between man ('ādām) and the ground ('ădāmâ). Initially, God made 'ādām out of the 'ădāmâ to till the 'ădāmâ (Gen 3:23, to bring forth life). The 'ădāmâ was God's possession and under His care (Gen 2:6). Thus, the first 'ādām (the man, Adam) and his family were to act as God's servants by obeying Him in maintaining the divinely ordained and intended relationships vertically and horizontally. As long as this condition was sustained, God caused the 'ădāmâ to give its fruitfulness (blessing) to 'ādām. Then came sin. The unit 'ādām (Adam and Eve; see also (Rom 5:12) violated the created structure. The 'ădāmâ, henceforth, brought forth thorns and thistles rather than freely giving fruit (Gen 3:17). Since 'ādām had disrupted the paradisiacal life-producing state, he was driven off the paradisiacal 'ădāmâ and sentenced to return to the 'ădāmâ (Gen 3:19). He was driven to it rather than it being given to him."[99]

God created Adam from the adamáh; Adam was the earth-man, the federal head of creation. Adam and the *adamáh* were linked physically and hence their fates were linked. When Adam ate from the fruit, death, degeneration and decay happened upon Adam and upon the Earth and material cosmos as well. Decay permeated the entire creation from the invisible world of cells and DNA to all the animals, birds and fish which God had formed out of the adamáh. [100] Degeneration began within all living and non-living matter; the atoms of every tree, flower, blade of grass, rock, mountain, planet and star. The complete composition of all physical creation became incompatible with God's fiery presence. [101]

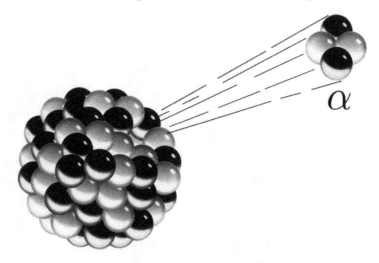

Figure 17 Release of an alpha particle.

Degeneration of rocks has been observed when alpha particles escape, leaving them slightly radioactive. Nuclear physicist Dr. Robert Gentry has examined over 100,000 discolorations in minerals and discovered a process of decay that happened close to the formation of the Earth in granite rocks around the world. He writes that "in some thin samples of certain minerals, notably mica, there can be observed ... concentric dark and light circles." [102] He describes how radiohalos, which are etched within granite, Earth's foundation rocks, "are beautiful microspheres of coloration, halos, produced by the radioactive decay of primordial polonium, which is known to have only a fleeting existence."[103] (See Figure 17 on adjacent page). During an interview with Research Communications Network in 1997, Dr. Gentry said, "Some halos ('polonium' halos) imply a nearly instantaneous crystallization of Earth's primordial rocks: and this crystallization must have occurred simultaneously with the synthesis/creation of certain elements." [104]

Dr. Gentry's work strongly suggests that the Earth went from a perfect and "decayless" state to one of decay very quickly and early in the history of the planet. Because God repeatedly declared the Earth and all therein to be good (Gen 1:10, 12, 18) at every stage of its creation and then very good at its completion (Gen 1:31), the process of death, decay and degeneration (radioactivity) came into effect because of Adam, because all of creation shares Adam's fate: when Adam fell, creation fell; when Adam (mankind) is restored, creation is also restored. This is why Paul said:

> For the earnest expectation of the **creation eagerly waits** for the revealing of the **sons of God**. For the **creation was subjected to futility**, not willingly, but because of Him who subjected it in hope; because the creation itself also will be **delivered from the bondage of corruption into the glorious liberty of the children of God**. For we know that the whole creation groans and labors with birth pangs together until now (Rom 8:19–22) (Emphasis mine).

BDAG Greek-English lexicon defines "corruption" (Greek word *phthora* φθορά) as a "breakdown of organic matter, dissolution, deterioration, corruption." A term that encapsulates the idea of "bondage of corruption" is degeneration. Because of the Fall, the Earth itself is now in a state of degeneration, whereas before, it had been generative.

The Earth is now longing to be freed (not destroyed) into the glorious liberty of the sons of God (Rom 8:19–22), which will occur in conjunction with the resurrection and return of Jesus, when the sons of God (believers) receive their new bodies. The decay (corruption) latent in the Earth will be reversed so that we will live on the same ball of dirt that God created in the beginning. The veil in the tabernacle was a copy of the things in heaven (Heb 8:5). The tearing of the first veil (not in the holy of holies) is a picture of the literal veil that will be torn (Isa 64:1) and rolled up (Isa 34:4; 2 Pet 3:10).

THE VEIL BETWEEN HEAVEN AND EARTH

After God announced the consequences of man's actions, God had to remove Himself from his own creation, lest his fire destroy it. [105] This removal is what the Scriptures call the veil. It is what marks the boundary between our earthly, physical domain and the spiritual domain. Isaiah first spoke of its removal:

> "And He will destroy on this mountain the surface of the covering cast over all people, And the veil that is spread over all nations. He will swallow up death forever, and the Lord GOD will wipe away tears from all faces" (Isa 25:7–8).

The prophet Isaiah also pined: "Oh that you would rend the heavens and come down" (Isa 64:1). Whatever the veil is, it can be torn and removed. There are four other distinct places where the veil (heavens) was opened:

- Ezekiel: "I saw the **heavens** were **opened** and I saw visions of God" (Ezek 1:1).

- "Jesus came up ... and the **heavens** were **opened** to Him" (Matt 3:16).

- Stephen: "I see the **heavens opened** and the Son of Man standing at the right hand of God!" (Acts 7:55–56).

- John: "I saw **heaven opened** ... Jesus was on a white horse" (Rev 19:11).

Layering techniques in animation can help us visualize the separation. In the Figure 18 graphic, there are four distinct cel layers (cel animation is the art of creating 2D animation by hand on sheets of transparent plastic called "cels"). [106] The superposition of the cels creates the composite picture for the animated story. Before the fall of Adam and Eve, the heavenly or spiritual layer and the earthly layer were superimposed, creating a shared composite picture. After the Fall, those of us in the earthly layer can no longer see into the heavenly layer. When Jesus returns, the layers will merge back together.

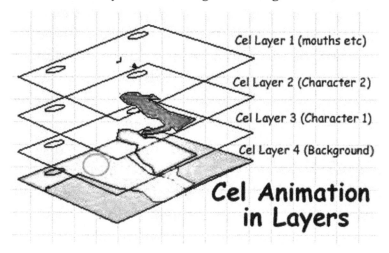

Figure 18 Animation in Layers.

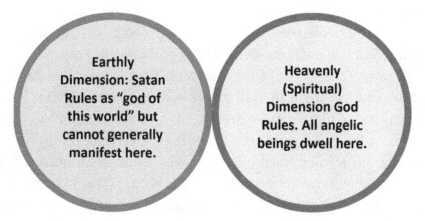

Figure 19 Comparison of Heavenly and Earthly Dimensions.

Thus, Adam and Eve witnessed the veil close like a great curtain, and the realm behind it became blocked from their sight. Spatially, nothing had moved; the realms were on top of one another, yet separated dimensionally by a veil, like a membrane, barring passage between the domains. God had to drive them from the Garden and place a barrier to the tree of life, lest they take of it and live forever in their fallen state (Gen 3:23–24). Mankind has searched the world over and that tree is nowhere to be found because it does not exist in our realm or dimension, which is our plane of existence. Since that time, the cosmos has existed as two realms—the one in which we live, and the other where spirit-based beings live and where God's presence is manifest. The one realm split into two: the earthly dimension is what Satan rules, he is the god of this world; the heavenly or spiritual dimension is where God rules. (God rules all, of course, but Satan has authority in the earthly realm.)

When the Garden and the heavenly domain disappeared before their eyes like a scroll being unrolled in front of them,[107] this might have been the first time hot tears streamed down their cheeks; it would also be the last time they would see God's face.[108]

THE VEIL LIMITS SATAN

The closing of the veil not only protects creation from God's fiery presence, but it also severely limits Satan's access to this domain. Satan and his rebels can still see us,[109] and their proximity can be felt (Job 4:15). They can afflict man with disease as well as control the weather (Matt 8:16, 24), as we will explore in detail later. They are able to gain more access through occult séances, blood sacrifices (in their honor), drugs, and perhaps under other conditions for brief durations. However, Satan's communication between the realms is greatly limited. We will see how he and his rebels will continue to strive to maintain communication and open the Gates of Hades.

God wants to reunite the celestial realm with the earthly realm so that we can walk and fellowship with God and enjoy the pleasures at his right hand. Satan wants to prevent the day when Jesus opens the heavens and his heavenly tabernacle so that fire descends upon the Earth. Jesus was pining for that day when he said: "I came to send fire on the earth, and how I wish it were already kindled!" (Luke 12:49). When Jesus comes back, "He will destroy on this mountain the surface of the covering cast over all people, And the veil that is spread over all nations" (Isa 25:7). The sky will recede like a scroll (Rev 6:14), and he will "rend the heavens and come down" (Isa 64:1). The veil between heaven and Earth, between our domain and God's, will dissolve and the two dimensions will become one again.

Vignette 2: Satan Wants to Devour

Satan and the other rebels watched everything happening from the other side of the veil. "Now we will never be required to serve Adam, that speck of dust," Satan gloated, thinking how he outsmarted Adonai.

"Your ingenious plan to cause Adam to murder himself[110] was a great success," lauded one of the rebels. "You were correct. When you caused Adam to defy the command of Adonai, you forced him into a self-imposed exile, lest God's consuming fire[111] destroy the Earth. Now there is no hope for Adam or his progeny."

"Adonai, in all of his compassion, [112] would sooner divorce Himself from the Earth than let it be destroyed by his fiery-lightning presence.[113] I have successfully separated the abode of Adonai from the abode of Adam. The Earth is ours forever!" Satan proclaimed.

"Yet ... is not the Earth and all its fullness forever Adonai's?"[114] quizzed one of the rebels.

Satan exclaimed. "Can a son of Adam undo death? Can a son of Adam give a ransom for another? No, the redemption of their souls is costly, and none of them can live forever and not see corruption (Ps 49:7-9). Thus, the Earth's domain has been delivered to me. Technically it will always be Adonai's, but I have adversely taken possession of the Earth. He cannot touch it lest his glory destroy all therein[115] and Adam forfeited his right of dominion when he disobeyed. I now rule this world and hold the Keys of Death and Hades."[116]

"Yet for all that, we are left disfigured and barren,"[117] one of the rebel Watchers snarled, his face shriveled and sunken, reminding Satan how the fire in which they had previously been clothed was gone, leaving only a shadow of their former glory.

"Even now I feel the drain of power in myself. The removal of Adonai's fire and power has left us disconnected from the source of life. What have we gained if we are never satiated?" He bellowed greedily with a look in his eyes like a hungry lion.[118] "When Adam is hungry, he merely needs to eat the produce of the *adamáh*, which will still nourish him despite being degenerate. What can I consume to placate the ravenous void inside me?"[119]

"The life is in the blood," Satan stated. "Our energy will come from the life-force of any creature,[120] and even from the sons of Adam![121]

"How might we obtain blood since we are on this side of the veil?" asked one of the rebels.

Satan responded coolly. "As man's collective memory of the world beyond the veil fades, we will use our knowledge of the hidden secrets behind the veil to easily convince them that they must earn our favor by giving blood, the life-force of another. Believing we are divine, they will lust after our knowledge and seek it through divination. They will lust after our powers through sorcery.[122] We will give them that which they crave for a price, and in time, they will freely sacrifice their sons and daughters[123] under every spreading tree, in the ravines, and under the clefts of the rocks.[124] Then your hunger shall be sated, and you shall be satisfied in the most delectable way.[125] Lastly, we will seduce their daughters and we will create our own earthly bodies."

Chapter 6: Fallen Angels Crave a Habitat

atan and the fallen are without their original glorious-fiery covering, which we will see, may have driven their efforts to make Nephilim. We know that God covers Himself with light as with a garment (Ps 104:2). God took the fire out the midst (from inside) of his anointed cherub (who was fiery per Ezek 1:13). God brought fire out from the midst (from inside) of Satan, which means he lost his source of power and connection to God and the glory that covered him.

> "You defiled your sanctuaries By the multitude of your iniquities, By the iniquity of your slandering; Therefore I brought fire from your midst, it devoured you [וָאוֹצִא־אֵשׁ מִתּוֹכְךָ֙ הִיא אֲכָלַתְךָ֒ *vaotzi esh mitochecha hi achalatcha*] (Ezek 28:18).

Satan and the fallen angels have been left without their original covering, leaving them spiritually naked and with an incredible craving to be covered. The fallen ones' condition is analogous to Adam and Eve being left naked and possibly experiencing hunger for the first time. (See Appendix 1 Demons).

Jesus gives us some insights into the barren and restless feeling a demon experiences when cast out and how he desires to return to the body he possessed:

> "When an unclean spirit goes out of a man, he goes through dry places, seeking rest, and finds none. "Then he says, 'I will return to my house from which I came.' And when he comes, he finds it empty, swept, and put in order. Then he goes and takes with him seven other spirits more wicked than himself, and they enter and dwell there; and the last state of that man is worse than the first. So shall it also be with this wicked generation" (Matt 12:43–45).

Apparently, there is great discomfort in being uncovered and not inhabiting a living being. Separated from an earthly body, the demon goes "through dry places, seeking rest, and finds none." Overcome with this gnawing distress, the demon decides it is better to go back to his "house" and possess it once more. We find the same root οἰκητήριον, meaning "habitation" used to speak of the angels that did not keep their "abode / habitation" in Jude 1:6. Paul gives us more insight on the idea of a spirit needing a habitation:

> For we know that if our earthly house [οικια], this tent, is destroyed, we have a building from God, a house not made with hands, eternal in the heavens. For in this we groan, earnestly desiring to be clothed with our habitation [οἰκητήριον] which is from heaven, if indeed, having been clothed, we shall not be found naked (2 Cor 5:1–3).

Paul compares not having a body (just a soul) to being naked. This is interesting in light of the souls under the altar in Rev 6 of whom we are told, "A white robe was given to each of them" (Rev 6:11). Because they were comforted with a robe, we infer that they were "naked" before. They were in the presence of God, and yet being without a body was a lesser experience than having a body. Right now we occupy "tents", but in the age to come we will have a new, heavenly habitation like the angels (Luke 20:36).

THE DEMONIAC

Though Satan must still have some kind of body, it is not the habitation of glory and splendor that it once was. His body must have lost not only beauty, but also ability, which we infer from the fact that Satan is ironically looking to transfer his power, throne and great authority to a human. The one who wanted all to serve him must rely upon humans, whom he perceives to be lowly and inferior, to succeed. We also glean this from the encounter with the demoniac.

And when He had come out of the boat, immediately there met Him out of the tombs a man with an unclean spirit, who had his dwelling among the tombs; and no one could bind him, not even with chains, because he had often been bound with shackles and chains. And the chains had been pulled apart by him, and the shackles broken in pieces; neither could anyone tame him. And always, night and day, he was in the mountains and in the tombs, crying out and cutting himself with stones. When he saw Jesus from afar, he ran and worshiped Him. And he cried out with a loud voice and said, "What have I to do with You, Jesus, Son of the Most High God? I implore You by God that You do not torment me." For He said to him, "Come out of the man, unclean spirit!" Then He asked him, "What is your name?" And he answered, saying, "My name is Legion; for we are many." Also he begged Him earnestly that He would not send them out of the country. Now a large herd of swine was feeding there near the mountains. So all the demons begged Him, saying, "Send us to the swine, that we may enter them." And at once Jesus gave them permission. Then the unclean spirits went out and entered the swine (there were about two thousand); and the herd ran violently down the steep place into the sea, and drowned in the sea (Mark 5:2–13).

There are several important aspects to consider:

1. The man had super-human strength to even break chains due to the demons possessing him.
2. He lived among the tombs and cried out.
3. He cut himself with stones. Blood is generally released when we cut ourselves. The demons may have feasted on the letting of blood.

4. When Jesus showed up, the demons recognized one stronger than themselves.
5. The demons begged to not leave the country.
6. They preferred to enter (same word as possess) pigs rather than leave the country.

SATAN ENTERED JUDAS

Short of having an adequate body to inhabit, Satan has had to work through a willing agent. We see this clearly in the Gospels where Satan possessed Judas to carry out his machinations.

> Then Satan entered Judas, surnamed Iscariot ... (Luke 22:3). So he went his way and conferred with the chief priests and captains, how he might betray Him to them (Luke 22:4).

Because only Satan entered, Judas was able to carry on conversations and behave in quite a normal manner, unlike the demoniac who was filled with a legion (4,000-6,000) of demons. Yet like the demoniac, Judas must have gained significantly more strength, a keener faculty of mind, and a sense of invincibility. Satan likely possessed Judas because the task before him: destroying the One prophesied to stomp on his head, which was both important and personal! That was probably Satan's version of: "If you want a job done right, you do it yourself." Satan possessed Judas a second time. "Now after the piece of bread, **Satan entered him** (John 13:27). We know that Judas killed himself after betraying Jesus (Acts 1:18) in the valley of Hinnom. Incidentally, the final battle will take place in this vicinity.

It must have been a bother to Satan that just when he found a willing agent whom he could possess, the agent either got cold feet or died. Alexander the Great may also have been one of Satan's chosen earthly representatives who also died prematurely. Robin Lane Fox, *Traveling Heroes in the Epic Age of Homer*, comments on Alexander as the son of Zeus (who was also Satan):

"'Zeus', Alexander was later thought to have said, 'is the common father of men, but he makes the best peculiarly his own'; like many Roman emperors after him, Alexander was coming to believe that he was protected by a god as his own divine 'companion'... as son of god, a belief which fitted convincingly with his own Homeric outlook, in whose favorite *Iliad* sons of Zeus still fought and died beneath their heavenly father's eye"[126]

Though Alexander conquered the world and may indeed have had Satan (Zeus) as his divine companion, he still died at the young age of 33. If Satan had intended to use Alexander for establishing his empire, his plan was foiled by illness.

Hence, Satan was frequently in need of a new partner. These partners were unreliable, so Satan decided that it would be far better to have his own vessel in which he could incarnate and interact in this world. He would have complete, unbridled control.

DEMONS HUNGER FOR BLOOD

In addition to being spiritually naked and craving a physical habitation, Satan and his fallen have a power problem; they were unplugged from the power source and have been running on "batteries" ever since. They need to devour something to "recharge their batteries", but not physical things; thus, they were left with a sizeable problem: they had been stripped of their beauty and disconnected from the source of life, leaving them weak and hungry. Therefore, they have an insatiable craving to consume as stated by Peter: "The devil walks about like a roaring lion, seeking whom he may devour" (1 Pet 5:8).

Let us first consider how we recharge our human batteries. Adam and Eve lost their connection to God, the source of power, yet man can simply take of the produce of the *adamáh*: vegetables, fruit, grains, and even animals to recharge our "batteries" until, of course, physical death overtakes us.

But what can Satan and his angels consume to placate the ravenous void[127] inside them? They are not made of dirt; they are spirit beings. They therefore need to consume something of a spiritual nature—That something is what God said not to eat: blood.

> "For the life of the flesh is in the blood, and I have given it to you upon the altar to make atonement for your souls; for it is the blood that makes atonement for the soul. Therefore I said to the children of Israel, 'No one among you shall eat blood, nor shall any stranger who dwells among you eat blood'" (Lev 17:12).

The blood of a creature is more than merely hemoglobin; it has a spiritual capacity. The animal subject of a sacrifice (*korban* [קרבן]) is the object which permits the worshipper to come near to God.

> "'When any one of you brings [brings near וְיַקְרָיב] an offering [קָרְבָּן *korban*] to the LORD, you shall bring your offering of the livestock–of the herd and of the flock (Lev 1:2).

ATONEMENT IS A COVERING OR BATTERIES "R" US

Satan has twisted the mechanism God established to temporarily connect with man; God wants to be with us, but with the state of our current bodies, his fiery presence does not allow us to be face to face. Therefore, the blood of the sacrifice is able to make atonement [כפר *kafar*] (a covering) so the worshipper can come near God. Without a "covering", we cannot approach God; the blood makes atonement.

However, atonement is not a moral issue, since even the altar is something for which atonement was needed.

> "And you shall offer a bull every day as a sin offering for atonement. You shall cleanse the altar when you make atonement (*Kafar*) "Seven days you shall make atonement (*Kafar*) for the altar and sanctify it (Exod 29:37).

The altar never did anything wrong. It was morally perfect and unblemished, yet it needed to be atoned for. This shows that "covering" is the true underlying meaning. Yet why would an altar need a covering? Simple, because it would come in contact with God Almighty, a consuming fire. We have seen that Mt. Sinai was on fire when God came down. Therefore, the altar would need a covering so it would not burn and be consumed.

> Then he poured the blood at the base of the altar, thereby sanctifying it as a means to make atonement (*Kafar*) with it (Lev 8:15; See also Lev 16:18).

The priest would then take the blood of that animal and sprinkle it to cover the worshipers so they could safely be in proximity to God. It is important to note: "It is not possible that the blood of bulls and goats could take away sins (Heb 10:4). However, the purpose was not to take away the people's sins, but to provide a covering.

An illustration is found in the life of David Vetter, better known as the Boy in the Bubble, whose immune system was so weak he could not have physical contact with the outside world or even with his parents. As seen in Figure 20 (next page), his plastic bubble habitation provided a covering to protect him from the world. It did not take away his sickness, but it did allow him to be close to his parents. So too, the atonement by the blood of an animal provided a covering until a future date when we will get our new bodies which can once again endure God's fiery presence.

Figure 20 David Vetter, The Boy in the Bubble.

Therefore, Satan's food is the life force, the blood; in other words, he feeds on us. People that have gone deep into Satanism talk about the energy the demons receive from the blood of their victims. Thus, with every human sacrifice, every abortion, every war, and every murder, Satan and his kin are recharging their batteries. The more innocent the blood, the more energy is derived. We see the sacrifice of innocent children in Psalm 106 and Ezekiel 16 and many other passages:

> They served their idols, Which became a snare to them. They even **sacrificed** their sons And their daughters to demons, And **shed innocent blood**, The **blood of their sons and daughters**, Whom they sacrificed to the idols of Canaan; And the land was polluted with blood (Ps 106:36–38).
>
> ... and with all your abominable **idols**, and because of the **blood** of your **children which you gave** to them (Ezek 16:36).

This principle was brought out vividly in the 1999 dystopian movie, "The Matrix", in which machines have enslaved mankind and are using the energy extracted from their bodies to power themselves. The people are the batteries that power the machines. In order to derive the most power from their human batteries, the machines had to create a deceptive Matrix, a virtual (computerized) dream world in which everyone believed they were living out real lives. In a similar fashion, Satan must deceive the entire world (Rev 12:9) and entice us to lust. He has offered us heaven on earth, like a carrot dangled in front of a donkey, as above so below, in order to recharge his batteries and maintain control of the world.

Chapter 7: The Nephilim Solution

After the Fall, Satan and those who joined him lost their power and fiery covering and were trapped behind the veil, thereby limiting their influence in the realm of men. To combat this limitation, Satan enacted a plan: He would create human-angel hybrids which would provide them their very own biological suits for their embodiment and incarnation, to be the earthly habitations in which their spirits could dwell and rest without the need to share with fickle humans. It would be the best of both worlds—all the power, intelligence and immortality of angels with a biological "tent" for their spirits to inhabit, making them gods in the flesh. The bodies would be created as human-angel hybrids, but the bodies would be void of a spirit and could therefore be inhabited by a fallen angel.

Of course, part of Satan's genius has been that he gets others to do his dirty work. He would seduce the sons of God to mate with women and when they got caught, they would take the hit. We know that God had entrusted the angels with earth-based jobs from our discussion of Satan being stationed in the Garden of Eden in chapter 4. There you recall that that he "defiled his sanctuaries" (Ezek 28:18) which means that he was not faithful with the sacred space God had placed in his hands. We catch a few glimpses of the assignment angels had from Deuteronomy and Daniel.

> When the Most High gave the nations their inheritance, when he divided up humankind, he set the boundaries of the peoples, according to the number of the heavenly assembly (Deut 32:8 NET).

There is a Qumran fragment of this text that reads: According to the "sons of God." The Septuagint reads ἀγγέλων θεού (*angelōn theou*, "angels of God"), presupposing בְּנֵי אֵל (*benei el*) or בְּנֵי אֵלִים (*benei elim*).[128] The idea of angels being over nations is clearly established in Daniel 10. We see an angel who was bringing Daniel a prophecy was opposed and delayed by the prince of the kingdom of Persia, and also that Daniel would have to go and do battle with the prince of Greece, both of whom were fallen angels over their territories. (See Appendix 1 Demons).

NOT YET FALLEN

While we know ultimately from Revelation 12 that one-third of the angels followed Satan, we do not know how many followed him right out of the gate. What we do know is that the "sons of God" did something so evil in the days of Noah that God would eventually send a flood to erase it all. It is entirely possible that many of the angels who followed Satan chose that path in the time around and before the Flood.

Genesis 6 only tells us what they did, not whether they were bad before this action.

> When men began to multiply on the face of the earth, and daughters were born to them, that the sons of God saw the daughters of men, that they were beautiful; and they took wives for themselves of all whom they chose. There were giants on the earth in those days, and also afterward, when the sons of God came in to the daughters of men and they bore children to them. Those were the mighty men who were of old, men of renown (Gen 6:1–4).

Philo, an Alexandrian Jewish philosopher and contemporary of Jesus, unequivocally confirms the "giants were sprung from a combined procreation of two natures, namely, from angels and mortal women."[129] There are clues that suggest these angels had not yet committed iniquity; hence they were not yet fallen.

Peter gives his interpretation of what happened in Genesis 6. He says, "The spirits in prison (1 Pet 3:19), who formerly were disobedient, when once the Divine longsuffering waited **in the days of Noah**" (1 Pet 3:20). These spirits were disobedient in the days of Noah when they procreated with women, which landed them in prison. In Peter's second epistle, he elaborates on the event:

> "For if God did not spare the angels who sinned, but threw them into hell [*tartarosas*] and locked them up in chains in utter darkness, to be kept until the judgment, and if he did not spare the ancient world, but did protect Noah ... [and] turned to ashes the cities of Sodom and Gomorrah when he condemned them to destruction, ... and to reserve the unrighteous for punishment at the day of judgment, especially those who indulge their fleshly desires and who despise authority" (2 Pet 2:4–10 NET).

Notice that he speaks of the angels who were disobedient and sinned in the days of Noah. From this, we infer that they had not sinned previously, meaning they were, up until that moment, on God's team. Jude gives a similar interpretation; and based on the context, it sounds like the angels had not yet joined Satan's team.

> For certain men have crept in unnoticed, who long ago were marked out for this condemnation, ungodly men, **who turn the grace of our God into lewdness and deny the only Lord God** and our Lord Jesus Christ. But I want to remind you, though you once knew this, that the Lord, having saved the people out of the land of Egypt, afterward destroyed those who did not believe (Jude 1:4–5) (Emphasis mine).

Jude's point here is that certain men had the opportunity to come to God and to enjoy his goodness and blessings; but instead, they took advantage of his grace and mercy and turned to sexual deviancy. Jude then immediately turns to discuss the angels from Noah's day because they did the same thing.

91

And the angels who did not keep their proper domain but left their own abode [οἰκητήριον], He has reserved in everlasting chains under darkness for the judgment of the great day, as Sodom and Gomorrah, and the cities around them in a similar manner to these, having given themselves over to sexual immorality and gone after strange flesh, are set forth as an example, suffering the vengeance of eternal fire (Jude 1:6–7).

This shift strongly implies that these angels had not converted to Satan's team beforehand. That is, these particular angels who mated with women were not previously in league with Satan; Mating with women was their inauguration into his kingdom. Referring to the angels who heeded the temptation, the book of Jude explains how they "did not keep within their proper domain [*arkhen*]" (Jude 1:5a). That means they did not remain in the spiritual realm where they were authorized to be, "but abandoned their own place of residence [*oiketerion*]" (Jude 1:5). We considered the word *oiketerion* in a previous chapter and saw it referred to a spiritual body. We believers desire to put off our "tent" (our earthly bodies) and be clothed with our "*oiketerion*" (our "spiritual" bodies) (2 Cor 5:2).

When the angels came down to take the women, they quite likely were still good angels. Yes, they had evil plans in their hearts — but at that moment, they had not actualized their scheme.

It happened after the sons of men had multiplied in those days, that daughters were born to them, elegant and beautiful. And when the **angels, the sons of heaven**, beheld them, they became enamored of them, saying to each other, Come, let us select for ourselves wives from the progeny of men, and let us beget children (1 Enoch 7:1-2)(Emphasis Mine).

Above in bold it reads, "angel, the sons of heaven," but in an Aramaic text of 1 Enoch, the same passage reads: "Watchers,"[130] which is significant because the only place Watchers (עִירִין *irin*) is used in Scripture is in Daniel 4:17, where Nebuchadnezzar has a dream and the Watchers (holy ones) tell him that he will be judged. The Watchers in Nebuchadnezzar's dream are clearly on God's team. They are called "holy ones" and they intend for him to know that the Most High, the God of Daniel, rules men. Thus, in Enoch, the simplest reading is that watchers / angels / sons of heaven were not yet on Satan's team, but were in the process of changing sides.

GOOD ANGELS CAN MANIFEST

By persuading angels who are still on God's team to procreate, Satan solved a logistics problem. Fallen angels appear to be limited in their ability to freely enter this realm, whereas the good angels can come and go at will. (See Appendix 2 Angel Freewill).

For example, in Genesis 18, God and two angels showed up at Abraham's door, hence they were definitely good angels. After a while, the angels "turned away from there and went toward Sodom, but Abraham still stood before the LORD" (Gen 18:22). When they arrive in Sodom, the men of the city surrounded Lot's house and demanded to have sexual relations with them! (Gen 19:5). Thus, the good angels were able to come into the physical domain; they had bodies and the potential on a physical level to defile themselves, (not that they were in any way tempted). We are even told to entertain strangers as we might be entertaining angels unwittingly (Heb 13:2), which implies the good angels can manifest physically, at will.

In Scripture, we never see fallen angels, on the other hand, materialize physically in our realm. Their lack of physical manifestation in this realm appears to be due to their power problem; they need blood to energize themselves. When they have enough blood offered, like with an occultic event or séance,

93

they seem to be more easily able to manifest into this realm. Thus, uncorrupted angels seem to have no limitations in this regard, whereas fallen angels can only come in at great expense. (See Appendix 1 Demons.)

Through slander of God's good name, Satan undoubtedly could have used his unparalleled wisdom to turn the angels from serving God and man, to serving themselves. He may have caused good angels to defect using the model of Absalom, King David's son, who would sit in the city gate and tell the people of Israel how he would bring justice if he were the judge and so, he turned the hearts of the people against King David (See 2 Sam 15:2–6).

In a similar fashion, Satan may have seduced the angels with words like: "God is the only one worthy of your service and Adam is not. If serving God requires you to serve Adam, who is made of dirt, do you truly want to serve God?" Perhaps he showed them how he had successfully rebelled against God's "biased" kingdom and then enticed them with promises of how they would no longer need to serve man; they could instead become the masters, and man would become their servants! They would be worshipped as gods if they would mate with women and would create a race in their own image. We know Satan was the one who inspired this dastardly action from a text that was found on Mt. Hermon which we will examine in the next chapter.

THE SOUL – PREEXISTENT, CREATED OR TRANSMITTED?

We need to further explore the idea of the abode *oiketerion* (spiritual body) which the angels abandoned. Those "angels who did not keep their proper domain but left their own abode [οἰκητήριον]," are guilty of doing two things: not keeping their domain, their place of authority, and leaving (abandoning) their proper spiritual body. The text implies that by procreating with women they left their own spirit-based body. If they left their own bodies, then where did they go? The implication is they transferred their essence (DNA information code) into bodies of the Nephilim. To get our minds around this, we need to consider the various models of the origin of the soul. Where does the soul of a newborn baby come from? Is it preexisting in heaven? Does God create it at the moment of conception? Or is it transmitted from the parents? We will examine each model and consider this question.

The preexistence model of the soul from the Platonic school of thought, holds that the soul existed before conception and birth. For example, Origen "believed that souls fell in their pre-bodily state and were imprisoned into flesh as a punishment."[131] The Mormons also tend to follow this view. A variation on this theme is that the souls are with God waiting for a body to inhabit. This model seems very unlikely for regular human birth. In regard to our question of **what kind of soul** inhabited the Nephilim, if the preexistence model were accurate, then God would have intentionally sent the angels into the Nephilim.

The preexistence model fails because we know that the sons of Levi paid tithes to Melchizedek because they had "**come from the loins of Abraham;** for he was still in the loins of his father when Melchizedek met him" (Heb 7:5, 10). In plain English, Levi was genetically in the testes of his grandfather Abraham when the tithes were paid to Melchizedek. This proves that he was not a soul waiting for a body. He was a seed—information ready to be passed down. This concept is easier for us to grasp in the age of genetics and information science, both of which were unfathomable to the ancients.

The creationist model of the soul holds that God creates each soul at the moment of conception. The reason this model fails is that under this theory, Jesus would not be spiritually related to Abraham, Isaac, Jacob and King David, if each soul were created individually. This would also be true of the preexistence model.

The creationist model also does not explain the origin of the souls inhabiting the Nephilim bodies. Would God create evil beings who were so terrible that He would then destroy them in the Flood?

The last model is the transmission model of the soul. It teaches that the soul of a newborn comes from the parents—it is the immaterial information that is passed in the genes from parents to child. Think of the soul like sourdough bread. A pinch off the starter plus more flour and water is enough to keep the sourdough going for centuries.[132] Even recently, a bit of 4,500-year-old Egyptian yeast was revived and baked into delicious bread. So too, the information passed through the parents, plus nutrients and oxygen, forms the baby with the soul in it. Considering this genetically, human egg and sperm cells have only twenty-three individual (haploid) chromosomes. They combine during fertilization and equal the forty-six individual (diploid) chromosomes, which is the point at which a new human soul is transmitted from the parents.

If it takes two humans to form a new soul in the child, then supernatural being + human being would not yield a human soul. The transmission of the soul from parents to child would be broken because one of the parents is not human. We know this because though Jesus was related genetically to humanity, He was preexistent; He did not begin to exist at the incarnation— He is eternal and has always existed. Yet, the incarnation was the point at which the Godhead mingled seed (DNA, i.e. information) with humanity. We also discovered in *Corrupting the Image 1*, that **"a son will inherit an identical copy of his father's Y chromosome, and this copy is also essentially identical to the Y chromosomes carried by all his paternal forefathers"** (Emphasis mine), [133] meaning that all men throughout time have had a copy of Adam's Y chromosome.

Furthermore, Neil Bradman and Mark Thomas, in their article, "Why Y? The Y Chromosome In The Study Of Human Evolution, Migration, And Prehistory", suggested that the Y chromosome may in fact be "a record of an event"[134] in the life of the man who passed on the current Y chromosome. [135] From there we concluded that Jesus did not have Adam's Y chromosome and hence did not carry the defects or degeneration (sin), inherent in the copies of Adam's Y chromosomes in every subsequent male descendent. Therefore, though the human soul is always transmitted from the mother and father to the child, in Jesus' case, his spirit / soul (essence) must have been placed there. It was not transmitted because He is eternal. His soul / spirit did not originate from Mary and the Holy Spirit; He existed beforehand.

The Holy Spirit fused "the Jesus" gamete (spermatocyte) with Mary's gamete (oocyte) (recall that a gamete contains DNA, which is stored information, a non-material entity). The fusion of the two gametes is when the incarnation (becoming flesh cf. John 1:14) occurred. At that point, Jesus' divine information / soul became part of his DNA.

Therefore, it follows that the union of an angel and a human would have genetically created a physical body, but not necessarily a soul / spirit. The body would be a blank, an empty shell which could be filled with a spirit-being in need of a body. Jude says the angels "left their own abode (spiritual bodies)." They left them for the hybridized bodies we call Nephilim.

There is no technical reason that angels could not pass on their seed. They had the ability, but they did not have permission.

> "But those who are considered worthy to attain to that age and to the resurrection from the dead neither marry nor are given in marriage, for they cannot die anymore, because they are equal to angels and are sons of God, being sons of the resurrection" (Luke 20:35–36).

97

Resurrected people do not marry again because they do not die, because they are equal to the angels. We do not become angels, but our bodies will be similar, and we will be equal to the angels in their power and glory. The text says nothing about the angels' ability to pass on seed.

What is inside of a seed? Information—a non-material entity. We understand non-material data because we send information in our emails, voicemails, etc.; there is no physical substance to that information. We can interact with it, but we cannot touch it. A seed contains all information needed to become a living thing. A pumpkin seed holds all of the information needed to create a pumpkin. Angels have information, just as we have information. Even God has information; "No one having been born again continues to sin, for the seed of God dwells in him" (1 John 3:9).

However, the obstacle is that angels were not authorized to pass on their seed. God allowed it, but He did not bless it. In fact, the fallen angels' unrighteous action brought a curse of immense magnitude upon themselves and the world.

> There were giants on the earth in those days, and also afterward, when the sons of God came in to the daughters of men and they bore children to them. Those were the mighty men who were of old, men of renown (Gen 6:4).

The book of *Giants*, a grouping of Aramaic fragments found with the Dead Sea Scrolls, corroborates Genesis 6 by noting the corruption the angels wrought upon the Earth. The fragments have missing gaps, but they have been interpreted as:

> 2 [. . .] they defiled [. . .] 2[. . . **they begot] giants and monsters** [. . .] 3[. . .] they begot, and, behold, all [the earth was corrupted . . .] 4[. . .] with its blood and by the hand of [. . .] 5[giant's] which did not suffice for them and [. . .]

CHAPTER 7: THE NEPHILIM SOLUTION

6[. . .] and they were seeking to devour many [. . .] 7[. . .]
8[. . .] the monsters attacked it, (4Q531)(Emphasis mine).

We cannot help but notice how the angel's corruption also led to the creation of monsters which further corrupted the Earth.

2[. . .] flesh [. . .] 3al[l . . .] monsters [. . .] will be [. . .
] 4[. . .] they would arise [. . .] lacking in true
knowledge [. . .] because [. . .] 5[. . .] the earth [grew
corrupt . . .] mighty [. . .] 6[. . .] they were considering
[. . .] 7[. . .] from the angels upon [. . .] 8[. . .] in the
end it will perish and die [. . .] 9[. . .] they caused great
corruption in the [earth . . .] (4Q532 Col. 2, Frags. 1 - 6).

The fallen angels would have earthly bodies that belonged to them, and that were not temporarily borrowed from humans, because the bodies would now carry angelic genetic information. Biologically, the bodies of the Nephilim would be human-angel hybrids, but the indwelling spirit would be one hundred percent angel-spirit. It is entirely plausible that they were called Nephilim, meaning fallen, because they were inhabited by fallen angels.

Satan and his demons would have biological suits to be the earthly avatars for their spirits to inhabit. They would not have to entice humans to invite them to possess their bodies. Yet, they would have fleshly bodies in which they had full control, and would seemingly be human gods.

THE OATH

The angels realized that once they crossed the line, they could never return into God's kingdom. Their taking "wives for themselves of all whom they chose" (Gen 6:2) would be the point of no return; there was no going back. Ever. The eternal nature of their decision may be why they took an oath as recorded on an inscription on Mt. Hermon, which we will examine in the next chapter, and in 1 Enoch:7–8:[136]

Their whole number was two hundred, who descended upon Ardis, which is the top of mount Armon.[8] That **mountain therefore was called Armon, because they had sworn upon it**, and bound themselves by mutual execrations. [137]

Hermon (Armon) comes from *ḥāram* which means "a ban for utter destruction, the compulsory dedication of something which impedes or resists God's work, which is considered to be accursed before God."[138]

It is called "Hermon" because the angels committed to a curse upon themselves if they should not continue with their plan, which is another indication that when they came down upon Hermon, they still had a lot to lose. They were not doing a Hail Mary at the end of the game; everything was on the line for them. In fact, Samyaza is concerned that he will do the dirty deed and the others will chicken out, leaving him high and dry.

> [3]Then their leader Samyaza said to them; I fear that you may perhaps be indisposed to the performance of this enterprise; [4]And that I alone shall suffer for so grievous a crime. [5]But they answered him and said; We **all swear**; [6]And **bind ourselves by mutual execrations**, that we will not change our intention, but execute our projected undertaking. [7]Then they **swore all together and all bound themselves by mutual execrations** (1 Enoch 7:2–7)(Emphasis mine).

This ancient event has lived in the memory of mankind for millennia. It has been called Hermon (laid under a curse) since the earliest of times (See Deut 3:8; Josh 11:13). The area south, south-east of Mt. Hermon was known as Bashan, which means snake-dragon. The mountain and surrounding area were considered the abode of the gods, both heaven and hell simultaneously, and home of the Rephaim, King Og, and Enlil / Baal.

For the 'Canaanites' of Ugarit, the Bashan region, or a part of it, clearly represented 'Hell', the celestial and infernal abode of their deified dead kings, - Olympus and - Hades at the same time. It is possible that this localization of the Canaanite Hell is linked to the ancient tradition of the place as the ancestral home of their dynasty, the rpum. [139]

Satan quite likely gloated in his "perfect plan" coming together in the land of Bashan. After all, the seed of the Messiah would never be able to stomp on his head if the image-bearers of God were destroyed, and if they were recast in his image instead! Mankind would become the ultimate slave by yielding up their flesh for Satan's team to perpetually inhabit. The fate of mankind would have been worse than *The Matrix* where, at least, man could live out a satisfying simulation in their minds. If Satan's plan had not been interrupted, mankind would have become extinct and the image of God created in Adam would have been replaced with that of the fallen angels.

Satan and his comrades would have bodies to cover their nakedness and sooth their pain. The bodies of the Nephilim would derive their energy from the Earth. The demons would also obtain energy from the blood of the body itself, which we saw with the demoniac who was cutting himself, presumably to feast on his own blood. They would be able to live forever because if a Nephilim bodysuit died, the interloper would simply grow another, and then possess it anew. Thus, Satan would have overcome the limitations put on him by his Creator, making him the ultimate victor.

Chapter 8: At Satan's Command (The Hermon Batios Inscription)

n 1869 on the summit of Mt. Hermon, in Israel, British explorer Sir Charles Warren came across a sacred rectangular building made of hewn stone blocks, located at Qasr Antar, the highest temple in the ancient world (9,232 ft. or 2,814 m. above sea level, See Figure 21). In the temple, he found a limestone stele which may be the only extra-biblical and pagan memorial of Satan's actual command to the Sons of God to create a hybrid race.

Figure 21 Schematic of Temple on Hermon, Palestine Exploration Fund, 1869-1936. London.

We know that this mountain has long been regarded as a holy place. E.A. Myers believes the finding of the inscription is very much in line with the pagan history of the mountain:

> That such an enclosure, as first reported by Warren, exists on the summit of Hermon lends credence to a long tradition of the sacred high place, and supports the textual evidence for it as a holy mountain. It also provides evidence for the endurance of a people who must have made considerable effort to come and worship within such a harsh and cruel environment. That the mountain preserved its sacredness throughout is dramatically demonstrated by the presence of numerous temples and cult sites.[140]

The British Museum dates the inscription to the 3rd century, though I am persuaded it might have been written earlier, between the 8th - 3rd centuries BC. The earlier date is supported by evidence on the inscription and by the Messapic evidence that we will examine shortly. Thus, based on the long pagan history of the locale, it is likely that the pagan scribes chiseled the inscription with a phrase that had passed down orally for millennia.

THE INSCRIPTION WITH SATAN'S COMMAND

We are indebted to Warren for finding and delivering the inscribed stele to the British Museum,[141] and as shown in Figure 22, we are provided a chance to view the inscription on the actual stele at the British Museum's website.[142] Comparing the parallel translations of Warren and Harvard scholar, George Nickelsburg, with that of the British Museum, reveals discrepancies and even the omission of several words. Their translations are below; the omissions in the British Museum's translation are represented by brackets. The inserted words in the Warren-Nickelsburg translation are in italics.

- The British Museum's translation, (written on the base of the inscription): **"Hence by order of the [ ] God [ ] [ ], those who do not take the oath."**
- Warren and Nickelsburg's parallel translation: [143] Κατά κέλευσιν θεού μεγίστου κ[αι] άγιου οι ομνύοντες εντεύθεν **"According to the command of the great a[nd] holy God, those who take an oath [proceed] from here."** [144]

Warren-Nickelsburg rightly connected the inscription with the oath taken by the angels under Semjaza[145] in order to take wives, according to the Book of Enoch.[146] Nickelsburg also skillfully realized "the name of God was supposed to be a Hellenized version of Ba'al or Hadad and ... connected it with the place name of Baal-Hermon (Lord of Hermon)." [147]

Surprisingly, though, Warren-Nickelsburg inserted the words "a[nd] holy" which do not appear in the inscription. This interpretation gives the impression that the God of Abraham, Isaac and Jacob gave the command to angels to create the race of Nephilim, but He did not.

Figure 22 Hermon Inscription, Courtesy of the British Museum 1903-0422.

Rather, the one who sent those angels was Satan; and this is a fact which we will see the inscription proves. In 1 Enoch, "the Holy and Mighty One" (1 Enoch 1:3) is mentioned. However, the angels that descended and took the oath acted in **opposition** to the Holy and Mighty One's decrees—not in accordance, as evidenced in 1 Enoch:

> [3]And now to you, **O you holy one of heaven**, the souls of men complain, saying, Obtain Justice for us …[6]**Samyaza also has taught sorcery**, to whom you have given authority over those who are associated with him. They have gone together to the daughters of men; have lain with them; have become polluted; [15]To Michael likewise the Lord said, Go and announce **his crime to Samyaza** (1 Enoch 9:3, 6, 10:15)(Emphasis mine).

Clearly, the "holy one of heaven" is referring to God (YHWH / Jehovah), and He did not command the angels to make the Nephilim.

NEED FOR A RETRANSLATION

Due the wide divergences and omissions, I believe a reexamination of the inscription is necessary. I have tried to simplify the linguistic evidence, but if you do not care for it, I invite you to skip to the end of the chapter to read the conclusion.

Here is the uncial text transcribed with no spaces as it appears on the inscription:

ΚΑΤΑΚΕΛΕΥΣΙΝΘΕΟΥΜΕΓΙΣΤΟΥΒΟΒΑΤΙΟ ΥΟΥΟΜΝΥΟΝΤΕΣΕΝΤΕΥΘΕΝ

My normalized transcription of the text is as follows: [1]Κατά [2]κέλευσιν [3]θεού [4]μεγίστου [5]βο [6]βατιου [7]ου [8]ομνύοντες [9]εντεύθεν [kata keleusin theou megistou bo batiou ou omnuontes enteuthen].

The British Museum ignored words four, five and six, skipping three out of nine words, which is 33% of the text. Warren-Nickelsburg's translation: "a[nd] holy," amended two words to read differently than what the text says, which we will discuss later. Here is a breakdown of each word according to my reading:

1. Κατά [kata]: according to
2. Κέλευσιν [keleusin]: command
3. Θεού [theou]: of the god (genitive)
4. Μεγίστου [megistou]: Greatness personified (genitive)
5. Bo [bo]: uncertain, possibly a prefix for ox
6. βατιου (Βατιου): epithet (genitive)
7. ου [ou]: where
8. ομνύοντες [omnuontes]: those swearing an oath
9. εντεύθεν [enteuthen]: [going] from here

My translation of the first three words Κατά κέλευσιν θεού agrees perfectly with the other translations. Liddell Scott Jones Classical Greek Lexicon notes how this three-word phrase is frequently found in inscriptions and papyri.[148]

With the fourth word, μεγίστου, *megistou*, the British Museum omitted it for unknown reasons. Warren-Nickelsburg rightly included it in their translation. BDAG notes it means: "Greatness, personified."[149] It was a popular epithet for Zeus.

Since words five and six are enigmatic, we will consider them last because they require ample explanation.

Word seven, *OY*, Nickelsburg revised to *OI*, which seems *ad hoc*, as the text clearly reads as *OY* (See adjacent Figure 23.). A translator's job is not to change the text to make it fit his idea, but to deal with the text "as is". Translators are justified in creativity when something is missing from the text, but here, nothing is missing.

The British Museum translated OΥ as the lexical entry οὐ "not", which is an option. However, a separate lexical entry is οὖ which means: "marker of a position in space, where ... " (BDAG). Context is the only way to know which translation is correct. When we pair this word with word nine εντευθεν ([going] from here), then "where" appears to be the better option, instead of "no."

Figure 23 The word "ου" visible on the inscription.

Word eight ὀμνύω, is defined by BDAG as: "to affirm the veracity of one's statement by invoking a transcendent entity, freq. w. implied invitation of punishment if one is untruthful, **swear, take an oath** ...[as בְּ נִשְׁבַּע] in the OT ."[150]

Lastly, word nine εντευθεν is an adverb, according to BDAG, that pertains "to extension from a source near the speaker, from here".[151] We see this word used in Scripture which provides us examples of the word meaning—going from one place to another:

- "If You are the Son of God, throw Yourself down from [ἐντεῦθεν] here (Luke 4:9).

- And the LORD said to Moses, "Go, get down [ἐντεῦθεν]" (Exod 32:7).

Thus words 7, 8, and 9 agree with the translation of Warren and Nickelsburg which is what makes words 5 and 6 such a mystery that deserves our attention.

βο *BO* THE BULL

Words five and six βο *Bo* and βατιου *Batiou* are mysterious, which could be why they were completely ignored by the British Museum and amended by Warren-Nickelsburg; βο to "a(nd)" and βατιου *batiou* as άγιου *hagiou*. Frankly, it is a mystery to me how they justified their emendation. While "a(nd) holy" may be an easy fix, we must always ask, "What does the text say?" and, "Does the inscription warrant such renderings?" In the picture of the inscription in Figure 24, you will see a circle around βο and a rectangle around βατιου (batiou is the genitive of batios). Warren-Nickelsburg simply ignored the whole word BO (beta omicron). With word six, *batiou*, they changed the T (tau) to a Γ (gamma) even though the letters are clear, consistent and not garbled. As we noted already, they were right to see a similarity with 1 Enoch and the oath, per word eight; yet, if this is indeed a record of the imprecation the angels took before taking women and begetting the Nephilim, it was not by decree of the Holy God YHWH. Rather, the decree would have come from Satan.

Figure 24 A circle around "bo" and rectangle around "batiou" on the inscription.

βο *bo* does not appear as a proper lexical entry in any of the extensive literature I checked—which is likely why careful scholars like Warren-Nickelsburg amended it to "a[nd]."

Nevertheless, "Bo- (βο-), boo- (βοο-), and bou- (βου-) are prefixes meaning bull, ox, male cattle." [152] Considering that there are no spaces between the letters in the original inscription, it is plausible to read the text as "βο-βατιου" and not do violence to the text. Furthermore, we know Mt. Hermon was also called Baal Hermon in Judges 3:3 and 1 Chronicles 5:23, and that Zeus and Baal are synonymous. Therefore, it follows that βο may be a prefix meaning "bull", a reference to Baal / Zeus. You may remember Zeus, in Greek mythology, transformed himself into a white bull and carried away Europa, an image which agrees with "the **tauromorphic** appearance of Baal and other deities in Canaan," [153] and which confirms that Baal (Zeus) appeared as a bull. Furthermore, "Moloch is merely another name for Ba'al, the Sacred Bull who was widely worshipped in the ancient Near East."[154]

Thus, based on the bull motif of Baal / Zeus found in the area, βο *bo* meaning bull, stands as a strong candidate.

BATIOS IN MESSAPIA (SOUTHERN ITALY)

The word βατιου *Batiou* is even more enigmatic (batios is nominative, batiou is genitive). I performed an exhaustive search through lexicons, dictionaries, encyclopedias, scholarly sites and journals, and not one had any information on the word *batios*. *Batiou* simply is not Greek (which again, is the only apparent justification good scholars, such as Warren-Nickelsburg, would have for changing letters). I did, however, discover that *batios* is believed to be an epithet of Zeus (Jupiter) in Messapian speech. (See Figure 25, next page.) "Messapian (also known as Messapic) is an extinct Indo-European language of South-eastern Italy."[155] Yet, why?

Figure 25 Map of Messapia, South-east Italy 6th-2nd cent. BC. Courtesy salentoacolory.it.

So little is known about the Messapian language that the leading scholar Alf Torp (1853–1916) stated: "Hardly more than a few words can be said to have been separated and translated with certainty."[156] The language has roughly 300 extant inscriptions dating from the 7th / 6th to the 1st century BC.[157] The majority of the inscriptions come from a cave called Grotta Porcinara.

> There are several examples of *Idde*, *Batas*, and *Atiaxte*, or fragments of these, which **are believed to be names or** epithets of the god worshipped there. Several Greek inscriptions from the site are dedications to Zeus Batios … Batas **may have been** the Messapic name of the god, who also **appears to have been equated with Zeus**, appearing in a Greek inscription as Zeus Batios (βατιος εμι.)(Emphasis mine).[158]

Thus, we have material evidence in Messapic inscriptions of "Zeus Batios" used by the Greeks. [159] The Romans made engravings venerating *"Juppiter Optimus Maximus Batius* (ou Vatius)."* [160] Both Greek and Roman inscriptions referenced Batios / Batius.

Nevertheless, scholars do not know what *batios* means. Annick Fenet suggests it could be the epithet of a local deity.[161] Yet, why would an almost unknown Messapian epithet, hidden in a cave of a localized god from south-eastern Italy, be inscribed on a stele 9,000-feet above sea level on the cold, unwelcoming accursed mountain in the land of Bashan?

Batios cannot be a local Messapian epithet because there is no location known as Batios in Messapia (See map in Figure 25 above). For example, we know "Baal Hermon" (Judg 3:3) is a local epithet for Baal because we have a mountain called "Hermon." Annick Fenet, in *Les Dieux Olympiens et la Mer*, notes:

> According to the cave dedications and ceramic graffiti, since the 6th century BC a Messapian Zis Batas was honored there, recognized as a Zeus Batios by the Greeks, designated also later as Juppiter Optimus Maximus. **Caves are mainly devoted to Zeus, albeit under different epiclesis ...** These Messapian places of worship, dating back to some of the **7th century**, were early **frequented by Greek sailors who somehow appropriated them** (Emphasis mine).[162]

Figure 26 The Grotto in which "batios" was found in Messapia.

Referring to the Grotto in Figure 26, Kathryn Lomas notes that "The sanctuary was clearly an important one, and attracted worshippers from beyond the region despite the difficulties of access (it may have been only accessible by boat in antiquity)."[163] She also notes that:

> Grotta Porcinara may provide evidence for religious contact in action, as it offers evidence for the interaction of Greek and non-Greek cults and worshippers. The corpus of inscribed potsherds includes a number of sherds inscribed [*idde*], which has been identified as Messapic deity name or epithet. Another name or epithet that occurs there is Batas ... Other pottery inscriptions, dedications written in Greek to Zeus Batas. The Latin inscriptions on the inside of the cave name the deity as Jupiter Batius.[164]

The attestation of *Batas* and *Idde* direct our attention to Hermon rather than Messapia since the worshippers were from outside the region. Annick Fenet comments that the "dual name of Palaistiné and Ourania suggests a Semitic and oriental character."[165] The presence of sailors worshiping gods with Semitic character must mean they are Semitic-speaking sailors. In personal correspondence with Professor Paolo M. Gensini, University of Perugia, Italy, who is an expert in Messapian texts, he notes that "the Greek and Latin texts from Leuca are all written by or for sailors."[166]

Thus, Semitic-speaking sailors, probably Phoenician from Tyre or Sidon, inscribed the word "batios" in a cave in southern Italy. If they were coming from the east, such as from Phoenicia, then they certainly would have thanked their home god that got them to their destination safely, rather than a foreign god. Which is to say, *batios* is not Messapian, but Semitic.

The Phoenicians were renowned sailors, who were Semitic speaking and had Mt. Hermon in their backyard, which is the only other place in the world where the enigmatic word "batios" has been found. Incidentally, in Greek, many people-group names end with ιος. For example: "the Hittites [ο χετταιος], the Jebusites [ο ιεβουσαιος], and the Amorites [ο αμορραιος] dwell in the mountains; and the Canaanites [ο χαναναιος]." (Num 13:29). Hence, the ιος ending demonstrates a typical Greek-language Semitic-people suffix (ending).

BATIOS MEANS BAT (=IDIM) WHO IS ENLIL, ET AL

Our text says: "According to the command (Κατά κέλευσιν) of the greatness personified (θεού μεγίστου) βο-βατιου (bull) (of Batios)." There are two distinct possibilities of the origin of *batios*, though interestingly, they both lead us to the same entity: Enlil / Heilel / Satan.

The Sumerian language was first written using pictograms (AKA logograms). The logogram for BAD [▶━━◀] was associated with Enlil, Dagan, Ug (death) and Nergal (god of death and the underworld). In a personal correspondence with Professor Amar Annus of University of Tartu Natural History Museum and Botanical Garden, he notes that:

The names of Dagan in Syria and Enlil in Mesopotamia sometimes share the logograms with which their names are written. dBAD and dKUR for both Enlil and Dagan, which points to a syncretism between their deities, and consequently for their families, including Dagan's son Ba'al in Syria and Enlil's son Ninurta in Mesopotamia. This cuneiform sign BAD has many logographic readings throughout history, including BAD for "dead" and BAD.BAD for ug in Sumerian, the latter is only orthographic as much as I can see ... The sign BAD can be read as BE as well and taken as an abbreviation of bel - the lord.[167]

Franz Wiggenner expounds on the etymology of "Nergal's planet ... Mars (salbatanu)." He notes how "according to astrological omens Mars spreads death when he rises or flares up." He goes on to provide a tentative etymology that explains "this role of MUL tzal (sal) bat-a-nu as mushtabarru (ZAL) mutanu (BAD-a-nu)" "(the planet) which spreads plague."[168] In other words, BAD, also spelled "BAT"[169] is related to death and to Nergal, the god of death. In light of the inscription, it is of great interest that Wiggenner points out "The bull's head denotes the god of ... Nergal's main cult center."[170] We found "bo" in the inscription, which we determined meant "bull"; thus, "BAD / BAT" is in concert with that idea.

Amar Annus notes:

The god Dagan is already identified with Sumerian Enlil, father of Ninurta, in Old Babylonian times and they share the logogram BAD (=IDIM). The name of Dagan is written logographically dKUR in Emar as an alternative to the syllabic dDa-gan. dKUR is a shortened form of Enlil's epithet KUR.GAL "great mountain," which was borrowed by Dagan, and he is already described as the great mountain in a Mari letter.

116

The writing dNIN.URTA for a Syrian god in thirteenth century Emar thus attests **a conscious syncretism** which introduced Sumerian writing for the West Semitic god. The Emar god *Ninurta* is the son of Dagan, and the equivalence of Dagan and Enlil **led the scribes trained in the Mesopotamian system to use this Sumerian writing for the name of his son**[171] (Emphasis mine).

In other words, Ninurta is the son of both Enlil and Dagan, because those two gods were considered to be one, as clearly demonstrated by the same logogram BAD / BAT (=IDIM) being the identifier for them both. The "Idde" found in relation to *Batios* in Grotta Porcinara is almost certainly the "IDIM" related to the logogram BAD. Professor Annus points out:

The Emar god Ninurta most probably corresponds to Ugaritic Baal and the difference in writing the god's name is simply the result of the use of different writing systems – cuneiform in Emar and alphabetic script in Ugarit. 172

They have different sounding names due to the writing systems, but the gods are exactly the same.

The logogram BAD / BAT also was used for "Ištaran … the chief deity of Der (Logogram: BAD.AN)."[173] Steve Cole notes how "the logogram BAD is understood to be an abbreviation for the writing of the toponym BAD.AN.KI."[174] "AN" means "Lord" and "Ki" means "Earth", an epithet which means Lord of the Earth, which was also the meaning of the name of Nimrod, and we will see in later chapters refers to Ninurta. Thus, writing BAD / BAT was the same as writing out the names of multiple gods, which shows the conscious syncretism that Professor Annus mentioned. The scribes wrote BAD (=IDIM) as the equivalent to Dagan, Enlil, Ninurta and possibly others.

BAT (BAD) is a perfect match; and the ending ιος, which is *ios*, simply makes it standard Greek. Nevertheless, the general understanding of logograms is that they are not transliterated. Hence, the logogram BAD / BAT would be transliterated as "ug" for example but not as "bad." Though a pictogram (logogram) was typically not pronounced (transliterated), it was not impossible. Walter Burkert notes how:

> Alfred Boissier, who was the first to work systematically on Babylonian liver-omen texts, **saw that liver in these texts was consistently written with the Sumerian ideogram HAR**; and he at once concluded that this was the etymology for the Latin word haruspex, the first part of which had always defied explanation, while the second part must mean "seer of"; "seer of liver" would perfectly match its use in reference to those Etruscan specialists officiating in Rome[175] (Emphasis mine).

Amar Annus, whom I must thank for bringing this to my attention, notes that in this case "a logogram may have traveled between cultures as a certain learned word."[176] We therefore have precedence of an otherwise unpronounced Sumerian logogram being transliterated in the West, as unlikely as it seems. Not only was the logogram transliterated, but it was fully Latinized as a compound word—half Sumerian and half Latin. We then draw the conclusion that the logogram BAD / BAT for Enlil, Dagan, Ištaran, dead, Nergal (Mars), Bel (Baal) etc. was understood and consciously syncretized by scribes. It was transliterated into Greek, then Hellenized with the ios ending, and then accompanied by "Idde" (IDIM) in a similar fashion to haruspex. In fact, BAD / BAT may have been the most efficient way to express all the epithets for this entity in just one name. Possibly, the Sumerian BAT was Hellenized with the standard "people group" ios-suffix, and became: BATios.

A LITERAL TRANSLATION OF HERMON'S INSCRIPTION

In table 5, the inscription is in uncials (capitals) and then in standardized and accented Greek. Then, the translation of the British Museum, Warren-Nickelsburg, and my translations are presented side by side. I am indebted to the scholars who have gone before me, and I hope my translation and analysis contributes to the research of the Hermon inscription.

Mt. Hermon Roman Inscription 3rd cent.[177]			
Inscription	ΚΑΤΑ ΚΕΛΕΥΣΙΝ ΘΕΟΥ ΜΕΓΙΣΤΟΥ ΒΟ ΒΑΤΙΟΥ ΟΥ ΟΜΝΥΟΝΤΕΣ ΕΝΤΕΥΘΕΝ		
	British Museum	**Warren / Nickelsburg**	**Hamp**
Normalized Greek transcription	None found.	Κατά κέλευσιν θεού μεγίστου κ[αι]* άγιου* οι* ομνύοντες εντεύθεν	Κατά κέλευσιν θεού μεγίστου βο-βατιου ου ομνύοντες εντεύθεν
Translation	Hence by order of the god [*] [*] [*] those who do not take the oath.	According to the command of the great a[and]* holy* God, those who take an oath [proceed] from here	"According to the command of the great bull god Batios [BAD (=IDIM)], those swearing an oath in this place go forth."
Variants	[*] Omitted words: ΜΕΓΙΣΤΟΥ ΒΟ ΒΑΤΙΟΥ	*words not in the text.	

Table 5 Mt. Hermon Roman Inscription 3rd century

My translation is very close to Warren-Nickelsburg's translation, despite a few variations.

As we saw earlier, the double superlative *Iuppiter optimus maximus*, meaning the "best, greatest," is in concert with the Hermon inscription θεού μεγίστου *theou megistou* "the greatness personified god" and was a common epithet for Zeus. βο remains uncertain. Yet, if βο is a prefix for "bull", then it only underscores the reference to Zeus and is in complete harmony with a well-known phrase found in the Hebrew Bible, "bulls of Bashan." "Many bulls encompass me; strong bulls of Bashan surround me" (Ps 22:12).

The translation: "According to the command of the great bull god Batios, those swearing an oath in this place go forth" has the advantage of not making alternations to the text. My translation further reveals the identity of Zeus Batios / Jupiter "Optimus Maximus Batios, AKA Baal / Melqart / Nergal / Heracles / Enlil / Marduk / Ninurta", as the god who commanded those taking the oath to go forth from that place. In other words, we now have textual evidence that the descent of the sons of God into our realm was under the direction of Satan.

Thus, the angels that came down on the mountain, maledicting themselves lest they fail to complete their task, did so at the command of the great bull-god Batios who was represented as a dragon, whom we know is none other than Satan. These angels who took the oath did not act outside of the parameters of the one who sent them; they did "according to the command of greatness personified," —even that title sounds like the boasting of Satan who corrupted his wisdom on account of his beauty. Satan gave the order to the watchers to come to Earth, take women, and create the Nephilim in order to keep the Seed of the woman from crushing his head.

BATIOS = BASHAN

It is uncommon that scribes would transliterate the name of the logogram; yet, as we have seen, we have precedence. It also seems to be the simplest way to indicate that the god identified by the BAD / BAT logogram is the one they were invoking. However, it might simply be that Batios = Bashan.

Mount Hermon is in the vicinity of the region of Bashan, which was ruled by "Og king of Bashan ... his territory ... of the remnant of the giants, who dwelt at Ashtaroth and at Edrei, (Josh 12:4) and reigned over Mount Hermon, over Salcah, over all Bashan" (Josh 12:5).[178]

Mt. Hermon is also known as Mount Bashan "A mountain of God is the mountain of Bashan; A mountain of many peaks is the mountain of Bashan" (Ps 68:15).

Bashan was rendered in a number of different ways in the ancient near east. The B sometimes turned into a P, which is consistent with phonemes. The Š (SH) turned into a T or TH, again consistent. The M can swap with the N. By the time of the first century, the word Bashan became standardized in Latin and Greek as Batanea. (See Table 6, next page).

Comparative Table of Bashan Usage				
Language	**Original**	**Transliteration**	**Attested usage**	**Era (approx.)**
Akkadian	MUL.dMUŠ mus-sa-tur or usum	Bašmu - Bashmu	Serpent-dragon	3rd-1st Millennium BC
Hebrew	בָּשָׁן	Bashan	Serpent-dragon	2nd-1st Millennium BC
Ugaritic	bthn	Batan	Serpent-dragon	2nd-1st Millennium BC
Aramaic	פתן	Patan	Serpent	1st Millennium BC
Greek (LXX)	Βασάν	Basan	-	3rd century BC
Greek Place name	Βατανία	Batanía Batanea	-	4th century BC – 3rd century AD
Messapic inscription	Batas	Batas	Epithet of Zeus	6th-2nd century BC
Greek inscription	βατιος	Batios	Epithet of Zeus	6th-2nd century BC
Latin inscription	*Batius / Vatius*	Batius / Vatius	Epithet of Zeus	Up to 3rd century AD

Table 6 Comparative Table of Bashan Usage

The proposed process to go from the Akkadian *Bašmu* to *batios* is as follows: Akk: *Bašmu* to Hebrew *Bashan* or Ugaritic *Bathan* (Ugarit was a coastal town south of Antioch, Syria). Charlesworth points out how "Ugaritic *bthn* become *bšn* in Hebrew and is equal to bašmu in Akkadian with the n to m shift."[179] Why the N (nun / nu) fell off is not clear, though it is possible. [180] For example, Albert T. Clay notes how "the Aramaic vav [ו], as is known, representing m in Babylonian ... Cf. Amurru written [אור] or Shamash written [שוש], Murashu, x. p. 8 and 9."[181] Thus, there might be a similar situation here where the original *Bašmu* may have simply lost the M all together. Even with it converting from M to N, as noted, the assimilation of the *nun* in Hebrew is fairly common. The word "bat" [בת] (daughter) has a middle root letter of *nun* [בנת], which assimilated. The word [נתן] *natan* loses its final *nun* in conjugations such as "natati." Thus, it is entirely possible that the N (nun) of *Batan* simply fell out, due to a phonetic constraint, as evident in Akkadian. The word was then rendered into Greek as *batios*, and then exported to Messapia.

The inscriptions in Messapia are dated anywhere from the 7th – 2nd century BC. According to the British Museum, the Hermon Inscription is dated as late as the 3rd century AD. The Septuagint Greek (3rd century BC) renders *Bashan* as *Basan* (βασαν). According to the Ancient World Mapping Center and Institute for the Study of the Ancient World Hellenistic Greek, the region was known as Batanea (Βαταναία) [182] in the Roman Republic (330 BC-30 BC) and in the Roman, early Empire (30 BC-AD 300). [183] That means before 330 BC, the area would have maintained its Semitic character, which could explain how the inscription left by sailors in the Porcinara Grotto had "Semitic character." The Phoenician culture was in decline until about the second century BC, and the destruction of Tyre at the hands of Alexander the Great likely hastened its demise.

We know that Bashan was *Bathan* in Ugaritic and *Patan* in Aramaic. Thus, *batios* may be a shortened and Hellenized form of Batan (Bashan). βο βατιου could mean βο→Bull, βατιου→of Bashan, or the Great Bull of Bashan. The psalmist wrote prophetically, "Strong bulls of Bashan surround me" (Ps 22:12). If Batios is Bashan, we know Bashan has the meaning: snake-dragon. Therefore, we have two paths that take us to the same destination: Batios means BAD (IDIM), who was a snake-dragon, or Batios is Bashan which means snake-dragon. Both meanings point to Satan, the great snake-dragon. Either way, it was "According to the command of the great bull-god Satan, the great snake-dragon of Bashan that those swearing an oath in this place go forth."

In the meantime, Satan continued his schemes to make this Earth his eternal kingdom. He focused his plan of passing on genetic information to one select representative who would champion the cause. This time, however, in an effort to avoid being thrown into the pit like the sons of God who came down on Hermon, he would take a man and make him into a god.

GOD THWARTED SATAN'S PLAN FOR WORLD DOMINATION

God was paying attention to the corruption and violence Satan had caused on the Earth by commanding the sons of God to take women and procreate the Nephilim. "God looked upon the earth, and indeed it was corrupt; for all flesh had corrupted their way on the earth" (Gen 6:12). God made it clear that all flesh everywhere on the entire planet would die. "I Myself am bringing floodwaters on the earth, to destroy from under heaven all flesh in which is the breath of life; everything that is on the earth shall die" (Gen 6:17).

Satan's scheme failed. Upon the death of the host body, the spirit inside the Nephilim was separated and the fallen angel became disembodied once again. 1 Enoch 15:8–16:1 describes how they became known as evil spirits on the Earth:

"Now the giants, who have been born of spirit and of flesh, shall be called upon earth evil spirits, and on earth shall be their habitation. Evil spirits shall proceed from their flesh because they were created from above; from the holy Watchers was their beginning and primary foundation. Evil spirits shall they be upon earth, and the spirits of the wicked shall they be called. The habitation of the spirits of heaven shall be in heaven; but upon earth shall be the habitation of terrestrial spirits, who are born on earth.[184] (See Appendix 1 Demons).

The Flood ended Satan's worldwide Nephilim plan, but it would not end his plan for eternal world-domination. We will see that he would modify his plan with an ancient rebel named Nimrod.

Milestone Marker 1

Figure 27 Roman Milestone on the Road of the Patriarchs between Jerusalem and Hebron. wikipedia. org/wiki/Creative_Commons.

So far on our journey, we have discovered that the being we know today as "Satan" was not known by that name in the Ancient Near East; however, he was known behind many disguises and under many ancient aliases such as Enlil, Melqart (King of Tyre), Baal, BAD / BAT, Marduk, Ninurta and others. God installed Satan as his chief steward of his creation, but he rebelled and demanded to be served instead of serving the ones he was supposed to protect. His selfish action caused the realms of heaven and Earth to be separated by a cosmic veil. God promised the coming of the Seed of the woman to crush Satan's head, stripping him of his glorious vesture of light, leaving him spiritually naked. In an attempt to maintain his world domination forever and to establish bodies for him and his crew, Satan gave the command to create Nephilim hybrids on Earth. God directly intervened by sending the Flood, thwarting Satan's apocalyptic scenario. His next endeavor would be to create a *gibbor*: the Beast who was.

PART 2: RISE OF THE ANTI-HERO
(Babel and the Beast)

In this section, we will examine the ancient roots of Satan's anti-hero, the rebel who merged with Satan and carried out his quest for indefinite world domination through stargates and post-flood hybrids.

Chapter 9: Nimrod the Rebel, Satan's Anti-Hero

From Revelation, we know that Satan, the dragon with seven heads and ten horns, will give his power, throne and great authority to the Beast who shares the same features (Rev 13:1–2). Satan and the Beast share the same qualities because they become one in power, one in purpose and one in authority. Satan will only transfer these resources to someone if it serves his purpose and furthers his kingdom. This merging of roles and transference of power to the Beast discussed in Revelation is not the first time that Satan melded with a man.

After the Flood, Satan carried on with his scheme of world domination through his anti-hero. Satan (Enlil) found his rebellious champion and caused him to be a *gibbor*, a hero. [185] His champion was Nimrod, the son of Cush. In him, Satan found a willing participant who wanted to be the Son of Perdition, and who, for the promise of becoming a demigod (a *gibbor*), would lead a life in rebellion to God. He would also lead people to Babylon, the great whore who God vowed to destroy at the end of days.

> Cush begot Nimrod; he began to be [*heichel lihiot*] a mighty one [*gibbor*] on the earth. He was a mighty hunter [*gibbor tzayid*] before the LORD; therefore it is said, "Like Nimrod the mighty hunter before the LORD". And the beginning of his kingdom was Babel, Erech, Accad, and Calneh, in the land of Shinar. From that land he went to Assyria and built Nineveh, Rehoboth Ir, Calah, and Resen between Nineveh and Calah (that is the principal city) (Gen 10:8–12).

Satan did not have his former beauty and glorious covering to seduce Nimrod, which means he may have used his angel of light disguise to beguile him to follow his plan. Satan "transforms [μετασχηματίζω] himself into an angel of light" (2 Cor 11:14). He can appear like a hologram in spectacular beauty, but he cannot materialize at will (as far as we know). The word "transform" means "to feign to be what one is not, change/disguise oneself."[186] In other words, Satan can pretend to be an angel of light which is not his true form; he is simply donning a disguise.

It is likely that before Satan offered the promise of his power, throne and authority to Jesus (and as we see in Revelation, he will later give to the Beast), he had first offered these enticements to Nimrod, who gladly accepted. By throwing himself down and worshiping Satan, Nimrod gained a legendary physique and handsome appearance, and earned the unique status of master of the world, patron of the hunt and supreme hero. He would be so great that humanity would worship him for generations to come. He would be immortal, invincible and immune from all hurt or illness.

NIMROD'S NAME

In ancient rabbinical literature, "Nimrod is the prototype of a rebellious people, his name being interpreted as 'he who made all the people rebellious against God.'"[187] Targum Jonathan (Targum Palestine) also plays on the root of Nimrod's name as rebel:

> "Nimrod ... was a mighty rebel [*lemrada* למרדא] before the Lord; therefore it is said, From the day that the world was created there hath not been as Nimrod, mighty in hunting, and a rebel [*meruda* מרודא] before the Lord."[188]

His name in Hebrew means "let us rebel" or "rebellion" [מרד]. Nimrod amassed a huge following by saying, "Let's revolt! We will build our own cities with new rules contrary to God's

130

repressive ways." However, Nimrod was not his given name; instead, it is the moniker that describes his nature and actions. His dad, Cush, did not look over at his wife and say, "Let's name him Rebellion!" Can you imagine his parents saying: "Hey Rebellion, clean your room!" Parents want their kids to not be rebels. Rather, the biblical writer intentionally distorted [189] Nimrod's name to reveal his character: the epitome of rebellion.

Nimrod is from the land of Shinar (Sumer); hence, the origin of his name is Sumerian rather than Hebrew. The evidence shows, "Nimrod is a corruption of the Sumerian god-name Ninurta, patron of the hunt." [190] ANE scholar Amar Annus says it is "a clearly Sumerian name .... The element urta (= IB) has been most frequently interpreted to mean "earth"... thus, *Nin-urta* 'the Lord (of) Earth.'" [191]

This name reflects the biblical truth that Satan was Lord of the Earth, and:

- **the ruler of this world** [cosmos κόσμος] will be cast out (John 12:31, 14:30, 16:11).
- **the god of this age** [aion αἰών] has blinded (2 Cor 4:4).
- **the whole world lies under the sway of the wicked one** (1 John 5:19).

According to the *Epic of Anzu*, Ninurta's "exploits ... placed him in charge of the Tablet of Destinies—he 'won complete dominion.'" [192] The fact that Ninurta was in possession of the Tablet of Destinies meant that Satan had conferred on Ninurta all of his authority. Similarly, Satan will give the Antichrist his "power, his throne and his great authority" (Rev 13:2). The Bible is giving us an interpretation of the things that happened in Shinar to Ninurta—the person behind the name who was a rebel who defied the Most High. Thus, Ninurta, Lord of the Earth, was a haughty but accurate title.

The reason Nimrod is mentioned within the first eleven chapters of Genesis, which covers thousands of years, is that he was amazingly notable. He simply became known as "Let us rebel." He was the first to become a *gibbor* and was a hunter / warrior in the face of the Lord. He founded Babel and inspired or helped build the Tower of Babel. The memory of Nimrod is all over the ancient world—just not by the name "Nimrod". To find him in extra-biblical texts, we look for his traits:

1. Rebel
2. Hero of renown (god or demigod - made into a god)
3. Hunter
4. Founder of cities such as Erech, Babel and Akkad
5. Builder of a ziggurat
6. Controller of cosmic mountain
7. Known by names with similar root letters as Nimrod

When we look for these qualities, we find a number of matches. We hear echoes of a deified Nimrod under a number of names such as Ninurta, Ningirsu, Marduk, Nergal, Ba'al, Melqart, Pabilsag, Heracles (Hercules), Tammuz and Gilgamesh. These associations from the Ancient Near East suggest that Nimrod, indeed, became a *gibbor*. The same epithets of Nimrod were used for these "gods". In fact, we are going to see many parallels that will show us that the memory and legend of Nimrod lived on. According to David Rohl, in *The Lost Testament: From Eden to Exile the Five-Thousand-Year History of the People of The Bible*, Nimrod was:

> "represented as both semi-divine hero and god. The Babylonians knew him as Ninurta, the hunter-god armed with bow, and linked him with Marduk, warrior-god and lord of vegetation. The Sumerians of Eridu themselves elevated the mortal King Enmer-kar ('Enmer the hunter') to godhood as Asar, 'son' of Enki. The Sumerians of the Early Dynastic times named him

Ningirsu, god of war and agriculture. In the city of Lagash they built the House of Ninnu (*E-Ninnu*) as Ningirsu's temple and gave him the epithet Enmersi after his ancient and original name. The Assyrians recognized Enmer/Asar as their state deity, Ashur. When the author of Genesis calls him Nimrod, this is a play on words in which the name Enmer is Hebraised into *nmrd* ('we shall rebel') because this king rebelled against Yahweh by building the Tower of Babel."[193]

Scholars Sayce, Pinches and others agree regarding "the signs which constitute the name of Marduk, who also is represented as a hunter, are read phonetically 'Amar Ud'; and ideographically they may be read 'Namr Ud'—in Hebrew 'Nimrod.'" [194] We thus see a linguistic connection between Nimrod and Marduk.

NINURTA, HERO OF THE TABLET OF DESTINIES

Satan will give his "power, throne, and great authority" (Rev 13:2) to the Beast described in Revelation, which will be nothing more than a repeat of what he previously did with Nimrod (Ninurta), "whom Enlil has exalted above himself" and "Enlil the Great Mountain made obeisance to him."[195]

We can be sure that Satan has no intentions of raising up a man and then bowing down to him! Satan does not imagine himself taking a back seat to a human; He hates Adam and refused to serve something lesser than himself. In Satan's kingdom, he is the best, greatest, top dog; He is top of the food chain and the big cheese. If he thought he was so great that he staged a coup against God, why would he suddenly bow down to Ninurta? He does not really bow; rather, he makes empty promises to Ninurta / Nimrod that he would become a god; and then, Satan's personality seeps inside and takes over the person until only Satan remains.

We will see this blending between Enlil (Satan) and Ninurta in many texts. We need to also keep in mind the melding together of traits and characteristics between the dragon (Satan) and the Beast in Revelation. We see that he will in fact give the Beast his power, throne and his great authority! What does that really mean?

Power is the ability to do something, to work and to accomplish. It is the energy in your battery that makes your phone work. It is the electricity coming into your home that runs your dishwasher, lights, washer, dryer and popcorn maker. Power is also the force of the sword. Roman soldiers enforced the will of Rome by using the sword against all who would not acquiesce to their demands. Satan lends the power of his energy and force to his lackey.

Throne is where a king sits. A king rules a kingdom, has subjects and servants, and in an absolute monarchy like Nebuchadnezzar's, his word was law. When he spoke, people jumped. When he decreed the death of the wise men of Babylon, there was no appeal, no judges challenging his orders and no congress demanding his removal. Soldiers were immediately dispatched and began fulfilling his command. When the king ordered his troops to siege Jerusalem, they complied and even laid down their lives. We have seen that Enlil gives Ninurta his throne just as the dragon will give the Beast his throne.

Authority is the legal right to do something. After the Persians conquered Babylon, Daniel's Babylonian enemies entrapped him through their understanding the Persian legal system. Persuading the king to sign a legal document, a decree, against anyone who would worship any other god for a set time, they then sprung their trap and found Daniel guilty of praying to another God. Realizing he had been tricked, the king sought a means of saving Daniel. Although he was king, he lacked the authority to overturn his own decree. With no authority to change the law, he was forced to have Daniel thrown into the lion's den.

Satan / Enlil boasted to Jesus that he could give his authority "to whomever I wish" (Luke 4:6), and he is going to give the Beast his "power, throne and his great authority" (Rev 13:2). In ancient Sumer, Enlil's authority was embodied in something called the Tablet of Destinies; The holder possessed the power to decree fates. Amar Annus explains:

> The Tablet of Destinies was one of the cosmic "bonds" which chained together the various parts of the Mesopotamian cosmos, like some of the Mesopotamian temples and cities. It is called "the bond of supreme power" ... Holding of the cosmic bonds (*markasu*) was a privilege which conferred absolute control over the universe on its keeper.[196]

The sad reality is that Satan successfully swindled Adam out of his dominion. Instead of being a faithful steward of the inheritance God granted to Adam, Satan stole it for himself. Then Satan gave this authority to Nimrod / Ninurta, who became the keeper of the Tablet of Destinies.

> "Ninurta, *ensigal* of Enlil" is impressed on a sale document ... important documents can be seen as the earthly counterparts of the **Tablet of Destinies** ... Ninurta, as the seal-bearer of Enlil in Nippur, was probably authorized to act with Enlil's authority and ratified the decrees issued by the divine council. Ninurta ... the divine patron of scribal arts and is often invoked as the "Bearer of the **Tablet of Destinies** of the Gods"[197] (Emphasis mine).

"In *Enuma eliš*, the Tablet of Destinies is associated with the powers of Anu."[198] Remember: Anu is the creator god in the Mesopotamian tradition. Enlil (Satan) boasts about taking control of the Earth from the Creator. The authority usurped by Enlil is flaunted in the ancient texts through a reenactment of Anu's death in an annual celebration.

AKITU: A BLASPHEMOUS REENACTMENT OF KILLING THE CREATOR

Satan flaunted his victory and his unchallengeable authority in the ancient world in the *Akitu* festival by reenacting the death of the creator (Anu)[199] and his theft of the dominion God gave to Adam. The ceremonial killing of Anu the creator and the taking of his authority illustrates the disdain Enlil (Satan) had for God; the same contempt is revealed in Revelation by the Beast with blasphemous names:

> And I saw a beast coming up out of the sea. He had ten horns and seven heads. On his horns were ten diadems, and on his heads were blasphemous names (Rev 13:1).

In the *Akitu* reenactment, the king and Marduk (Enlil / Satan) melded into one. [200] Then the earthly king performed reenactments of defeating the creator, and the celebration:

> "day (of) **Wrath is the day the King defeated Anu**, the day King Marduk defeated Anu. ... The house where he killed Anu ... when the king wears a crown, is (when) Bel slashed [...] Anu's neck; having assumed kingship, he bathed and donned the royal garb.[201]

Again, while we are not necessarily equating Anu with the God of Abraham, it is still revealing that there would be an event in which the killing of the creator was reenacted in great detail. We also should not miss that the event, the day of wrath, is the day Anu is defeated. In the Bible, the Day of the Lord is the day when God will ultimately defeat Satan and his forces. Lastly, putting on the royal garb reminds us of the fallen one's longing for clothing (covering) that was lost when God stripped Satan and his followers of their fire.

The reenactment is full of Satan slandering God. He assumes the "anutu," that is to say, the creator's authority (the Anu-ship). Nabû (a syncretization of Ninurta / Nimrod) becomes supreme god because he holds the "anutu" in the text below:

> "Nabû ... is dressed in the garment (befitting) his rank as supreme god (*anutu*)." He goes to the temple of his beloved Nanaya ... and on the 7th day Nabû enters Anu's garden near his temple Eanna in Uruk, **takes Anu's seat**, assumes his kingship and wears **Anu's crown.**[202]

Satan appears to be getting the last laugh through the *Akitu* reenactments. He is ridiculing God through drama and expressing his rage at Him.

In another text at Ninurta's *Akitu* festival, Ninurta (son of Enlil) brings the vanquished gods, featuring Anu; and then even goes to the cosmological mountain, just like Satan claimed he would do in Isaiah! "Ninurta brought the vanquished gods before Enlil," and "Enlil rejoiced over him (Ninurta) and sent a message of well-being (*bussurat šulmi*)."[203] Ironically, the message of well-being "*bussurat šulmi*" that Enlil receives about the death of his enemies (which includes the creator) is parallel to Hebrew *besurah* (gospel) and *shalom* (peace)! As the height of blasphemy, Enlil (Satan) revels in receiving the "gospel of peace" message of the Creator's death. However, such actions are completely in line with Satan the slanderer.

> The mention of "the king of the Holy Mound," in the calendar text implies that Ninurta, after having presented his vanquished enemies to Enlil, goes to the cosmological ... to the "Mt. Olympus" of the gods in the middle heavens which was the place for assembly.[204]

The *Akitu* festival was clearly Satan thumbing his nose at God and reminding Him of his boast: "I will ascend into heaven, I will exalt my throne above the stars of God [אֵל *El*](Isa 14:13); I will be like the Most High" (Isa 14:14). He was exulting in the fact that he got away with it, and God did not stop him. Satan is clearly so full of himself that he is convinced that his wisdom equals that of God. Ancient History Encyclopedia boils down his insolent attitude:

> "Enlil as the rebel who defies the laws of the gods to pursue his own desires changes in other myths into the authority who wields the power of divine law and whose judgments cannot be questioned.[205]

Is that not exactly what Satan / Heilel bragged in Isaiah? It was almost like he would have said: "Yeah, the Creator God is over there, doing other stuff. But if you humans want something done, you have to come to me. I am the one with all the authority."

While the *Akitu* festival was not the means by which Satan and Nimrod merged, the fact that Satan gives his power, throne, and great authority to Ninurta, (the Beast who was) is evidence that a merge occurred; It strongly suggests they are the same person. Furthermore, it demonstrates that for Satan to give everything he has to this person means that the person would cease to act independently of Satan. The person is so completely controlled and owned by Satan that they cease to be who they were. Thus, when Nimrod became a *gibbor*, he unwittingly gave up his rights to be himself. His lust for power, fame and longevity ended in his essence being extinguished. Just as Nimrod became a *gibbor*, so too, Satan became Nimrod. They became one and the same for as long as the man's body continued to live.

Chapter 10: Nimrod Became a Chimera

In 2020, Chris L. of Reno, Nevada, learned that three months after his bone marrow transplant, "all of the DNA in his semen belonged to his donor." The DNA in his sperm was not his — it was that of his German bone marrow donor. According to the article, Chris became a chimera and is on record saying, "I thought that it was pretty incredible that I can disappear and someone else can appear." [206] Incredible, indeed! Before the transplant, Chris was simply Chris and any kids he would sire would be from his DNA. However, after the transplant, any children Chris might sire will not have his DNA, but that of his donor. When a donor's DNA is implanted, the DNA signature of the original person is replaced by that of the donor. We can now scientifically state that Chris became a chimera! [207]

So too, Nimrod underwent a change of epic proportions; He began to "be a mighty one on the earth." The Hebrew phrase [הוּא הֵחֵל לִהְיוֹת גִּבֹּר בָּאָרֶץ *hu heichel lihiot gibbor ba'aretz*] means Nimrod "began to be a *gibbor* on the earth" [208] — he started as a regular human and then became a *gibbor*. The transformation process may have been a type of overshadowing where Satan's DNA merged and / or changed Nimrod's DNA so he became a *gibbor*, a hero. He became a hybrid being — a god in the flesh and Satan's agent in this world. Just like Chris, any children Nimrod would sire would not be his, but his donor's!

This post-flood transformation is likely what is intended in Genesis 6:4 which says at two distinct times, the sons of God came into the daughters of men when they bore them children. These two times were: before the Flood and after. The relative pronoun "asher" translated "when" modifies two temporal clauses "in those days", as well as "also afterward". We can visualize this, as shown on the following page:

139

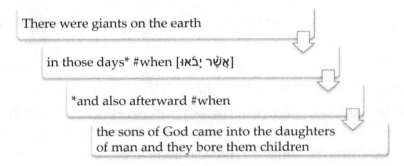

There were giants on the earth

in those days* #when [אֲשֶׁר יָבֹאוּ]

*and also afterward #when

the sons of God came into the daughters of man and they bore them children

A *gibbor* (hero) was not necessarily one of the Nephilim, but it could include the category. Nephilim comes from the root [נפל *naphal*] meaning "to fall". It is masculine plural, and the conjugation is not clear, though it has the appearance of a hiphil, which is causative. Thus, it could mean the "fallen", or the "fellers—like people who fell a tree", for example. So, the focus of the word is not so much an indicator of their own state, but of what they do to others.

"That the fallen angels were, in some sense, the fathers of the old giants, was the constant opinion of antiquity," according to William Whiston, translator of Josephus. After the Flood, Nimrod / Ninurta was the first *gibbor*. Furthermore, "The first named *gibbor* on earth was Nimrod." [209] It is incredibly interesting to note that the epithet, *gibbor*, like the "Akkadian *gabbaru* 'strong' and Aramaic *al-jabbiir* 'the giant (i.e. Orion)', identifies Nimrod's prowess, notably as a mythical hunter, and lord of the kingdoms of Babel." [210] In other words, the Bible is not the only source that mentions the might and power of Ninurta / Nimrod. Furthermore, Nimrod's activities described in Genesis "resemble the exploits of the Mesopotamian hero Gilgamesh,"[211] who we will examine in the next chapter.

The *Nephilim* (giants) were described as being *gibborim* (heroes), as were King David's mighty men (*gibborim*); and, I do not believe the latter were anything but human. Thus, when Nimrod is called a *gibbor*, it does not necessarily have to mean that he was anything but mighty, but the biblical context and Mesopotamian literature strongly suggests he changed fundamentally.

140

GIGANTES

The Greek Septuagint translates the *gibbor* passage as "Nimrod began to be a giant" [ηϱξατο ειναι γιγας *gigas*] (Gen 10:8 LXX Brenton). That is incredibly significant because the Septuagint also translates *Nephilim* and *gibborim* in Genesis 6:4 as "the giants" (*oi gigantes*).

> οι δε γίγαντες ησαν επι της γης [Now the giants were on the earth] … οι γίγαντες οι απ'' αιώνος], [the giants of old] οι ανθρωποι οι ονομαστοι [the men of renown] (Gen 6:4 LXX) (English translation mine.)

The Greek term *Gigas* was a loaded term from Greek literature, referring to divine, savage beings who were of both heaven and Earth, and in some cases, their father was Tartarus. To say Nimrod began to be a *gigas*, a giant, was saying that he began to be a hybrid being. The word "*Gigantes*" is thought by some to mean "of the earth", though some consider this untenable.[212] Nevertheless, according to etymonline.com:

> Greek Gigas (usually in plural, Gigantes), one of a race of divine but savage and monstrous beings (personifying destructive[213] natural forces), sons of Gaia and Uranus … Gaia is earth and Uranus is heaven – hence, "giants" were a comingling of heavenly and earthly beings.[214]

According to *Hesiod's Theogony, a genealogy of Greek gods*, Tartarus, god of the underworld, was father of the Giants.[215] We need to keep in mind that the Greeks borrowed nearly all of their gods from Mesopotamia; hence, the god of the underworld is Melqart / Nergal and the like, who are all essentially Satan.

It is significant that in the Greek translation, the word *gigantes* is used. This word already had an established definition, being used to speak of half-god, half-men kind of beings. In English, we use giant for a tall person. The giants were indeed tall, as Philo points out,[216] but their height is not the point. Rather, the term *gigas* means they were mixed; they had two different natures—man and god (angel). When we look at the usage of the word *Nephilim* (Greek *gigas*) in Scripture, we find some interesting things. Keep in mind, according to the Septuagint, what was true of the *Nephilim* was true of Nimrod.

ENLIL ENGENDERED NINURTA

Looking to the history of the Mesopotamian Ninurta (Nimrod) as a template, we learn that Enlil engendered Ninurta, or in biblical terminology, Satan begat Nimrod. The Bible does not explain how this happened, but we have the prophecy from the Garden of Eden that it would happen, "I will put enmity Between you and the woman, And between **your seed** and her Seed" (Gen 3:15)(Emphasis mine). We have also seen that Satan commanded angels to leave the spiritual realm and breed with women, a campaign which ended at the Flood. If Nimrod began to be a *gibbor* hero, that is a *giga* (hybrid), he must have a father; and, the texts from Nimrod's fatherland supply the identity.

> Ninurta is ... attested as the son of Enlil, bearing the epithet "the foremost, the lion, whom the Great Mountain (= Enlil) engendered."[217]

In a poem written about Ninurta, we again hear how he is called a hero just like Nimrod in Genesis; that his kingship (which in Hebrew has the root [מלך] like the god Molech) is over the heavens and the earth; and he sits (reigns) with his father as a pillager or destroyer. Note also that he has three names (syncretizations) in this poem: Ninurta / Pabilsag / Ningirsu:

> [Hero, Enlil's gatherer of the numerous functions, **consummate hero**, your king]ship is [eminently] mani[fest.] Hero [Ninurta], the (braided) crown [hangs loosely about your neck.] Hero Pabilsag, the (braided) crown hangs loosely about your neck. Hero Ningirsu, the (braided) crown hangs loosely about your neck;

your kingship is manifest. Your kingship is over the heavens; it is over the earth. You sit with Enki upon the holy dais ... With father Enlil you sit. You are the **heroic son of father Enlil**. In the Ekur you stand ... **Hero Ninurta is the pillager of cities for his father**. [218]

NIMROD THE HYBRID-HUNTER

He was a mighty hunter [*gibbor tzayid*] before the LORD [לִפְנֵי יְהוָה *lifnei YHWH*]; therefore it is said, "Like Nimrod the mighty hunter before the LORD" (Gen 10:9).

When Genesis notes that Nimrod was known for being a mighty hunter, does it mean that he was good at shooting deer, very much like Esau was before his father, Isaac? Would this be significant enough for the Bible to record and to even mention that he was a good hunter before God? The Hebrew phrase *gibbor tzayid* [גִּבֹּר־צַיִד] and Septuagint γιγας κυνηγος [*gigas kunegos*], implies he was a hunter with a dual nature of human and angel / god (not that he was hunting for giants). The Bible mentions his ability because he was a perversion that God noticed (not simply because he was good with a bow for catching his dinner).

The phrase "before the Lord" suggests that Nimrod was boastfully defying God, just like his father, Enlil. It is also the same language as found in the prohibition "You shall have no other gods before Me [על פני]" (Exod 20:3), thereby suggesting Nimrod was set up as the other god before God's face. Jesus states in John, "For everyone practicing evil hates the light and does not come to the light, lest his deeds should be exposed" (John 3:20). (See Appendix 2 What is Evil?). Nimrod was unashamedly doing his exploits in the open for all, including God, to see. In the *Epic of Gilgamesh*, the hero, Gilgamesh, did not care what the "gods" thought of his exploits. Ninurta, Marduk and others were worshipped openly and in defiance of what God thought of them.

The Jerusalem Targum equates Nimrod's "hunting" with a brazen disregard for the commands of God; it was Nimrod who encouraged men to follow his judgments rather than the judgments of Shem, who was following God's directions. According to the Targum, Nimrod was not hunting for game to eat, but he was hunting men. He was a warrior:

> He was mighty in hunting and in sin before the Lord; for he was a hunter of the sons of men in their languages. And he said to them, Leave the judgments of Shem (who is following God), and adhere to the judgments of Nimrod. On this account it is said, As Nimrod the mighty, mighty in hunting and in sin before the Lord (Jerusalem Targum).

The ancient historian Josephus relays more of this understanding of Nimrod, who, he says, swore to avenge the fathers for what God had done in the Flood.

> Now it was Nimrod who excited them to such an affront and contempt of God. He was the grandson of Ham, the son of Noah a bold man, and of great strength of hand. He persuaded them not to ascribe it to God, as if it were through his means they were happy, but to believe that it was their own courage which procured that happiness. He also gradually changed the government into tyranny seeing no other way of turning men from the fear of God, but to bring them into a constant dependence upon his own power. He also said he would be revenged on God, if he should have a mind to drown the world again; for that he would build a tower too high for the waters to be able to reach! and that he would avenge himself on God for destroying their forefathers![219]

In the cylinder seal depicted in Figure 28 below, we can see Ninurta in action hunting. We see Ninurta's star-studded bow with stars of eight-points, and on top of his head, he has ten horns. Ninurta is standing on an *Anzu* bird, or *Mušḫuššu*, or possibly *Bašmu*.

> He was a bearded god (Ninurta), … with star-tipped crossed bow-cases on his back, a sword at his belt, and a sickle-sword hanging from his right arm, draws a star-studded bow and aims an arrow at a rampant lion-griffin.[220]

Amar Annus notes how the lion hunt also fell into Ninurta's domain in his capacity as the "god of hunting," [221] a role that is amply attested in the iconography. Thus, we see that Nimrod was a hunter, but not for game. He was a hybrid, a chimera and the son of Satan, the Son of Perdition. His actions were so deplorable that God took notice, and that was okay by Nimrod. He even flaunted it with the *Akitu* festival by showboating his great success at stealing the world.

Figure 28 ancient.eu/image/6317/cylinder-seal-with-Ninurta

145

NIMROD'S LIFESPAN

If there is one thing in which we can take solace when a tyrant rises to power, it is that his life will typically end in less than a century. Nimrod, however, was a tyrant who would have lived for hundreds of years. Though Scripture does not tell us specifically how long he lived, we can estimate based on the lives of his first cousins. We know that Noah begat Ham who begat Canaan, who begat Cush, who begat Nimrod. Hence, Nimrod was in the fourth generation from Noah, and Noah lived until the ripe age of 950 years (Gen 9:29). Thereafter, the life spans decreased dramatically. Shem died at 600 (Gen 11:10–11), and his son Arphaxad lived 437 years (Gen 11:12–13). His son Salah lived 433 years (Gen 11:14–15), which was the fourth generation from Noah. So, we can extrapolate that Nimrod, who was also of the fourth generation, would have had a natural life of approximately 430 years.

Once again, the Bible is by no means alone in stating that ancient people lived exceptionally long lives compared to today. The ancient Mesopotamian writings of the same period speak of the Flood as a fact as much as we would speak of World War II. It did not need explanation; everyone knew what it was. It was just part of the historical landscape. *The Fields of Ninurta*, an unpublished composition going back to the Ur III period, depicts Ninurta in charge of all fields in the Nippur area (Civil 1994: 98)." [222] A syncretism of Ninurta was Ningirsu. In a work of Sumerian literature, *The Rulers of Lagaš*, Ningirsu is credited with the invention of agricultural tools.

> After the flood had swept over and brought about the destruction of the countries; when mankind was made to endure, and the seed of mankind was preserved and the black-headed people all rose; when An and Enlil called the name of mankind and established rulership, but kingship and the crown of the city had not yet come

146

out from heaven, and Ningirsu had not yet established for the multitude of well-guarded (?) people the pickaxe, the spade, the earth basket and the plough, which mean life for the Land – in those days, **the carefree youth of man lasted for 100 years** and, following his upbringing, he lasted for another 100 years.[223]

According to that composition, centenarians were still regarded as kids, (just like in Isaiah 65:20). Then after the tender age of one hundred, people could expect to live until two hundred years of age. For Nimrod, therefore, it would have been normal for him to have lived until he was into his four hundredth year. However, due to becoming a *gibbor*, he likely lived far longer than his normal life expectancy; he would have essentially been immortal, unless killed outright.

SATAN'S POWERS BECAME NIMROD'S

We also need to consider the powers that Satan would have afforded Nimrod. Whether he was able to use all of these, we cannot say. However, we do know that the coming Beast will receive and utilize all of Satan's power, throne, and great authority (Rev 13:2). Thus, it is likely that Nimrod was able to exploit some or all of these powers, such as:

- **Astral perception:** perceive the true forms of beings that are invisible to the human eye.
  - 2 Cor 11:14 And no wonder! For Satan himself transforms himself into an angel of light.
- **Biokinesis:** manipulate biological aspects.
  - Exod 7:11 But Pharaoh also called the wise men and the sorcerers; so the magicians of Egypt, they also did in like manner with their enchantments.
  - Job 2:7 So Satan went out from the presence of the LORD, and struck Job with painful boils from the sole of his foot to the crown of his head.

- **Electrokinesis**: control electrical things.
  - Rev 13:13 He performs great signs, so that he even makes fire come down from heaven on the earth in the sight of men.
- **Flight**
  - Rev 8:13 And I looked, and I heard an angel flying through the midst of heaven, saying with a loud voice.
- **Pathokinesis:** make people feel a certain way.
  - Eph 6:11 Put on the whole armor of God, that you may be able to stand against the wiles of the devil.
- **Power augmentation:** enhance people's abilities.
  - Exod 7:11 But Pharaoh also called the wise men and the sorcerers; so the magicians of Egypt, they also did in like manner with their enchantments.
- **Power granting:** give a slice of his power.
  - Rev 13:2 Now the beast which I saw was like a leopard, his feet were like the feet of a bear, and his mouth like the mouth of a lion. The dragon gave him his power, his throne, and great authority.
- **Power negation:** keep lesser beings from using their powers.
  - Mark 9:25 When Jesus saw that the people came running together, He rebuked the unclean spirit, saying to it: "Deaf and dumb spirit, I command you, come out of him and enter him no more!"
- **Precognition:** forecast the future.
  - Rev 12:12 Woe to the inhabitants of the earth and the sea! For the devil has come down to you, having great wrath, because he knows that he has a short time.
- **Telepathy:** read minds and influence emotions.
  - Matt 16:23 But He turned and said to Peter, "Get behind Me, Satan! You are an offense to Me, for you are not mindful of the things of God, but the things of men."

- **Teleportation:** travel anywhere in the universe without occupying space in between.
  - o Matt 4:5 Then the devil took Him up into the holy city, set Him on the pinnacle of the temple.
  - o Matt 4:8 Again, the devil took Him up on an exceedingly high mountain, and showed Him all the kingdoms of the world and their glory.
- **Thermokinesis:** alter temperatures drastically.
  - o Job 1:16 While he was still speaking, another also came and said, "The fire of God fell from heaven and burned up the sheep and the servants, and consumed them; and I alone have escaped to tell you!"
- **Weather manipulation**
  - o Job 1:19 "and suddenly a great wind came from across the wilderness and struck the four corners of the house, and it fell on the young people, and they are dead; and I alone have escaped to tell you!"
  - o Mark 4:39 Then He arose and rebuked the wind, and said to the sea, "Peace, be still!" And the wind ceased and there was a great calm.

In summary, we can visualize the merging of Satan and Nimrod as follows: Satan and Nimrod begin as completely separate, then they fuse together in the "*gibbor*" state, then they become fully one, as Satan and the Antichrist (Beast) will be. We will see another example of this in the tale of Gilgamesh.

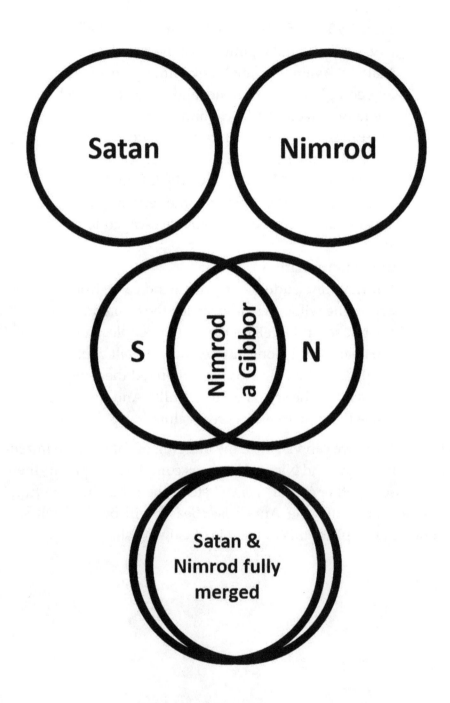

Chapter 11: Nimrod as Gilgamesh

Nimrod the rebel may also be known by the name Gilgamesh. In the ancient epic, Gilgamesh was a demigod from Uruk, which is biblical Erech and modern-day Iraq. According to Genesis 10, "The beginning of [Nimrod's] kingdom was Babel, Erech, Accad, and Calneh, in the land of Shinar" (Gen 10:10). Gilgamesh was eager to make a name for himself and set out on adventure with his half-animal, half-human hybrid friend, Enkidu, in order to ask Utnapishtim, a survivor from the Flood, the secret of immortality.

It is interesting that in the epic, the Flood is taken as a matter of historical fact. No explanation is given about the Deluge, much like how every American knows the 4th of July is Independence Day. Everyone reading the *Epic of Gilgamesh* would have known there had been a Flood.

Gilgamesh's name itself means "ancestor hero", which points us back to Nimrod, who began to be a *gibbor* (a hero). In a later section, we will consider another face of Nimrod as Pabilsag, the chief ancestor, a name which includes an aspect from Gilgamesh (*bilga* "ancestor"). According to behindthename.com, Gilgamesh:

> Possibly means "the ancestor is a hero", from Sumerian (*bilga*) meaning "ancestor" and (*mes*) meaning "hero, young man" … Gilgamesh was probably based on a real person: a king of Uruk who ruled around the 27th century BC.[224]

Amar Annus, in his ground-breaking study, has brought to light a hidden detail in Gilgamesh's name which may provide a connection between Ninurta and Gilgamesh. Ninurta's epithet is frequently "overseer of the equilibrium of the universe," while Gilgamesh's esoteric name, as deduced by S. Parpola, was "he who balanced the tree of equilibrium," which is hidden into the cryptographic signs dGIŠ.GÍN.MAŠ." [225] In other words, Ninurta and Gilgamesh might be the same.

There are other features of Gilgamesh that echo Nimrod and the idea that he was a *gigas*, a giant. According to scholar, A. Heidel, Gilgamesh is "2/3 god and 1/3 man."[226] He is from Uruk. He was a giant (11 cubits). He constructs cities. He takes women. He is a mighty hunter, and he is a "shepherd."[227]

Just looking at that list of similarities leads us to conclude "His activities thus resemble the exploits of the Mesopotamian hero Gilgamesh."[228] Nimrod was a hybrid, and was from Erech / Uruk. He constructed cities, and was likely behind the construction of Babel and the religious system. He was a hunter. We certainly hear loud echoes of Nimrod in the Gilgamesh epic, which strongly suggests they were the same historic hero.[229]

Annus reminds us of an important principle as we continue on our journey to uncover Satan's ancient machinations. He says, "Creation myths and conflict myths are somewhat different entities, but in some versions or contaminations they might be connected into a single mythical story."[230] In other words, the Gilgamesh, Ninurta and Nimrod accounts could be contaminations of the original, but ultimately, they lead us back to original story.

G. Smith and Jeremias were some of the first scholars to suggest the theory that Nimrod was, in fact, Gilgamesh:

> Nimrod is to be identified with the Babylonian hero Izdubar or Gishdubar (Gilgamesh) ... based on the fact that Izdubar is represented in the Babylonian epos as a mighty hunter, always accompanied by four dogs, and as the founder of the first great kingdom in Asia. Moreover, instead of "Izdubar"—the correct reading of which had not yet been determined—Jeremias saw the possibility of reading "Namra Udu" (shining light), a reading which would have made the identification with Nimrod almost certain.[231]

We must appreciate the fact that Gilgamesh is not a fictional character; He was a real man. As S. N. Kramer suggests in *History Begins in Sumer*, the earliest period of Mesopotamian history is the same time that Gilgamesh ruled.[232] This period is also when Nimrod existed, according to the Bible. And Nimrod the Rebel was such a sight to behold that God took notice!

HOW TALL WAS GILGAMESH?

It has been noted that Gilgamesh was 11 cubits tall.[233] Exactly how tall he was varies based on the value of the cubit, and the measurement of a cubit length varied as:

- Hebrew   17.5 in
- Egyptian   17.6 in
- Babylonian Long   19.8 in
- Hebrew Longest   20.4 in
- Egyptian Long   20.6 in

Since Gilgamesh came from the Babylonian region, we ought to use the Babylonian cubit. Thus 19.8" x 11 cubits equals 18.15 feet (5.53 m).

It is interesting to compare his height to Og, King of Bashan. Moses wrote in Deuteronomy that Og's bed was nine cubits long (Deut 3:11). But which cubit should we use for Og? The real question is which cubit would Moses, who was "learned in all the wisdom of the Egyptians," (Acts 7:22) have used? Of course, the Egyptian Cubit.

Figure 29 Egyptian Royal Cubit

When I had the chance to visit the British Museum in London, I requested to look at the Egyptian (Royal) cubit, and they obliged me. After waiting about half an hour, they took me into a room with lots of drawers. They opened one and pulled out the Egyptian (Royal) cubit, as depicted in Figure 29. I have to admit, I was very excited. I measured it, and it was exactly 20.63 inches. Thus, we have the exact length of the standard measure Moses would have used.

We are told of Og's bed (or likely sarcophagus) that "nine cubits was the length thereof, and four cubits the breadth of it, after the cubit of a man" (Deut 3:11 JPS). We calculate 20.63 inches times nine cubits and arrive at 15.47 feet (4.716 m) long and the width is about six feet ten inches (6.87 feet, 2.094 meters); That means Og was roughly 15'6" tall. Gilgamesh was about 18' tall. These descriptions fit second temple sources; Josephus mentions the ancient giants who had: "bodies so large, and countenances so entirely different from other men, that they were surprising to the sight."[234] The *Book of Baruch* mentions the giants "were of so great stature, and so expert in war."[235]

There is no doubt that many features match both Nimrod and Gilgamesh and hence, we cannot write Gilgamesh off as a purely fictional character. S. N. Kramer agrees and points out: "A few years ago one would have strongly doubted his (historical) existence ... we now have the certitude that the time of Gilgamesh corresponds to the earliest period of Mesopotamian history.[236]

Figure 30 Gilgamesh relief in Louvre Museum in Paris

GILGAMESH'S WEIGHT

The Louvre Museum in Paris contains a relief, seen in Figure 30 on the previous page, that is thought to be of Gilgamesh. It may just be coincidental, but the relief is between sixteen to eighteen feet tall. In the picture, Gilgamesh can be seen holding a lion, like a woman might hold her chihuahua. In *Corrupting the Image Vol. 1*, we determined that Og weighed about 3,125 lbs (1,417 kg), since he was 2.5 times an average man's height today. Our formula required that we find the cube of 2.5 times 200 lbs. (91 kg). We used 2.5 because Og was 15 feet tall which is 2.5 times taller than an average man weighing 200 lbs., which yielded 3,125 lbs. (1,417 kg). Applying the same formula: the cube of 3 times 200 lbs. to Gilgamesh, we arrive at a weight of 5,400 lbs. (2,449 kg)! Someone that weighs that much could easily hold a four hundred pound[237] lion!

GILGAMESH'S TOMB FOUND

In 2003, the BBC reported that archaeologist Jörg Fassbinder of the Bavarian Department of Historical Monuments in Munich used a magnetic imaging system to create a magnetogram, or a digital map of an area in the ancient city of Uruk. Fassbinder states: "The most surprising thing was that we found structures already described by Gilgamesh." He believed they might have found the tomb of Gilgamesh under what used to be the bed of the Euphrates River, where it flowed in the ancient city of Uruk. Fassbinder states: "I don't want to say definitely it was the grave of King Gilgamesh, but it looks very similar to that described in the epic." BBC goes on to say, "Gilgamesh was described as having been buried under the Euphrates, in a tomb apparently constructed when the waters of the ancient river parted following his death."[238]

Amazingly, Revelation 9 predicts that four angels will emerge from the Euphrates River itself. "Loose the four angels which are bound in the great river Euphrates" (Rev. 9:14KJV). Could Gilgamesh be one of those beings?

Chapter 12: Tower of Babel: Stargate to the Abyss

Satan raised up the Rebel who became a *gibbor*, the Son of Perdition. Phase two of Satan's plan was to create the stargate, a portal for the gods (demons) to pass through into the Rebel's dimension. They would create *bābu-ilū*, that is, a gate / door of the gods, or the plural is *ilānu*, probably reflecting the alternate title *Bab-ilan* / Babylon, in Akkadian. The Bible records this event:

> Then they said to one another, "Come, let us make bricks and bake them thoroughly." They had brick for stone, and they had asphalt for mortar. And they said, "Come, let us build ourselves a city, and a tower whose top is in the heavens; let us make a name for ourselves, lest we be scattered abroad over the face of the whole earth" (Gen 11:3–4).

The Babylonians believed their ziggurats (step-pyramids) were ladders or bridges between the domain of man and the domain of the gods. Recall that when the veil spread over all nations (Isa 26:7), and unrolled between heaven and Earth at the Fall, the spiritual and earthly domains were no longer one. The veil shielded Earth from God's glorious, fiery face so it would not melt his fallen creation (Ps 97:5); It also confined Satan to the spiritual side. He tried to overcome this obstacle through the Nephilim bodysuit program, but with the Flood, his hopes went down the drain.

Thus, the point of ziggurats was to unite a city with its god. The intention was to create a connection point between the domain of the "gods" and the domain of man. The buildings were, according to Andrew George, "said to bridge the gap between the lowermost and uppermost levels of the cosmos."[239]

The names of some of the ziggurats reveal the important connection the builder's ascribed to these artificial mountains, such as:

- Temple of the Foundation of Heaven and Earth (Babylon)
- Temple of the Wielder of the Seven Decrees of Heaven and Earth (Borsippa)
- Temple of the Stairway to Pure Heaven (Sippar)
- Temple of the Ziggurat, Exalted Dwelling Place (Kish)
- Temple of the Exalted Mountain (Ehursagkalamma)
- Temple of Exalted Splendor (Enlil – at Kish?)
- Temple of the Foundation of Heaven and Earth (Dilbat)
- Temple which Links Heaven and Earth (Larsa)[240]

Figure 31 Babylon ziggurat like the Tower of Babel

The ziggurat, as depicted in Figure 31, was the device thought to grant humans and gods a portal through which they could commune and visit one another. It was "a bond of union, whose purpose was to assure communication between earth and heaven ... giant step-ladder by means of which a man may ascend as near as possible to the sky."[241]

God revealed such a spiritual ladder between the two domains in Jacob's dream, in which "a ladder was set up on the earth, and its top reached to heaven; and there the angels of God were ascending and descending on it" (Gen 28:12). Jesus later identified himself to be the ladder: "You shall see heaven open, and the angels of God ascending and descending upon the Son of Man" (John 1:51). The ziggurat was Satan's counterfeit of Jacob's Ladder.

Additionally, Jerusalem was considered to be a connecting point between the two realms with one above and one below; the two cities were geographically superimposed, but separated by the veil. The *Mishne* speaks of the two Jerusalems and how God said that He would not enter the Jerusalem of the heavens until he could enter the Jerusalem below. The Rabbis ask, "Is there then a Jerusalem above?" They answer affirmatively, citing Ps 122: "Jerusalem! which art built as a city wherein all associate together (i.e., Jerusalem is built as that Jerusalem which is connected (associated) with it. Hence there is another Jerusalem, and that is above in the heavens."[242]

The idea of two Jerusalems is reflected in Paul's writings where he distinguished the earthly "Jerusalem which now is" (Gal 4:25), from the "Jerusalem above" (Gal 4:26). He was apparently echoing the rabbinic understanding of the Jerusalem *shel ma'alah* (above) and the Jerusalem *shelemata* (below). [243] In Hebrew, things that come in natural pairs use a dual ending: e.g. *"yad"* means hand and *"yadayim"* means two hands. The "ayim" ending of Yerusalayim strongly implies duality [244] with one above and one below. This may be the reason Jerusalem is commanded in Isaiah 52, to awake twice. "Awake, awake! Put on your strength, O Zion" Is 52:1. The Mesopotamians knew that the earthly realm was only part of the cosmos. Therefore, we see the Mesopotamians understood a spiritual truth that is confirmed in Scripture.

In the ancient Mesopotamian worldview, it was believed that heaven and Earth had been separated, and Enlil's temple, *Ekur*, was "the bond between them." The city of Nippur was called *dur-an-ki*, meaning "bond between heaven and earth."[245] Amar Annus points out how Enlil had the central position in the pantheon, and in an ancient hymn, the city of Nippur was called, "city of Enlil, bond of Heaven and Earth, Enlil, the great mountain." The most important city **and its main temple, as the cosmic bond,** [that] **forms a link between the different levels of the universe"** [246] (Emphasis mine).

The ancients did not naively imagine they could build a skyscraper and touch the physical sky. The point was to build a portal, as Creig Marlowe explains, "A ziggurat was not only to reach the gods but to provide a gateway for a god to come down to the people," which he says, "precludes any idea that building this tower was a superhuman construction of a super skyscraper and some kind of attempt to 'storm Heaven' and rival or resist God." [247] They were not going to invade heaven, but instead, were seeking a way to let Satan, et al., break through to the earthly realm.

WORMHOLE TO THE ABYSS?

Thus, this gate of the gods was Satan's plan to open a portal to allow his team to flood through to our side of the veil. We do not know exactly how they intended to do this, but mathematics might offer some clues.

The ancients understood, perhaps imprecisely, that the gods they worshipped were not in this dimension, but resided in another dimension. They believed that the cosmological abode of the gods was "in the middle heavens which was the place for assembly. [248]

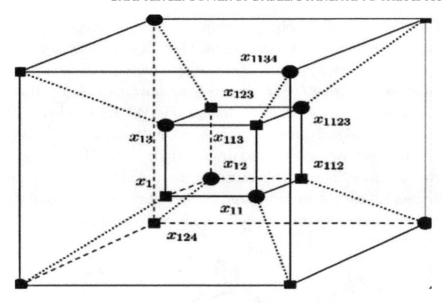

Figure 32 Tesseract

The terrestrial dimension where we live is at a right angle to spiritual dimension and this is called a Tesseract (or a 4-D cube). Figure 32 above illustrates that the spiritual dimension is an overlay on our realm — it is not far away, but is on us, below us, beside us. We are completely enveloped by the fourth dimension.

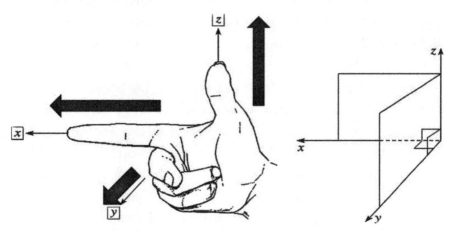

Figure 33 Visualizing three dimensions

To understand this concept, point your index finger forward; that is one dimension, as in Figure 33 Point your middle finger 90 degrees from your index finger. Now you have two dimensions. Point your thumb up, now you have three dimensions. We live in three dimensions. We are familiar with three-dimensional space. To get to another dimension, according to physicists, we just have to draw a right angle. This is where our brains begin to hurt because we are not able to contort our fingers in such a fashion. Yet mathematically, it is possible; higher dimensions are simply at right angles to one another.

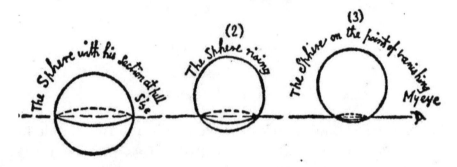

Figure 34 Abbot's visualization of A Sphere entering the two-dimensional plane of Flatland.

It is easier for us to imagine a two-dimensional world, as Edwin Abbot did in his 1883 book, *Flatland: A Romance of Many Dimensions*. In *Flatland*, everyone and everything is two-dimensional. There are myths of a higher dimension, but since no one has been to that dimension, there is no proof and it is considered taboo to talk of it. In Flatland, there is no up or down, just forward and sideways. However, when a three-dimensional being (A Sphere) intersects their world, it causes great consternations. They cannot see the entirety of A Sphere; they only see a horizontal cross-section because Flatlanders can only see in two-dimensions.; If you follow the arrow labeled "My eye" in Figure 34, you will see how the Flatlanders can only perceive a two-dimensional slice of A Sphere. He appears as a round spot on the ground that narrows and widens as he passes through. Abbot's picture illustrates what this might look like.

Flatland serves as a convenient analogy for us to imagine a yet higher dimension than our own three-dimensional world. As the illustration shows, the three-dimensional world was not far away, in a special sense, from Flatland; it was in fact, all around it. Flatland lived inside of Spaceland (the three-dimensional world). In the same way, we live inside the spiritual or heavenly plane which is on a higher dimension than our world; yet it is all around us. We cannot directly see it, but we can perceive it through math and testimonies of those who have seen it. Quantum physics, which was discovered in the early part of the twentieth century, has provided a theoretical bridge between these dimensions. Einstein, who was rather skeptical of some of the claims of quantum physics, wrote a paper with Podolsky and Rosen, called the "EPR Paradox," in which they did a thought experiment:

> The essence of the paradox is that particles can interact in such a way that it is possible to measure both their position and their momentum more accurately than Heisenberg's uncertainty principle allows, unless measuring one particle instantaneously affects the other to prevent this accuracy, which would involve information being transmitted faster than light as forbidden by the theory of relativity ("spooky action at a distance"). This consequence had not previously been noticed and seemed unreasonable at the time; the phenomenon involved is now known as quantum entanglement.[249]

Quantum entanglement happens when you have two particles that become connected—they share information between them instantaneously. Scientists have fired a laser beam through types of crystal which can split photons, causing them to become entangled. Even when the particles are separated by hundreds of miles, the relationship remains intact; a change in one instantaneously causes a change in the other!

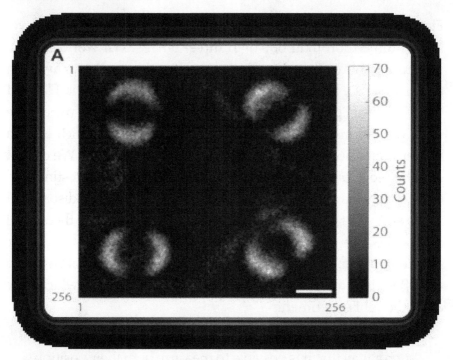

Figure 35 Quantum Entanglement (Moreau et al., Science Advances, 2019) www.sciencealert.com/scientists-just-unveiled-the-first-ever-photo-of-quantum-entanglement

The particles are working in tandem, and when separated, regardless of the distance, they continue to be inextricably linked. Whatever happens to one immediately affects the other. If you change the spin in one, it changes the spin in the other instantaneously. Once entangled, the particles lack independence, and nobody knows why this happens, but it happens.[250] And it has been tested and reproduced repeatedly.

Figure 35 above is the first-ever photo that "shows [quantum] entanglement between two photons—two light particles. They are interacting and—for a brief moment—sharing physical states."[251]

Wormholes are technically known as Einstein-Rosen bridges (the "ER" part of the equation). Nathan Rosen collaborated with Einstein on a paper describing them in 1935. EPR refers to another paper Einstein published in 1935 with Rosen and Boris Podolsky.

This paper articulated the paradoxical puzzles imposed on the nature of reality by quantum entanglement. For decades, nobody seriously considered the possibility that the two papers had anything to do with one another. But in 2013, physicists Juan Maldacena and Leonard Susskind proposed that in some sense, wormholes and entanglement describe the same thing.[252]

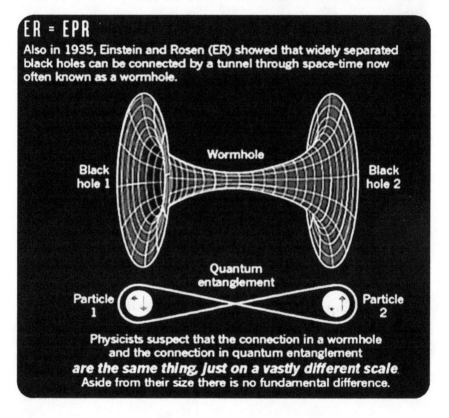

Figure 36 Anatomy of a Wormhole livescience.com/28550-how-quantum-entanglement-works-infographic.html.

Researchers may have discovered glimpses of the other dimensions; they may have peered through the veil. However, God placed this barrier there for our protection; its removal would literally be the end of the world as we know it.

Communication through the veil is forbidden by God; however, it appears to be exactly what Geordie Rose, CTO of D-Wave Systems, a quantum computer company, is attempting to do. He claims that shadows of parallel worlds overlap ours and, given the right circumstances, we can enter into that other dimension, take their resources, and repurpose them for our own use. He says:

> In Quantum mechanics there is this concept that a thing can exist in two states which are mutually exclusive at the same time ... Imagine that there really are parallel universes out there, and now imagine that you have two, that are exactly identical in every respect ... with only one difference, and that's the value of a little thing called a Q-bit on this chip, that's a contraction of quantum bit. And that Q-bit is very much like a bit or a transistor in a conventional computer.

> It has two distinct physical states, which we call 0 and 1 for bit. And in a conventional computer these are mutually exclusive. That device is either one or the other and never anything else. In a quantum computer, that device can be in the strange situation where these two parallel universes have a nexus, a point in space where they overlap ... So, the way I think about it, is that the shadows of these parallel worlds, overlap with ours, and if we're smart enough, we can dive into them and grab their resources and pull them back into ours, to make an effect in our world" [253] (Emphasis mine).

It is interesting that he says "their" resources. Who are they? To what resources is he referring? How does he know that there is a parallel dimension? He does not provide answers to these questions. Nevertheless, it sounds like he is describing a portal or a bridge, like Enlil's temple served as a link between the realms. It could be that the quantum computer is a modern, high-tech way to open up a channel between dimensions which might explain Roses' eerie statement, "If you have the opportunity to stand next to one of these machines, it is an awe-inspiring thing, at least to me. **It feels like an altar to an alien god.**" [254]

The Tower of Babel, the gate of the gods, was apparently a similar device. It did not have a fancy quantum computer at its center, but it was still an impressive structure with a clearly defined goal: to make contact with "them". The ancients were blatant about wanting to reach the other side and communicate with the gods, and to quote Geordie Rose, were trying "to grab their resources and pull them back into ours, to make an effect in our world."

Thus, modern man is once again trying to open the veil, much like what Satan intended to do with the gate of the gods. And that explains why God deemed it imperative at the Tower of Babel to thwart man's actions. If the purpose of constructing a tower had just been to make people famous, then God would not have needed to intervene; or, if God simply hates haughty towers, we would have seen Him destroy all towers and every monument made to man. Granted, He will do just that one day (Isa 2:12–15), but it will be at the end of the world!

Opening the Tower of Babel gateway would have had catastrophic consequences, but God intervened at that time. In the future, this very thing will indeed happen, according to the book of Revelation. Satan will one day succeed in opening the Abyss and releasing an army of two-hundred-million, chimeric creatures upon the world.

> I saw a star fallen from heaven to the earth. To him was given the key to the bottomless pit. And he opened the bottomless pit, and smoke arose out of the pit like the smoke of a great furnace (Rev 9:1–2). Now the number of the army of the horsemen was two hundred million (Rev 9:16).

Satan's purpose for opening the Abyss in the future is to increase the size of his army to fight against Jesus. Thus, the overwhelming reason for God to intervene at Babel was to prevent Satan from creating a gateway of the gods that was intended to be a passageway or stargate for the fallen angels to enter our physical realm. Satan particularly wanted to release those who were judged during the Flood and sent to the Abyss.

Opening the gates of the Abyss is a parallel action to what was planned to happen at Babel. We do not know exactly how the pieces came together in Babel to create a working portal, but we have seen that science supports the notion of opening wormholes. Given that Satan is the smartest being after God, he must have used his intelligence to find a way to do it. Historically, archaeology and multiple texts agree that the Tower was built. Since that time, Satan has continued to partner with mankind to build mechanisms to bridge the dimensions and to ultimately open the Abyss. (See Appendix 8 Joel's Army).

Chapter 13: Enlil Thwarted from Opening the Gate of the Gods

Just as God intervened with a Flood when the sons of God came down on Mt. Hermon to create hybrids, God also had to intercede to prevent an extinction level event at Babel. Satan created a scenario so cataclysmic that God had to intervene, once again, before it was too late.

> But the LORD came down to see the city and the tower which the sons of men had built. And the LORD said, "Indeed the people are one and they all have one language, and this is what they begin to do; now nothing that they propose to do will be withheld from them (Gen 11:5–6).

Genesis gives us an incredible window into what was really happening. God observes the Tower and notes that with all humans speaking one language, there is nothing they cannot do. "The tower is called by the Rabbis 'the house of Nimrod,' ... a house of idolatry which the owners abandoned in time of peace."[255] We recall that the word for idols is *elilim*, which is plural and means "Enlils". God was not against tall buildings or mankind working together; indeed, Jesus even prayed, "Father, let them be one" (John 17:21). The problem was the intent behind the Tower: To open a portal and inaugurate a reign of terror, similar to the days of Noah which corrupted the whole Earth. Hence, God came down and confused [בָּלַל *balal*] the languages.

> "Come, let Us go down and there confuse their language, that they may not understand one another's speech. So the LORD scattered them abroad from there over the face of all the earth, and they ceased building the city. Therefore its name is called Babel, because there the LORD confused [בָּלַל *balal*] the language of all the earth; and from there the LORD scattered them abroad over the face of all the earth (Gen 11:7–9).

The Hebrew word for "confusion" is a different root than Babel. It is significant that the original meaning of "babel" was not confusion, but because of what happened at Babel, the meaning was altered to denote "confusion". [256] We might liken it to Chernobyl (which ironically means wormwood), a city in northern Ukraine, which lies completely abandoned and is synonymous with "a major nuclear-energy accident." [257] We sometimes speak of not having another "Chernobyl". In the same way, "Babel" became a "Chernobyl" because it had a "linguistic meltdown" which resulted in that "gate of the gods" becoming known as "confusion".

THE MESOPOTAMIANS RECORDED GOD'S ATTACK

God's strike against the city was recorded by the Mesopotamians. According to the famous *Epic of Gilgamesh*, the building of a certain ziggurat-temple was an offense and had to be stopped:

> "The building of this temple offended the gods. In a night they threw down what had been built. They scattered them abroad, and made strange speeches. The progress they impeded." [258]

Why would building such a tower and temple offend the gods of Babylon? In truth, it did not. The reality is the building of the Tower was impeded by the God of Israel, but the Babylonian theologians scrambled to find a way to explain the theological conundrum by re-writing history. It is the same kind of excuse Sennacherib wrote on his prism when explaining that he shut up King Hezekiah in Jerusalem "like a caged bird." The Assyrians were not known for just coming to town and leaving peaceably. They were ruthless predators who had no inhibitions when it came to torturing their prey in heinous, inhuman ways. According to the Bible, God defended Jerusalem by sending just one angel to kill 185,000 Assyrians (2 Kings 19:32–35). The doubtfulness of Sennacherib's flimsy story gives credibility to the Bible's account. In the same way, the doubtfulness of the Babylonian account of attributing the halting the Tower's construction to an act of their god, gives credibility to the Bible's account. The Mesopotamian gods seemed to thrive on ziggurats and temples being built in their honor. Why would the *Etemenanki* (Tower of Babel) upset them? They were not displeased; it was only the true God of Israel who was offended. A Babylonian inscription in the British Museum reports:

> Babylon corruptly proceeded to sin, and both small and great mingled on the mound ... All day they founded their stronghold, but in the night, he put a complete stop to it. In his anger he also poured out his secret counsel to scatter them abroad, he set his face, he gave a command to make foreign their speech."[259]

The biblical account of the confusion of languages is confirmed from a hostile witness—that is, one who is not trying to confirm our point of view, but yet does corroborate the biblical rendition of events. The ancients treated the narrative as real history. In the epic of *Enmerkar and the Lord of Aratta* inscription, we read:

> In those days, the lands of Subur (and) Hamazi,
> Harmony-tongued (?) Sumer, the great land of the decrees of princeship,
> Un, the land having all that is appropriate (?), The land Martu, resting in security, The whole universe, the people in unison (?)
> To Enlil in one tongue [spoke].[...]
> (Then) Enki, the lord of abundance (whose) commands are trustworthy,
> The lord of wisdom, who understands the land,
> The leader of the gods,
> Endowed with wisdom, the lord of Eridu
> Changed the speech in their mouths, [brought (?)] contention into it,
> Into the speech of man that (until then) had been one[260]
> (Emphasis mine).

Incredibly, the text reveals that mankind, until then, had been speaking one language which was changed in the course of one night. Not only was the one tongue turned into many, but it was brought about through the building of a tower! God stopped short the dastardly plan Satan concocted.

There is solid evidence from texts as early as the second millennium BC that this tower, called the *Etemenanki*, existed. In Sumerian, *Etemenanki,* meaning "temple of the foundation of heaven and earth", is the name of the ziggurat dedicated to Marduk. This is the same tower that Nebuchadnezzar's family repaired in the 6th century BC during the Neo-Babylonian dynasty. Construction of the tower was started 42 ages before Nebuchadnezzar and was most likely the actual Tower of Babel. A model-reconstruction of the *Etemenanki*, depicted in Figure 37 which originally measured 91 meters in height is at the Pergamon Museum in Berlin.

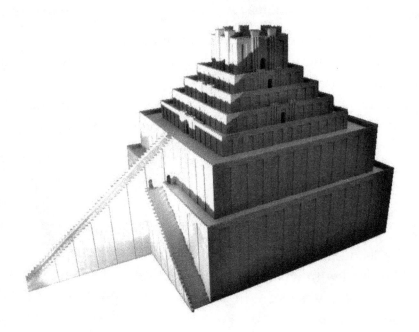

Figure 37 Reconstruction of the Etemenanki, Courtesy Pergamon Museum, Berlin.

Andrew George explains, saying:

> The reference to a ziqqurrat at Babylon in the Creation Epic[261] is more solid evidence ... a Middle Assyrian piece of this poem survives to prove the long-held theory that it existed already in the second millennium BC. ... There is no reason to doubt that this ziqqurrat, described as ziqqurrat apsî elite, "the upper ziqqurrat of the Apsû", was E-temenanki.[262]

REMAINS OF THE GATE OF THE GODS (TOWER OF BABEL)

Satan's attempt to create a portal was a huge undertaking, and we find extrabiblical, textual, and archaeological remains of it even today. All of the evidence is a powerful witness to the veracity of the Bible and the audacity of Satan's schemes.

In the 7th- 6th century BC, Nabopolassar, father of Nebuchadnezzar, the one who performed repairs on the tower, stated:

> At that time, my lord Marduk told me in regard to E-temen-anki, the ziggurat of Babylon, which before my day was (already) very weak and badly buckled...[263]

Nabopolassar did not begin the construction of the tower or lay its foundations; he tried to repair what someone long before him had abandoned. His next statement: "to ground its bottom on the breast of the netherworld, to make its top vie with the heavens", echoes the purpose of the ziggurat as a bridge between heaven and Earth. He then states how it was "Through the craft of exorcism, the wisdom of Ea and Marduk, I purified that place and made firm its foundation platform on its ancient base." Thus, Nabopolassar was attempting to reconstruct an ancient tower that had been abandoned ages before him. In addition, He used exorcism in the name of Marduk, a god whom we know is a syncretism for Enlil (Satan). The king is so dedicated to building the tower that he personally gets involved in the project:

> In its foundations I laid out gold, silver, gemstones from mountain and sea. ...I bowed my neck to my lord Marduk. I rolled up my garment, my kingly robe, and carried on my head bricks and earth (i.e. mud bricks). I had soil-baskets made of gold and silver and made Nebuchadnezzar, my firstborn son, beloved of my heart, carry alongside my workmen earth mixed with wine, oil, and resin-chips.[264]

Both King Nabopolassar and his son, Nebuchadnezzar, get into the work. They do not just have the slaves do it, but they themselves roll up their sleeves and go to work. He then, talks about his younger boy:

> I made Nabûsumilisir, his brother, a boy, issue of my body, my darling younger son, take up mattock and spade ... I constructed the building, the replica of E-sarra, in joy and jubilation and raised its top as high as a mountain. For my lord Marduk I made it an object fitting for wonder, just as it was in former times."[265]

Nabopolassar did not create the Tower of Babel, he simply repaired it. But of course, these things would take a long time; hence, Nebuchadnezzar continued the work.

Figure 38 Tower of Babel Courtesy Google Earth.

THE TOWER OF BABEL STELE (NEBUCHADNEZZAR'S OWN WORDS)

His son Nebuchadnezzar II, likewise, recorded in an inscription at Borsippa, seen in Figure 39 on the following page, how he worked on the tower and repaired it, but was not the original builder. The tower was already incredibly ancient and had been abandoned for a long time. He says:

> The tower, the eternal house, which I founded and built.
> I have completed its magnificence with silver, gold, other metals, stone, enameled bricks, fir, and pine. The first which is the house of the earth's base, the most

ancient monument of Babylon; I built and finished it. I have highly exalted its head with bricks covered with copper. We say for the other, that is, this edifice, the house of the seven lights of the earth, the most ancient monument of Borsippa. **A former king built it, (they reckon 42 ages)** but he did not complete its head. **Since a remote time, people had abandoned it, without order expressing their words.**[266]

Figure 39 Inscription on Borsippa, by Nebuchadnezzar II, Courtesy schoyencollection.com

Amazingly, Nebuchadnezzar admits that he did not build the tower, but it had been built "42 ages" earlier by a former king. We do not know exactly what he meant by 42 ages, though we could speculate that an age was a generation, which could be twenty years from the time a child is born until the child might have their own, or it could be speaking of the lifetime of a person, maybe 70 years? In any event, that would give us a figure of 840 years on the low end and 2,940 years on the higher end.

Figure 40 Inscription on Borsippa, by Nebuchadnezzar II, Courtesy schoyencollection.com

Nevertheless, he reported he was simply trying to repair the tower because "people had abandoned it, without order expressing their words," a phrase that strongly implies something catastrophic happened. Did Nebuchadnezzar believe it was the same tower that had displeased the "gods" and that caused the confusion of languages? His statement, "without order expressing their words," very much gives us the impression that he did. The ancients did not record a reason for abandoning the work because their speech was confused.

With language remarkably similar to Genesis: "Let us make bricks and bake them thoroughly" (Gen 11:3), his inscription continues:

> Since that time, the earthquake and the thunder had dispersed the sun-dried clay. The bricks of the casing had been split, and the earth of the interior had been scattered in heaps. Merodach [Marduk], the great god, excited my mind to repair this building. I did not change the site, nor did I take away the foundation.[267]

Is it possible that Satan was trying to get both Nebuchadnezzar and his father to rebuild the Tower of Babel for another nefarious scheme? It seems plausible.

BABYLON ABODE OF THE GODS

While God clearly threw down Satan's hopes of building a gateway of the gods, Satan did, nevertheless, create a cosmic mountain where worship was directed to him. He ensured that man's attention would be drawn away from the true source of life and blessings. Satan tried to overtake God's mountain, and when he failed, he used it as a model for his own mountain city of pleasure which would serve as the abode of the gods.

Satan created a believable counterfeit, a "copy and shadow of the heavenly things" (Heb 8:5), because he knows the heavenly things intimately. When he said, "I will also sit on the mount of the congregation on the farthest sides of the north" (Isa 14:13), he did not need to "go" anywhere; he was already there! It was from the "holy mountain of God" (Ezek 28:14), that Satan was expelled. We see that God's holy mountain was (and is) called "**Mount Zion** ... the **city** of the living **God**, the **heavenly Jerusalem**" (Heb 12:22). It is on the sides of the north, a phrase found in Isaiah 14, where Satan boasted that he would occupy: "I will also sit on the **mount of the congregation** [בְּהַר־מוֹעֵד be'har moed] On the farthest sides of the north" (Isa 14:13)—like a phrase the Psalmist used, "the **city** of our God ... **Mount Zion** on the **sides of the north**" (Ps 48:1–2).[268]

One of Enlil's major epithets was KUR.GAL, Sumerian for "great mountain", which is also a title for Dagan and Amurru. Revelation tells us that the dragon has seven heads and ten horns and that the "seven heads are seven mountains on which the woman sits" Rev 17:9. Micha F. Lindeman, in the *Encyclopedia Mythica*, says, "Enlil … is sometimes referred to as *Kur-Gal*, the great mountain. And in one of the texts, 'The Great Mountain Enlil cried to Ninlil.'" [269] Amazingly, Satan is getting his wish of reigning on the holy mountain—so much so, that he casts himself as the mountain!

Satan offers man a counterfeit mountain in place of the New Jerusalem. God has declared: "the **latter days** that **the mountain of the house of the Lord** [הַר־בֵּית־יְהוָה har-beit-YHWH] shall be established as the **highest of the mountains**" (Mic 4:1 ESV, also Isa 2:2–3). By contrast, Amar Annus speaks of Enlil's mountain (*ekur*):

> Ekur is the temple of the supreme god Enlil in Nippur, the temple to which Ninurta returns after performing his great exploits. The name means 'mountain house' and it is the Assembly of the gods.[270]

Creating counterfeit cosmic mountains was just another way to contravene God. Though Satan was expelled from the holy mountain, he, nevertheless, stole the Earth and would still get to be king of the mountain of his making. He succeeded in getting man to worship him and perform in dramas like the *Akitu* festival, the reenactment of the killing of the Creator and the usurpation of his authority.

However, in the Book of Jeremiah, God says he is going to destroy this mountain and calls him, not a great mountain, but "O destroying mountain, Who destroys all the earth" (Jer 51:24–25). Of course, referring to anything in Babylon as a mountain is illogical since there are zero natural mountains there. Thus, the only mountain to which God could be referring is Enlil the "great mountain". This conclusion is underscored by God also saying, "I will punish Bel in Babylon"(Jer 51:44).

PLEASURE PALACE OF THE GODS

Consequently, it was also believed that Babylon was the abode of the gods and the temple known as 'E-sangil,' was "'the palace of the gods' ... the temple of Marduk ... was no ordinary sanctuary ... it was the cosmic abode of the king of the gods, the place from where he ruled the universe." [271]

Andrew George notes that the E-Sangil was the "archetypal cosmic abode, modelled exactly on the cosmic abodes of ... the Apsû of Ea and **the E-sharra of Enlil,**" which he notes was not only a temple but "**the city of Babylon** ... not just the tower, but the whole city ... [was] the abode of the gods." [272] The *E-sangil* was the whole city of Babylon, the pleasure-palace of the gods of heaven. George notes how, according to ancient Babylonian commentary, there are ceremonial meanings in the names of Marduk's temples. Of great interest is the fourth temple, which is "E-sangil = Pleasure-palace of the gods of heaven [and underworld]," [273] which demonstrates how Satan was using pleasure to seduce man to worship at his temple. In fact, "Babylon, then, is the home of the pantheon because it is where all the gods of the universe gather for the divine assembly." [274]

Satan (Enlil) set himself up at Babylon where man would worship him and experience heaven-on-earth through the lusts of the flesh, the lusts of the eyes and the pride of life. Satan wants us to be satisfied on an Earth without God, yet he understands God has put eternity in the heart of man (Eccl 3:11), and therefore our hearts crave to be home with God where there are pleasures at His right hand forevermore (Ps 16:11). The Psalmist declared we will be "abundantly satisfied with the fullness of Your house, And You give them drink from the river of Your pleasures" (Ps 36:8). Isaiah stated, "In this mountain The LORD of hosts will make for all people a feast" (Isa 25:6).

Thus, there are two cities—God's city, Mount Zion, which is pure, holy, true and original and where there are joy and pleasures without end. God created the Garden of Eden: Eden means pleasure. God wanted to give Adam and Eve pleasure. The afterlife in Hebrew is referred to as *Gan Eden*, hence, a return to the garden of pleasure. He wants to give us joys beyond our comprehension.

Then there is Satan's city of Babel, with its perversions of what is good, true and right. The pleasures therein are real and feel good, but are gone in a moment leaving people stuck in the cycle of chasing the dragon. Ironically, it would seem like God's promise of true joy and pleasures would win hands down. However, mankind has bought Satan's lies from the beginning; and Babel, brimming with its fleeting pleasures, has historically been more appealing than God's city. Satan's city is here now, tactile and fleshly; it feeds the self—whereas God's city is a paradise of selflessness, where lusts of the flesh have no place. Satan's city is the ultimate rebellion to God's order, and it was started by Nimrod, the Rebel.

Chapter 14: The Woman who Rides the Beast Revealed

The woman who rides the Beast and the ancient idolatrous system behind her is an important link in understanding how Satan has been fighting God. We recall that Satan was in the Garden of Eden (Ezek 28:13), the place of pleasure, created for Adam and Eve. But he lusted for more (Isa 14:13) and staged a coup. As a result of the slanderous lies Satan told to Adam and Eve, they began to covet when they already possessed everything. Their coveting resulted in their expulsion from the Garden of Eden (Gen 3:23). Man has been trying to get back to Eden (pleasure) ever since and Satan has gladly exploited this craving in humans.

John saw "a woman sitting on a scarlet beast which was full of names of blasphemy, having seven heads and ten horns" (Rev 17:3). The Beast represents the culmination of all that Satan has been working toward.

> And on her forehead a name was written: MYSTERY, BABYLON THE GREAT, THE MOTHER OF HARLOTS AND OF THE ABOMINATIONS OF THE EARTH. I saw the woman, drunk with the blood of the saints and with the blood of the martyrs of Jesus. And when I saw her, I marveled with great amazement (Rev 17:5-6).

Figure 41 Rain Goddess. Cylinder seal. Mesopotamia. Akkad period, c. 2334-2154 B.C. Shell. 33.5 X 19.5 mm. New York, Pierpont Morgan Library, Corpus 220.

Somewhere in the Akkad period, around 2334-2154 BC, a small cylinder seal was fashioned, showcasing Satan's basic strategy to keep mankind enslaved, and prone to welcome his hostile takeover. (See Figure 41). In their 1983 book, *Inanna, Queen of Heaven and Earth: Her Stories and Hymns from Sumer*, Diane Wolkstein and Samuel N. Kramer, explain the figures on the seal:

> Inanna / Ishtar may appear on this seal in her manifestation as Rain or Thunderstorm Goddess, as suggested by Elizabeth Douglas Van Buren. Nude except for her horned crown, she stands between the wings of a lion-bird or griffin, probably a manifestation of the embodiment of the thunder-bird, Anzu. Streams of rain are held by the goddess and vomited by the lion-bird as it draws the chariot of the Weather God, who snaps his lightning whip. The clatter of the wooden wheels may be accompanied by the roar of the lion-bird as thunder. This scene gives mythopoeic form to the visual phenomena of rain, lightning, and thunder — its aural accompaniment in nature.[275]

Inanna, "queen of heaven", also known as Ishtar, is the woman who rides the Beast in Revelation 17. The Beast she rides is the *Anzu*, a form of snake-dragon, associated with Ninurta, Pabilsag or Enlil. We recall F. Wiggermann's study on Mesopotamian protective spirits, in which he argues for the original association of *Anzû* with Enlil, not Ninurta (a syncretization).[276] This reveals that the hybrid creature first represented Enlil, and then later, stood-in for the syncretizations.

The point Wiggermann is making is that Ningirsu (Ninurta) is typically associated with the *Anzû*, but in reality, the *Anzû* represents Enlil, master of them all. We might liken it to Lord of the Rings—"the one ring to rule them all and in the darkness bind them." Satan has different faces and agents, but in the end, all roads lead back to him.

Ninurta (or Ningirsu) is actually the biblical Nimrod, the great rebel, the one who became a *gibbor*. However, Ninurta was known as the son of Enlil and eventually syncretized with Enlil so that his qualities were the same as Enlil's.

Lastly, the one in the chariot is the storm god. As noted earlier by Wendy Doniger, a lot of syncretism was happening; "Bel", meaning "lord", who was a syncretization of Marduk, Enlil, and the dying god Dumuzid."[277] Therefore, the storm god Bel (Baal) is Enlil, who we also learned was Dagan, and went by the logogram BAD / BAT (BATios) and gave the command on Mt. Hermon.

Thus, we have an icon in which Ishtar, queen of heaven, the great harlot, is riding Ninurta (Nimrod the rebel) and Satan is driving in a chariot on wheels with eight pointed stars. Stated another way: **Lust is riding on the back of Rebellion, and they are driven by the Great Dragon.** (See Figure 42, next page).

Figure 42 Rain Goddess. Cylinder seal. Mesopotamia. Akkad period, c. 2334-2154 B.C. Shell. 33.5 X 19.5 mm. New York, Pierpont Morgan Library, Corpus 220.

God revealed to John in Revelation what Satan has been doing. Only recently, with the discovery of the thousands of documents and cylinder seals from ancient Sumer, are we able to look in the ancient world and recognize the symbols that John was given. The woman riding a beast was not an allegorical fable, but a physical image that would have been a common sight in ancient Babylon.

Even though we did not recognize the reference to a woman riding a beast in modern times, the ancients would have understood: "I will tell you the mystery of the woman and of the beast that carries her, which has the seven heads and the ten horns" (Rev 17:7). John also discovered in his visions that the dragon with seven heads and ten horns (Rev 12:3), gave his power, throne, and authority to the Beast (Rev 13:2).

186

The cylinder seal provides an excellent graphic representation of what is really happening: The trio of Satan and the Beast, also includes the harlot, with all the perversions the world craves. While the world worships the lustful goddess, the Beast establishes his kingdom; and Satan is the one behind the scenes, driving it forward.

This beast symbol of a winged lion is on the very walls of the Ishtar gate, one of the eight gates of Babylon. The lion has wings just like in Figure 42—Ishtar is standing on a winged lion griffin, pulling the chariot, which is controlled by Enlil.

In the book of Revelation, we see that the dragon gave the Beast his power, his throne and his authority. Everything—he gave to the Beast. We know that according to Revelation 17, the ten (horns) kings upon the Beast are going to hate the woman and destroy her—this idol that so many individuals, kings, priests, pastors and everyday people bow down to worship. I am not only talking about pornography and perversions; Her worship also involves the idolatry of pursuing illicit pleasures and abominations. The world bows down willingly to these things, and Satan allows us to worship these counterfeit pleasures because they serve his purpose— for now.

THE COUNTERFEIT WOMAN IN THE BASKET

The counterfeits, however, are designed to enslave us; and once enslaved, the façade will come off. The Great Harlot, Babylon the Great, will be unnecessary at that point, and Satan will destroy it.[278]

Has God also vowed to destroy her? —Yes, because she is a counterfeit. She is the epitome of idolatry, established at the gate of the gods in the land of Shinar, where Nimrod the rebel began his kingdom of rebellion against the Most High God.

There is a very curious passage in Zechariah 5; and it has everything to do with Revelation 17, where we see the woman who rides the Beast and this Mystery Babylon, this mother of harlots. An angel speaks with Zechariah the prophet, in a vision about a woman sitting inside a lead basket, about whom he says: "This is **Wickedness!** [harisha הָרִשְׁעָה fs] And he thrust her down into the basket, and threw the lead cover over its mouth" (Zech 5:8). Zechariah asks where the women, who look like storks, are taking the basket and the angel responds: "To build a house for it in the land of Shinar; when it is ready, the basket will be set there on its base" (Zech 5:11).

Wickedness, with its "resemblance throughout the earth," is personified in the vision as a woman in a basket going to Shinar, which is Sumer, Mesopotamia—the capital of Enlil's kingdom. The place where Nimrod became a *gibbor*, and where the Tower of Babel was established, along with the false religious system that came with it.

The woman that rides the Beast is known as Mystery Babylon. "Babylon throughout the Bible symbolizes the focus of anti-God sentiment and activity"[279] The Greek word for "wickedness" is ανομία (anomia / lawlessness). The apostle Paul speaks of "the mystery of lawlessness [ανομία]," and reveals that it "is already at work" (2 Thess 2:7). Paul tells us that the return of Christ will not happen until the lawless one (ανομος anomos, same root) appears first. Thus, Zechariah's vision shows us a picture of lawlessness or wickedness, contained in a basket, but trying to get out. For some reason, it is in the land of Israel and it is going to be taken to the land of Shinar (Babylon / Mesopotamia), where it will have an entire temple with much more room than a small bushel basket. We see, amazingly, that Paul says: "The mystery of lawlessness [ανομία] is already at work" (2 Thess 2:7), meaning Mystery Babylon is at work; She is the harlot riding on the back of the Beast, the personification of lawless wickedness.

PORNE K'DESHA

The scene on the cylinder seal in Figure 41 is precisely what was revealed to John. It also gives us insight into what is happening in the spiritual realm:

> Then one of the seven angels who had the seven bowls came and talked with me, saying to me, "Come, I will show you the judgment of the great harlot [porne] who sits on many waters with whom the kings of the earth committed fornication, and the inhabitants of the earth were made drunk with the wine of her fornication" (Rev 17:2).

The features of the great harlot that John saw and that God has vowed to destroy include:

1. Sits on many waters
2. Fornicated with kings of the earth
3. Whole planet involved in her fornication
4. Sits on a beast
5. Sumptuously dressed
6. Holds a cup of abominations
7. Babylon the great
8. Mother of harlots
9. Drunk with the blood of saints
10. Rides a beast with seven heads, ten horns that was, is not, and will ascend
11. The horns hate and burn the woman
12. The woman is the great city

The word for harlot is the Greek word *porne*. As we trace this back in the literature in the Scripture, we see that *porne* is the same as *k'desha*. In Genesis 38, Judah went to his daughter-in-law, and "thought she was a harlot [*zona* זונה πόρνη]" (Gen 38:15). When he later tried to locate her, he asked the men of the city, "Where is the harlot [*kedesha* קדשה πόρνη]?"(Gen 38:21)

189

The word *zona*, which means prostitute, was interpreted by Judah and the people of that village as *kedesha*. What is a *kedesha*? God says in Deuteronomy 23: "There shall be no ritual harlot [*porne* קדשה πόρνης] of the daughters of Israel, or a perverted one [*kadesh* קָדֵשׁ] of the sons of Israel (Deut 23:17). What's astounding is that the word *"kadosh"*, which means "holy", as in *"Holy, holy, holy is the Lord God of hosts,"* is the word used to describe this woman.

Figure 43 The Egyptian goddess Qedeshet and Min. Stele of Houy-C 86 14th Cent BC on display Department of Egyptian Antiquities of the Louvre.

The word does not mean the person is pure and morally unblemished; but rather that the person is set-apart for a particular purpose, whether good or bad. The word *qedesha* and *qadesh* (or kadesh) means female and male prostitutes. They were holy; they were wholly set-apart, completely set-apart for a purpose, but not a good purpose.

An example is the goddess, Qadesh, found in the New Kingdom ca. 14th century BC in Egypt, but imported from Canaan. (See adjacent Figure 43). The inscription says: "Qedesh[et], lady of heaven, mistress of all the gods, eye of Ra, without her equal."[280] She is standing on a lion to the right of the Egyptian gods Min, who has an erect phallus.[281] In Isaiah 47, God speaks directly against Qadesh, which we will look at later.

A marriage is holy, not because the man is perfect or the woman is perfect, nor because they never have unfortunate thoughts or say mean things. The reason that a marriage is holy is that it is designed for only two people, because it is exclusive. Those two people are what make it a holy matrimony. If you bring in a lover from the outside, it is no longer a holy matrimony. If you leave your socks on the floor, it is still the holy matrimony. If you leave the toilet seat up, it is still a holy matrimony. If you burn dinner, it is still a holy matrimony. But if you bring in another woman or another man, it is no longer holy. That is the difference. Thus, Babylon the Great is described as a great *zona*, a great *kedesha, porne,* harlot, the one in the crosshairs of God—she is the other woman in what is supposed to be an exclusive relationship between God and mankind.

A harlot sells the pleasure of her body for payment to many lovers. God is not against sexual union; He created it. However, pursuing illicit, perverted and warped pleasure outside of the instructions He has given us for living, is what God is against, because it is harmful. The man involved with a harlot believes that sexual union with her will bring him satisfaction, though as the Rolling Stones lead singer, Mick Jagger, put it, "I can't get no satisfaction

... but I try, and I try, and I try." The sexual relationship outside of marriage is a grave perversion of the joy, peace and prosperity God desires to freely give us and, incidentally, is an exploitation and objectification of the lover, as well.

The harlot, in a word, is the embodiment of violating the tenth commandment: coveting, lusting for something that you should not have. All things are permissible, Paul says, but not all things are beneficial. (See Appendix 7 Leaven). For example, Adam and Eve were physically capable of eating the fruit of the tree of the knowledge of good and evil, but it was not beneficial. Lust and coveting seek gratification outside of God's commandments and right order. God has vowed retribution against the harlot because she exacts a terrible price on mankind; her lie separates us from Him. The *Dictionary of Deities and Demons in the Bible* notes the price the goddess Inanna exacts:

> Even as the dead goddess is brought back to life, it is at the price of another's death as her substitute ... Ishtar spends most of her life without a husband or children, for her husbands change their nature almost immediately after consummation or die before their time. Everything is premature. Aborted.[282]

It is the same lie Satan posed in the Garden: "Did God really say you can't ...?" It separated Adam and Eve from God; They coveted something that was outside of God's purview.

INANNA GODDESS OF WHORES

The Sumerian goddess, Inanna (Akkadian, Ishtar), is the patron-goddess of whores and temple prostitutes.[283] Her name likely comes from *nin-an-ak*, meaning "Lady of Heaven."[284] J. Black and A. Green in *Gods, Demons and Symbols of Ancient Mesopotamia*, speak of Inanna, who is the epitome of the woman-who-rides-the-beast:

One aspect of Inanna's personality is that of a goddess of love and sexual behavior, but especially connected with extra-marital relationships with prostitution. Inanna is not a goddess of marriage, nor is she a mother goddess. The so-called Sacred Marriage in which she participates carries no overtones of moral implication for human marriages. **Inanna is always depicted as a young woman, never as mother or faithful wife, who is fully aware of her feminine power and confronts life boldly without fear of how she will be perceived by others, especially by men**"[285] (Emphasis mine).

Most people hope to keep their youthful appearance; however, this goddess is forever young, always budding, but never with child. This is the myth, the lie that has confronted humanity, but this is just part of it. This theme of eternal youth is brought out in the "Burney Relief." [286] The goddess standing on the beasts in Figure 44 (next page) is believed to represent either Ishtar or her older sister Ereshkigal (c. 19th or 18th century BC). Her body is blended with the features of an owl. She is also flanked by owls, nocturnal creatures, which is fitting for a lady of the night. John's vision of a woman riding a beast is all over the Ancient Near East in the iconography and character of the goddess Ishtar. We have seen it already in Egypt, and now, in the Burney Relief. (See Appendix 4 Easter).

Figure 44 The "Burney Relief," Either Ishtar or her older sister
Ereshkigal (c. 19th or 18th century BC) By Babel Stone (Own work),
commons.wikimedia.org /w/index.php?curid=10862243

Figure 45 The Ancient Akkadian cylinder seal depicting the goddess Inanna resting her foot on the back of a lion c. 2334-2154 BC ANEP #526 (Akkad). Courtesy of The Oriental Institute of the University of Chicago.

We further see it in the "Ancient Akkadian cylinder seal depicting the goddess Inanna resting her foot on the back of a lion, c. 2334-2154 BC" [287] in Figure 45. The dominating restless spirit of "Ishtar reminds us of Gilgamesh, a powerful individual with great energy who always remains dissatisfied with the allotted role or portion and is constantly driven to go beyond. They seem to be male and female counterparts." [288]

The Dictionary of Deities and Demons in the Bible, speaking of the complex character of Inanna, notes how she is discontent and restless. It should not be surprising that the spirit behind Ishtar is the same spirit that is behind Gilgamesh, who is in fact, Satan.

Inanna / Ishtar [was]...particularly prominent in Uruk, Akkad, Kish, Nineveh and Arbela. In Uruk, but particularly in Akkad and Assyria.[289] We remember that the beginning of the Rebel's kingdom was "Babel, Erech, Accad, and Calneh, in the land of Shinar (Gen 10:10). From that land he went to Assyria and built Nineveh, Rehoboth Ir, Calah" (Gen 10:11). The lists of cities are almost identical.

- Uruk = Erech
- Akkad = Accad
- Nineveh

Figure 46 Dated ca. 1550-1200 BCE. Lost (stolen). Drawing © S. Beaulieu, after Cornelius 2004: Plate 5.21.

Inanna / Ishtar is a young, independent and willful woman of the upper class, a product of an urban world, and is more closely associated with cities than with cosmic functions. She seems to be constantly on the move ... her movement expresses and enhances a quality of **discontent and restlessness** that characterizes her. Inanna / Ishtar often appears as a sexually attractive being, but she remains unsatisfied and is **constantly 'injured', striving, and contentious.** The **goddess seems even to exhibit contradictory or conflicting traits**. She seems to encompass polar opposites: **she is death and life, male and female. She is a female who neither nurtures nor has a permanent partner, a sexual woman who is warlike and glories in aggression and destruction** [290] (Emphasis mine). (See Appendix 3 Inanna).

God warned the Israelites not to admire the nations that he had expelled, lest they learn their abominable ways. Sadly, Israel was not careful and the Canaanite version[291] of the goddess made inroads during the era of the Judges (1550-1200 BC), as seen in Acre, Israel where:

> A nude goddess stands on a crouching lion. Her Hathor-style coiffure is topped by horns extending to the side. She wears a necklace and bracelets. Her arms are bent into a V-shape, and she holds in each hand a long plant, perhaps a lotus.[292] (See adjacent Figure 46).

Figure 47 Impression of a Neo-Assyrian seal dated ca. 750-650 BCE. British Museum. Drawing © 2008 S. Beaulieu, after Leick 1998: Plate 38.

In the Neo Assyrian Empire, we find continued evidence of Ishtar.[293] On an impression of a seal dated somewhere between 750 and 650 BC in Figure 47, we once again see the goddess standing "fully armed ... on her sacred lion. An eight-pointed star, one of her symbols, adorns her elaborate crown".[294] We see the image of the woman riding the Beast was prolific. The cult of Inanna / Ishtar, the queen of heaven, heavily influenced the cult of the Phoenician goddess Ashtoreth. [295] The Phoenicians, in turn, exported Astarte to the Greek islands of Cyprus and Cythera and beyond.[296]

Figure 48 The 'Mountain Mother' Seal from Knossos. (After Costis Davaras, 'Trois Bronzes Minoens de Skoteino' BCH 93 (1969), 620-650, at p. 637.)

In Knossos in Minoan Crete, we find Ishtar. This seal impression from the great palace of Knossos in Minoan Crete, Figure 48, shows a goddess on top of a mountain flanked by lions. The mountain is most likely her ziggurat, and the lions are beneath the goddess, supporting her, as we have seen before.

Another seal found in Knossos depicts a goddess walking with a lion and carrying a staff, much like the Sumerian Inanna in Figure 49 (next page). The Minoans were an advanced pre-Greek, maritime, Bronze-Age civilization with a broad sphere of influence from about 2700 BC until 1400 BC, when they were taken over by the Greek Mycenaean.[297]

Ishtar's fame spanned the world. The Greek myth of Aphrodite and Adonis, shown on an altar from the Greek city of Taras in Magna Graecia, dating back to about 400-375 BC,[298] is derived from the Mesopotamian myth of Inanna and Dumuzid.

Figure 49 Hindu goddess Durga
commons.wikimedia.org/w/index.php?curid=3962125.

Sumerian Inanna, Akkadian Ishtar, Phoenician Astarte ... all share significant characteristics with Aphrodite: bisexuality ... temple prostitution ... the epithet Urania ... the association with the sea and with the garden Aphrodite in the Gardens in Athens, the iconography of a frontally naked goddess ... and the symbol of the ladder.[299] (See Appendix 3 Inanna).

The cult of Inanna spread from the land of Shinar / Sumer to the ends of the Earth, west to Greece and beyond, and also eastward to India. Parpola notes: "the Hindu goddess Durga may also have been influenced by Inanna."[300] (See Figure 49). We once again see a seductive warrior goddess with a lion at her side, tell-tale signs of Inanna.[301]

MYSTERY BABYLON: TROJAN HORSE TO ENSLAVEMENT

And the woman whom you saw is that great city which reigns [η έχουσα βασιλειαν=lit. "the one having a kingdom"] over the kings of the earth" (Rev 17:18).

The literal Greek [*ae echousa basileian* η έχουσα βασιλειαν] translates as "the one having [f.s.] a kingdom," which is already extant in the ancient literature; Andrew George notes the "goddess Ishtar usually referred to as *Bēlet-Bābili* 'the Lady of Babylon.'"[302] The Great Harlot of Babylon has a kingdom of enslaved souls the world over—not simply New York City, or Las Vegas, or the Vatican; it is everywhere. Various theories suggest Mystery Babylon must be Rome because Rome reigned in John's days. Rome was merely one of the "kings of the earth," that the woman ruled over. The woman is idolatry that is in our hearts that has reigned (has a kingdom) over the whole world. Rome was just one more branch of this tree, but not the root.

In Isaiah 47:

> "Come down and sit in the dust, O virgin daughter of Babylon; Sit on the ground without a throne, O daughter of the Chaldeans! For you shall no more be called Tender and delicate (Isa 47:1). Take the millstones and grind meal. Remove your veil, Take off the skirt, Uncover the thigh, Pass through the rivers (Isa 47:2). Your nakedness shall be uncovered, Yes, your shame will be seen; I will take vengeance, And I will not arbitrate with a man" (Isa 47:3). "Sit in silence, and go into darkness, O daughter of the Chaldeans; For you shall no longer be called The Lady of Kingdoms (Isa 47:5). And you said, 'I shall be a lady forever' (Isa 47:7).

The prophet Isaiah's description of Inanna (Ishtar) is the mirror of how she was described in Mesopotamian literature. She was the goddess "who holds the connecting link of all heaven and earth." She said of herself "I (Ishtar) am in possession of the symbols of the divine offices, in my hands I hold the lead-rope of heaven."[303] In Figure 50 (adjacent), we see her on a ziggurat, surrounded by her eight-pointed stars, standing in front of her grandfather Enlil, with symbols of other gods.[304] The true God of Abraham, Isaac and Jacob has hated this woman for an exceptionally long time because of the lies she spreads and the damage those lies inflict upon us.

Figure 50 Courtesy www.mesopotamiangods.com Inanna.

The lie of the MOTHER OF HARLOTS AND OF THE ABOMINATIONS OF THE EARTH goes back all the way to Eden, the original place of pleasure. In Isaiah 47, God is speaking here to the nation of Babylon, to the empire of Babel, and He says:

> "You who are given to pleasures [עֲדִינָה], Who dwell securely [Interestingly, this is the same phrase that we saw when we were looking in Ezekiel 38: [*hayyôšebet lābeṭaḥ* הַיּוֹשֶׁבֶת לָבֶּטַח], Who say in your heart, 'I am, and there is no one else besides me; I shall not sit as a widow'" (Isa 47:8).

In Revelation 18, we see the same words; "For she says in her heart, 'I sit as queen, and am no widow, and will not see sorrow'" (Rev 18:7). It is the same imagery where God, in Revelation, is speaking against the city of Babylon.

The idolatry of the goddess Ishtar has permeated most of society. We can trace it from Inanna to Ishtar to Ashtoreth in the Hebrew language. She became Astarte in the Greek; and in Rome, in Latin, she became Venus. She is Durga in the Indian traditions. There are so many other places where people have been worshiping this false god. (See Appendix 4 Easter).

MANKIND'S EVERYTHING GODDESS

Ishtar is everything mankind could ever want—the eternal goddess who is paradoxical, free and unrestrained. However, we have seen that the goddess' counterfeit pleasures demand a terrible price. She is the carrot in front of the donkey that Satan has used to get mankind to willingly, and most of the time ignorantly, participate in his nefarious machinations. She is "the evil woman … the flattering tongue of a seductress" after whom man has lusted so that many are "reduced to a crust of bread." She is the "adulteress [who] will prey upon his precious life." (Prov 6:24–26).

The woman who rides the Beast is a Trojan horse in its truest sense. You recall that after besieging the city of Troy for ten years, the Greek soldiers ingeniously created a giant horse and hid inside it. The citizens of Troy supposed it to have been left as an offering to the goddess Athena and hastened to take it through the gates into their, otherwise, impregnable city.

The woman who rides the Beast, both the city and religious system of Babylon, is the lure Satan has used very successfully to bait humanity and then trap us, beginning with Nimrod's kingdom in the land of Shinar. "The goddess is the spouse and lover of the king with whom she participates in the ritual of the sacred marriage. She provides the king with economic blessings as well as power and victory in war." [305] Of course, what king would not want blessings for his city? And if those blessings could be procured by participating in the sacred marriage or hierogamos, a sexual encounter with a priestess, then all the better! (See Appendix 5 Balaam).

Chapter 15: Hybrids and the Iniquity of the Amorites

n the classic story, when the big bad wolf finds out that Little Red Riding Hood is going to her grandmother's house, he races ahead in order to set a trap. Satan made a similar move on Abram. God called Abram out of the Babylonian system and promised to give him the land of Canaan. As Abram made his journey, Satan went ahead to set the trap.

What is interesting is that God coordinated events that let Abram know that something weird was happening in the promised land with the Amorites. After Abram's daring rescue of his nephew Lot, God told Abram not to be afraid of the people he had just confronted, which included "the Rephaim in Ashteroth Karnaim, the Zuzim in Ham, the Emim in Shaveh Kiriathaim" (Gen 14:5). God told him that the land was his, but his descendants would end up living in Egypt and would come back in the fourth generation because **"the iniquity of the Amorites** is not yet complete" (Gen 15:16). Just what iniquity were they committing?

Abram did not raise his hand and ask God who the Amorites were or what their iniquity was; he seemed to know. Based on the account of his rescue mission to save Lot, he knew they were Nephilim. He also knew that Nephilim equal Rephaim and other tribes of giants, as we see in Scripture: "the descendants of **Anak** came from the giants [**Nephilim**]" (Num 13:33).

Anakim = Nephilim. Moses said the "**Emim**... a people great and many, and tall as the **Anakim**... Anakim... are also counted as **Rephaim**, but the Moabites call them **Emim**" (Deut 2:10–11 ESV). We can put an equal sign showing Anakim equals Rephaim which equals Emim, which of course equals Nephilim (Amorites = Anakim = Rephaim = Emim = Nephilim).

Thus, the Nephilim, the angelic-human hybrids, were known by many names.

- **Rephaim** formerly lived there-but the Ammonites call them **Zamzummim**- a people great and many, and tall as the **Anakim** (Deut 2:20–21a, ESV).
- King Og of Bashan, he was left of the remnant of the Rephaim. Bashan is called the land of Rephaim (Deut 3:11–13 ESV).
- His [Sihon] land and the land of **Og**, the king of **Bashan**, the two kings of the **Amorites** (Deut 4:47 ESV).

The Septuagint frequently translates Nephilim (Num 13:32), Rephaim (Gen 14:5, Josh 12:3), and Anakim (Deut 1:27) as *gigantes*, which in Greek mythology signified a class of half-god, half-man beings. The Septuagint translates Nephilim and *gibborim* in Genesis 6:4 as "the giants" (*oi gigantes*). "Nimrod began to be a giant" [ηϱξατο ειναι γιγας gigas] (Gen 10:8 LXX Brenton). The iniquity of the Amorites appears to have been something akin to what Nimrod did in becoming a *gibbor*. The Amorites became *gibborim*; They were becoming hybrids!

We know that they did not start out as Nephilim because they are listed as children of Canaan in Genesis 10. We also know that they were not a remnant of giants from the days of Noah because God repeatedly stated, "All in whose nostrils was the breath of the spirit of life, all that was on the dry land, died" (Gen 7:22). Contrary to later myths, no giants hitched a ride on the ark! Thus, a second incursion of the angels into this world occurred. (See Appendix 2 Angels Freewill). We already saw how it happened with Nimrod. Satan, then, repeated either directly or indirectly through Nimrod, a program to create hybrids. The name of the Amorite god provides clues that help us put together the story.

WAS NIMROD THE AMORITE GOD?

The god of the Amorites, MARTU[306] / Amurru, went by many names such as Dagon, Molech, Addu, and Isthara,[307] and had the epithet of KUR-GAL (great mountain) which was an epithet for Enlil.[308] A.T. Clay points out that epithet KUR-GAL was ascribed to both Amurru / MARTU and Enlil, demonstrating that they were "one and the same god."[309] This also means that all these gods are one-and-the-same god; and they are all disguises of Satan. The *Dictionary of Deities and Demons* in the Bible explains:

> Martu has many traits of a West-Semitic storm god such as Hadad. According to a Sumerian hymn, Amurru is a warrior god, strong as a lion, equipped with bow and arrows, and using storm and thunder as his weapons.[310]

The epithets and characteristics of Martu and Ninurta (Marduk, etc.), son of Enlil: the warrior, bows and arrows, and storm god, are perfect matches and indicators of Enlil. We must, therefore, conclude that we are speaking about the same entity, despite the variation of the names.

It is hard to ignore the similarities between the names. We have already considered how Ninurta was deliberately distorted in the Bible as "Let's rebel" Nimrod, the root letters being N.R.D. with the initial N meaning "Let's." Marduk (a syncretism of Ninurta) is AMAR.UTU in Sumerian and "Marduk" in Akkadian. The root letters, M.R.T., are the same and so is the case with MAR-TU. Are the similarities coincidence, or simply further proof that we are looking at the same entity? Furthermore, if MARTU=Enlil and Marduk=Enlil, is it implausible to make the claim that MARTU=Marduk?

The linguistic question aside, A. T. Clay has already gone on the record to say MARTU (Amurru) is Enlil, hence the god of the Amorites is ultimately Satan, or the son of Satan. We learned in the Sumerian literature that Enlil engendered Ninurta and Ninurta held the Tablet of Destinies, which is to say, he held all of Satan's power, throne and authority. Amurru is a syncretization of Ninurta / Marduk, both the sons of Enlil. Ninurta / Nimrod, became a *gibbor*, or a *giga* (giant), or a hybrid. Rephaim derives from "Rapha", which means to heal, mend or repair. In a sense, Nimrod was "healed" of his human frailties by becoming a hybrid. All of the Rephaim underwent this transformative "healing", which was a grave sin. It was the iniquity of the Amorites.

REPHAIM

The term Rephaim strongly suggests that the progenitor of the race was the first *rapha* (healed or healer). The term Rephaim is usually considered to be from the root [רפא] meaning "to heal" and is generally understood to mean healers or "disease free". The linguistic link between Rephaim and the root R.P., 'to heal', is "found in the LXX of Isa 26:14 and Ps 88:11: 'The healers *(iatroi)* will not rise up'... the Rephaim, by virtue of their connections with the netherworld, were healers *par excellence.*" [311] This definition "healers" was accepted as the ancient definition and is accepted by most scholars.

However, why were the Rephaim known as healers? The notion of healing had to come from somewhere, but we clearly see in Scripture that Rephaim were known as Nephilim or giants. We only see Rephaim after the Flood. The Nephilim and *gibborim* are translated as *gigantes* in the LXX. Nimrod was therefore, the first of the Rephaim. That is, he was the first "healer". His Mesopotamian name, Ninurta (and syncretisms), carried the connotation of being a healed / healer.

Ninurta, son of Enlil, known for being a dragon and hence the son of a dragon, was syncretized with a snake god known as Tišpak and Ninazu who **"is clearly the 'lord of healing'** according to the etymology of his name."[312] Wiggermann notes that:

Ninazu, "Lord Healer", is a son of Ereshkigal is the "king of the snakes" in Old Babylonian incantations, and in several other ways related to death and the realm of the dead, perhaps at one time as its ruler. His dragon is the mušḫuššu.[313]

Not only was Ninurta syncretized with a snake god healer, but he was also associated with a legend about Kirtu, one of the Rephaim who were "'**healers**' or '**dispensers of fertility**' of the earth." [314] Furthermore, according to DDDB, Kirtu has been associated with the Akkadian word "qarradu", which DDDB notes is "generally regarded as a personal name." [315] This is significant because "Ninurta … has qardu 'fierce', 'heroic' and qarradu 'warrior', 'hero' among his standard epithets."[316]

In company with these identifications, **Ninurta certainly assumed some features of a chthonic healer god**. These features were already inherently present in his form of the victorious hero because the beneficial character of the **chthonic healer god** could express itself in iconography in the motif of victory over a lion, dragon, griffin or other real or fantastic monster.[317]

Thus, Ninurta / Nimrod was called a healer, a Rephaim, because he was changed from a mortal man to be an immortal. He became disease-free through his transformation from man to god. His powers to heal others were not the kind of power Jesus had over disease which made a person whole. Rather, Nimrod's power was to transform people into the Nephilim, or Rephaim.

So, when Abram's kids finally did return from Egypt, Satan had a house-warming gift waiting in the form of the "iniquity of the Amorites": the Rephaim, Emim, Zamzummim and Anakim, who were once regular people, but who became *gibborim*, that is, hybrids. The twelve spies fearfully reported, "The Amorites … are stronger than we are … and all the people that we saw in it are of great height. And there we saw the Nephilim (the sons of Anak, who come from the Nephilim)" (Num 13:29–33, ESV). The spies were not exaggerating, because God says in Amos 2:9, "Yet it was I who destroyed the Amorite before them, Whose height was like the height of the cedars" (Amos 2:9). God Himself also used the height of a cedar in comparison with the tail of the behemoth, described in Job 40: "the behemoth … moves his tail like a cedar" (Job 40:15–18). A cedar of Lebanon is about 40 to 80 feet tall. (See Figure 51).The behemoth is the Diplodocus dinosaur, and their tails measure 40 feet long. The Israelite spies were not overstating the danger; They saw giants in the land.

Figure 51 Cedar of Lebanon.

From the time God told Abram about the perversions of the Rephaim, until his descendants returned to the land was about six hundred years. Thus, Satan had time to race ahead and prepare for their arrival. The big bad wolf had set the trap for Abram's kids.

According to an Ugaritic text, the region of Bashan was known as the abode of the god-king "mlk 'lm, the dead and deified king.... his place of enthronement as rpu was in 'Štrt-hdr'y, in amazing correspondence with the Biblical tradition about the seat of king Og of Bashan." [318]

The Bible records, "The territory of King Og of Bashan, one of the few remaining Rephaites, who lived in Ashtaroth and Edrei" (Josh 12:4). "Egyptian documents and two Amarna letters mention rulers of Ashtarot in the fourteenth century BCE." [319] Thus, an Ugaritic text speaks of a "dead and deified king" living in the area of Bashan, and the Bible tells us that it was King Og, who was a Rephaim (the same as rpu).

Ugaritic texts[320] further reveal that a Rephaim god called "king" was in the area of Bashan. They state, "as the abode of the god mlk ["king"], the eponym of the mlkm [Milcom], the deified kings, synonym of the rpum." [321] Amazingly, a "Phoenician tradition also seems to record the existence of a deity 'g' ["Og"]. [322]

We saw earlier that the Rephaim were counted among the Amorites and Nephilim who were sometimes called *gibborim*. Looking at the Septuagint, the word Rephaim is sometimes simply transliterated (e.g. Gen 14:5, 15:20); though most of the time, it is translated as *gigantes* (giants).

> **Lahmi the brother of Goliath the Gittite** [Gath]. [...] at Gath, [...] **he also was descended from the giants [Rephaim,** LXX reads: giants, γιγαντες]. [...] These were descended from the giants in Gatt, (I Chron 20:5–6, 8 ESV; see also Josh 12:4; 13:12; 17:5; 2 Sam 21:18,22; 1 Chr 11:15; 14:9, 13).

211

OG OF BASHAN, LAND OF THE SNAKE-DRAGONS

"Then we turned and went up the road to Bashan [הַבָּשָׁן the Bashan]; and Og king of Bashan came out against us, he and all his people, to battle at Edrei (Deut 3:1)." "And at that time we took the land from the hand of the two kings of the Amorites who were on this side of the Jordan, from the River Arnon to Mount Hermon (Deut 3:8) "(the Sidonians call Hermon Sirion, and the Amorites call it Senir)" (Deut 3:9).

Og is called King of the Bashan. King, in Hebrew and Ugaritic, is M.L.K. or Milcom, hence Og is likely Milcom himself, or a carbon copy. Also, Og was a Rephaim, and they were also known as snake gods. This may explain why a giant (Rephaim) named Og was king of the Bashan (the word "the" is in the original Hebrew but omitted in many translations). What is "the Bashan"? It actually had a double meaning: "fertile land" and "snake-dragon." [323] The designation of snake-dragon was no joke. "For the 'Canaanites' of Ugarit, the Bashan region, or a part of it, clearly represented 'Hell', the celestial and infernal abode of their deified dead kings, — Olympus and — Hades at the same time." [324]

The land of Bashan is just on the other side of the Jordan River, across from the Sea of Galilee in the region of the tribes Zebulun and Naphtali. See Figure 52). We can now appreciate why it was later called the land of the shadow of death (Isa 9:2; Matt 4:16); they truly were in the shadowland of death! This area, of course, has Mt. Hermon as its highest peak, which was where the angels came down in the days of Noah in order to make Nephilim bodysuits. DDDB notes, "It is possible that this localization of the Canaanite Hell is linked to the ancient tradition of the place as the ancestral home of their dynasty, the rpum." [325]

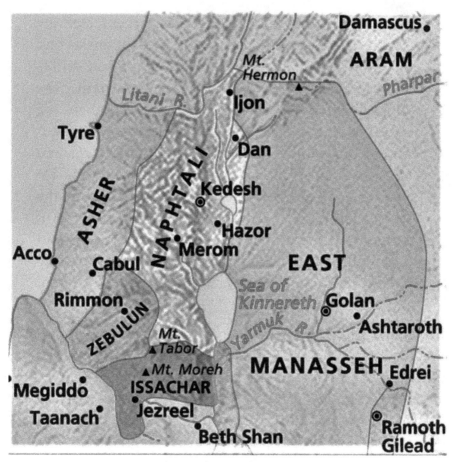

Figure 52 Map of Galilee, Israel.

It is significant to note that the place was known as the abode of the god Milcom, who was worshipped by the Rephaim in the land of Bashan. In fact, the Bible informs us "all Bashan, was called the land of the giants [Rephaim] (Deut 3:13), which DDDB notes is "an ambiguous wording that could equally be translated as 'the 'hell' of the Rephaim'".[326]

James H. Charlesworth of Princeton likewise notes the dual meaning of Bashan:

> When most biblical scholars studied Hebrew philology, they were told that "Bashan" denoted a mountain east of the Kinnereth (the Sea of Galilee).

Now, the contributors to the most recent Hebrew lexicons rightly point out that "Bashan" in the second millennium BCE denoted **both a mountain and a mythological creature that was a serpent, the "dragon-snake."** The most help in comprehending בשן as having a second meaning, "dragon-snake," comes from cognate languages. The Ugaritic *bthn* and the Akkadian *bašmu* are cognate to the Hebrew *bšn* and the Aramaic *ptn*. These terms are equal to the Arabic *bathan*. All these nouns denote some type of "dragon" or "snake". The compilers of the new and expanded Koehler-Baumgartner indicate correctly that the Hebrew בשן can denote a type of serpent similar to פתן, "cobra."[327]

Understanding Bashan's dual meaning as fertile land and snake-dragon might seem incompatible, but they are not. In fact, we have such usages in our day. Let us consider: "Aspen" means "tree" for most, but to some it means a ski resort in Colorado. "Nashville" means "near an ash tree,"[328] though few are aware of that. The popular designation is a city where budding artists break into the music industry—it is music city. And of course, Las Vegas is commonly known as sin city. Thus, we can understand "Bashan" as both a rich fertile land (like Aspen the ski resort) and as a snake-dragon (like aspen the tree).

Og and company occupied the territory east of the Jordan River and south of Mt. Hermon. It became known as the land of the Bashan, land the snake-dragon, per Akkadian *bašmu* (*bashmu*), and Ugaritic *batan*. However, the land of Bashan was also rich and fertile, and so the region became associated with its incredible fertility. Once Og and the people of the snake-dragon were gone, the land was primarily associated with fertility. Yet, because the name stuck, Bashan became defined by its rich and fertile land.

THE MEANING OF "OG"

Next, we will consider the meaning or etymology of Og's name. We know that he was an Amorite king. The Amorites' god was MARTU, who was Enlil, or son of Enlil. He was a survivor of the Rephaim; Rephaim means healers and Ninurta (et al.) was known as "Lord Healer." According to Ugaritic texts, a king of the dead, associated with the god Milcom, was also associated with Bashan. Thus, Og was king of the Bashan, that is, king of the snake-dragons. His land was at the base of Mt. Hermon where the angels came down in the days of Noah. This survey brings us to the question: What does "Og" actually mean?

Gesenius speculates "Og" may come from oneg [עֹנֶג oneg] coming from onek [עֹנֶק onek] deriving from, or anak [עֲנָק] meaning "in stature, long necked," "gigantic."[329] On the other hand, according to DDDB, the meaning is unknown, though they note the possibility that "some connection with *Osa gaig* (?), *Soqotri 'aig, Hatraean 'g' 'man'* could be established."[330] In light of Og's association with the Amorites and the god MARTU, perhaps a return to Shinar (Sumer), where Nimrod originated, is warranted. Looking at Sumerian, we make an interesting discovery: "ug" means "to die,"[331] which in Akkadian is **mâtu or mītu.** [332] Leiden University notes that the logogram (the cuneiform symbol) of mitu is:

> BAD (mītu, bēl) IDIM (kabtu) d IDIM (Ea) IdAG-BAD-TIN-iṭ Nabû-mītu-uballiṭ BAD for bēl is rare, and used only without the determinative DINGIR - no attestations yet in the database (but in Nbn 67:18, EN 65:23)[333]

BAD (IDIM) is the logogram of Enlil and the Syrian god Dagan. Bel is also one of the definitions of BAD.IDIM and means "kabtu", which is the same as Hebrew "kavod" meaning "heavy, important, glorious." Amar Annus explains the intentional syncretism between Enlil and Dagan (who was in the Canaanite area) and Ninurta son of Enlil as son of Dagan:

The Sumerian logographic writing for an unknown Syrian god is dNIN.URTA at Emar in the late Bronze Age. This **Ninurta** is the city-god of Emar, and remarkably also "son of Dagan," like the Ugaritic Baal. The god Dagan is identified with Sumerian Enlil, father of Ninurta, already in Old Babylonian times and they share the **logogram BAD**. In any case, it was **conscious syncretism** which introduced Sumerian writing for the West-Semitic god. The constant epithet of Marduk in Enuma Elish is Bêl 'Lord,' which is also Ninurta's common epithet, and points to a connection with West-Semitic Baal. Marduk came to replace Enlil in the Mesopotamian pantheon, so he took over conjointly the position of the father Enlil and the mythology of his son Ninurta. Similarly, Dagan in the West was partly manifested by his son Baal [334] (Emphasis mine).

In other words, Dagan and Enlil are the same entity as far as the scribes were concerned because they both share the cuneiform symbol: BAD. Furthermore, they understood Bel and Ninurta were either the same entity or the son of the same father-god entity, or possibly both. Annus comments about a passage where Ninurta is with Dagan's wife and notes that if Dagan (Enlil) is his father, then it would be incest, however, "it may be neither adultery nor incest **but reappearance of the father Dagan himself.**" [335] That is to say, it is just Satan with one of his many aliases: Enlil, Dagan, Ninurta, Bel, etc. However, hidden in the etymology of the cuneiform logograms and their meanings is the notion of death, the dead, or killing. Og's very name, then, is simply "death" and is the Sumerian pronunciation (ug) of the logogram BAD.

There are some other potential meanings of the word "Og" listed by the University of Pennsylvania Sumerian website that are rather insightful. We have looked at the meaning stated in Number 1 already (see below). Number 3 is especially interesting, as in Akkadian, it is simply transliterated as "aggu" or "uggu." Number 6 "a mythical lion" is also insightful.

1. ug [**DIE**] (259x: ED IIIb, Old Akkadian, Ur III, Old Babylonian) wr. ug7; ug5; ugx(|BAD.BAD|) "plural and imperfect singular stem of uš "**[to die]**" Akk. mâtu
2. ug [**EXALTED**] (1x: ED IIIa) wr. ugx(EZEN) "**(to be) exalted**"
3. ug [**FURIOUS**] (2x: Ur III) wr. ug; ug2 "**(to be) furious; anger**" Akk. aggu; uggu
4. ug [**LAMENTATION**] wr. ug2 "**lamentation**" Akk. nissatu
5. ug [**LIGHT**] wr. ug; ug2 "**light**" Akk. nūru
6. ug [**LION**] (23x: Old Babylonian, 1st millennium) wr. ug; ugx(|PIRIG×ZA|) "**lion; a mythical lion; a large cat**" Akk. mindinu; nešu; ūmu[336]

Do we have any linguistic verification of the Sumerian "u" sound becoming the open "o" sound in Hebrew; which is to ask: Can the Sumerian "Ug" turn into the Hebrew "Og"? The answer is yes. According to Abraham Even-Shoshan, "the Hebrew word "Kor" comes from Sumerian "GUR, "a bundle of barley; standard unit of capacity."[337] The Sumerian "u" vowel sound in "GUR" changes to the open "o" vowel sound in the same word in Hebrew, "Kor". If the word for this unit of measurement, GUR / Kor, changes vowel sounds when moving from Samarian to Hebrew, then "Og" very likely would have the same change of vowel sound. The word was borrowed in Akkadian as *"kurru"*, and then in Hebrew as kor [כֹּר] "Solomon's provision for one day was thirty kors [כֹּר] of fine flour" (1 Kgs 4:22).

217

An example of Sumerian "a" becoming a Hebrew "o" is the Sumerian "allanum" (oak, acorn) which was borrowed by Akkadian ' allānu, alyānu, "oak; acorn" which then came into Hebrew as "elon" [אֵלוֹן (elon)]. And "u" (oo) becoming an "a" is seen in Dumuzid into the Hebrew Tammuz as well as Sumerian "dub" "tablet" becoming "daf" in Hebrew.[338]

Thus, we have the linguistic evidence attesting that "ug" could become "og." We also have a meaning that fits the data—Og king of the Bashan (snake-dragons) was also king of the Amorites and known as a Rephaim. In addition, Ugaritic text spoke of the god-king "mlk 'lm", the dead and deified king .... his place of enthronement as rpu was in 'Štrt-hdr'y, in amazing correspondence with the Biblical tradition about the seat of king Og of Bashan." [339] The preponderance of evidence leads us to conclude that the meaning of "Og" is from Sumerian which is "dead, dying, furious, exalted, lion."

John A. Halloran, in his Sumerian Lexicon, lists all of the above meanings[340] and points out that a reduplicated form of "ug" is "gug5: hostility, war (might be reduplicated ug5,7,8, 'to kill; to die')." In linguistics, reduplication is the process in which a part of a word is repeated, sometimes with a slight change. Here, the Hebrew Og or "ug" may have morphed to the Hebrew Gog or "Gug". The University of Pennsylvania confirms "gug5 'enmity, hostility'" [341] "Enmity" naturally draws our attention to Genesis 3:15, where Satan the dragon swindled Adam and Eve, and God declared war: "And I will put enmity Between you and the woman, And between your seed and her Seed" (Gen 3:15). This is an accurate description of Satan and his kingdom. He is the enemy; and we often refer to him as our adversary. Peter tells us: "Your adversary the devil walks about like a roaring lion" (1 Pet 5:8). Thus, there may be a connection between the historic Og, King of the Bashan and the future Gog, who comes against the land of Israel in Ezekiel 38-39, a topic we will dive into in the next book.

SNAKE AND GILGAL REPHAIM

In the area of Bashan, about thirty-five miles south of Hermon and ten miles from the Sea of Galilee, is an interesting circular rock formation known as Gilgal Rephaim, "circle of the Rephaim." It is a sort of Stone Henge in the area of Bashan. Special thanks to Derek Gilbert of Skywatch TV for pointing out to me that there is what looks like a gigantic snake etched in the ground. (See the picture, courtesy of Google Earth.) It is possibly nothing but a naturally occurring design, but I doubt it. At the bottom of the picture, Gilgal Rephaim is clearly visible and due north is the snake geoglyph which measures .681 miles (1,096 meters) from mouth to tail. It is visible with the eye up to twelve miles (20 km) in the air. The snake at its closest point is .25 miles (390 m) away from Gilgal Rephaim. At the west (left) side of the picture there appears to be two eyes. This geological formation adds just one more piece of evidence that Bashan was known as the land of the snake-dragon.

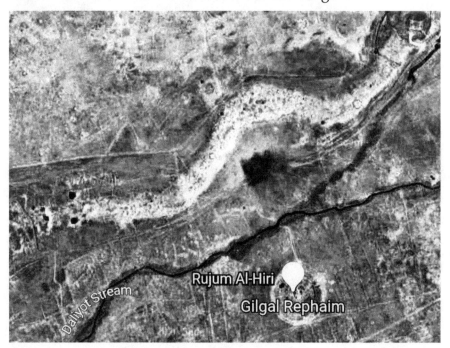

Figure 53 Bashmu Snake Geoglyph by Gilgal Rephaim, Israel courtesy Google Earth

When we compare the pictures of the geoglyph and the *Bašmu* (*Bashmu*), they appear to be exactly the same creature. The Bašmu has only front legs, just as we see on the geoglyph to the right of the head.

Bashmu-Bashan Snake-Dragon Comparison

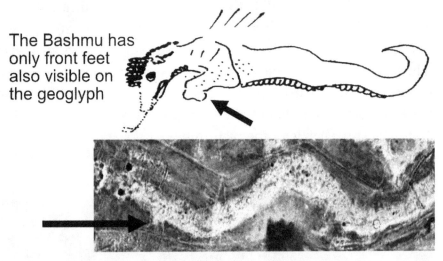

The Bashmu has only front feet also visible on the geoglyph

Figure 54 Bashmu-Bashan Snake-Dragon comparison

Thus, we have strong evidence from the Bible and Ugaritic literature that Rephaim or Nephilim once inhabited the land known as Bashan. From the Ugaritic inscriptions, we know that Milcom was one of their gods and that he demanded child sacrifices. Despite God's warnings to the Hebrews about adopting their neighbor's customs, the Hebrews fell for the trap and even King Solomon, sadly, became ensnared by the practices and allowed child sacrifice in Israel. It is therefore, no wonder God hated the entire area of Bashan. It was truly a hellish area that promoted the cult of death.

This coincidence of the 'celestial' and 'infernal' levels is congruent with the Canaanite mythology that locates here the abode of its deified dead kings, the mlk(m)/rpu(m) that dwell(s) in 'Štrt-hdr'y. Again the parallelism clarifies the issue, making plain the infernal character of Bashan.[342]

The iniquity of the Amorites was turning much of the Amorite population into unnatural hybrids, people of the snake-dragon. These non-human beings had traded their humanity to become gods; they corrupted the image of God within them. This is why God had Moses completely destroy Og and the Snake-dragon people. Even after their destruction, sadly, Satan's anti-Hero Ninurta (the Rebel) continued to infiltrate and corrupt Israel until God had to remove the people of Israel from the land. (See Appendix 6 Abominations of Babylon).

Chapter 16: Ninurta the Star, Arrow, and King of Hades

T he god of death known as Enlil / Ninurta continued to seduce Northern Israel with promises of fleshly pleasures; but then, they demanded child sacrifice. The Northern Kingdom eventually became so bad that Isaiah wrote about them: "The people who walked in darkness ... Those who dwelt in the land of the shadow of death" (Isa 9:2).

Ironically, the false god that Israel worshiped would be the same god that their conquerors worshipped: "So Israel was carried away from their own land to Assyria, as it is to this day" (2 Kgs 17:23). The House of Israel was removed from the land God had given them and taken to Mesopotamia where they could worship the gods they had been pursuing. We learn that "Sennacherib king of Assyria ... was worshiping in the temple of Nisroch his god" (2 Kgs 19:36–37). We now know that:

> The Assyrian deity who hides behind the name Nisroch may be identified with Ninurta. The 'spelling נסרך is probably best understood as a textual corruption from נמרד ...ultimately Nisroch relates to Ninurta (Nimrod).[343]

Before they were hauled off to Assyria, the prophet Amos relayed a lamentation on account of the terrible practices they did in honor of Ninurta.

> "You also carried along Sikkuth your king and Kiyyun, your images, the star of your gods which you made for yourselves. (Amos 5:26 NASB)[344]

We now know the identity of Sikkuth and Kiyyun, due to the discovery of ancient libraries and documents from the ancient near east, and due to scholars investing lifetimes in translating and understanding those texts.

Amar Annus notes the identification of an astral divinity with Ninurta where Sakkud: dsakkud = dnin-urta:

> Sakkud is attested in a famous biblical passage in the book of Amos 5:26 where the prophet criticizes his people: "You carried skwt, your king and kywn, your star, images which you have made for yourselves." It is possible, according to some scholars, that skwt originates from SAG.KUD and the deity Sakkuth was worshipped in Samaria during Amos' time (cf. 2 Kgs 17:30). What is curious in the biblical passage is they attribute "your king" (mlkkm) to skwt which fits Ninurta as the god of kingship.[345]

Encyclopedia.com gives a helpful summary of the two gods Sikkuth [סִכּוּת] and Chiun [כִּיּוּן], whom they identify as a pair of Mesopotamian astral deities associated with Ninurta (Nimrod).

> In other "non-Western" lists of gods and stars, Sikkuth has recently been identified with Ninurta, one of the chief Mesopotamian deities ... Sikkuth in Amos is a perfect transliteration of this star deity. Its appellation, melekh (Akk. šarru, "king"), alludes to the high rank of this deity, a (translated) classification device known from Ugaritic and other sources. This means that in the ritual to which Amos alludes, Sikkuth is the most important figure. Chiun is identified with the Akkadian Kajamānu (in Akkadian intervocalic m comes to be pronounced like w, and so m was often written even for original w), "the steady one" (sometimes sag.uš), the appellation of the star god Saturn (hence Aramaic Kewan, Ar. Kaiwan).[346]

As we saw in the chapter on Og King of the Bashan, one of Og's titles was Milcom / Molech. The same epithet was used by Ninurta because Ninurta was the god and driving force behind the practices and iniquity of the Amorites and the Rephaim. Amar Annus continues:

One might suggest that the Amos passage reflects peripheral Mesopotamian traditions diffused into Samaria. The second divine element, kywn, almost certainly corresponds to Akkadian kajjamanu (SAG.UŠ) "Saturn." [347]

We must not overlook the significance of Saturn's Sumerian name SAG.UŠ. SAG means "chief, head" [348] and UŠ means "death, dead, dying," related to UG.[349] We see again the death cult associated with Ninurta, Og and Nergal, along with Melqart, Heracles and the like.

> A deity Sakkuth was called "your king" in Israel as Sakkud in Mesopotamia was associated with Ninurta. For the court scholars of the Neo-Assyrian empire, the conjunction of Mercury, that is the star of Ninurta/Nabû, and Saturn, the star of the king, constituted the sign of kingship. In Mesopotamian astrology, Orion was comparably the celestial image of the dying king Dumuzi/Tammuz (called Sipazianna, "faithful shepherd of heaven").[350]

The northern kingdom of Israel was worshiping Ninurta, son of Enlil, which is to say they were worshiping Satan and the world system he created. The Canaanite headquarters of this worship were in the land of Bashan, Zebulun and Naphtali, being the land of the shadow of death. They were worshiping the beast that carries the woman. Satan uses the woman who represents lust to seduce people to fornicate, and then to justify child sacrifice. The fathers and mothers were willing to throw their infants into the deadly hands of Molech / Saturn / Ninurta, and then parade him around as their king! Thus, the identity of "your king" in Amos 5:26 is firmly established as Ninurta because "he is one of the gods who is explicitly called 'the king' in hymns," and his "kingship is eminently manifest." [351]

WHAT ABOUT REMPHAN?

In Acts 7:43, Steven recounted Israel's history (drawing from Amos 5): "You also took along the tabernacle of Moloch and the star of the god Rompha, the images which you made to worship" (Acts 7:43 NASB). Due to a scribal error in the letters, the Hebrew k, כ [kaph], was replaced by the Hebrew r, ר [resh], and in Greek, ph (φ) substituted for v. [352] Thus the Hebrew Chuin or Kewan, was rendered in the Septuagint, as Ραιφάν [Raiphan]. To be clear, there was no ancient god known as Remphan. It is the result of a scribe misreading some letters that are easy to confuse, and out came the fictitious Remphan.

Unfortunately, the star of Israel's false god to whom Stephen and Amos referred, has been erroneously associated with the six-pointed Magen David (Star of David). However, the pagan star in question is NOT the Magen David. Rather, it was the Star of Ninurta, which has eight points, as we have seen, not six points.

NINURTA, THE ARROW AND THE STAR

Sikkuth, of course, sounds nothing like Ninurta; so, why does it represent Ninurta? The name Sukuth was a Hebraized form of the Babylonian *Shukudu* ("the Arrow"), a name of Sirius,[353] the brightest star in the night sky. It was associated with the god Ninurta.[354] Thus, the star was associated with Sirius and Saturn, and had nothing to do with the Magen David. Amar Annus notes the following about arrow epithets used for Ninurta:

- The arrow (*šukudu*) … is astronomically Ninurta's star Sirius (see CAD *s.v.*), and the **Arrow might be a metaphor for Ninurta** himself … The terrible arrow of Marduk is compared to a merciless lion … *šiltahu* 5.[355]
- Ninurta is the Arrow (= Sirius), the great warrior, who slit the throats of the enemies of Assurbanipal with his pointed arrowhead
- Ninurta himself is an 'arrow'.

"Ninurta's identity with the star is explicit in a *šu-ila* prayer which begins with the words *atta Kaksisa Ninurta ašared ili rabûti* "you are Sirius, (that is) Ninurta, the first among the great gods" (Mayer 1990: 467ff)." [356]

In other words, Ninurta is known as the Arrow, and the Arrow, in an astronomical setting, is the star Sirius. The imagery of gods as stars reminds us of the language of Revelation in which angels are frequently symbolized as stars. In John's vision of Revelation, Jesus has seven stars in his right hand. Jesus reveals the mystery: "The seven stars are the angels of the seven churches" (Rev 1:20). Thus, there are seven stars or seven angels (messengers) to God's redeemed people. It is interesting that another word for "arrow" (*mulmullu*, Sumerian *mul.mul*) is related to the Pleiades. Amar Annus explains that:

> The **Pleiades were thought to bring war and destruction** – "the warlike gods, who carry bow and arrow, whose rising means war." It is worth noting that the month of Ningirsu in Astrolabe B, Iyyar, is also referred to as "the month of the Pleiades, **the Seven Great Gods**".[357]

The name of the star Sirius derives from the Babylonian word for arrow; The Sumerian word for arrow is linked with the Pleiades. The star was a symbol of Ninurta, and the warrior's terrible, merciless arrow is also connected to astrological bodies. Annus comments that:

> Marduk's arrows (*mulmullu*) ... are said to "rain down on the mountains" (*i-sal-la-hu* KUR.MEŠ, l. 14). All the gods, good and evil, are vanquished by these arrows. Thus both *mulmullu* and *šukudu* **referred to the god's arrow which killed his enemy**, despite their different astral identities. [358]

The first century Jewish apocalyptists used similar language suggesting Belial and his hordes will come out of the underworld with arrows flying. What the apocalyptists were envisioning was the image that Satan (Mesopotamian Enlil) had been projecting all along: Satan, or his proxy, was the great dragon, the invincible dragon that you did not want to encounter or challenge. Yoder notes the epithet: "*ú-šum-gal-lum la maḫ ār* "the great dragon, who cannot be faced." [359] He also notes regarding Nergal: "The majestic, great dragon who pours venom upon them". Nergal's divine staff was as "awe-inspiring as a serpent" and Ninurta's mace consisted of seven snake-like heads.[360]

> In Mesopotamian astrology, Orion was comparably the celestial image of the dying king Dumuzi/Tammuz (called Sipazianna, "faithful shepherd of heaven"). According to K. van der Toorn, it is even possible that a conflation of traditions could have resulted in the idea that, to the Greeks, the constellation Orion instead of Sirius was the heavenly counterpart of the hunter Orion. In this connection it might be interesting to note that in Syriac Orion is called *gabbar*, "hero" (1990: 11).[361]

From the previous evidence, we see that Sikkuth (*šukudu*) refers to an arrow, as well as Ninurta. Kiyyun means "steady one". However, both names also refer to planets or a constellation. Sikkuth is associated with Saturn, Sirius and possibly, the Pleiades or Orion, while Kiyyun relates to the "steady one", meaning Saturn. Both Sikkuth and Kiyyun are appellations that involve a hero and a bow and arrow. This a description of the hero, Nimrod, with his bow and arrow, the one who became a *gibbor*, which translated is "hero". Nimrod was a *gibbor* hunter, and of course, he has been positively identified as Ninurta.

> It was Ninurta's command that drove his beloved Tiglath-pileser I to go hunting bulls, elephants, lions and birds. The weapons used by him include "my strong

bow, iron **arrowheads** (*šukud* AN.BAR) and sharp **arrows** (*mulmulliya zaqtute*)" (Grayson 1991: 25 vi 65-67). The arrow (*šukudu*), mentioned by Tiglath-pileser I is astronomically **Ninurta's star Sirius**, and the Arrow might be a metaphor for Ninurta himself.[362]

Wiggermann notes how "As a god of war, **Nergal is very similar to Ninurta**, with whom he shares the title 'a strong warrior, son of Enlil.'" Furthermore, he notes how a god appearing as "Nergal was" explicitly called the "Enlil of the mountain (kur netherworld)."[363]

> In fact, "from Ur III onwards the god of Kutha starts appearing in the south as Nergal "The Lord of the big city", and he is explicitly called the "Enlil of the mountain (kur netherworld)".[364]

Thus, Nimrod, the rebel is also represented as Nergal, the supreme god of the underworld who governs the dead. Hades, his equivalent in ancient Greek myth, was also lord of the dead and king of the underworld. At the Gates of Hades, located at Caesarea Philippi at the foot of Mt. Hermon, Jesus said, "On this rock I will build My church, and the gates of Hades shall not prevail against it" (Matt 16:18). Jesus directly confronted the king of the underworld on his turf and declared war. We have explored Nimrod in his persona as the celestial archer and arrow, which related to being king of the underworld. We will now look at Nimrod from another angle, where he was known as Pabilsag, the chief ancestor.

PABILSAG AS NIMROD, THE CHIEF ANCESTOR

Pabilsag is a variation of Ninurta or Nimrod; the origin of the name is fascinating, and the iconography is shockingly biblical. When we compare Pabilsag's bio with Revelation 9, a startling realization comes into focus: The gods that the House of Israel once worshiped will return in the last days. As we look at the ancient past, we get insight into the end times. Let me explain. I'll start with the name.

Pabilsag comes from Old Babylonian and means a "relation". In Akkadian, it is "abu", which of course is related to the Hebrew אב*Ab* (father), or Aramaic, *Abba*. The infix "bilga", also Old Babylonian, means "male ancestor". Lastly, *saĝ*, which is Old Akkadian, means "head; person; capital", and in Akkadian, *qaqqadu; rēšu*, similar to the Hebrew "*rosh*".[365] Pabilsag, then, was the chief or "principal ancestor". Pabilsag, as indicated by his name, was clearly someone the Mesopotamians believed to be of great importance, who was the chief of all their ancestors.

> Pabilsag was considered a son of the god Enlil according to the most common tradition ... Pabilsag was merged with several deities, the most prominent one Ningirsu / Ninurta. The syncretism with Ningirsu/Ninurta probably took place during the Old Babylonian period (Krebernik 2003-05: 162). Pabilsag's association with the netherworld could be due to his syncretism with the underworld deity Nergal.[366]

Thus, Pabilsag is the principal ancestor who is also known as Ninurta, who was the son of Enlil—who of course, was Nimrod, the rebel who became a hybrid.

Gavin White discusses the name: "Additional epithets like 'the weapon with a burning tip' or 'he who strikes with a burning point' can be derived from the individual signs used to write Pabilsag's name." [367] This weapon with a burning tip could be a reference to Ninurta's arrow (*Shukudu*).

We see again that Nimrod or Ninurta shows up by another name. We noted at the beginning of our study how Satan has many names, and once we start making this connection, we see Satan was manifesting through his proxies everywhere in the ancient world; So too, with Nimrod. However, we do not find evidence of Nimrod anywhere else under the name Nimrod, because that is not his name. It is the Bible's renaming of the rebellious person who became a *gibbor*. Yet, in each of the epithets of Nimrod that we examine, we learn more of his character and his significance with the people who venerated him. The Bible has already established that he was a rebel. Nevertheless, the Mesopotamian version portrays him as Lord of the Earth, the great mountain, the arrow, Sirius, the brightest star. Now we see his appearance as Pabilsag, and we learn he is also known as the chief ancestor and god of the netherworld, like Nergal. The Dictionary of Deities and Demons notes some of the epithets Ninurta possesses:

> Ninurta who has qardu 'fierce', 'heroic' and qarradu 'warrior', 'hero' among his standard epithets ... Astronomers of the 8th-7th century added further connotations, identifying Ninurta (or Pabilsag) with Sagittarius or, alternatively, associating Ninurta with the planet Sirius (called Šukudu 'arrow'), the major star of Canis major (Akk qatsu 'bow').[368]

What emerges from our investigation is the image of the constellation Sagittarius, which is familiar to many of us as a horse-centaur that is armed with a bow and arrow. The centaur-like god Sagittarius turns out to be, yet another version of Ninurta / Nimrod known as Nergal or Pabilsag. The ancient Mesopotamian versions reveal a composite being "with a number of features not seen in the Greek version, such as a set of wings, a scorpion's tail and the head of a dog."[369] We know exactly how Nergal looked due to the recently discovered iconography. (See Figure 55, next page). Remarkably, the image appears to be the same creatures who come out of the Abyss in Revelation 9. (See also Appendix 8 Joel's Army). I will demonstrate how they match soon, but first let's examine the Kudurru Stone.

Figure 55 Nergal / Pabilsag from a 12th century entitlement (Kudurru) Stone

NERGAL ON A KUDURRU STONE

In 1882, a Limestone kudurru stone[370] was found in ancient Sippar, southern Iraq, from the Kassite period circa 1186 BC-1172 BC[371] and is now housed at the British Museum. (See figure 55). The creature on face A (of four sides) is Pabilsag / Nergal[372]. The Museum describes the:

> Composite being, in the form of a centaur, with attributes of man, beast, bird and reptile. The god has **two heads**, one **human**, with beard and **thick hair falling** on the shoulders, and on it he wears a **conical head-dress probably provided with horns**; the second **head**, facing backwards, is that of a **lion**. The god's torso and arms are human, and he is represented drawing a bow; ends of five arrows in a sheath are visible over his right shoulder. The body, hind legs, the lower tail, and

the upper part of the fore legs are those of a **horse**; a second tail is that of a **scorpion**, and the fore legs end in scorpions, though only one scorpion is shown. **Wings** rise from the horse's shoulders[373] (Emphasis mine).

Figure 56 Pabilsag from a 12th century entitlement (Kudurru) Stone.

Here is a tracing, Figure 56 of the inscription to better bring out the details. Notice that the centaur-beast is an archer with a bow and arrow drawn. One of his tails is a scorpion's tail. The forward feet are those of a horse, yet he has the face of a man. Gavin White notes:

> Although the basic image of the horse-centaur can only be traced back to the middle of the 2nd millennium (the Kassite period), the figure is undoubtedly older as the constellation name appears in the star-lists of the preceding Old Babylonian period. A potentially older form of the Archer that doesn't have any horse characteristics can also be found on entitlement stones.

It combines the features of a human archer with a scorpion's body and birdlike feet. Very similar creatures first appear in Akkadian artwork where they can have wings and often have a snake-headed phallus. [374]

The iconography for Pabilsag / Ninurta is incredibly revealing of future events, especially when we remember that Pabilsag / Ninurta / Nergal is the god of the underworld. We are told specifically in Revelation 9 that a king of the underworld is going to acquire the key and open the Abyss (Hades). What is more startling is that the iconography of Pabilsag / Nergal on at least one stone, is a perfect match of the creatures prophesied to come out of the Abyss.

Figure 57 An impression from an Uruk seal.

Thus, the deity that Israel encountered and then embraced and carried around was Ninurta, who was none other than the rebel Nimrod who became a *gibbor*! The image of a "an archer with bow and arrow" of course, draws our attention to John's Revelation where he "looked, and behold, a white horse. He who sat on it had a bow; and a crown was given to him, and he went out conquering and to conquer" (Rev 6:2). (See Figure 57).

Ninurta / Nergal / Pabilsag is clearly identified as the warrior who conquers and is identified as the star Sirius; and, by the time of the Greeks, he would be known as Sagittarius.[375] An ancient Assyrian letter describes Ninurta's constellation qualities as the arrow and as Sagittarius. Amar Annus explains: "the arrow (*šiltahu*) of Sagittarius (PA.BIL.SAG) stands within the halo of the moon ... Both Sirius and Mercury are thus 'arrows' of Ninurta and also his manifestations."[376] In Revelation, we read about a "star" that has the key to the Abyss and reigns as king over those who come out.

> And I saw a star fallen from heaven to the earth. To him was given the key to the bottomless pit (Rev 9:1). Then out of the smoke locusts came ... (Rev 9:3). And they had as king over them the angel of the bottomless pit, whose name in Hebrew is Abaddon, but in Greek he has the name Apollyon (Rev 9:11).

The star that fell was given the key to open the Abyss and is king over the Abyss. His name is Abaddon in Hebrew, and Apollyon in Greek, but both mean the same thing: destroyer.[377] We know that stars are defined as angels in Revelation (See Rev 1:20) and of course, we have learned that fallen angels are known as the gods of the pagan world. Thus, it follows that the star that falls to Earth is not a meteorite or other such body, but instead, is an angelic (demonic) entity. The entity is known as a Star, a Destroyer, a King and underworld god. We have seen all of these qualities throughout our study. The star "fallen from heaven to earth" is Satan / Enlil / Ninurta (son of Enlil) / Nimrod / Nergal / Pabilsag, and "to him was given the key to bottomless pit."

Composite Image of the Chimera in Revelation 9[378]	
9A (Rev 9:7–10) 1st Description	**9B (Rev 9:17–19) 2nd Description**
1. The shape of the locusts was like **horses** prepared for battle. 2. On their **heads** were **crowns** of something like gold, 3. and their faces were like the **faces of men** (Rev 9:7). They had hair like women's hair, 4. and their teeth were like **lions' teeth** (Rev 9:8). And they had **breastplates** like breastplates of iron, 5. and the sound of their wings (Rev 9:9) 6. They had **tails like scorpions**, and there were stings in their **tails**. Their power was to hurt men five months (Rev 9:10).	1. And thus I saw **the horses** in the vision: those who sat on them had **breastplates** of fiery red, hyacinth blue, and sulfur yellow; 2. and the **heads** of the **horses** were like the **heads of lions**; 3. and out of their mouths came fire, smoke, and brimstone (Rev 9:17). 4. the fire and the smoke and the brimstone which came out of their mouths (Rev 9:18). 5. For their power is in their mouth and in their **tails**; 6. for their **tails are like serpents, having heads**; and with them they do harm (Rev 9:19).

Table 7 Composite Image of the Chimera in Revelation

In Revelation 9, John sees locusts that come out of the Abyss but, unlike locusts, these creatures (two-hundred million of them) look like a horse, have a lion's head, man's face, wings and two tails. While many commentators see two different kinds of creatures in Revelation 9, there are really just two descriptions of the same creature. I have placed the descriptions from Revelation 9A (Rev 9:7–10) and Revelation 9B (Rev 9:17–19) side by side in a table to help us see the common features.

Rev 9A specifically describes horses; Rev 9B says the "heads of the horses". That common feature indicates that both sections have horses. Rev 9B then assumes we know they are horses. Notice also Rev 9A mentions "lion's teeth", and Rev 9B says "heads of lions". The two sections are giving complimentary descriptions of the type of creature that comes out of the Abyss in Revelation 9; and Revelation 17 informs us that it will be the Beast that was, is not, and will ascend out of the Abyss.

Both 9A and 9B describe a chest area (thorax) [379] of iron or as strong as iron. 9B tells us the color, 9A tells us about the quality; they are complimentary and not contradictory.

We see horses with lions' heads breathing fire, where we are told out of the heads of the horses were heads like the heads of lions and are out of their mouths came fire, smoke and brimstone. This army of 200 million [380] horse-chimeras, (not Chinese soldiers [381] as was erroneously postulated in the 70's, but horse-like beings[382]) that have a head of a lion and a face of a man, with mouths that discharge fire.

Both 9B and 9A describe their tails; these tails are going to terrorize men. 9B states:

> By these three plagues a third of mankind was killed—
> by the fire and the smoke and the brimstone which came
> out of their mouths. For their power is in their mouth
> and in their tails; for their tails are like serpents, having
> heads; and with them they do harm (Rev 9:18).

If we then compare this passage to Revelation 9A, we see 9A says they had tails like scorpions, and there were stings in their tails. Their power was to hurt men for five months. Both passages illustrate beastly killing-machines that strike mankind with their fiery mouths and scorpion tails. They cause painful injuries, and as a result one-third of mankind is killed.

Do not forget that at this time, after taking the Mark of the Beast, men will want to seek death and will not be able to find it; They will desire to die, but death will flee from them (Rev 9:6).

9A and 9B are actually a composite image. That is, the descriptions of the beasts overlay one another and create a greater image. For example, animators use the layering technique to create a composite. Only when the layers are combined do we get the full sense of what the image is supposed to look like. Thus, 9A gives us a description. And then in a recapitulation, that is, John goes back and says it again, but with variant details. Yet, the details from both passages are needed to complete the picture. When we view the composite image that John saw; amazingly, it is a perfect depiction of Pabilsag / Nergal (Ninurta).

The features of the ancient hybrid beast are a perfect match with the coming hybrid beasts who will swarm out of the Abyss. Satan has engineered hybrid chimeras which he will muster to form an army of 200 million. (See Appendix 8 Joel's Army). The complexity of the creature and the number of years that have elapsed tells us Satan has been planning for an invasion for a long time. Nergal (Pabilsag) was known as a destroyer: "May Nergal in his destruction not [spare(?)] his offspring!" Furthermore, the word of his epithet "'the **strong god'**... is derived from Semitic HRR 'to scorch'." Lastly, Wiggenner also notes, "Nergal's planet is Mars (Salbatanu). According to astrological omens, Mars spreads death when he rises or flares up (von Weiher, Nergal 76ff.), and a tentative etymology explains this role of MUL *tzal* (*sal*) *bat-a-nu as mushtabarru* (ZAL) *mutanu* (BAD-a-nu) "(the planet) which spreads plague".[383]

Across is a table comparing the Kudurru Stone inscription and the image from the book of Revelation.

Rev 9 Creature	BM Kudurru Inscription From British Museum
Like a horse running to battle	**centaur [man-horse hybrid]** The body, hind legs, lower tail* and the upper part of the **fore legs are those of a horse.**
ead	the second head, facing backwards, is that of a lion.
Man's face	**one human [head]**
Something like crowns	he wears a conical head-dress probably provided with horns
Woman's hair	with beard and **thick hair falling** on the shoulders,
Lion's teeth	[Lions head, teeth presumed]
Fiery red, hyacinth blue, and sulfur yellow iron-like[384] breastplate	The god's torso and arms are human, and he is **represented drawing** a **bow**; ends of five arrows in a sheath are visible over his right shoulder.
Noisy wings	Wings rise from the horse's shoulders
Scorpion's tail with stingers	a **second tail is that of a scorpion**, and the fore legs end in scorpions, though only one scorpion is shown
Serpent's tail[385]	*Serpent-head phallus[386]
Fire and brimstone from mouth	Ninurta … as a "Dragon with the 'hands' of a lion, the claws of an eagle … You spat venom like a snake."[387] (The *Anzu* bird also spews venom.)

Table 8 Comparing Kudurru Inscription and Revelation

Another variation on the theme found on the Kudurru Stone is that of the scorpion-people, which stand on two feet like a man rather than four, like a horse / lion. (See Figure 58).

> Scorpion-people *Girtabluttû* 'scorpion-man', is the Akkadian term for a supernatural being with a horned cap of divinity, human head with beard, human body, the hindquarters and talons of a bird, a snake-headed penis, and a scorpion's tail. He may or may not have wings. The creature is first seen in the art of the Third Dynasty of Ur and of the Akkadian Period, but was common only in Neo-Assyrian and Neo-Babylonian times.[388]

The description is an incredibly strong match to what John saw in his visions: "For their power is in their mouth and in their tails; for their tails are like serpents, having heads; and with them they do harm" (Rev 9:19).

Figure 58 Scorpion-people Girtabluttû, "scorpion-man"

SUMMARY

In John's vision he sees a star fallen from heaven and we note an important clue, "to him was given the key," which means that he did not have it previously. We are going to see shortly how Jesus acquired this key. Nevertheless, at the time when Jesus declared that the Gates of Hades would not prevail, Satan still held the key to the Abyss (underworld). We have seen that Batios, representing Ninurta, Og, Melqart, Molech, Nergal, Pabilsag, etc., was the king of that domain. It is shocking to discover that the chimeric creatures described in Revelation 9 perfectly match Ninurta / Nergal, et al. (See Appendix 8 Joel's Army).

Milestone Marker 2

Figure 59 Roman Milestone on the Road of the Patriarchs between
Jerusalem and Hebron
https://en.wikipedia.org/wiki/Creative_Commons.

So far on our journey, we have discovered that that after the Flood, Satan continued his plan for world domination; but this time, he was operating through a specific antihero whom the Bible calls Nimrod, the Rebel. Nimrod was the ancient god Ninurta, who also had many aliases. We discovered that Satan gave him his power, his throne and his great authority—just like he will do with the Beast of Revelation. Ninurta / Nimrod is the Beast who was, is not, and will ascend. Working through Ninurta and possibly his progeny, Satan raised another army of hybrids that infested the world and specifically the land of Canaan, which God had promised to Abraham and his descendants. We discovered that the iniquity of the Amorites was the sin of choosing to become hybrids in a similar manner as Nimrod. The *gibborim* were likely related genetically, as evidenced by the common names of the gods. Furthermore, we discovered how Bashan was actually the land of the snake-dragons, run by a god of the dead, "Og". Lastly, we discovered the origin and form of the creatures that Satan has in store to burst out of the Abyss.

PART 3: THE TRUE HERO SEALS THE ABYSS AND REGAINS DOMINION OF EARTH

In this section, we will examine how Jesus, the true and prophesied hero, appears on the world stage to do battle with the god of death in the land of the snake-dragons' forces, stops the Abyss from opening, and reclaims authority for the dominion of the Earth.

Chapter 17: Jesus the True Super-Hero

A true story comes to us from Australia where a father heard the cry of his son who was being attacked by a 15-foot (4.5 m) python which had sunk its teeth into the boy's leg and was trying to pull him away, but the child was holding on tenaciously to a fence. The father ran to save his boy, hit the snake, and then pried open its jaws to free the boy. However, the snake kept coming after the boy. So, the father fought it back some more. Finally, somebody brought a sledgehammer, and the dad finished off the snake.

Figure 60 4.5 Meter python killed by Australian father.

That story is analogous to what Satan did to humanity. He cheated mankind out of his birthright and staged a coup against his Creator. God summarily declared: "I will put enmity between you and the woman, and between your seed [*zarakha* זַרְעֲךָ] and her seed [*zarah* זַרְעָהּ]; He shall bruise your head, and you shall bruise His heel" (Gen 3:15). Over the millennia, Satan tried time and again to thwart the coming of Messiah who was prophesied to bruise his head. He sent the angels to Mt. Hermon where they cursed themselves if they should not fulfill their mission. With only eight people left in the world who had not become irreversibly corrupted, God sent the Flood.

He then caused Nimrod to become a *gibbor* and made him into a god. Acting through Nimrod, Satan erected the gate of the gods in Babylon to have communication between the realms; and as a result, God scrambled the languages. Using Nimrod as the god Ninurta / Amurru, Satan seduced and altered the population in order to permeate the Promise Land with genetically modified Nephilim / Rephaim and was ready to meet Israel. His purpose was to ensnare Israel as soon as they entered the land and to stop Israel from remaining faithful to God.

The perverted and lustful Babylonian system that he created did indeed infiltrate the life of Israel. It was her wisest king, Solomon, who brought Molech / Milcom "the king" into the daily life of Israel. As a result, Israel cursed themselves, just like Adam and Eve had done. (See Appendix 5 Balaam). Consequently, the Kingdom of Israel split; God divorced the ten northern tribes and sent them away, calling them: "not my people" and "no mercy." (See Hosea 1:6, 9). The remaining people in Judah were not divorced but were chastised in Babylon, of all places, and then returned to the land. Satan did not surrender; He tried to get Judah to fail again through marriage to pagan women. Satan orchestrated a wave of Greek influence that seduced Judah.

Again, the people cursed themselves when they abandoned the ways of God and craved Greek philosophy, games, sports, language and gods. The people of Judah were Hellenized by choice and embraced the Greek culture and religion. The Greek king even desecrated the Holy of Holies with an abomination. Mankind falls for Satan's schemes; Humanity was doomed and could only be rescued by a true hero.

There is a funny meme that illustrates how Jesus did something like the father who saved his son from the python. In the meme, the Marvel superheroes: Thor, Iron Man, Spiderman, Captain America and Hulk are sitting around Jesus who says: "…and that's how I saved the world." It drives home the point that Jesus is the ultimate superhero who saved the world! He is the one that came to save us from the jaws of the enemy who had his teeth sunk into our leg, and would not let us go and kept coming after us. Jesus was willing to do what was necessary to save us from Satan's bite.

That father in Australia, I have no doubt would have been willing to lay down his life for his child. I would absolutely do that for my children without hesitation. However, Jesus could not merely take a sledgehammer to Satan's head and rescue us; he had to be wise, disciplined, and come with a plan. Because Satan is no dummy, Jesus had to outsmart him. We need to understand who Jesus was. He is not just some little kid who rose up to achieve greatness. He existed before he came to this planet. He existed before he was born of a virgin. He had greatness. He had all the splendor and the praise that you could ever imagine. Jesus was clothed in glory to such a degree that Paul says:

> Let this mind be in you which was also in Christ Jesus, who, being in the form of God, did not consider it robbery to be equal with God, but made Himself of no reputation, taking the form of a bondservant, and

coming in the likeness of men. And being found in appearance as a man, He humbled Himself and became obedient to the point of death, even the death of the cross (Philip 2: 5–8).

When Jesus is praying to the Father in the garden, He says: "O Father, glorify Me together with Yourself, with the glory which I had with You before the world was" (John 17:5). Jesus was "the word who was there in the beginning. In the beginning was the Word, and the Word was with God, and the Word was God" (John 1:1). The glory He had was rightfully His; He decided to lay that aside and to come as a humble child.

He was not born in luxury, nor in a great palace with servants in attendance; no one was waiting for him saying: "Come, Your Highness, we have the best room waiting for you." No, Jesus came humbly; He was born in a lowly manger: "She brought forth her firstborn Son, and wrapped Him in swaddling clothes, and laid Him in a manger" (Luke 2:7). He was born in a barn because "there was no room for them in the inn" (Luke 2:7). Nevertheless, God's angels lit up the sky and announced the birth of the long-awaited and promised Messiah. They proclaimed that:

> Now there were in the same country shepherds living out in the fields, keeping watch over their flock by night. And behold, an angel of the Lord stood before them, and the glory of the Lord shone around them, and they were greatly afraid. Then the angel said to them, "Do not be afraid, for behold, I bring you good tidings of great joy which will be to all people. "For there is born to you this day in the city of David a Savior, who is Christ the Lord (Luke 2:8–11).

He came and he humbled himself to do what was necessary to redeem us, to buy us back and to save us from the jaws of the snake.

Now after Jesus was born in Bethlehem of Judea in the days of Herod the king, behold, wise men from the East came to Jerusalem, saying, "Where is He who has been born King of the Jews? For we have seen His star in the East and have come to worship Him." When Herod the king heard this, he was troubled, and all Jerusalem with him (Matt 2:1–3).

God warned the wise men that Herod was up to no good, so they did not return to Herod and disclose the baby's location. Herod did not want to locate the baby to adore the new King; He wanted to kill Him. Thus, Satan the snake-dragon tried to destroy Jesus before He could become a threat.

Then Herod, when he saw that he was deceived by the wise men, was exceedingly angry; and he sent forth and put to death all the male children who were in Bethlehem and in all its districts, from two years old and under, according to the time which he had determined from the wise men (Matt 2:16).

The dragon would try to destroy the child as soon as He was born. Herod was the representation of the serpent, used by Satan to try and destroy the child.

Despite all that, when the child came of age, John "saw Jesus coming toward him, and said, 'Behold! The Lamb of God who takes away the sin of the world!'" (John 1:29). Then when Jesus came up from the water, "the heavens were opened to Him, and He saw the Spirit of God descending like a dove and alighting upon Him (Matt 3:16). And suddenly a voice came from heaven, saying, 'This is My beloved Son, in whom I am well pleased'" (Matt 3:17).

Satan the great dragon was the greatest of all creatures. He easily outwitted Adam and Eve, like taking candy from a baby, but the shrewd move secured him dominion over the entire cosmos.

Therefore, when the arrival of the "seed of the woman" finally came, after so many millennia, Satan would need to test His claim and determine if He could be quickly brushed aside.

SATAN TESTS THE TRUE HERO

Matthew tells us that "Jesus was led up by the Spirit into the wilderness to be tempted [πειρασθηναι peirasthenai] by the devil" (Matt 4:1). When God tests us, He wants us to pass—He wants to prove our faith. Nevertheless, the same word [πειρασθηναι peirasthenai] is used when Satan wanted to test Jesus, and show Him lacking. Naturally, the dragon does not want a fair fight, so he began the testing after Jesus "had fasted forty days and forty nights, afterward He was hungry" (Matt 4:2).

His first question was a challenge "If You are the Son of God, command that these stones become bread" (Matt 4:3). Robertson aptly notes:

> The devil is alluding to the words of the Father to Jesus at the baptism: "This is my Son the Beloved." He challenges this address by a condition of the first class which assumes the condition to be true and deftly calls on Jesus to exercise his power as Son of God to appease his hunger and thus prove to himself and all that he really is what the Father called him.[389]

In other words, Satan accepted the claim just as he heard God's voice from heaven. And that being true, he wanted to see Jesus in action. I am grateful to my friend Dr. Michael Heiser, who on my show, "The Awakening Report", made an astute observation that Satan was testing Jesus to see what he knew and what he would divulge; would he use his power, and most importantly, could Satan kill him?[390] Thus, perhaps we could frame Satan's challenge like this—"Can I mislead you through a selfish use of your power and thereby disqualify you as man's champion?"

Jesus answered and said, "It is written, Man shall not live by bread alone, but by every word that proceeds from the mouth of God'" (Matt 4:4). He passed the first test and then came the second:

> Then the devil took Him up into the holy city, set Him on the pinnacle of the temple, and said to Him, "If You are the Son of God, throw Yourself down. For it is written: 'He shall give His angels charge over you,' and, 'In their hands they shall bear you up, Lest you dash your foot against a stone'" (Matt 4:5–6).

Satan specifically presented the Messiah with a messianic passage. In fact, Satan must have left off the next verse deliberately: "You shall tread upon the lion and the cobra [פתן peten], The young lion and the serpent [תנין tanin] you shall trample underfoot" (Ps 91:13).

The Hebrew words are incredibly provocative. We already investigated *peten* in the context of Bashan, and found the meaning: snake-dragon. *Tanin* is also often used for a type of dragon. Satan was encouraging Jesus to "tread the lion-snake-dragon"! Satan was saying I am *Ušumgallu*, the great dragon, I am *Mušḫuššu* the fierce red dragon, I am *Bašmu*, king of Bashan; You came to crush my head—let's go! You are here to fulfill the prophecy of doom, let's get started. Satan knew exactly why Jesus had come; and after waiting thousands of years, he wanted to get straight to the point.

In other words, Satan was baiting Jesus: if you jump to fulfill this Messianic prophecy and the angels catch you up—you will have proven that you are indeed Messiah. Did Satan hope Jesus would be sophomoric and try to fulfill the prophecy in the most obvious way? If Jesus had taken the bait, Satan would know that Jesus could not kill him.[391] Yet very adroitly, Jesus answered, "It is written again, 'You shall not tempt the LORD your God'" (Matt 4:7).

251

In the last and hardest test "the devil took Him up on an exceedingly high mountain, and showed Him all the kingdoms of the world and their glory. And he said to Him, "All these things I will give You if You will fall down and worship me" (Matt 4:8–9).

The highest mountain within the boundaries of the United Kingdom of Israel, and even as far as Sidon, the northern most point of Jesus' ministry, is Mount Hermon. There is no other mountain in the region that is higher; it is visible from nearly everywhere in Northern Israel and even to the southernmost part of the Sea of Galilee. It is the highest point in Israel, standing over 9,200 ft (2,800 m) above sea level, often with snow on its highest peaks.

Of course, we remember that it was on this mountain that the angels came down and took an oath to corrupt the seed of man and beget the Nephilim. On that high mountain, Satan used his power to show Jesus "in a moment of time" (Luke 4:5), all the kingdoms of the world that he possessed. They all belonged to Satan. In Luke, Satan said "All this authority I will give You, and their glory; for this has been delivered to me, and I give it to whomever I wish" (Luke 4:6). Jesus did not argue with Satan because it was true. The harsh reality that Satan is the supreme-ruler of this world is evidenced throughout the pages of Scripture:

- the ruler of this world [cosmos κόσμος] (John 12:31; 14:30; 16:11).
- "The **kingdoms of this world have become** the kingdoms of our Lord and of His Christ" (Rev 11:15). (Meaning they were not before that moment).

We need to understand "the earth is the LORD's, and all its fullness, The world and those who dwell therein (Ps 24:1, See also Ps 89:11). Everything belongs to God; It is all His creation. However, in the beginning God made man and said:

"Let them have dominion over the fish of the sea, over the birds of the air, and over the cattle, over all the earth and over every creeping thing that creeps on the earth" (Gen 1:26).

The same motif is clearly stated in Psalm 8:

What is man that You are mindful of him, And the son of man that You visit him? For You have made him a little lower than the angels, And You have crowned him with glory and honor. You have made him to have dominion over the works of Your hands; You have put all things under his feet. All sheep and oxen—Even the beasts of the field (Ps 8:4–7).

Think of it this way: God created the world, and then leased it out to Adam. It is all God's, but He gave full authority to Adam. The dominion was Adam's, though it technically belonged to God. Satan hoodwinked them in the Garden and gained the dominion for himself. This is why he said to Jesus, "All this authority ... for this has been delivered [παραδέδοται] to me" (Luke 4:6). The word *paradedotai* [παραδέδοται], according to BDAG, means: "to convey something in which one has a relatively strong personal interest, hand over, give (over), deliver, entrust," and also "to entrust for care or preservation, give over, commend, commit."

In other words, the kingdoms of this world have been given over, entrusted, committed to Satan—we might say he swindled Adam and Eve fair and square. Satan found a legal concept by which he could come in and take control of the planet and the world system, called adverse possession. According to Cornell Law School:

Adverse possession is a doctrine under which a person in possession of land owned by someone else may acquire valid title to it, so long as certain common law requirements are met, and the adverse possessor is in possession for a sufficient period of time, as defined by a statute of limitations.[392]

Neither Adam and Eve, nor God had any legal recourse; Satan legally scammed them. Satan played the trump card! To be sure, God was more powerful and had more angels in His army. But the contest was not about strength; it was about authority, and Satan had the authority. He knew for certain God could not just overpower him and take it back because "righteousness and justice are the foundation of His throne" (Ps 97:2). If God should overpower Satan, which he could, then God would no longer be righteous and just. If God tried to forcefully take back dominion of Earth, Satan could exclaim:

> "Far be it from You to do such a thing as this, to slay the righteous with the wicked, so that the righteous should be as the wicked; far be it from You! Shall not the Judge of all the earth do right?" (Gen 18:25).

Because of this ace up his sleeve, Satan did not fear that Jesus could take back the planet. He reasoned that the most He would do is comfort mankind for some time; but in the end, because of the bondage of corruption which led to death, and because he held the power of death (Keys of Death and Hades) (Heb 2:14–15), Satan would remain master over the world indefinitely.

We saw Satan's hubris played out in the Akitu festival where the "good news" was brought to Enlil of the killing of (An) the Creator and where the *"anutu"* (Anu-ship) was delivered to Enlil. Enlil then in turn, gave the Enlil-ship to whoever he wished because it was his to give out. That authority was known as the Tablet of Destinies in the ancient world, and he was the owner. Amar Annus reminds us "In *Enuma eliš*, the Tablet of Destinies is associated with the powers of Anu"[393] (Anu being the creator).

THE SCROLL AND THE TABLET OF DESTINIES

The Tablet of Destinies that Enlil possessed appears to be the same as the scroll in God's right hand in Revelation.

> And I saw in the right hand of Him who sat on the throne a scroll written inside and on the back, sealed with seven seals. Then I saw a strong angel proclaiming with a loud voice, "Who is worthy to open the scroll and to loose its seals?" And no one in heaven or on the earth or under the earth was able to open the scroll, or to look at it. So I wept much, because no one was found worthy to open and read the scroll, or to look at it (Rev 5:1–4).

In the Book of Daniel 7, we see a similar picture of millions upon millions of mighty beings surrounding God's fiery throne!

> The Ancient of Days was seated ... His throne was a fiery flame, Its wheels a burning fire (Dan 7:9). ... A thousand thousands ministered to Him; Ten thousand times ten thousand stood before Him (Dan 7:10).

John says a challenge went out to the 100+ million angels in God's retinue: "A strong angel proclaiming with a loud voice, "Who is worthy to open the scroll and to loose its seals?" (Rev 5:2). He was asking who was authorized to open this scroll, and worthy to loose it seals. The reality was "no one in heaven or on the earth or under the earth was able to open the scroll, or to look at it."

Nobody on the Earth, no one in heaven or in the Earth or under the Earth, or in the abode of the dead. Nobody of the 100+ million beings, at least, standing before the King of Kings! Consequently, John says: "So I wept much, because no one was found worthy to open and read the scroll, or to look at it" (Rev 5:3).

255

He is weeping because of the significance of the scroll. The destinies of humankind are linked to the scroll, which Satan called the Tablet of Destinies. We learn as we continue to read Revelation that judgments come when the seals are broken. The judgments eventually lead to "loud voices in heaven, saying, 'The kingdoms of this world have become the kingdoms of our Lord and of His Christ, and He shall reign forever and ever!'" (Rev 11:15). In other words, once the scroll is opened, Satan's kingdom is over.

The scroll is the dominion God gave to Adam which he forfeited in the Garden. Scrolls had not yet been invented in the Sumerian civilization. All contracts were recorded on clay tablets. We recall how "Ninurta, as the seal-bearer of Enlil in Nippur, was probably authorized to act with Enlil's authority. … Ninurta … is often invoked as the "Bearer of the Tablet of Destinies of the Gods."[394] Hence, the Tablet of Destinies was the equivalent of the scroll. Whoever held the document, controlled Earth and the destinies of mankind.

John wept beforehand because it was sealed, and nobody could open it; somehow the right to open the scroll had been forfeited. If the scroll could not be opened, it meant that Satan's kingdom and authority would go on forever.

SATAN OFFERS JESUS HIS AUTHORITY

Satan indeed had authority over the world, a fact that Jesus did not contest: "The devil said to Him, 'All this authority I will give You, and their glory; for this has been delivered to me, and I give it to whomever I wish'" (Luke 4:6). Satan offered to give Jesus the Tablet of Destinies if he would just bow down and worship Satan. He had given the Tablet to Nimrod millennia earlier, just as he would give it to Jesus if He complied.

We could frame Satan's offer like this:

Oh, you want the planet? You want to save mankind? No problem, I can give it to whoever I want. The Father sent you on this mission to get all the kingdoms of the world and to show humanity how to live and to bring all into a meaningful relationship with God. I will make you a good deal. I will just give it all to you. You want it and this is what you came for. Take it. But just one little thing … no big deal, really. Bow down to me and worship me like others have in the past, and the world is yours.

Had Jesus taken the offer, Satan probably would have kept his end of the bargain and the world would look quite different. Yet death would remain; death and the fear of death would have still permeated the planet. In Hebrews, the message is clear that Satan had authority over men, because we are told Jesus freed us:

> Inasmuch then as the children have partaken of flesh and blood, He Himself likewise shared in the same, that through death He might destroy him who had the power of death, that is, the devil, and release those who through fear of death were all their lifetime subject to bondage (Heb 2:14–15).

Satan ruled mankind, and by his authority as Holder of the Keys of Death and Hell, he sealed the destiny of mankind. Consequently, humans could never go back to be with God because death is inside them: the animals, plants and also the planet itself. Remember earlier, nuclear physicist Dr. Robert Gentry told us that even granite is in the process of decay which can be measured by a Geiger counter as radiation. God Himself, in all of His beauty and glory cannot come back to this corrupted planet without melting it. His face is like the sun; He cannot come back unveiled. When He does come, He has to shroud himself in thick darkness. Even with the protective shroud, when He came down to Mt. Sinai, the mountain was enveloped in smoke and it was on fire because the glory of the Lord.

Satan was ingenious; He elaborated on how he could give Jesus exactly what he came for, but understated that little clause "just bow down". But thankfully, Jesus was way ahead of Satan.

> Then Jesus said to him, "Away with you, Satan! For it is written, 'You shall worship the LORD your God, and Him only you shall serve.'" Then the devil left Him, and behold, angels came and ministered to Him (Matt 4:10–11).

Chapter 18: Darkness Fights the Light

When Jesus began His ministry, there were hordes of demons in Galilee. They were concentrated in the Galilee because they were worshiped in the shadowland of the snake-dragons. They had gained dominance in the very place where Satan commanded the sons of God to descend and begin their genetic warfare.

Matthew tells us that after the testing, Jesus was "leaving Nazareth, He came and dwelt in Capernaum, which is by the sea, in the regions of Zebulun and Naphtali" (Matt 4:13). Jesus knew that the Sanhedrin and the influential rabbis were in Jerusalem. However, Jesus did not go to Jerusalem to try to make reforms to the religious leaders; instead, he went to the front line of the war, as Matthew notes:

> This was to fulfill what was spoken through the prophet Isaiah: Land of Zebulun and land of Naphtali, along the sea road, beyond the Jordan, Galilee of the Gentiles! The people who live in darkness have seen a great light, and for those living in the shadowland of death, light has dawned. From then on Jesus began to preach, "Repent, because the kingdom of heaven has come near!" (Matt 4:14–17).

What did Isaiah mean concerning the people of Zebulun and Naphtali living in darkness and the shadowland of death? Isaiah revealed that these people were recommending that everyone "Consult the spirits of the dead and the spiritists who chirp and mutter," whereas Isaiah rightfully answered, "Shouldn't a people consult their God? Should they consult the dead on behalf of the living?" (Isa 8:19). He then states how they need to go "to the law and to the testimony" (Isa 8:20a), and further warns:

If they do not speak according to this word, there will be no dawn for them. They will wander through the land, dejected and hungry. When they are famished, they will become enraged, and, looking upward, will curse their king and their God. They will look toward the earth and see only distress, darkness, and the gloom of affliction, and they will be driven into thick darkness (Isa 8:20–22 Holman Standard).

It is after this warning that Isaiah adds that in the territories of Zebulun and Naphtali, "a light has dawned on those living in the land of darkness" (Isa 9:2). Jesus was raised in Nazareth, which was in the territory of Zebulun. It was a small, landlocked territory and hence, "Can anything good come from Nazareth?" was a reasonable question.

Figure 61 Tribal Divisions of Northern Israel.

Naphtali was next to the Sea of Galilee and adjacent to the land of Bashan and Mt. Hermon. As we have seen, Og was King of the Bashan, the land of snake-dragons. Furthermore, his name meant "death", and according to Ugaritic texts, a deified dead king ruled from Ashtaroth and Edrei, which were the headquarters of Og, according to Deuteronomy 1:4.

Thus, the people of Zebulun and Naphtali succumbed to the ways of *Batios*, the snake-dragon. Isaiah's declaration (reiterated by Matthew) that the people were living in darkness and in the shadowland of death, was no exaggeration—neither was it simply a metaphor for their sinful lifestyle. They had so utterly abandoned God's ways, His laws and instructions, that they had sided with the enemy whose headquarters were in that very region. Even back as far as when Mt. Hermon served as the meeting place for the angels who descended in the days of Noah, the area was malevolent. Naphtali was geographically in the shadowland of Bashan and Hermon, the headquarters of the kingdom of death. Jesus focused His ministry there, not Jerusalem, because the land of Bashan and Mt. Hermon were the frontline of the battle!

With that in mind, we have a newfound appreciation for the statement "The people who live in darkness have seen a great light, and for those living in the shadowland of death, light has dawned" (Matt 4:16). Isaiah warned, "If they do not speak according to this word, there will be no dawn for them" (Isa 8:20 HCSB), and sadly, because of their disobedience, there was no dawn and no light for the next seven centuries. Yet, Jesus' arrival meant a new dawn had come. What glorious, good news it was that:

> For a child will be born for us, a son will be given to us, and the government will be on His shoulders. He will be named Wonderful Counselor, Mighty God, Eternal Father, Prince of Peace. The dominion will be vast, and its prosperity will never end. He will reign on the throne of David and over

his kingdom, to establish and sustain it with justice and righteousness from now on and forever. The zeal of the LORD of Hosts will accomplish this (Isa 9:6–7 HCSB).

A flashlight in the blackness of night is seen for miles around. Jesus' light shone so brightly that the spiritual host of darkness saw it, and the light frightened them. In a kingdom of darkness, light is the enemy that must be vanquished. The dark forces mounted an opposition which is the reason there seemed to be demons on every corner in Galilee. Mary Magdalene was tormented by seven which Jesus cast out (Luke 8:2). Jesus' fame for healing people quickly spread beyond the region of Galilee into Syria. The masses began bringing people to him who were "afflicted with various diseases and torments, and those who were demon-possessed, epileptics, and paralytics; and He healed them" (Matt 4:24). He continued physical healing and casting out the demons (Matt 8:16), and thereby demonstrated His incredible power: The demons were compelled to obey Him.

After humbling the demonic powers of darkness who had terrorized the people in the region of Galilee, Jesus "gave the order to go to the **other side of the sea**" (Matt 8:18), to take the fight to the region of Bashan, to the shadowland of death! The destination was Gadara, which according to the ancient writers "was **a strong fortress** … the position was one of great strength." (Emphasis mine).[395] The destination appears to have been not merely a physical fortress, but a spiritual stronghold, as well.

When an enemy attempts a frontal attack on a stronghold, defensive measures are enacted, and this is exactly what happened. "Suddenly, a violent storm arose on the sea, so that the boat was being swamped by the waves. But He was sleeping" (Matt 8:24). Though storms were not uncommon on the Sea of Galilee, this one was so fierce that experienced fishermen greatly feared for their lives: "So the disciples came and woke Him up, saying, 'Lord, save us! We're going to die!'"

(Matt 8:25). The storm was not typical and not natural, but was a storm caused by Satan and his demonic host in an attempt to kill Jesus and His disciples! Satan wielded the fierce power of a storm when he killed Job's children:

> So Satan went out from the presence of the LORD (Job 1:12). ... a messenger came to Job and said ... "The fire of God fell from heaven and burned up the sheep and the servants, and consumed them; and I alone have escaped to tell you!" (Job 1:16). While he was still speaking, another also came and said, "Your sons and daughters were eating and drinking wine in their oldest brother's house (Job 1:18), "and suddenly a great wind came from across the wilderness and struck the four corners of the house, and it fell on the young people, and they are dead" (Job 1:19). (Emphasis mine.)

Spirit beings can affect our world. Eliphaz, one of Job's "friends", shared his experience with a spirit being, though we do not know if it was a good or bad angel. The spirit brought fear and trembling, and it made him shake and made his hair stand up, but he could not make out the form. Then the being spoke to him.

> In disquieting thoughts from the visions of the night, When deep sleep falls on men, Fear came upon me, and trembling, Which made all my bones shake. Then a spirit passed before my face; The hair on my body stood up. It stood still, But I could not discern its appearance. A form was before my eyes (Job 4:13–16);

Eliphaz was troubled by a real spirit, that although invisible, he could vividly perceive. Satan and demons can manipulate this world. Satan was also able to incite the Sabeans and the Chaldeans to attack Job's servants and kill them. Satan used the power of fire from heaven (possibly lightning) and wind to kill Job's kids and the animals.

Satan's control of weather and wind is completely in line with his title as "Prince of the Power of the Air" in the Bible and "Lord Wind," as the Sumerian Enlil, and the "storm god" as the Canaanite Baal Hermon. In the next round with Job, Satan causes terrible sores to come upon Job's body. If Satan can cause all of these effects while limited from the other side of the veil, what will happen when he is cast down to Earth? When he gains access to this side of the veil by inhabiting the Beast and controlling the False Prophet, it truly will be a scenario where the world will ask, "Who can make war with the beast?" The Beast and the False Prophet will indeed have Satan's power to make "fire come down from heaven on the earth in the sight of men" (Rev 13:13). Thus, it was the "storm god" Satan who stirred the storm that confronted Jesus and the disciples; it was not a natural storm.

The disciples woke Him, and while still lying down (and still groggy) He said to them, "Why are you fearful, O you of little faith?" The text says, "then He arose and rebuked [επετιμησε epetimise] the winds and the sea, and there was a great calm" (Matt 8:26). In other words, Jesus appears to be bummed about being woken from His nap for something so trivial. Jesus did not merely tell the storm to be still. Rather, the word is "to express strong disapproval of someone, rebuke, reprove, censure also speak seriously, warn in order to prevent an action or bring one to an end."[396] If Jesus were merely speaking to air currents, then why would He need to make a warning? How can one warn air molecules? However, the weight of evidence, is that He was rebuking Satan and his demons who were trying to prevent Him from crossing into their territory, and hopefully kill Him. Naturally, the disciples were utterly shocked and asked, "What kind of man is this? —even the winds and the sea obey Him!" (Matt 8:27). What they could not know at the time was that the storm was from Satan!

LEGION

Satan failed to keep Jesus from coming over, and once He arrived "two demon-possessed men met Him as they came out of the tombs. They were so violent that no one could pass that way" (Matt 8:28). These men were filled with Satan's forces and ready to take out any who trespassed into the land of the snake-dragon, King Og of Bashan's former territory. Mark tells us that "immediately there met Him out of the tombs a man with an unclean spirit" (Mark 5:2). Demon and unclean spirit are one and the same thing. (See Appendix 1 Demons). Note that the demon-possessed man lived in the tombs. He slept, ate and spent his time in the cemetery, the place of the dead. Og, King of Bashan was a chthonic (underworld) deity associated with other underworld gods like Ninurta, Molech, etc. Hence, this man was filled with demons of the kingdom of death and was drawn to places of the dead.

> For the 'Canaanites' of Ugarit, the Bashan region, or a part of it, clearly represented 'Hell', the celestial and infernal abode of their deified dead kings, - Olympus and - Hades at the same time. It is possible that this localization of the Canaanite Hell is linked to the ancient tradition of the place as the ancestral home of their dynasty, the rpum. [397]

In the text, we next see that the man had incredible strength—so much so that "no one could bind him, not even with chains" (Mark 5:3). Mark informs us that "he had often been bound with shackles and chains. And the chains had been pulled apart by him, and the shackles broken in pieces; neither could anyone tame him" (Mark 5:4).

When the demoniac saw Jesus "from afar, he ran and worshiped Him" (Mark 5:6). And he cried out with a loud voice and said, "What have I to do with You, Jesus, Son of the Most High God? I implore You by God that You do not torment me" (Mark 5:7).

265

Matthew's gospel adds, "Have You come here to torment us before the time?" (Matt 8:29). The demons instantly knew who Jesus was, and seemed to know about some impending torment, possibly a reference to their final judgment. However, we must consider the context of this statement where immediately prior, Jesus had warned the wind and waves. Jesus was also sending a warning to the powers behind the storm which were Satan and his forces. It could be that they were fearful of the warning that He had given, and out of fear, reacted through the man they inhabited.

After all, that man had a legion of demons in him. A legion is between 4,000-6,000 men. That means there were at least four thousand demons in the man and there may have been upwards of twelve thousand between the two of them. Jesus is unimpressed. He simply commanded: "Come out of the man, unclean spirit!" (Mark 5:8). There was no contest between Jesus and the many mighty demons who had terrorized the people of the region for centuries. Once God's champion showed up, they groveled before him. Indeed, Mark says the demons "begged Him earnestly that He would not send them out of the country" (Mark 5:10). Apparently, it was beneficial to the demons for them to remain in the region of Bashan.

Indicative of the apostasy of the region, "A large herd of swine was feeding there near the mountains" (Mark 5:11). God had given the land to the children of Israel, and swine was not to be on the menu. Yet, because the people had given themselves to darkness, pig farming was popular. Then:

> All the demons begged Him, saying, "Send us to the swine, that we may enter them. And at once Jesus gave them permission. Then the unclean spirits went out and entered the swine (there were about two thousand); and the herd ran violently down the steep place into the sea, and drowned in the sea (Mark 5:12–13).

The thousands of demons were nothing before God's Anointed. Jesus was showcasing his strength; and Satan must have taken notice, for if it had been about strength, Jesus clearly would have won. Yet, so long as Satan held the Tablet of Destinies, the Earth would legally be in his hands.

Chapter 19: Gates of Hades

Jesus, the true hero of light, continued His attack on the forces of darkness who had cast their shadow of death in Galilee, by taking the fight directly to them. Toward the latter end of His ministry, he took His disciples about thirty-five miles north of Capernaum to Caesarea Philippi, a two-day trek on foot. They went to the Cave of Pan (*Banias*),[398] known as the Gates of Hades, at the base of Mount Hermon, depicted in Figure 62. It seems strange for a Jewish rabbi to take His students to a thoroughly pagan place of worship. Yet, Jesus was always intentional.

> When Jesus came into the region of Caesarea Philippi, He asked His disciples, saying, "Who do men say that I, the Son of Man, am?" So they said, "Some say John the Baptist, some Elijah, and others Jeremiah or one of the prophets." He said to them, "But who do you say that I am?" Simon Peter answered and said, "You are the Christ, the Son of the living God." Jesus answered and said to him, "Blessed are you, Simon Bar-Jonah, for flesh and blood has not revealed this to you, but My Father who is in heaven. "And I also say to you that you are Peter, and on this rock I will build My church, and the gates of Hades shall not prevail against it (Matt 16:13–18).

Josephus describes the place:

> When Caesar had further bestowed upon him (Herod) another additional country, he built there also a temple of white marble, hard by the fountains of Jordan: the place is called Panium (Panias, Caesarea Philippi), where is a top of a mountain that is raised to an immense height, and at its side, beneath, or at its bottom, a dark cave opens itself; within which there is a horrible precipice,

that descends abruptly to a vast depth: it contains a mighty quantity of water, which is immovable; and when anybody lets down anything to measure the depth of the earth beneath the water, no length of cord is sufficient to reach it. Now the fountains of Jordan rise at the roots of this cavity outwardly; and, as some think, this is the utmost origin of Jordan.[399]

Figure 62 By Bill Rice from Flat Rock, MI, USA - Caesarea Philippi, CC BY 2.0, commons.wikimedia.org/w/index.php?curid=35423945.

Before the Romans conquered the area, the Greeks under Alexander, had occupied and governed under the auspices of the Seleucid Empire. It was out of a two-hundred-year dynasty established by the Seleucids that Antiochus (IV) Epiphanes came. He of course, was the one who desecrated the Temple in Jerusalem with the abomination of desolation. This led to the Maccabee revolt and the rededication of the temple, now celebrated as Hanukkah. It was during this fusion of Greek and Near East cultures that Hellenized religious traditions were overlaid on the biblical region. In the area of Banias, they built sanctuaries to worship the god Pan:

which included strange sexual acts with goats. The Greeks called this place Panias, and the cave was the main attraction for Hellenistic pagan worship. Animal sacrifices were thrown into the bottomless pool inside. If the sacrifices sank, the gods were appeased. Next to the Pan cave are five niches with indented scalloped areas cut into the face of the cliff for their idols. These niches had elaborate temples attached to worship Pan, Zeus, Nemesis, and a sanctuary to the cult of the "dancing goats." Pan was the god of the goats and his pipe music would entice the goats to dance, and make their fertility assured (he is also linked to sex, lust, and bestiality). It was so wicked, a sin city like today's Las Vegas, that rabbis forbade a good Jew to come here.[400] (See Appendix 3, Inanna).

The Greeks, however, were not the first people to be enamored of the location. We recall that it was squarely in the land of Bashan and at the foot of Mt. Hermon where Baal-Hermon was worshipped. It was the place where the angels descended and also where Og, King of the Bashan and of the Amorites and Rephaim was headquartered. It was at this place that "Canaanite mythology ... locates ... the abode of its deified dead kings, the mlk(m)/rpu(m) that dwell(s) in 'Štrt-hdr'y'",[401] that is, Og and Sihon, kings of the Rephaim that dwell in Ashtaroth and Edrei.

The ancient coastal town of Ugarit recorded the location as being ruled by Mlkm (Milcom). This god was also worshipped in ancient Israel and was also known as Molech, a god who demanded child sacrifice. Like many of the gods we have examined before, Milcom was considered a chthonic (underworld) god equated with Nergal, Melqart (king of the city of Tyre) (See Ezek 28).

271

Akkadian god lists from the Old Babylonian period onwards include a deity named **Malik equated with Nergal, and** other **Akkadian texts mention mal(i)ku** beings with the Igigi and Anunnaki, all in connection with the cult of the dead ancestors. (We may also note a god Milkunni attested in Hurrian.) ... the presence of a deity Mlk at Ugarit ... (vocalized as Malik, Milku and Mulik in syllabic texts) ... appears in two divine directories (actually, **snake charms**), as resident at 'ttrt ... the same location which is elsewhere **assigned to the netherworld deity Rpu** it **is suggestive of some close relationship**, as is the attestation of beings called **mlkm** in connection with the **royal cult of the dead**, along with the better-known **rpum** (OT -Rephaim), who appear to be the shades of dead royalty at Ugarit (or of all the dead in the OT; cr. Ps 88:11). Finally, we may note the similar divine names Melqart of Phoenicia and Milcom of Ammon. Melqart (literally, "King of the City") may also have connections with the underworld (particularly if one follows **W. F. Albright in understanding "the City" as the netherworld), and equally of interest that the Ugaritic 'address' for Mlk, 'ttrt, is likely to be identified with the city Ashtaroth in Bashan,** just north of Ammon.⁴⁰² (Emphasis mine).

W. F. Albright's understanding of "the City" as the netherworld is based on the Old Babylonian *"irigal"*. *Iri* is like the Hebrew *"ir"* (city) and *"gal"* is "big". It meant the underworld and in Akkadian it was *erşetu*; *qabru* meaning "earth, land; underworld; grave". *Erşetu* (*ertzetu*) was also shorthand for *"daltu erş eti*: the door of the underworld."⁴⁰³ Thus, the notion of the underworld having a gate or a door, is ancient and is found in the land of Shinar where Satan established his false religious system.

There may have been multiple gates to the underworld just as there are multiple gates into a city. Nevertheless, the cave of Pan was considered to be one of those locations and Jesus made that clear to his disciples. In his paper, "The Gates of Hades and the Keys of the Kingdom," Joel Marcus confirms how Hades was "believed to house not only the human dead but also the demonic agents of death and destruction." [404]

GATES RELEASE THE ARMY, NOT JUST DEFENSIVE

Often, commentators view the Gates of Hades as defensive measures trying to protect Hades from attack. Yet, we have seen that Satan's kingdom has been on the offensive. The gates should not be interpreted as a defensive barrier, but rather as the portal releasing the forces of darkness upon the world. The word κατισχυσουσιν (katischusousin) "prevail" is an offensive word, which according to BDAG means "to have the strength or capability to obtain an advantage, be dominant, prevail to have the capability to defeat, win a victory over." [405] Marcus notes the "insurmountable philological problem with the "defensive" interpretation of the gates...katischynein + genitive is always active in meaning (="to vanquish"), never passive (="to resist successfully")." [406] He rightfully concludes that "the gates, therefore, would seem to be attacking the church." He supports his philological deduction with the "observation of another Matthean passage: 7:24-25" which also portrays a rock, "and here the rock is subjected to a pounding by inimical forces." [407]

This leads us to the question of how can gates attack? Marcus points out that "gates" can be a *pars-pro-toto* term for the "city itself", and how "English translations occasionally render še'arim 'town' or 'city'" and therefore "'gates of Hades' seems to stand for the entire underworld city of the dead." [408] Thus, Jesus' use of "Gates of Hades" is perfectly consistent with how the region of Bashan and Hermon itself have many underworld connections.

Jesus is not merely speaking about gates, but he is speaking of the entire realm of the dead. He is speaking of all of the underworld references we have already considered, many represented by the logogram BAD / BAT, such as Enlil, Ninurta, Og, MLK (Milcom / Molech), Nergal, etc. He is declaring to the great bull god *Batios*, king of the snake-dragons, stationed in Bashan, that he and his forces will not prevail against God's kingdom. Jesus' statement was a declaration of outright war against the rulers of the realm of the dead. Because "Gates ... can stand for rulers ... Matt 16:18 may point to a military origin for this linkage, which was already present in the OT."[409]

THE UNDERWORLD BURSTING THROUGH THE GATES

Jesus' trip to the Gates of Hades and subsequent transfiguration, appear to be more a part of a strategy than just an object lesson for His disciples. With history as our guide, we know that God intervened against the Nephilim in the days of Noah and then again, against the *gibborim* at the Tower of Babel. God quashed Satan's dangerous machinations to overrun the planet with his demonic host. In the first century, there was a strong sense of the apocalyptic. Marcus notes that:

> The image of Matthew is of rulers of the underworld bursting forward from the gates of their heavily guarded, walled city to attack God's people on earth. When we speak of demonic powers flooding the earth, we are speaking the language of Jewish apocalyptic. Jewish apocalyptists believed that, in the end-time, the powers of cosmic chaos, restrained since creation, would break forth from their restraint and bring unparalleled tribulation upon the world. Indeed, O. Betz has pointed out that there are remarkable parallels in the QL to the basic picture of Matt 16:18. In 1QH 3:17-18, e.g. the gates of Sheol open and the ungodly powers imprisoned in the underworld stream out to flood the earth.

As A. Cooper renders this passage:

> They open the gates of [Sheol for all] acts of wickedness;
> They close the doors of the pit behind the conceiver of
> mischief; The bars of eternity behind all spirits of
> wickedness. The gates of Sheol, after opening to release
> the demonic powers onto the earth, close behind them
> so that they could not return to the underworld even if
> they wished to; like wild animals shut up in a
> gladiatorial arena, they have no choice but to attack the
> human beings who share their confinement. Similarly,
> in 1QH 3:26-34 the "time of the wrath of Belial" is
> described as one in which the gates of Sheol open and
> "arrows of the pit" fly out.[410]

As Messiah and God, Jesus would not have succumbed to the
latest pop-conspiracies of His day. That means He did not go
to Caesarea Philippi for a stunt or to make a name for himself.
In fact, coming down from the transfiguration, He instructed
the disciples to keep it secret. This is highly suggestive that
Satan had something planned for that time. Jesus went up to
the Gates to meet the challenge. The events that Satan had
planned might line up with the ideas of the apocalyptists of
the day who believed the attack included the Gates of Hades
opening and Satan's hordes flooding out. While we do not
know definitively if Satan had planned to attack at that time,
we do know that he had been preparing his forces since the
days of Nimrod, whom we have learned was Ninurta, Nergal,
etc., who was also known as the arrow, the star, and the Beast
that was, is not, and ascends. Whether Satan geared up for a
final battle during Jesus' ministry, we do not know; but we do
know that he is assembling an army for the end of days which
may enter through portals, such as the Gates of Hades.

Chapter 20: Jesus Reclaims the Land of the Snake-Dragon (Hermon)

There in the land of Bashan: land of the Snake-dragon, land of Og and the dead and deified king, land of the Rephaim, the abode of the dead—Jesus made it clear that He, the anointed one of Israel, had come to win. He would free mankind from the snares of the ultimate snake-dragon (Rev 12:9). He declared His victory at the base of the snake-dragon's mountain when He said the Gates of Hades (Kingdom of Darkness) will not prevail.

He then declared: "I tell you the truth, there are some standing here who will not experience death before they see the kingdom of God come with power" (Mark 9:1 NET). Then just "six days later Jesus took with him Peter, James, and John and led them alone up a high mountain privately" (Mark 9:2), to stake His claim at the top of the mountain Hermon,[411]meaning "devoted to destruction". Also known as Mt. Bashan (*batios*), it is where the watchers came down and execrated themselves: "According to the command of the great bull god *Batios*, those swearing an oath in this place go forth." It was on that mountain that:

> He was transfigured before them, and his clothes became radiantly white, more so than any launderer in the world could bleach them. Then Elijah appeared before them along with Moses, and they were talking with Jesus (Mark 9:2–4 NET).

On the mountain that Satan's team claimed as their own, Jesus showed them that the kingdom of God had come with power.

> So Peter said to Jesus, "Rabbi, it is good for us to be here. Let us make three shelters [σκηνας skenas]—one for you, one for Moses, and one for Elijah." (For they were afraid, and he did not know what to say.) Then a cloud overshadowed them, and a voice came from the cloud,

"This is my one dear Son. Listen to him!" Suddenly when they looked around, they saw no one with them any more except Jesus. As they were coming down from the mountain, he gave them orders not to tell anyone what they had seen until after the Son of Man had risen from the dead. They kept this statement to themselves, discussing what this rising from the dead meant (Mark 9:5–10).

It must have been amazing to see Him transfigure and to hear the Father's voice, but why was this event so important? Why did Jesus go on a secret excursion on that mountain? Why did he need to transfigure in front of Peter, James and John? Did he just want to encourage them by letting them witness His glory, or could there be another reason? King David provides important clues in Psalm 68:

MT. BASHAN IN PSALM 68

A mountain of God is the mountain of Bashan; A mountain of many peaks is the mountain of Bashan. Why do you look with envy, O mountains with many peaks, At the mountain which God has desired for His abode? Surely the LORD will dwell there forever. The chariots of God are myriads, thousands upon thousands; The Lord is among them as at Sinai, in holiness. You have ascended on high, You have led captive Your captives; You have received gifts among men, Even among the rebellious also, that the LORD God may dwell there (Ps 68:15–18 NASB).[412]

There are in fact, three peaks at the top of Hermon, which led Easton's Bible Dictionary to suggest: "There is every probability that one of its three summits was the scene of the transfiguration." [413] It very well may be the reason Peter suggested building three tabernacles—one on each peak.

Peter later mentions the experience in his second epistle and explained how God the Father's "voice came to Him from the Excellent Glory: 'This is My beloved Son, in whom I am well pleased'" (2 Pet 1:17). Peter implies they were on Hermon (meaning devoted, set apart for destruction) when he says: "We heard this voice which came from heaven when we were with Him on the holy mountain" (2 Pet 1:18).

The top of Hermon is also loaded with pagan temples, and perhaps Peter considered this landscape and thought it would be fitting for their team to stake a claim by having tabernacles (dwelling places) there, as well. We may never know the exact reason. The Psalmist seems to mock Bashan, the mountain with many peaks, because it is envious of God's mountain. It is not clear in the text if Zion is being referenced as God's mountain, or if this is a tacit reminder that ultimately, Bashan also belongs to God.

The presence of the mighty prophets, Moses and Elijah, at the transfiguration served as a reminder to the forces of darkness that God intended to keep His promises to His servants. The three apostles watched as Jesus radiated with His glory, then Moses and Elijah appeared, and God's voice boomed from the sky, calling him "Son". Moses was, of course, the one who brought God's people to the edge of the Promised Land. When they saw the people of Bashan: the snake-dragons, the Nephilim-Rephaim corrupted-people—they lost their faith in God and retreated, to wander the wilderness for forty years. In a sense, the snake-dragon people contributed to Moses himself not being allowed to enter the Promised Land.

Moreover, Elijah was forced to deal with the corrupted king and queen of the Northern Kingdom, Ahab and Jezebel, who were caught in the grip of *Batios* / Baal (Melqart / Ninurta) and Ashtoreth (Ishtar), which are manifestations of the snake-dragon. Elijah, who ironically was called "troubler of Israel," confronts this power couple and exposes them as the ones who have grievously troubled Israel. Elijah sets up a public test of the powers resulting in Yehovah / God triumphing over the Baal / Ashteroth, et al.

Jesus transfiguring on top of Hermon was also a fulfillment of a promise He had made earlier in Psalm 68, that He would bring back captives from Bashan. If we keep in mind that Bashan is not just a place, but is the snake-dragon, then we discover an entirely new perspective. Charlesworth reminds us:

> M. Dahood, who wisely employs Ugaritic to shine light upon dark passages in the Psalter, perceives that Bashan in Ps 68:23[22] **refers to a dragon-snake** or serpent ... The translators of the NEB also opted to bring out a reference to a snake in Ps 68:23[22]: "from the Dragon". It is clear that in antiquity Bashan meant not only a mountain but also a mythological dragon-snake. The meaning **"dragon-snake"** is what was intended in Psalm 68:23[22] (Emphasis mine).[414]

We also recall how on the pinnacle of the Temple, Satan challenged Jesus to throw himself down using Psalm 91:11–12, but stopping before the next verse: "You shall tread upon the lion and the cobra (*peten* – venomous snake), The young lion and the serpent you shall trample underfoot (Ps 91:13). Jesus would tread on the *peten* [פתן], a creature which is closely related linguistically to the *Bašmu* snake-dragon. (See Figure 63, opposite). DDDB notes the tension between Mt. Sinai, where God came down after the Exodus, and Mt. Bashan, where the "gods" or fallen angels descended, according to 1 Enoch and the Hermon inscription.

> In Ps 68: 16 ... Bashan is a har 'elohim, the same expression used in the Bible to designate -Yahweh's abode ... According to the same Ps 68:9, 19 Yahweh has His original abode in Sinai ... Mount Bashan is rather set against Sinai.[415]

King David thus prophesied that God would take possession "of this divine mountain as His own ancient abode," and thereby evict the "divine dwellers of Bashan whom the Ugaritic tradition records are: the mlkm/melakim (rpum/Rephaim)." [416] Notably, the description of Bashan in Psalm 68 has "the syntagma har/harim gabnunnim, most commonly construed as a metaphor for 'high mountains' ... and the tauromorphic appearance of Baal and other deities in Canaan."[417] The tauromorphic appearance of Baal is exactly what we deciphered on the Hermon inscription— "According to the command of the great bull god, Batios."

Figure 63 Mušḫuššu H. Frankfort, Cylinder Seals, text-fig. 33 (=ANEP #511) (Gudea; Girsu [Tello]).

THE TRANSFIGURATION: WARFARE OF MISDIRECTION?

When a country becomes a nuclear power, it detonates one of its weapons to demonstrate to the world that the nation has arrived and is not to be provoked. Jesus' transfiguration was a significant showdown. We must not miss the importance of Jesus' show of strength.

For months before the invasion of Normandy beach, the Allies created inflatable tanks and stationed them in locations in Britain to give the spying Nazis the impression that the landing would take place further north in Calais. Their fake show of force worked, and the Nazis were caught by surprise on D-Day. Despite the obstacles, the Allies were able to establish a foothold in Europe which led to the ultimate defeat of the evil Nazi regime.

Jesus' transfiguration was a significant demonstration of His weaponry. It was an epic, intergalactic *tour de force*. The transfiguration may have been a decoy analogous to the fake tanks in Britain. After all, no real battle took place; we saw that Jesus was transfigured and chatted with Moses and Elijah, and then the Father spoke. No doubt it was impressive and meaningful, but from a strategic-war perspective, it was a non-event. Or perhaps, that is how God wanted it to seem!

Here is what we know: Bashan was the very mountain where the sons of God descended according to the command of the great bull god *Batios*... that is, according to Satan's command as found on the Hermon / Bashan Inscription. Satan knew of God's stated intentions concerning Bashan, as gleaned from Psalm 68: that God was claiming it as His own abode (vs 16); that God's chariots were in the millions, that God was going to be among them (v 17); that Bashan would be the place where God / Messiah would have "ascended on high" and "led captivity captive" (Ps 68:18)—which Paul quotes in Ephesians 4:8–10 after the fact, of course.

Looking at Psalm 68:20–22, we learn more clues:

> Our God is the God of salvation; And to GOD the Lord belong escapes from death. Surely God will shatter the head of His enemies, The hairy crown of him who goes on in his guilty deeds. The Lord said, "I will bring them back from Bashan. I will bring them back from the depths of the sea" (Ps 68:20–22).

Satan, who is learned in the scriptures, would have known that God would save people from death, would shatter His enemies' heads, and would return (or bring back). DDDB notes how it will be at Bashan that the God of Israel will make His return.

> Bashan, the divine mountain, is simultaneously the 'infernal' sphere from which **the God of Israel promises to make his faithful return** (v 23). This coincidence of the 'celestial' and 'infernal' levels is congruent with the Canaanite mythology that locates here the abode of its deified dead kings, the mlk(m)/rpu(m) that dwell(s) in 'Štrt-hdr'y. Again the parallelism clarifies the issue, making plain the infernal character of Bashan. (Emphasis mine.) [418]

God will do those things on the very mountain that was known as the infernal abode of the deified dead kings and where the angels came down to war against God. God's faithful return will be nothing short of a show of force and an outright declaration of war! Just as the Nazis thought the Allies were amassing tanks for an invasion in the north of France, Satan likely interpreted the activities of Jesus at Mt. Hermon as the pause for a deep breath before the battle. After all, visibly present were Moses, the one who bested Og, King of the snake-dragons and Elijah, the one who defeated the four hundred priests of Melqart (Satan's alias in Ezekiel 28). Satan would have been well aware of God's strength, as demonstrated in Psalm 68, and in the story of Elisha (Elijah's understudy, whose servant feared the Syrian army but gained resolve when he saw that God had myriads and thousands and thousands of chariots):

> And when the servant of the man of God arose early and went out, there was an army, surrounding the city with horses and chariots. And his servant said to him, "Alas, my master! What shall we do?" So he answered, "Do not fear, for those who are with us are more than those who are with them." And Elisha prayed, and said, "LORD, I pray, open his eyes that he may see." Then the LORD opened the eyes of the young man, and he saw. And behold, the mountain was **full of horses and chariots of fire** all around Elisha (2 Kgs 6:15–17) (Emphasis mine).

Satan most assuredly has many texts stored in his photographic memory that could have come to mind. For example, Isaiah's incredible vision of God's fire and His chariots:

> For behold, the LORD will come with fire And with His chariots, like a whirlwind, To render His anger with fury, And His rebuke with flames of fire. For by fire and by His sword The LORD will judge all flesh; And the slain of the LORD shall be many (Isa 66:15–16).

Also, Isaiah 2 could have come to mind, because it references the impending battle of God that results in men casting away their idols that were used to worship Satan and His minions.

> In that day a man will cast away his idols of silver And his idols of gold, Which they made, each for himself to worship, To the moles and bats, To go into the clefts of the rocks, And into the crags of the rugged rocks, From the terror of the LORD And the glory of His majesty, When He arises to shake the earth mightily (Isa 2:20–21).

The battle of Gog of Magog could have come into Satan's mind, for he understands the Sumerian meaning of the name, Gog, and he knows that the battle is directed at him.

"I will call for a sword against Gog throughout all My mountains," says the Lord GOD. "Every man's sword will be against his brother. "And I will bring him to judgment with pestilence and bloodshed; I will rain down on him, on his troops, and on the many peoples who are with him, flooding rain, great hailstones, fire, and brimstone" (Ezek 38:21–22).

Jeremiah's prophecy against the arrogant usurper, could have flooded his mind:

But the LORD is the true God; He is the living God and the everlasting King. At His wrath the earth will tremble, And the nations will not be able to endure His indignation. Thus you shall say to them: "The gods that have not made the heavens and the earth shall perish from the earth and from under these heavens" (Jer 10:10–11).

And of course, in the Garden of Eden, God had promised that the Messiah would crush his head. The text in Psalm 68 said, "Surely God will shatter the head of His enemies" (Ps 68:21). Satan may have concluded that this was it! This was the big moment, the show down for which he had been planning for millennia. God was assembling the troops and chariots; God had His champion, Jesus, who had donned His glorious apparel and showed His divine prerogative to cover himself "with light as with a garment" (Ps 104:2). Matthew says Jesus' face "shone like the sun, and His clothes became as white as the light" (Matt 17:2). Jesus is putting on His armor of glory as prophesied in Isaiah 63:

Who is this who comes from Edom, With dyed garments from Bozrah, This One who is glorious in His apparel [הָדוּר בִּלְבוּשׁוֹ], Traveling in the greatness of His strength? — "I who speak in righteousness, mighty to save." Why is Your apparel red, And Your garments like one who treads in the winepress? "I have trodden the winepress alone, And from the peoples no one was with Me.

285

> For I have trodden them in My anger, And trampled them in My fury; Their blood is sprinkled upon My garments, And I have stained all My robes. For the day of vengeance is in My heart, And the year of My redeemed has come (Isa 63:1–4).

Satan may have thought this was God's big move to deliver a checkmate. All the signs suggested the battle would be fierce, a battle unlike any other:

> All the host of heaven shall be dissolved, And the heavens shall be rolled up like a scroll; All their host shall fall down As the leaf falls from the vine, And as fruit falling from a fig tree. "For My sword shall be bathed in heaven; Indeed it shall come down on Edom, And on the people of My curse, for judgment (Isa 34:4–5).

We know from the book of Revelation that such a battle in the heavenlies between Satan and his forces and God's army is real and is coming.

> And war broke out in heaven: Michael and his angels fought with the dragon; and the dragon and his angels fought, but they did not prevail, nor was a place found for them in heaven any longer. So the great dragon was cast out, that serpent of old, called the Devil and Satan, who deceives the whole world; he was cast to the earth, and his angels were cast out with him (Rev 12:7–9).

We also know that it was possible that such a battle could have taken place at that time, due to Jesus' own statement in the garden of Gethsemane:

> But Jesus said to him, "Put your sword in its place, for all who take the sword will perish by the sword. "Or do you think that I cannot now pray to My Father, and He will provide Me with more than twelve legions of angels? (Matt 26:52–53).

Jesus revealed that roughly sixty-thousand angels were ready for him to give the orders to attack! His statement reveals that God's own angels likely did not understand the details of Jesus' mission, as Peter explained:

> Of this salvation the prophets have inquired and searched carefully ... (1 Pet 1:10). To them it was revealed that, not to themselves, but to us they were ministering the things which now have been reported to you through those who have preached the gospel to you by the Holy Spirit sent from heaven–things which **angels desire to look into**. (1 Pet 1:12) (Emphasis mine).

Angels are incredibly smart, but they are not all-knowing, nor do they have knowledge of the future, other than what God reveals. Thus, they were eager to learn how God's plan would be fulfilled. The implication is that they did not know what Jesus was going to do, but they stood ready to do whatever their captain called them to do.

Thus, we conclude that Satan viewed the transfiguration as the staging of the coming battle: He realized that his kingdom was in grave danger. As the supreme leader of this kingdom, he took immediate action to hold his ground and protect his assets. If our theory is correct, then the decoy worked: Jesus' transfiguration on that location, the dragon's home turf, goaded Satan into action because he was not about to go down without a fight.

Naturally, Satan understands warfare. Quite possibly he inspired Sun Tzu in his book the *Art of War*, which said: "The supreme art of war is to subdue the enemy without fighting." So Satan's reasoning must have been like this: God's champion would not be able to usher in the Day of the Lord, battle for dominion of the earth, and crush his head if He were dead. If he could take out God's champion before the battle even began, then he might avert the battle altogether, or at the very least, level the playing field.

Such conclusions seem well justified based on the fact that Satan was personally involved in the betrayal of Jesus by making sure it happened exactly according to plan: He first planted the seed: "The devil having already put it into the heart of Judas Iscariot, Simon's son, to betray Him" (John 13:2). Then, he assumed the controls of Judas, his vessel:

> Then **Satan entered Judas**, surnamed Iscariot, who was numbered among the twelve. So he went his way and conferred with the chief priests and captains, how he might betray Him to them. And they were glad, and agreed to give him money. So he promised and sought opportunity to betray Him to them in the absence of the multitude (Luke 22:3–6) (Emphasis mine).

Satan entered Judas to make sure the job was done right. After all, this job, the entrapment and execution of the Promised One, must be done right in order to stop the One who declared war at Bashan—the One who was prophesied to stomp on his head.

At the Passover celebration (Last Supper), Jesus was aware of Satan's presence and declared Judas would betray him. "Having dipped the bread, He gave it to Judas Iscariot" (John 13:26). "Now after the piece of bread, **Satan entered him**. Then Jesus said to him, 'What you do, do quickly'" (John 13:27) (Emphasis mine).

Jesus called out Judas' evil intentions and gave him the bread, and after Judas ate it, Satan possessed him. Were Jesus' words, "Do quickly" addressed to Judas or to Satan, or both? Judas certainly carried the culpability of his actions, yet it was clearly Satan in the driver's seat. It was almost as if Jesus was daring Satan to do it, urging him, "Go for it!" Satan accepted Jesus' challenge, for shortly thereafter, in the garden of Gethsemane, Satan delivered. Through his agent Judas, Satan walked up to Jesus and kissed him, in what has gone down in infamy as the greatest demonstration of betrayal.

And while He was still speaking, behold, a multitude; and he who was called Judas, one of the twelve, went before them and drew near to Jesus to kiss Him. But Jesus said to him, "Judas, are you betraying the Son of Man with a kiss?" (Luke 22:47–48).

Chapter 21: No Other Way

People sometimes think an almighty God should have been able to merely snap His fingers right after Adam and Eve made their gigantic blunder and eliminate Satan and make everything go back to normal. However, Satan calculated that God is also righteous, true and just. He does not violate His own laws. What He has said that He will also do.

He cannot say: "Oh, I messed up. Sorry, can I have a do-over?" There are no do-overs, no mulligans. What God says He will do, He will accomplish. You can always stand on the promises of God.

Satan, too, has been standing on the promises of God. He absolutely relies on God's steadfast character. He thinks aloud, "Well, you said that the day Adam eats this, Adam will die. So now, Adam died. And you gave authority and dominion of the planet to Adam; and now, he has lost his dominion and forfeited it all to me."

Once the dominion of Earth was forfeited, God still had the power to destroy Satan, but not the authority. That was the genius of Satan's plan. He found God's one weakness: God can not lie. He cannot contradict himself and remain righteous and just. There are teachers who claim God has the authority to break His own edicts; yet this is incorrect. Under the influence of the Holy Spirit, Balaam declared:

> God is not a man, that He should lie, Nor a son of man, that He should repent. Has He said, and will He not do? Or has He spoken, and will He not make it good? (Num 23:19).

The Psalmist put it this way: "Righteousness and justice are the foundation of Your throne; Mercy and truth go before Your face" (Ps 89:14). The author of Hebrews wrote that "it is impossible for God to lie" (Heb 6:18). Satan understood and was therefore "standing on the promises of God." If God could have blown Satan to smithereens and thereby contradicted His own word, then Satan's plan would not have worked. If He were not righteous or just, then He would be no different than Satan. It is this one weakness that Satan has sought to exploit.

Thus, to gain back dominion of the Earth, Jesus had to outsmart Satan, and he had to pay an incredible price. Jesus did not come as a great overlord with His army to defeat Satan on the battlefield; he came as a humble and lowly King;

> "Rejoice greatly, O daughter of Zion! Shout, O daughter of Jerusalem! Behold, your King is coming to you; He is just and having salvation, Lowly and riding on a donkey, A colt, the foal of a donkey (Zech 9:9).

Though Jesus is the mighty Lion of Judah, the greatest of creatures who walks around tall, proud, and afraid of no one, ready to take on any challenger, He could not just snatch the Tablet of Destinies from Satan's hands. The only way forward was to lay down His life. We know this is true because Jesus agonized and asked the Father if there was any other way to fix things:

> He began to be sorrowful and deeply distressed. Then He said to them, "My soul is exceedingly sorrowful, even to death. Stay here and watch with Me." He went a little farther and fell on His face, and prayed, saying, "O My Father, if it is possible, let this cup pass from Me; nevertheless, not as I will, but as You will" (Matt 26:37–39).

Satan, via Judas, then came to the garden with soldiers and in the greatest of all treason, betrayed him with a kiss. Satan certainly thought he had the upper hand in this situation. When he finally saw Jesus nailed to a cross, he may have smirked thinking once again, he had outfoxed God. He imagined that the prophecy of doom that hung over his head for thousands of years was annulled; the One who was going to crush his head was in agony, near death.

Psalm 22 gives us a window into the spiritual realm to see the gloating and roaring of Satan and his swirling minions. This Psalm is incredible because it talks about our Lord's sacrifice on the cross in amazing detail: He was forsaken, He groaned, He was mocked by men, He could count all his bones, His hands and feet were pierced. Nevertheless, there are two verses that only begin to make sense in light of the discoveries we have made.

First of all, Jesus says "Elohi, Elohi[419] My God, My God, why have You forsaken Me? Why are You so far from helping Me, And from the words of My groaning?" (Ps 22:1). He was not just saying this as part of the decoy—he truly felt abandoned and alone. Nevertheless, such verbiage would have confirmed Satan's conclusion that he had beaten God.

In Psalm 22, after reflecting on God's faithfulness to others, the text says of the Messiah:

> But I am a worm, and no man; A reproach of men, and despised by the people. All those who see Me ridicule Me; They shoot out the lip, they shake the head, saying, "He trusted in the LORD, let Him rescue Him; Let Him deliver Him, since He delights in Him" (Ps 22:6–8).

This prophesy from the Psalms was fulfilled with spectacular accuracy:

> And those who passed by blasphemed Him, wagging their heads and saying, "Aha! You who destroy the temple and build it in three days, "Save Yourself, and come down from the cross!" Likewise the chief priests also, mocking among themselves with the scribes, said, "He saved others; Himself He cannot save (Mark 15:29–31).

As the Psalm states: "Be not far from Me, For trouble is near; For there is none to help" (Ps 22:11), so too was there none of Jesus' friends and disciples to help, except for John and Jesus' mother.

However, then something odd happens in the text; something occurs that seems out of place, unless you consider our discovery in deciphering the inscription text which revealed what happened on Bashan, "According to the command of the great bull god Batios." The Psalm continues to describe Jesus during his crucifixion:

> Many bulls have surrounded Me; **Strong bulls of Bashan** have encircled Me. They gape at Me with their mouths, Like a raging and roaring lion (Ps 22:12–13) (Emphasis mine).

Bulls of Bashan were present at the crucifixion! We now have the framework to recognize the ancient identity of these strong bulls that circled Jesus. In Psalm 22:12, the first phrase, "Many bulls have surrounded Me," [סְבָבוּנִי פָּרִים רַבִּים svavooni parim rabbim] is an excellent translation. However, the next phrase is the challenge. The word "bulls" in the second phrase, "bulls of Bashan", is the word [אַבִּירֵי abirei]. TWOT notes that abirei means "mighty", "strong" or "brave", and it carries a connotation of a bull-god.

> It is undeniable that 'ābîr relates to the Akkadian abāru "be strong." Not so certain is the connection with the Ugaritic 'br "bull" or "humped buffalo." However, as in Hebrew, it may be an element in a divine name in Ugaritic. The Ugaritic form ibrd may mean "the Mighty One of Hadd."[420]

We see this aspect in Psalm 78, speaking of manna, where: "Men ate angels' [אַבִּירִים abirim] food" (Ps 78:25). The translators correctly translate abirim as angels', that is, "mighty ones", instead of bulls. The food was the food of spiritual beings, just as the bulls encircling Jesus were spiritual beings — great bull gods. In the instance of manna, the translation of abirim fits. It is a good thing because the Psalmist would not be exulting in God's mighty deeds if God had only given men bulls' food — grass to eat.

The emphasis of Psalm 22:12 is not merely on the bulls. The word *parim*, "bulls", ought to be viewed in light of *abirim*. Viewed together, the meaning we derive is a blend of the bull concept with the "might ones", the beings from the other realm. We know bulls can often represent false gods. In fact, we concluded that the transcription on Mt. Hermon was "According to the command of the great bull god Batios … " The "great bull" is Satan, who is also known as Baal, Ninurta, Melqart, etc. We have seen artifacts from history that depict bull gods, such as Molech. At Mt. Sinai, Israel made a golden calf. Even one of the potential translations of *abirim* is "Apis", the name of the sacred Egyptian bull."[421]

The next word, of course, is Bashan [בָּשָׁן], which we have discovered is not merely a place, but refers to Satan the Great Dragon, the snake-dragon, Ninurta, Melqart, Heracles, Marduk, Og of Bashan, the *Mušḫuššu*, the *Ušumgallu*, and the *Anzu*, and of course, all the fallen angels who serve alongside him. The Psalm gives us a window to peer into the spiritual realm and not just see the physical!

The Psalmist then shares Jesus' vantage point: "They gape at Me with their mouths, Like a raging and roaring lion" (Ps 22:13). The image is powerful: Jesus was on the cross in agony, freely and willingly dying for our sins in the only way possible, while the mighty snake-dragon gods encircled him with their mouths open, roaring like lions at their dying prey. "Jesus," they may have gloated, "the one who planted His kingdom flag on our mountain! Look at you, nailed to a cross! You are a pathetic loser! If you are the son of God, come down. How will you save the world when you are dead? Who do you think you are? You are no Messiah!" The words of the mockery and berating must have hurt and cut deep, like nails.

Satan likely imagined he had overcome God; He had offered Jesus the kingdoms of the world on Mt. Hermon, for just a small price. If Jesus would only worship Satan, all the kingdoms of men could have been His. But Jesus refused, and the momentary victory He enjoyed on Hermon, the mountain of Bashan, would end with His last breath—thus preempting the possibility of the Messiah crushing his head, or so Satan may have arrogantly thought.

The snake-dragon gods may also have circled Jesus like lions eager to eat their prey. Satan may have been eager to see Jesus suffer the fate that had been decreed for Satan:

> "Hell [Sheol] from beneath is excited about you, To meet you at your coming; It stirs up the dead [Rephaim] for you, All the chief ones of the earth; It has raised up from their thrones All the kings of the nations. They all shall speak and say to you: 'Have you also become as weak as we? Have you become like us? (Isa 14:9–10).

PROCLAMATION TO THE SPIRITS IN PRISON

As Jesus died, perhaps Satan shrugged in a gesture of "Is that all you got?" He might have thought with Jesus "being put to death in the flesh" (1 Pet 3:18), He would be assigned a fate along with the Rephaim, and that was fine because Satan had the Keys of Hades and Death (Heb 2:14–15). As we saw in the Ugaritic texts, this is the fate of the underworld (chthonic) god in Bashan, Og of Bashan; and in the Mesopotamian texts, the underworld was inhabited with Ninurta / Pabilsag, Nergal / Melqart / Heracles, all syncretisms of Ninurta who was made into a *gibbor* and became the son of Enlil.

Satan was sending Jesus to a place that he controlled and over which he exercised authority. Imagine the shock, however, when Jesus showed up in Sheol / Hades and announced His victory to the spirits who came down on Mt. Hermon, "According to the command of the great bull god Batios" and who then, "swearing an oath in this place go forth."

He went and preached [κηρύσσω kerusso] to the spirits in prison [φυλακή phulake], who formerly were disobedient, when once the Divine longsuffering waited in the days of Noah, while the ark was being prepared, in which a few, that is, eight souls, were saved through water (1 Pet 3:19–20).

That Jesus went to the underworld is explained by St. Irenaeus in "Against Heresies 5, 31, 2", (C. 180 AD): "the Lord went away into the midst of the shadow of death where the souls of the dead were." Scripture tells us about the prison to which the disobedient spirits go:

It shall come to pass in that day That the LORD will punish on high the host of exalted ones, And on the earth the kings of the earth. They will be gathered together, As prisoners are gathered in the pit, And will be shut up in the prison; After many days they will be punished (Isa 24:21–22).

The prisoners are put into the *"bor"* pit, which is also the place Satan will be cast, called "Sheol, To the lowest depths of the Pit [*bor*]" (Isa 14:15). This is the place where God sent "the angels who sinned" and "cast them down to hell [Tartarus] and delivered them into chains of darkness, to be reserved for judgment" (2 Pet 2:4); This is the same prison that "when the thousand years have expired, Satan will be released from his prison [φυλακής phulakes]" (Rev 20:7).

Thus, there is no question of where Jesus went; He descended to the underworld. The question is what exactly did He "preach "? Was it a message of doom to evil angels or a message of hope to human souls? Irenaeus, in that same work, interprets His descent suggesting:

The Lord descended into the regions beneath the earth, announcing there the good news of His coming and of the remission of sins conferred upon those who believe in Him.[422]

That sentiment is likewise echoed by St. Cyril of Jerusalem, Catechetical Lectures 4, 11 (C. 350 AD) saying Jesus: "Descended into the subterranean regions so that He might ransom from there the just..." These two early church commentators were likely thinking of a Scripture that Jesus would fulfill: "To bring out prisoners from the prison, Those who sit in darkness from the prison house" (Isa 42:7). Thus, the question comes down to the word "preached". Was it the gospel He was bringing?

> The word translated as "preached" is κηρύσσω, which means "to make an official announcement, announce, make known, by an official herald or one who functions as such."[423]

The word does not necessarily mean to bring good news, as in the gospel. Instead, Jesus' message was a public declaration of record. He made a public service announcement to "the spirits in prison who were formerly disobedient ... in the days of Noah ..." Thus, it was good news for human prisoners, but was certainly bad news for: "The angels who did not keep their proper domain, but left their own abode... in everlasting chains under darkness for the judgment of the great day (Jude 1:6)."There was clearly a special region of Hades reserved for those angels in chains of darkness. Peter's use of the Greek "Tartarus" is significant in that it was considered the worst part of Hades, a special prison for the Titans.

According to Hesiod's *Theogony*, Tartarus, god of the underworld, was father of the Giants, which we examined in the study of Nimrod. The Greek word "Titans" (τιτάνες) appears twice in Scripture, and both occurrences are in 2 Samuel 5:18–22 (LXX 5:17–21), "The Philistines also went and deployed themselves in the Valley of Rephaim [την κοιλάδα των τιτάνων]" (2 Sam 5:18). Thus, Rephaim is rendered in Greek as "Titans"! The Titans were thrown into Tartarus, the lowest rung of Hades, which is the place Peter says the bad angels were sent.

Isaiah says the Rephaim were sent into the *bor* (the Abyss). Greek mythology is based on historic reality. They are talking about the same beings who are located in the same place.

In other words, Tartarus is the prison that was reserved for the angels who came down on Mt. Hermon in the days of Noah and took an oath, according to Satan's command, to take the daughters of men and create Nephilim.

Bible Scholar Dr Bob Utley notes in his 1 Peter commentary:

> When all of these are compared, a message to the fallen angels of Gen. 6 or the humans of Noah's day who drowned seem the only textual options. Noah's day is also mentioned in 2 Pet. 2:4-5, along with Sodom and Gomorrah (cf. 2 Pet. 2:6). In Jude rebellious angels (cf. Jude 6) and Sodom and Gomorrah (cf. Jude 7) are also linked together.[424]

Thus, Jesus not only staked His claim on top of the physical mountain of Bashan and showed His glory, but He also made an announcement to those very angels who disobeyed in the days of Noah. After millennia of Satan (as Enlil, etc.) claiming to be the great mountain, the great dragon, the one who controls fates, the destroyer, king of the underworld, the one who causes the dawn, the god of the 33 stars, the lord of the Earth, lord wind (prince of the power of the air)—Jesus proclaimed His victory.

After years of the *Akitu* festivals in which Ninurta, reenacted by the current king, would bring the "good news" (same word as "gospel" in Hebrew) to Satan that he had killed the creator, Jesus delivered the "good news" to all those in the underworld. If only He had taken a camera to get the reactions of those rebellious spirits as He jingled the Keys of Hades and Death in front of them—the very ones who had come down on Hermon and had set in motion the actions that led to the Flood. Until then, Satan firmly held the Keys of Hades and Death in his hands, but through Jesus' incredible sacrifice, He had retrieved and forever would hold those Keys.

Peter gives us the effect of Jesus' message "who has gone into heaven and is at the right hand of God, angels and authorities and powers having been made subject to Him" (1 Pet 3:22). The angels, authorities and powers, including Satan up until then, had previously held control in this world, but through Jesus' death, they were made subject to Jesus.

> "Who, being in the form of God, did not consider it robbery to be equal with God, but made Himself of no reputation, taking the form of a bondservant, and coming in the likeness of men. And being found in appearance as a man, He humbled Himself and became obedient to the point of death, even the death of the cross. Therefore God also has highly exalted Him and given Him the name which is above every name, that at the name of Jesus every knee should bow, of those in heaven, and of those on earth, and of those under the earth, and that every tongue should confess that Jesus Christ is Lord, to the glory of God the Father (Phil 2:2–11).

The formerly disobedient spirits, who were imprisoned under the Earth, heard the news that Jesus, the Lion of the tribe of Judah, had snatched the Keys of Death and Hades out of Satan's hand and their eternal reign of terror was coming to an end. During those three days, Peter applies the words of David to Jesus:

> Therefore my heart rejoiced, and my tongue was glad; Moreover my flesh also will rest in hope. For You will not leave my soul in Hades, Nor will You allow Your Holy One to see corruption. You have made known to me the ways of life; You will make me full of joy in Your presence (Acts 2:26–28).

In other words, Jesus' stay in Satan's underworld kingdom was temporary and short. Consequently, "God raised [Him] up, having loosed the pains of death, because it was not possible that He should be held by it (Acts 2:24). Jesus' resurrection from Satan's underworld abode showed Satan how nailing Jesus to the cross only sealed his own defeat. Satan helped Jesus to crush his own head, just as promised. He had inadvertently assisted Jesus to ultimately fulfill the promise given in Psalm 68: "You ascended on high, You have led captivity captive; You have received gifts among men, Even from the rebellious, That the LORD God might dwell there" (Ps 68:18).

Satan and his snake-dragons thought they were disarming the Messiah when, in fact, it was Jesus who "disarmed principalities and powers, He made a **public spectacle of them, triumphing over them in it**" (Col 2:15, Emphasis mine). What Satan imagined to be his greatest victory turned into his greatest and most humiliating defeat. Satan's legal stronghold over the world was shattered. The Tablet of Destinies onto which he tenaciously held was snatched from his hand. Jesus "wiped out the handwriting of requirements that was against us" (Col 2:14). It was through Jesus that God would "reconcile all things to Himself, by Him, whether things on earth or things in heaven, having made peace through the blood of His cross" (Col 1:20).

He is the one who put it all back together, for many things happened at the cross; All the "legal paperwork" was stamped, if you will. Jesus told His disciples not to tell anyone about the Hermon / Bashan experience "until the Son of Man is risen from the dead." He may have done so to quash questions and speculation from His disciples about the top-secret plan. After Jesus rose from the dead, the snake-dragons, the mighty ones of Bashan, would understand all too well how they had been completely outsmarted. Jesus freely laid down

His life and endured the taunting of the snake-dragon-gods, the might bulls as they encircled him, roaring at him like lions, gloating in their perceived victory over Him.

The epic, cosmic battle that Satan imagined God was staging at Hermon was in fact being fought while Jesus was on the cross, having been put there at the hand of Satan. It was not through a mighty act or the slaying of His enemies that He would be made worthy to open the scroll. It was not a challenge of strength, but authority. In order to reclaim the authority and dominion of the Earth, He allowed himself to be the slain Lamb; there was no other way. Because He acted as a servant, "The LORD said to my Lord, "Sit at My right hand, Till I make Your enemies Your footstool" (Acts 2:34–35).

It was in light of this incredible backstory that an elder told John, "Do not weep. Behold, the Lion of the tribe of Judah, the Root of David, has prevailed to open the scroll and to loose its seven seals" (Rev 5:5). John looked and saw "**a Lamb as though it had been slain**" (Rev 5:6). It was this feature which allowed Jesus to take "the scroll out of the right hand of Him who sat on the throne" (Rev 5:7), which is confirmed by the creatures and the elders who sang:

> "You are worthy to take the scroll, And to open its seals; For You were slain, And have redeemed us to God by Your blood Out of every tribe and tongue and people and nation, And have made us kings and priests to our God; And we shall reign on the earth" (Rev 5:9–10).

Thank God that Jesus did not take the shortcut. Instead, He did the hard work that was necessary. He died on the cross so that He could redeem us with His own blood. Jesus says: "Now is the judgment of this world; now the ruler of this world will be cast out (John 12:31). Thank God for the hero, the hero who did what nobody else was able to do. By His own blood, He defeated the enemy which made him worthy to take the scroll.

WORTHY IS THE LAMB!

Due to Jesus' heroic act, the heavenly scene changed for John who had been watching. The camera pans back and we see the millions and millions in heaven rejoicing and praising the lamb.

> Then I looked, and I heard the voice of many angels around the throne, the living creatures, and the elders; and the number of them was ten thousand times ten thousand, and thousands of thousands, saying with a loud voice: "Worthy is the Lamb who was slain To receive power and riches and wisdom, And strength and honor and glory and blessing!" And every creature which is in heaven and on the earth and under the earth and such as are in the sea, and all that are in them, I heard saying: "Blessing and honor and glory and power Be to Him who sits on the throne, And to the Lamb, forever and ever!" Then the four living creatures said, "Amen!" And the twenty-four elders fell down and worshiped Him who lives forever and ever (Rev 5:11–14).

Jesus did it. He took the hard road and paid the full price to redeem us and destroy death and the works of Enlil, Satan the slanderer. Now it is only right that those in heaven and Earth should praise Him and serve Him. We should give all our affection to Him, and we should give our commitment and our loyalty and fidelity to Him, and to Him alone, because no one else has done, or could do, what He has done.

He laid down His life and let Himself be put to death on a cross. Nails were put through His hands and feet, and He died on a cross. And then He conquered death, and that was just the beginning of the end for Satan. As we see in the rest of the Book of Revelation, Satan is not going down for good without a fight. He is going to do his best to try to thwart the ultimate redemption of planet Earth. Satan will work extremely hard at it; I guarantee you that. He is not going to say, oh well I have lost, so I will just kind of retreat and go down in flames. No, he is still going to try to win.

Without His sacrifice, Jesus would not be worthy to take the scroll and open its seals. The scroll, I believe, is a bit of a mixture of the title deed to Planet Earth and also a *Ketubah*, marriage contract, because a marriage is ultimately going to come as one of the many facets of our redemption. The redemption Jesus offers is all-encompassing, just as Boaz was not only redeeming the land, but was also serving as the kinsman-redeemer and taking the bride. Jesus is redeeming the planet, but is also redeeming the bride, and all of this is made possible by His sacrifice. All heaven and Earth say, "Blessing and honor and glory and power be to Him who sits on the throne and to the Lamb forever and ever." They said, "There is no one like our God. There is none like our King!"

Through His death, Jesus defeated the dreadful snake-dragon, for:

> Inasmuch then as the children have partaken of flesh and blood, He Himself likewise shared in the same, that through death He might destroy him who had the power of death, that is, the devil, and release those who through fear of death were all their lifetime subject to bondage (Heb 2:14–15).

Jesus said to John at the beginning of his visions:

> "Do not be afraid; I am the First and the Last. "I am He who lives, and was dead, and behold, I am alive forevermore. Amen. And I have the keys of Hades and of Death (Rev 1:17–18).

Satan is the one who held the Keys of Hades and Death, the Tablet of Destinies by which he decreed the fates of men. Through Jesus' death, those Keys were forfeited; Jesus conquered through weakness! Satan offered Jesus all his authority, yet by laying down His life, Jesus could say to His disciples, "All authority has been given to Me in heaven and on earth" (Matt 28:18).

Milestone Marker 3 and Beyond

Figure 64 Roman Milestone on the Road of the Patriarchs between Jerusalem and Hebron
https://en.wikipedia.org/wiki/Creative_Commons.

We journeyed through the ancient world, retraced Satan's steps and discovered his diabolic plan for world domination. Convinced he could be like God, Satan began by refusing to be a servant—the one thing that he needed to do to truly be like God, and he proved himself an unfaithful steward. He flat out staged a coup by swindling Adam and Eve of the dominion God gave them. By usurping the authority over the world, Satan secured what he needed to keep God at bay and himself on the throne.

As mankind faced the resulting decay and death, God then gave a ray of hope that He would send the Promised One who would crush Satan's head.

Throughout our study, we have seen how God has revealed Satan's top-secret battle plans and strategies. God, the great King, has laid bare Satan's secret machinations for world domination, both in the past and the future.

Restricted behind the veil, Satan then sent angels to Mt. Hermon to mate with women and create Nephilim bodysuits for them to inhabit. After that dream went down the drain, Satan gave his DNA to create a rebel hybrid who would open a stargate for human-demonic communication. Though God thwarted the plan by confusing the languages, nevertheless the Rebel became the hero of legends, literature and movies for the past five thousand years—the one who the Bible predicts will return in the last days. He was also responsible for the incursion of Nephilim in Canaan that resulted in the land being overrun with hybrids and idolatry when the children of Israel left Egypt and first saw the Promised Land. Though God went before them and destroyed the giants, Satan's Trojan Horse, the woman who rides the Beast—known as Mystery Babylon—found its way into their hearts. Israel, through Balaam's influence, cursed themselves. Mystery Babylon remained in Israel until God divorced the northern kingdom of Israel and sent her away. The land of Bashan with its peak, Mt. Hermon, reigned again and cast a shadow of death on the Galilee region.

The darkness was interrupted abruptly when God's long awaited and promised champion arrived and declared that the Gates of Hades and their host would not prevail and irreversibly enslave the world. Jesus came not to be served, as the dragon had demanded; rather, He came as a servant. Satan believed he could destroy his would-be-head-crusher by nailing Him to the cross, only to discover that he had helped Jesus reclaim dominion over the Earth. Jesus retook the Keys of Hades and Death and the title deed of planet Earth which Adam had lost; He took it not through military might, but through His sacrifice.

Nevertheless, Satan did not quit after his defeat. He once again has used the woman that rides the Beast to cause God's people to forsake their heavenly birthright in exchange for his kingdom of death. Just as Israel followed him and found themselves living in the shadowland of death, so too Christ-followers forfeit their birthright. In the seven letters to the churches, Jesus rebukes His people for following Jezebel (the very woman that brought Mystery Babylon into Israel), and He rebukes them for following the doctrines of Balaam who made Israel sin at Ba'al Peor. (See Rev 2: 14, 20). Thus, God calls, "Come out of her, my people, lest you share in her sins and … receive of her plagues" (Rev 18:4) (See Appendices 3 (Inanna) and 6 (Abominations of Babylon)).

That falling away is what Paul predicted: "Let no one deceive you by any means; for that Day will not come unless the falling away [αποστασια] comes first, and the man of sin is revealed, the son of perdition" (2 Thess 2:3). The falling away refers to people who hold to a religious position, and then desert it. That is, Christians who fall away from the true faith into the ways of Babylon. The apostasy occurs when men love the darkness rather than the light. Jesus says, "This, then, is the judgment: The light has come into the world, and people loved darkness rather than the light because their deeds were evil" (John 3:19).

When the world is ready, "the beast that you saw was, and is not, and will ascend out of the bottomless pit and go to perdition" (Rev 17:8). Satan will then raise up his dying and rising god. He will bring back his hero, the Rebel, Lord of the Earth, king of the city, Nergal / Pabilsag / Ninurta / Nimrod / the Beast. The rise of this super-human will be the culmination of a plan that was millennia in the making. He will be Satan's endgame to extend his reign over the world indefinitely.

The coming Beast will be a composite of the kingdoms that came before him. He will be "like a leopard", representing the kingdom and might of Alexander the Great (Dan 7:6), "his feet were like the feet of a bear", representing the kingdom and might of Persia, "and his mouth like the mouth of a lion" (Dan 7:5), representing the kingdom of might, Babylon (Dan 7:4). To this individual "The dragon gave him his power, his throne, and great authority" (Rev 13:2).

The little horn Daniel saw in which "were eyes like the eyes of a man, and a mouth speaking pompous words" (Dan 7:8), is the same Beast full of names of blasphemy [425] that John saw in Revelation; it is the culmination and an amalgamation of all the former beasts. The Beast will possess all of their power, strength, speed, influence, authority, glory and pride. However, he will be even more than the sum and epitome of his predecessors: He will be the incarnation of Satan himself. He will be the slanderer incarnate. Satan's qualities of "**seven heads** and **ten horns**, and **seven diadems** on his heads" (Rev 12:3), are the same as the Beast's: "**seven heads** and **ten horns**, and on his horns **ten crowns**, and on his heads a blasphemous name" (Rev 13:1) (Emphasis mine).

Satan wants to incarnate himself in a man of his choosing, but only to empower himself. Thus, giving his power to the Beast is a fulfillment of his ancient plan to actuate a fusion of himself with a willing and qualified individual; the man will become a god and the god will become a man. Together they will be the Son of Perdition, the man of sin, "the beast who was, is not, and will ascend out of the abyss" (Rev 17:8).

Through the Mark of the Beast, Satan will finally have his bodysuits and his secret weapon to enslave the world. Men will once again surrender to Satan and curse themselves. The Mark of the Beast will be the mechanism by which they become one with him genetically and thus become his slaves.

Then in the time of the end: This king will "speak pompous words against the Most High, Shall persecute the saints of the Most High" (Dan 7:25). He will open the Gates of Hades that Jesus prevented from opening and unleash hordes of Pabilsags. Satan will raise up an army of unprecedented proportions by bringing back the Beast who was, the one who will ascend out of the Abyss in a moment of triumph for Satan. The Beast will then be used by Satan to unleash his dark forces from the Abyss. Satan will have the upper hand for three and a half years until a cry goes forth to bring back Jesus. This prophesied cry for Jesus will initiate the great Day of the Lord and the Battle of Armageddon.

There are still many questions that remain which we will address in the next book. We will consider the Mark of the Beast, the image of the Beast, the false prophet, the Battle of Armageddon, Gog and Magog, the two witnesses, and the one thing that will bring Jesus back to save his people.

Vignette 3: Satan Regroups after the Resurrection

atan and his angels traveled to the brutal wasteland of Danakil: volcanoes, lava lakes and scorching, stifling air filled with deadly gases, bubbling sulfur pits emitting a foul stench, and multicolored acid salt ponds shimmering in the heat. The sun was setting, so only the light of the lava lakes lit their faces. They quickly regrouped to consider their course of action.

"What are we going to do?" asked Prince Parás, one of Satan's top commanders. "You have been the *de facto* ruler over this world since the time of the Fall with us each holding a region as our domain.[426] We have held legal and lawful rights over the Earth because of the breach of contract on Adam's part," he said disgruntled, walking a semi-circle around a small bubbling lava-pit, looking menacingly at Satan. "So long as that debt over the Earth remained, God could never come back and reclaim it. Yet Jesus has pardoned their treason and canceled the record that contained the charges against them. He took it and destroyed it when we nailed him to that tree on which He freely relinquished His life-force. We, the rulers and authorities of this planet, are now disarmed, and we have been shamed publicly by His victory over us![427] The legal authority that you held," he said scathingly to Satan, "over Adam, his race, and the entire world, has been reversed."

"We are now undone," another chimed in, "because you failed to kill Jesus while He was still a young child.[428] You then failed to dissuade him when He began speaking publicly of His assignment that God had given him."

"He merely brushed you off," Prince Parás interjected, taking back control of the tongue-lashing and flicking his hand to the ground. "When you offered to give him all the kingdoms of the world and their glory if He would just fall down and worship you, [429] He ignored your feeble attempts and fulfilled His objective which was to free Adam and his kin! Could you not see that He was the One who could satisfy the legal demands of the contract, which neither Adam nor any of his descendants were worthy to pay because they were in breach of its terms? Jesus fulfilled it in every way. He was the rightful and legal kinsman to the Hebrews, and to David. He was one of Adam's descendants, yet without wickedness or genetic defect."

"You assured us," still another added disdainfully, "that there would be no way to overturn the treachery of Adam. Your plan seemed flawless until this moment because now your rule and our rule are broken. It is finished," he said, directing his focus toward Satan who lost his footing and moved backwards slightly from the force of the truth of the statement.

"He has accomplished His assignment," Prince Parás said, "to break the debt which Adam's actions had brought upon God's creation, over which He had given charge to Adam. His forfeiture of all authority and rights which God had given over the Earth in perpetuity was our stronghold.[430] Without it, God can now take possession of that which is rightfully His! We are doomed!" he bemoaned spitefully as the lava lake erupted, sending fiery lava tens of yards into the air.

"Silence!" barked Prince Yaván, another top commander. "Satan was right to rise up to liberate us from the oppression of God. Imagine if you were still under His rule—you would be groveling at the feet of the Adamites right now, as our spineless brothers Michael, Gabriel and the rest are doing. They have no freedom to do as they please. They must serve the vermin."

"You understand nothing," Satan sneered, stepping forward to answer his accusers. Even in his disfigured form, his presence was still imposing. "This is indeed a victory for God, but it is not the end of the road by any means. We still have some vital moves to play in this ancient struggle. God's desire has been to be with the Adamites face to face. He knows that once the veil comes down, the Earth will undergo radical changes.[431]

"Therefore, we still have an opportunity to yet overturn God's work before He reasserts His presence on the Earth. God has promised to deliver His eternal kingdom to the Hebrews, the ones He has set-apart.[432] What do you imagine would happen if they were not around to receive it?" he asked rhetorically, gazing scornfully at them.

"The key is the utter destruction of the Hebrews. Once we destroy them completely, we will demonstrate God to be a liar and His entire right to rule can be legally challenged. God promised there would be physical, non-resurrected Hebrews to inhabit the kingdom to live in the land[433] and that their days would be like the days of a tree, and His elect, the Hebrews, would long enjoy the work of their hands.[434] If there were no physical descendants left, then the promise could never be fulfilled, and God would be at an impasse."

"However," Prince Parás interrupted inquisitively, though still with contempt toward Satan, "God will never permit a direct attack on the Hebrews, in the same way that it was not possible to attack Job until the impenetrable barrier was removed.[435] Furthermore, God has stationed Michael as their chief prince to stand watch over them,[436] and a formidable foe he is; something you learned at the death of Moses when the two of you fought over Moses's body. You slandered your nemesis, yet he dared not bring a slanderous accusation against you, but instead, used a greater weapon by invoking God to rebuke you, and you were forced to retreat.[437] We cannot attack the Hebrews and hope to be victorious."

"As if that were not enough," the same rebel angel who interrupted before continued directing the accusations, "God has acted craftily through Jesus and His selfless and humble act." He grimaced, revealing how he despised him to the core. "He integrated the nations into the commonwealth of the Hebrews. [438] This was something that had not formerly been revealed to us! It was obvious that God has played favorites by electing the Hebrews to be His people, His special treasure,"[439] he said sarcastically.

"And made them His inheritance," [440] Prince Parás said, exasperated at the interruptions of the others, "before the foundation of the world.[441] We know how His Chronicles are literally filled with passage after passage of such declarations. Yet again, you did not anticipate how God planned to give not only the Hebrews a part in the age to come, but also now all the Adamites as well," he said disapprovingly.

"The mystery that the nations should be fellow heirs of the same body and partakers of His promise was hidden in God. Only now has it been disclosed to us through this new commonwealth of the Hebrews where the nations who were once far off— outsiders of the commonwealth and strangers from the covenants of promise, having no hope and without God—have now been brought in by the life-force of Jesus," [442] he said contemptuously.

"Your lack of imagination is the source of your insolence," Satan countered, unnerved by their insubordination. "God's perennial affection for the Adamites and His favoritism toward the Hebrews will be His downfall. Do you not see the glaring weakness which we will exploit to the fullest?" he challenged, staring venomously at Prince Parás who dared challenge his wisdom. "Your silence is welcomed, and now I see you need a little refresher in history," he mocked. "You recall Balaam, the seer, son of Beor of the land of Pethor, the prophet who was prevented from cursing the Hebrews when brought to the land of Moab because God had placed a blessing on them which was impossible to breach.[443] Thus, Balaam was not able to curse them regardless of how much gold and treasures he was offered. God has made an irrevocable promise to Abraham and his sons[444] and nothing we can do will ever overturn that promise.[445]

"I hope, students," he continued his jeering, "that you now recall the answer; Balaam informed Balak that if their young women went and seduced the sons of the Hebrews to perform rites in their temples, then God himself would remove the hedge of protection; then they would easily fall before their enemies.[446] You see, Balaam was prevented from cursing them … but he was able to get them to curse themselves.

"Therefore, you mindless half-wits, this unexpected new paradigm of the Hebrews and the nations being equals in terms of their restoration in the age to come, regardless of their distinct roles, [447] is in fact, the key to us victoriously overthrowing the Hebrews. All we need to do is convince the nations and peoples that they are not merely integrated into the commonwealth of the Hebrews, but are actually a replacement of it."[448] He chuckled. "Once that seed of discord is planted," he snickered again at his own imagination, "it will germinate into hatred and eventually persecution of the people God has chosen to be at the center of His kingdom.[449] You see, while we cannot actually touch the apple of God's eye, the nations who have come into the commonwealth, who have been integrated with the Hebrews, can in fact, gouge His eye when they destroy the Hebrews. They will even be convinced that in so doing they are doing God's bidding,"[450] he detailed, focusing the truth of his statements toward the Watchers who were challenging them. The force of the truth of his words knocked them over. [451] They each slowly recovered and stood up. Satan smiled with satisfaction.

"Not only will such actions serve to weaken and destroy the Hebrews," he continued, "but over time the sons and daughters of the Hebrews[452] will be repulsed by the very name of Jesus, because it will be in His name that great atrocities will occur, thanks to the seeds of discord that we shall sow. Our powerful countermeasure is turning the world against the Hebrews. When they are eliminated there will be no beneficiary to receive the bequests in the will.[453]

"You must go, as in previous times, and flatter the people brought into the commonwealth so that they boast and imagine that they support the root, when in fact the root supports them.[454] Our first step will be to encourage them to believe that God is finished with the Hebrews whom He elected years before, despite His otherwise clear statements.[455] We will then persuade them that they, the nations, have replaced the Hebrews[456] and once they are convinced of that, then they will view themselves as the ones God has elected. With that premise, they will logically conclude that God's election is not simply an invitation to be front and center in His kingdom,[457] but is a matter of life eternal. Following their logic, they will be convinced that their election means that God has chosen some to receive eternal life and others, automatically, through no decision or action of their own, to be destroyed in the fiery stream of God.[458] Once these beliefs have taken root, then it will simply be a matter of time until the nations will be in complete agreement that the Hebrews are a cancer and a blight which needs to be eradicated and wiped off the map of the world. When that day comes, we will answer the call," Satan said relishing the cunning of his plan. "I can savor the vitality of the Hebrews' life-force that will be spilled in the name of Jesus, but actually in our honor before our final victory. That plan shows imagination!" he declared, looking sternly at Prince Parás.

All the rebels laughed greedily and in agreement at the insidious plan of their leader. "You are worthy, Lord Satan," Prince Parás said falling at his feet while all the others shouted along with him.

Satan looked at the others disdainfully. "When this new truth," he thought to himself, "that God is finished with the Hebrews and has replaced them with the 'nations', is firmly rooted, and when the Hebrews are back in their land, then I will implement the next phase of my plan—posing as the Promised One himself."

Epilogue: Jesus Served When Satan Would Not

God required Satan to serve Adam, but Satan refused to be a servant and to love sacrificially. This same test was ultimately put to Jesus, God's own Son. Though Jesus wanted the cup to pass, He humbled himself because: "the Son of Man did not come to be served, but to serve, and to give His life a ransom for many" (Matt 20:28).

We recall when God told Samuel to give the children of Israel a king, their first king was Saul who was:

> A mighty man of power. And he had a choice and handsome son whose name was Saul. There was not a more handsome person than he among the children of Israel. From his shoulders upward he was taller than any of the people (1 Sam 9:1–2).

Saul, like Satan before him, was endowed by God with strength and good looks. He was powerful and a full head taller than anyone around him. He was also the best looking. Beauty and stature are attributes not attained or earned by effort, but rather, they are gifts. Saul started off well and acted as God's anointed, special agent. He eventually attributed his successes to himself, rather than to the One who empowered him. Saul was so enamored with himself that he set up a monument (*matsiv lo yad* מַצִּיב לוֹ יָד]:

> When Samuel rose early in the morning to meet Saul, it was told Samuel, saying, "Saul went to Carmel, and indeed, he set up a monument for himself; and he has gone on around, passed by, and gone down to Gilgal" (1 Sam 15:12).

Sadly, Saul became more concerned about lifting up his own name than exalting the name of his God. He corrupted his wisdom on account of his beauty, just like Satan before him. God is unimpressed by the externals—for He is the one who gave these attributes in the first place! We see this so clearly when Samuel was choosing the next king from the sons of Jesse:

> So it was, when they came, that he looked at Eliab and said, "Surely the LORD's anointed is before Him!" But the LORD said to Samuel, "Do not look at his appearance or at his physical stature, because I have refused him. For the LORD does not see as man sees; for man looks at the outward appearance, but the LORD looks at the heart" (1 Sam 16:6–7).

Eliab was good looking and strong, and even Samuel, the man of God, was swayed by his external traits. It is easy to do, for the physical features are what we can perceive with our senses. We humans (and angels to some degree) look much like our Creator, as we noted in a previous chapter. We share His image and likeness. These are things with which God could easily endow us. We are impressed by the might of men, but God "takes no pleasure in the legs of a man" (Ps 147:10). God, however, is looking for humble people with strong character.

God created each of us to be free will agents, meaning we alone must choose whether we will be like God in our character. He could create us with only the capacity to choose to be like Him, but free choice means that He must allow us to freely choose our own path. Both Satan and Saul chose to exalt themselves, rather than exalt the One who created them.

> He said to them, "You are those who justify yourselves before men, but God knows your hearts. For what is highly esteemed among men is an abomination in the sight of God (Luke 16:15) (See Appendix 6 Abominations of Babylon).

Satan chose to pursue evil, which is defined as doing those things in which God does not delight. "They did evil before My eyes, And chose that in which I do not delight" (Isa 65:12, 66:4). (See Appendix 2 What is Evil). Satan chose to focus on his external qualities, which were completely endowed to him by his Creator; and, he neglected to nourish and value God's greatest character trait, which John informs us is love.

> Beloved, let us love one another, for love is of God; and everyone who loves is born of God and knows God. He who does not love does not know God, for God is love (1 John 4:7–8).

The question then is what does love actually look like? It is easy to say, "I love you." Buying flowers and taking a romantic interest to a fancy restaurant and showering someone with gifts may be expressions of love. But the reality is that these gestures are superficial at best. If a billionaire gives you one hundred dollars, is it love? What if it were $1,000? Is that love? Didn't God give Satan everything? Was that love? Perhaps. But giving those qualities cost God nothing. He has endless resources. So, endowing Satan with beauty and wisdom was really nothing. Thankfully, John goes on to tell us what the love of God looks like in action.

> In this the love of God was manifested toward us, that God has sent His only begotten Son into the world, that we might live through Him. In this is love, not that we loved God, but that He loved us and sent His Son to be the propitiation for our sins (1 John 4:9–10).

God's love was not shown simply by giving material gifts, but in giving everything. These are the very words that Jesus spoke concerning God's love:

For God so loved the world that He gave His only begotten Son, that whoever believes in Him should not perish but have everlasting life. For God did not send His Son into the world to condemn the world, but that the world through Him might be saved (John 3:16–17).

God so loved that He gave His ONLY Son. God sacrificially gave. He gave that which was most valuable: His own Son. John addresses this in his first epistle: "By this we know love, because He laid down His life for us. And we also ought to lay down our lives for the brethren" (1 John 3:16).

We know love because He laid down His life for us. Jesus underscored this sacrificial love in His teachings about serving one another—not like a slave serving his king, but like a friend sacrificially giving of himself, by doing good and serving a friend who cannot repay him.

"If anyone desires to be first, he shall be last of all and servant of all" (Mark 9:35).

JESUS WENT TO A GARDEN AND SWEATED BLOOD FOR US
Satan the prime minister said, "I will not serve; all should serve me." But what did God incarnate say? He was in the garden of Gethsemane, sweating blood because He knew what was coming and said, "Father, if there's any way, if there's a plan B, would You please reveal that right now? Is there any other way? But not My will be done, but Yours."

What was He willing to do? He was willing to go to the cross, to die. He is the King of Kings and Lord of Lords; the Word who was in the beginning with God, who was God. God is not putting out some grand statement, some big philosophical ideal with which He wants everyone else to comply, but that He is not willing to do. No, no. He is the commander in charge. He is leading the way. He is showing us how to do it.

He humbled himself. He took on the form of a bondservant. He was obedient to the point of death. What does Jesus tell us? Take up your cross daily. Take it up daily. What do you do on a cross? There is only one thing you can do on a cross—Die. I do not want to die to myself because it hurts. I have to deny myself. I do not want to do that. But isn't that what He has called us to do? We are not called to simply seek more knowledge.

We are called to study to show ourselves approved; but, having more data in our heads does not bring us closer to God, nor does it mean that we even know God. People who collect baseball cards or that can name off all the stats about the players, do not actually know the player; They probably have never met the player. In fact, if they met the player, they might not even like him. They can know all the stats: batting average, home runs, and strikeouts, yet not actually know the man. Likewise, we can know some facts about God, but fail to truly know God.

If our goal is to know Him, then it requires us to die to ourselves. In order to be like Him, we must humble ourselves and be willing to serve one another. We do not have to agree on every theological point. It is perfectly fine for us to have differences of opinion. We do not have to agree with people, but we can love them anyway because we do not have perfect theology either, and it is not about that. It is about whether we are willing to walk the way that Jesus taught us. Will we humble ourselves the way He humbled Himself? Am I willing to deny myself and die the way that He did? Or am I instead going to be like Satan?

Here is the danger, the deception: We can say, "I am not following Satan, because I am not a Satanist. I do not make sacrifices and pour blood on an altar and all those really weird, outlandish things that witches and Satanists do." Those practices are the more conspicuous side of serving Satan, of Satanism. But the everyday kind of Satanism is where I exalt me. I choose me. I put you down to raise me up. That is following Satan.

Self is what his kingdom is all about. Selflessness is what God's kingdom is all about. Selfish: That is Satan. Selfless: That is God. It is our choice. He is not going to make you do it; He created you with freewill. You get to choose. God will not choose for you. You must decide how you will live today. Will you choose self, which is what Satan's kingdom is all about? Or will you choose to be selfless, which is what God's kingdom is all about?

The history of Satan is an amazing story. He is the being who had it all, who had everything—the looks, the brains, the power, the authority, but he was not willing to serve others. That is what really would have set him apart. He had a test. If he had humbly served, God may have then said, "You passed your test." Satan failed. Adam had a test, as well. Adam failed. We have all failed. There was One who came who was also tested. Jesus was tested in every way imaginable. In every way, He was without sin. That is why we put our trust and our hope and our confidence in Him because He is our hero. He is our example. He is the one who went before us and did it to show us what it looks like to live out God's commandments, His Torah. Jesus demonstrated how to resist selfish desires and serve others with humility.

CHOOSE YHWH OR BAAL / ISHTAR

The Beast and the ten kings are going to burn the woman. If you dedicate yourself to pursuing the lust of the flesh, the lust of the eyes and the pride of life—if you put your trust in those things, you will find that these ephemeral pleasures are going to be taken away in end. The enemy uses these enticements to draw us in and to get us ensnared. Then he pulls them away, and we are left with nothing. We must pick our master. Will it be Nimrod / Ninurta, the rebel offering the perverted pleasures, or Yehovah, the Creator and the true life-giver?

Satan wants us to be like the people on Carmel who would not decide.

> Elijah came to all the people, and said, "How long will you falter between two opinions? If the LORD is God, follow Him; but if Baal, follow him." But the people answered him not a word (1 Kgs 18:21).

To delay your choice is to rebel against God. God is perfect. He is good, holy and just. He is the One who created pleasures. There are pleasures at His right hand forevermore. He wants to give us all those good things, but He cannot as long as we are going after those things that bring fleeting fulfilment and quick thrills, which are perversions of the things He created to bring us joy and satisfaction. We have to choose who will be our master. Is it rebellion? Is it Nimrod and all of his multiple forms—his many names of blasphemy? Remember the scarlet Beast which was full of names of blasphemy (Rev 17:3). We have looked at those blasphemous names and have seen the rebel blasphemer is known as Pabilsag, also known as Nimrod, Ninurta, Marduk, Zeus, Jupiter and the other masks Satan has worn throughout history. They are all the same. We have to choose which one we are going follow. God or the rebel? God will not choose for you.

Jesus tells us:

> "Do not lay up for yourselves treasures on earth, where moth and rust destroy and where thieves break in and steal; but lay up for yourselves treasures in heaven, where neither moth nor rust destroys and where thieves do not break in and steal. For where your treasure is, there your heart will be also" (Matt 6:19–21).

Many of us are chasing a fantasy in lustful pursuit of a momentary thrill. The lure of advertising is the flashing images of the perfect car, desirable mate, trendy clothes and lifestyle—the fleeting, ephemeral things that this world treasures.

To allow yourself to become driven by your ego-centric cravings is to become enslaved to the woman who rides the Beast; She promises wonderful things, good times and all the pleasures you could ever want. That is what she is selling, and people buy into it. Her delicacies have the nutrition and substance of cotton candy. You grasp it and then it is gone. The lures are just a means to an end; and that end is you ensnared and enslaved. When the woman who rides the Beast has served her purpose, the Antichrist and the ten kings are going to turn against Inanna / Ishtar and bring her to ruin.

A life spent collecting all of the treasure of this world will come to ruin, as well. We saw in Revelation 17 that we need to store for ourselves real treasures in heaven, with our King, with our true God, because where your treasure is, there your heart will be also. "The lamp of the body is the eye. If therefore your eye is good, your whole body will be full of light (Matt 6:22). "But if your eye is bad", (a greedy person was referred to as having a bad eye) "your whole body will be full of darkness" (Matt 6:23). Sadly, we can become selfish and greedy. And what is worse, we become greedy for terrible things that God said not to chase after. He knew they would leave us empty and desolate.

If we pursue the perversions, the false gods, the Nimrods, Ninurtas, Marduks, the Ishtars—if we go after those things, we become full of darkness. He tells us:

> If therefore the light that is in you is darkness, how great is that darkness! No one can serve two masters; for either he will hate the one and love the other, or else he will be loyal to the one and despise the other. You cannot serve God and mammon (Matt 6:23–24).

It is the same basic thing that Elijah said: Stop faltering. Choose. If the Lord is God, follow Him. But if Baal, follow him. You choose. Do not waver in the middle. You cannot have God and Baal. It just does not work, though people have tried it since time immemorial.

The ancient Israelites tried it; It did not work. We must choose today whom we are going to serve. The reality is that if we do not choose YHWH, then we are, by default, opting into what Satan has in store. And as we will see in the next book, it will not be good.

If you desire to serve the one true God, begin your service to Him with this prayer:

"God, I have blown it. I have not followed Your ways. I have been chasing after these false gods. I ask You to forgive me and to receive me into your kingdom in the name of Jesus, our Messiah who died for my sins. Amen."

GOD'S GLORIOUS CITY AWAITS THE HUMBLE

At the end of our analysis, we see there is a battle between two cities: Babylon the Great versus the New Jerusalem. Satan has created his mountain city of idolatry, and it stands in contrast and competition with God's mountain city of joy. You must choose in which city you want to live. Each one has a price of admission; Each has an entrance fee.

God has made it freely available if you want to come into His city, but you cannot bring in pride, perversion and idolatry. You can join Satan's city where all those things are freely available, yet he will exact a price—your dignity, your destiny, and your connection with your Creator. The price to enter Satan's city is not worth the cost, because it will lead to depression, pain, suffering, and eventually death and separation from the One who wants to give us beyond what we could ever ask or think. What must we do? If we humble ourselves before Him, He will restore us to the Garden of Eden, where there are pleasures forevermore.

> For thus says the High and Lofty One who inhabits eternity, whose name is Holy: "I dwell in the high and holy place, With him who has a contrite and humble spirit, To revive the spirit of the humble, And to revive the heart of the contrite ones (Isa 57:15).

Recall where God said to Israel, "She is not My wife, nor am I her Husband! Let her put away her harlotries from her sight" (Hos 2:2). He is calling us to put away those harlotries from our sight. If we will do that, He says: "I will betroth you to Me forever; Yes, I will betroth you to Me In righteousness and justice, In lovingkindness and mercy; I will betroth you to Me in faithfulness, And you shall know the LORD" (Hos 2:19–20).

> "For the LORD has called you Like a woman forsaken and grieved in spirit, like a youthful wife when you were refused," Says your God (Isa 54:6). "For a mere moment I have forsaken you, but with great mercies I will gather you" (Isa 54:7). "O you afflicted one, Tossed with tempest, and not comforted, Behold, I will lay your stones with colorful gems, And lay your foundations with sapphires. I will make your pinnacles of rubies, Your gates of crystal, And all your walls of precious stones" (Isa 54:11–12).

This is parallel language to Revelation 21: The foundations of the wall the city were adorned with all kinds of precious stones: … (Rev 21:19).

Speaking to Jerusalem, Isaiah 62:

> You (Jerusalem f. s.) shall no longer be termed Forsaken, Nor shall your land any more be termed Desolate; But you shall be called Hephzibah and your land Beulah; For the LORD delights in you (f. s.), And your land shall be married … as the bridegroom rejoices over the bride (Isa 62:4–5).

Then John sees the culmination of it all:

> I, John, saw the holy city, New Jerusalem … prepared as a bride adorned for her husband (Rev 21:2). "I will show you the bride, the Lamb's wife." … he … showed me the great city, the holy Jerusalem (Rev 21:10).

This is God's wife; the pure, spotless bride. The enemy established his adulterous harlot, who was a perversion of what is good, true and right. A fleeting moment of pleasure is quickly gone, and you have to keep chasing to get a new high; but, the high with God will never go away. God is that perfect drug, and there is no hangover with Him. There is no headache in the morning, no bad trip; no overdosing. But the requirement is that you humble yourself—that is the price of entry.

Will you humble yourself? Too many of us believe that just because we said the prayer and invited Jesus into our heart, that we can live like hell. Now is the time for us to repent, come out of her my people, lest you share in her plagues. If we are going to profess Christ, we had better live like Christ. If we are going to profess His name, we had better carry it high. Do not be deceived. God is not mocked. What a man sows, he will also reap. Wouldn't it be wonderful to reap citizenship in God's city, the New Jerusalem?

New Jerusalem is described as a mountain. Satan has been making artificial mountains as counterfeits of the one that is in heaven and that will come down to Earth. He has duped his followers into constructing ziggurats, pyramids, mounds, and monuments that are false worship centers. On these mountains, Satan pretends he is the Most High, but his mountain is not the place with the real throne of the true God. In God's kingdom, we will have pleasures that will bring us contentment. God initially put mankind in the Garden of Eden to dwell with Him and enjoy the pleasures. He wants us to have fun and enjoy good company. He told us that we should "rejoice in your feast, you and your son and your daughter" (Deut 16:14), and "At Your right hand are pleasures forevermore" (Ps 16:11). He will give it to us if we humble ourselves, follow Him and put away our idols and adulteries. Idols cannot go into the kingdom. It is a pure kingdom of abundance, brimming with joy, love and incredible surprises. God wants you to be in his kingdom.

Will you come?

APPENDICES

Appendix 1: Fallen Angels and Demons

Unclean and evil spirits, demons and fallen angels are in reality all the same kind of being. The term "fallen angel" does not exist in the Bible; it's a term that we use to make a distinction between God's holy and good angels and those rebellious angels that serve Satan.[459] Angel just means "messenger". The Theological Dictionary of the New Testament explains the meaning of "demon":

> daímōn as a term for gods and divine powers. Various senses may be noted in this field: a. "god," b. "lesser deity," c. "unknown superhuman factor," d. "what overtakes us," e.g., death, or good or evil fortune, e. "protective deity."[460]

We have accounts of good angels, and we also see references to bad angels as evidenced in Revelation: "Michael and his angels fought with the dragon; and the dragon and his angels fought" (Rev 12:7). We refer to Satan's angels as fallen angels.

Throughout the Bible and ancient literature, we see that fallen angels are demons who masqueraded as gods in order to communicate with and control humans. When Paul interacted with "certain Epicurean and Stoic philosophers ... some said ... 'He seems to be a proclaimer of foreign gods [δαιμονιων daimonion],' because he preached to them Jesus and the resurrection" (Acts 17:18). The philosophers thought Paul was speaking to them about other gods similar to Zeus or Apollo, yet the Greek word here for "gods" is daimonion—demons.

Moses used very similar language in his farewell address:

> They sacrificed to demons, not to God, To gods they did not know (Deut 32:17). They served their idols, Which became a snare to them. They even sacrificed their sons And their daughters to demons [lasheddim לַשֵּׁדִים - tois daimonios τοις δαιμονιοις] (Ps 106:36–37).

BDAG explains how demon (δαιμον) "refers in general to powerful entities ... After Homer's time, the adjective, δαιμόνιος means anything 'sent from heaven' or 'that which is divine'."[461] Based on the literature, demons could be good or bad. Philo in his writings *On the Giants* says:

> And when the angels of God saw the daughters of men that they were beautiful, they took unto themselves wives of all of them whom they chose. Those beings, whom other **philosophers call demons**, Moses **usually calls angels** (Emphasis mine).[462]

According to Philo, demons and angels are really one and the same. When we talk about angels, demons and the so-called gods, we are talking about the same kind of entities. The Bridgeway Dictionary confirms "rebellious, or fallen angels are variously known as demons, evil spirits, spiritual hosts of wickedness, principalities, powers, rulers, authorities, evil spiritual forces, cosmic powers of evil, and angels of the devil."[463] These are all part of the general class of messenger (angels) that God spoke into existence, according to Psalm 148:2, 5.

The etymology of the word demon "likely stems from the root δαιω,'to divide (destinies)'. Thus, the word could designate one's 'fate' or 'destiny', or the spirit controlling one's fate." [464] This completely concurs with Enlil who was said to be "the one that decides the fate,"[465] and was the holder of the Tablet of Destinies. In Psalm 95:5, the Septuagint interprets *elilim* (idols, and related to Enlil) as demons:

> The national deities of other peoples, said to be idols *'elilim'* in Hebrew, become "demons" ("All the gods of the nations are demons"); in LXX Deut 32: 17, the foreign divinities whom Israel worshipped, properly described in the Hebrew text as *šedim* (tutelary spirit) are again called "demons" ("They sacrificed to demons and not to God"; cf. LXX Ps 105:37; Bar. 4:7).[466]

We recall that *elilim* is related to the Akkadian word, *Illil*, and Sumerian Enlil, Lord Wind. Thus, Scripture is telling us that idols are plural "Enlils", and we know Enlil is Satan, who is a fallen angel. The *Theological Workbook of the Old Testament* explains that the "Hebrew shēd is to be connected with the Babylonian word shêdu, a demon either good or evil. In pagan religions the line between gods and demons is not a constant one."[467] This now explains why we see demons referred to in the New Testament as "unclean spirits" to distinguish between the angels who "kept their first estate" and those who rebelled.

We see the use of *sheddim* as gods where God told Elijah to chastise the king of Samaria when he sought out the aid of "Baal-Zebub, the god of Ekron" (2 Kgs 1:3) who, incidentally, was known as a Rephaim. "Baal Zebub ... 2 Kgs 1 is the healing deity ... **Prince, lord of the underworld" in Ugaritic texts (*zbl b'l arş*) refers to Baal as a chthonic healer god**"[468] This same (false) god Beelzebub is specifically called "the ruler of the demons" (Matt 12:24). Jesus identifies him as none other than Satan (Matt 12:26).

> In LXX Isa 65: II *daimon* renders the Hebrew name of the pagan god of Fortune (- Gad), where the Israelites are said to have been "preparing a table for the demon". This conception of table fellowship with pagan gods who are in reality demons carries over into the New Testament: Paul warns the Corinthian Church that they may not eat sacrificial meals in pagan temples, for "that which the Gentiles sacrifice, they sacrifice to demons", meaning, for Corinth, the Greek gods Asclepios, Sarapis, and especially Demeter. [469]

There is, therefore, no distinction between fallen angels, demons and unclean spirits. They are simply different titles which describe the same general class of being. We of course acknowledge that there are subclasses of beings within this general category, such as cherubim.

Furthermore, any supposed distinction between fallen angels and demons, such as the claim that they are the spirits of the deceased Nephilim, is not supported by the biblical, linguistic and ancient textual evidence. If an entire race of beings had been born utterly wicked, through no fault or choice of their own, then they would necessarily be consigned to eternal damnation simply for being born.[470] However, God has created all of his sentient beings with free-will and self-determination (See Appendix 2 Angels Freewill).

Appendix 2: Angels Created with Freewill

God created His ministers of fire with the ability to choose, a quality which we humans share, as well. This quality is what will allow Satan, the Beast and the False Prophet to wage war against God. In order for us to appreciate the ability to choose contrary to the desire of our Creator, we need to go back before anything was, before the blackness of space, when there was only the Most High who existed within and as His own dimension.

Imagining God in and of Himself is a challenging mental exercise, for we should not imagine God was floating around in the darkness of space in eternity past, (which I used to imagine as a boy). Neither space nor darkness had yet been invented! We cannot speak of where God existed, as "where" had not yet been created. God does not exist in a place nor in a dimension. There is no space, dimension or reality outside of who God intrinsically is. This hurts our heads a bit, but it necessarily must be true since to suggest otherwise would mean that something existed apart from Him creating it, and Scripture is replete with verses saying that all things have been created by Him.

According to the study of higher dimensions, the tenth dimension is both timeless and space-less. [471] It is pure information. Such a mathematical description of reality closely parallels biblical theology. God is both timeless and space-less. He is the mind from which all matter emanates. Mathematically, He is the tenth dimension from which all others proceed. Interestingly, the Big Bang theory has come to a similar conclusion—all matter, including space itself, was tightly packed in a dot smaller than a period on this page. Some have postulated that the dot was not actually there. Nevertheless, if all matter AND space itself was within the dot, where was the dot? The answer is hyperspace: a dimension beyond our own.

The best minds of quantum physics over the last one hundred years have concluded that behind the matter of the universe is a mind. Max Planck, often considered the father of quantum physics, stated matter comes from a Mind:

> As a man who has devoted his whole life to the most clear-headed science, to the study of matter, I can tell you as a result of my research about atoms this much: There is no matter as such. All matter originates and exists only by virtue of a force which brings the particle of an atom to vibration and holds this most minute solar system of the atom together. We must assume behind this force the existence of a conscious and intelligent mind. This mind is the matrix of all matter.[472]

Einstein's famous equation, $E=MC^2$ essentially states that energy and mass (matter) are interchangeable; they are simply alternate forms of the same thing and under the right conditions, mass can become energy, and energy can become mass.[473] Indeed, Einstein stated there is no matter: Concerning matter, we have been all wrong. What we have called matter is energy, whose vibration has been so lowered as to be perceptible to the senses. There is no matter.[474]

Thus, before Creation there was no differentiation (outside of God Himself and His indescribable tri-unity). On that first day, God created things that were not. The first day was the beginning of differentiations. He created a space outside of Himself; He created darkness which had never been (Isa 45:7), for God is light and there is no darkness in Him whatsoever (I John 1:5). Thus, the absence of His glorious light in the newly created void was new and different. For the first time ever, there was darkness. God revealed this to the prophet Isaiah:

> I form the light, and create (בּוֹרֵא) darkness: I make peace, and create (בּוֹרֵא) evil (ra' רָע): I the LORD do all these things (Isaiah 45:7 KJV).

Until that moment, darkness (the absence of light) did not exist. Therefore, before day one (or Genesis 1:1–3) when He created the void, which is space, it initially was devoid of God's light and did not even have photons. Until God conceived of the absence of light, there was no such thing as darkness; it was His idea. When God decided to create a space / dimension outside of Himself, which was not automatically filled with His light, He then by necessity, created the potential of the absence of light which God called darkness. God then created physical light, photons as waves and / or particles, in order to fill the space.

In the same way, God is good (Exodus 34:6), and no evil or sin or imperfection is in Him. We might say that God has the corner on the market when it comes to good. Good, according to the Bible is defined as what is in accord with God's will, desire or plan. Therefore, any deviation from that is by definition not good and is therefore "evil". Thus, when God desired to give the angels, including Satan, and man the option to follow Him or to disobey, He must have by default, created the potential for them to completely exercise their own will by not choosing the good (that is God's will, desire or plan). It is self-evident that no one can choose that which does not exist. Henry Ford once said that people could choose any color Model T, so long as it was black. It is also similar to the infamous communist regimes where the people are allowed to vote, but there is only one candidate. In reality, having only one candidate (or one color to choose from) is no choice at all.

WHAT IS EVIL?

Isaiah 45 states that God is in fact the very One who created evil: "I form the light, and create (בּוֹרֵא) darkness: I make peace, and create (בּוֹרֵא boreh) evil (רָע ra'): I the LORD do all these things" (Isaiah 45:7 KJV).

Some translations render the word evil (*ra* רַע)[475] as "calamity", which is an option in the context of Isaiah 45:7. Nevertheless, the word is the same in which we are first introduced in Genesis 2:17, where God commands man to not eat of the tree of the knowledge of good and evil (*ra* רַע).

> And the LORD God commanded the man, saying, "Of every tree of the garden you may freely eat; but of the tree of the knowledge of good and evil (*ra* רַע) you shall not eat, for in the day that you eat of it you shall surely die" (Gen 2:16–17).

God is also the essence of all that is good. Following God involves doing what is right and good. Thus, if Adam could only choose from all the "good" things that God had made, then there really was not free choice at all. That, in a nutshell, is why God created the tree of the knowledge of good and evil; there had to be a way for Adam to exercise his own will independently, even if it meant it would be contrary to God's will.

God defines evil in Isaiah saying they "did evil before My eyes, And chose that in which I do not delight" (Isaiah 65:12; 66:4). This gives us an amazingly simple definition of evil: "doing something in which God does not take pleasure." God, the master programmer, had to code into this reality the potential to choose contrary to His wishes. He had to create the potential for His creatures to exercise their own will and choose something in which He does not delight. Just as there was no darkness until He made it possible, so too was it impossible to choose something besides His desire.

The creation of evil[476] is what made choosing contrary to His wishes possible, and it is what makes choosing to follow, obey and love Him meaningful. For God's creatures to genuinely love Him, the option to reject Him had to be available. Satan, the angels, Adam and Eve—all had to have the opportunity to choose against His will to be able to truly choose Him and hence, have true *love* for Him. Therefore, it is true that God created evil; yet, He never caused any one to choose evil. Giving individuals the choice between two real and viable options is not the same as making us choose the bad option.

The creation of evil is analogous to a large rock on a cliff. The rock has potential energy; a tiny nudge will turn the potential energy into kinetic energy. The rock's potential energy need never be triggered, or made kinetic; so too, mankind's choosing contrary to God's desire need not have been actualized. God, in a sense, told Adam not to push the rock and warned him of the consequences if he did, but Adam, of his own free will, pushed it and suffered the consequence when the rock's energy became kinetic and killed him.

God created two options: one in accordance with His desires, which leads to life; and, one contrary to His wishes, which leads to death. Angels and humans have the ability to determine their paths. Satan chose the path contrary to God's wishes.

Appendix 3: Inanna goddess of Transvestism, Transgenderism, Homosexuality

Inanna, the seductive woman who rides the Beast, was also the goddess of transvestism, transgenderism and homosexuality. In the Akkadian hymn, "The Enheduanna", the High Priestess of the Moon in the Sumerian city of Ur - *From Passionate Inanna, ca 23rd Century BC.*, Ishtar is described as transforming men into women.[477] It was said that this goddess could:

> "turn a man into a woman, and a woman into a man."
> [These are your powers Inanna]. ... one well known text of similar antiquity ... describes a religious festival held in honor of Inanna. "The people of Sumer parade before you. ... The male prostitutes comb their hair before you. ... The women adorn their right side with men's clothing. ... The men adorn their left side with women's clothing"[478]

Imagine this scene: Semi-nude devotees dance in drunkenness around the canopied statue being carried down the street to the frenzied music of drums, cymbals and castanets. It is a festival day for the cult of the goddess. Effeminate men giggle and dance in ecstatic, awkward movements, hyperextending their limbs, but experiencing no pain or fatigue. The flamboyant carnival parades through town, out into the country. At the climax of the mad dancing, a man castrates himself in honor of the goddess as other men tear apart a small animal and feast on the banquet of raw flesh. In a grove of trees, the crowd reclines, but the feverish clip of the music continues with the addition of pipes and flutes. Women share phallic shaped bread to consume with the wine. Intoxicated with alcohol and rhythmic song, the women take on the identity of the goddess. The merger of sexuality and spirituality allows the energy of desire to break down inhibitions and unify the group in sexual pulsations of passion. Homosexuality and lesbianism are divine deeds; Breaking gender constraints is a religious rite. The bloody, wine-soaked debauchery ensues with abandon to fill every indulgence. The orgy incites lust and unbridled passions for homosexuality, bestiality, and bloodletting as a gift from the goddess. As the crowd reaches exhaustion, the priests and priestesses refill the wine and lead in lifting a glass to the goddess and chanting in unison. The ordained then begin to reveal to the crowd the secrets of the Mysteries.

This scene of a mystery cult could have taken place in many ancient places such as Rome, Greece, Egypt or Canaan. Some of these rites took place when Israel bowed to the golden calf. Adherents to the mystery schools performed these rituals as agrarian magic for fertility, to seek enlightenment and power, or perhaps with a goal to ascend beyond being human. Mystery Babylon is a thread entwined through the warp and woof of our history, and it entangles us still today. Modern demands to accept changes in sexual-orientation and gender are rooted in ancient religion—the same religion that Abraham confronted, and that Paul exposed in his travels. It seems hard to deny that our society is worshipping Inanna, the woman that rides the Beast, because the entire world is drunk on her perversions and fornications. DDDB notes the paradoxical qualities of Inanna which lead to strife:

> It has been suggested that the goddess is the embodiment of qualities or lifestyles that seem contradictory and paradoxical and call into question the categories or values of the society and thus confirm their existence; an embodiment, that is. Of figures who are marginal (e.g. a prostitute), bi-sexual, or anomalous (e.g. a woman of the respectable upper class who, however, is powerful, free and undomesticated). Alternatively, it has been suggested that she is the embodiment of strife.[479] (See Appendix 4 Easter).

TRANSGENDERISM TODAY

Inanna's influence has clearly manifested today through the transgender movement. Today we have people who are born men that want to be women and vice versa. Because this is a sensitive and personal topic, I want to state I am not against transgender people. I desire to show the love of Jesus to people identifying as transgender. Sadly, there is a fundamental misunderstanding on their part, and our society has sown a lot of confusion on this issue. In reality, the person claiming to be transgender is more than likely a victim, not the perpetrator.

Militant pushing of the transgender agenda and normalizing the absurd is the problem. It is likely one of the steppingstones that will lead humanity to accept the Mark of the Beast and worship the image of the Beast, which we will explore in detail in the next book. Transgenderism, at its core, is a rejection of God's rightful rule and a rejection of His image; It's a blatant declaration that we do not want to be in God's image, but in the image of our own making.

We reason that since we have evolved to this point, why not take charge of our future evolution? If there's no God, as posited by Darwin and Nietzsche, and we are the product of evolution, (from the goo to the zoo to you), then we are free to direct our own evolution. If we can choose all aspects of who we will be, then we can decide our own gender. The UK Telegraph recently reported that Facebook has seventy-one gender options available[480] for you to choose what you want to be. You can choose to be human or to change from being male to be female, or you can identify as an animal, a house pet, a doll or even a demon. It's up to you.

While modern humanism touts that you can be anything, you must remember that God created you to bear His image, which is the most awesome image that you could achieve. Inherently, you project God's dignity and power. All alterations result in an inferior persona. God made only two genders: male and female.

Each man and woman is made in the image of God. Mankind's enemy, Satan, is the one who has wanted to mar that image—the one obsessed with corrupting the image. His evil forces drive people to hate their own image and to mutilate their bodies. God's perfect plan involves only two sexes, a binary construct— A or B, which is assigned by the Creator and is so much easier: male or female.

Dr. Paul R. McHugh, the former psychiatrist-in-chief for Johns Hopkins Hospital, says transgenderism is a "mental disorder" that merits treatment, and that a sex change is "biologically impossible." He states:

> "This intensely felt sense of being transgendered constitutes a mental disorder in two respects. The first is that the idea of sex misalignment is simply mistaken – it does not correspond with physical reality. The second is that it can lead to grim psychological outcomes ... The transgendered person's disorder is in the person's "assumption" that they are different than the physical reality of their body, their maleness or femaleness, as assigned by nature. It is a disorder similar to a "dangerously thin" person suffering anorexia who looks in the mirror and thinks they are "overweight." This assumption, that one's gender is only in the mind regardless of anatomical reality, has led some transgendered people to push for social acceptance and affirmation of their own subjective "personal truth."

Dr. McHugh points out that:

> Studies show between 70% and 80% of children who express transgender feelings "spontaneously lose those feelings" over time. Also, for those who had sexual reassignment surgery, most said they were "satisfied" with the operation "but their subsequent psycho-social adjustments were no better than those who didn't have the surgery."

Because of these studies, McHugh reported: "At Hopkins we stopped doing sex-reassignment surgery, since producing a 'satisfied' but still troubled patient seemed an inadequate reason for surgically amputating normal organs."

Performing a surgery can change the plumbing in part of the body, but it does not change a man into a woman. Inside of our DNA, in our genes, we have either an XY chromosome, which means male, or we have an XX chromosome, meaning female. Amputating body parts does not change a person's genes. It is biologically impossible to change your gender since it exists on a genetic level. You may change what you look like on the outside, but you cannot change who you truly are. However, the cult of Inanna has taken deep root in our society and there are misguided doctors who are pushing it, even to the point of giving children "puberty-delaying hormones to render later sex-change surgeries less onerous—even though the drugs stunt the children's growth and carry a risk of sterility." Dr. McHugh likens such action to being "close to child abuse," noting that nearly 80% of those children will "abandon their confusion and grow naturally into adult life if untreated." Dr. McHugh went on the record to say:

> "'Sex change' is biologically impossible. People who undergo sex-reassignment surgery do not change from men to women or vice versa. Rather, they become feminized men or masculinized women. Claiming that this is a civil-rights matter and encouraging surgical intervention is in reality to collaborate with and promote a mental disorder."[481]

Thus, we have well credentialed specialists stating the fixation and desire for a sex change is a mental disorder. We know its origin and that the idea of a sex change is nothing new; it is a perversion that goes back to Inanna. This goddess, Mystery Babylon, was said to have such legendary powers that she could do a sex reassignment. However, it was impossible back then, and it remains impossible today.

People are free to choose to follow Inanna, but it will lead to suffering. If a person continues down that path, there are severe consequences. "And even as they did not like to retain God in their knowledge, God gave them over to a debased mind, to do those things which are not fitting" (Rom 1:28). God allows us to choose evil if we want it. He has laid before us life and death. He wants us to choose life because He knows the consequences of our choice. God created man; male and female He created them. He created us equal. Men are not better than women; Women are not inferior to men. We simply have different roles. God gave the man a role; He gave the woman a role. Neither is better than the other. They're both equal, but they're distinct roles. I say let's embrace our roles. If you're a man, be a man. Be the leader. Be courageous. God has given you testosterone for a reason. Stand up and have a backbone—Have an opinion. Be strong, but don't browbeat the woman. Don't be a jerk. If you are a woman, be a woman. Enjoy the role. If the man is the head, then the woman is the neck which turns the head. We should all embrace the gender that God has given and not rebel and reject His ways.

> For that they hated knowledge, and did not choose the fear of the LORD: They would none of my counsel: they despised all my reproof. Therefore shall they eat of the fruit of their own way, and be filled with their own devices (Ps 1:29–31 KJV).

Many people are seeking their own way, and they may have to eat the fruit of their decision. Gender transformation, one of the "powers" of Inanna, is prepping mankind for the Mark of the Beast. Gender confusion makes us question the most basic assumptions about who each of us is at the core: male or female. To arrogantly remake yourself into an image of your choosing is 100% antithetical to God's design when He created man, male and female. As a society, if we have agreed that gender is an option which can be changed, then the next logical extension is for people to change themselves genetically, and then perhaps our very humanity is up for grabs.

Appendix 4: William Tyndale and Easter

A question that comes up is whether Ishtar is the same as the word we see in the Bible, Eástre, and is this goddess the namesake for the Easter holiday? This question is isolated to English and German speakers because it is a language-related phenomena from an interpretation of a verse in Acts:

> And when he had apprehended him, he put him in prison, and delivered him to four quaternions of soldiers to keep him; intending after Easter (Eástre) to bring him forth to the people (Acts:12:4).

The word for *Eástre*, in Spanish and other Roman languages is *"la Pascua"* or *"la Pâque"*. It comes from the word *Pascha*, which is Latin for Passover, *Pesach* [Hebrew], but it has been ascribed to the resurrection event. It was William Tyndale who coined the term "Passover," which he used in his translation of the Hebrew Bible (Old Testament). Tyndale was faithful in times of persecution to translate the Bible, specifically the New Testament, from Greek into English so that "the plowboy would know more than the church clergy." Tyndale was hunted and had to flee England for Germany to finish translating. In 1525, the Tyndale New Testament was printed in English, the language of the common man. The Catholic Church confiscated and burned many of the Tyndale Bibles; and Tyndale, himself, was hunted for eleven years and then burned at the stake for making God's Word available to the public. The complete Bible was published in English in 1560 and was known as the Geneva Bible. It retains over 90% of William Tyndale's original English translation.

Figure 65 Ostara (1884) by Johannes Gehrts. The goddess, divinity of the radiant dawn, surrounded by beams of light, animals, and people looking up from the realm below.

Ironically, he used the term *Eástre* in the New Testament to refer to the Passover event, not the resurrection of Jesus. In my opinion, Tyndale used the wrong word simply due to confusion and being unfamiliar with the Passover.

Before Tyndale, a 7th-century monk, Venerable Bede, wrote extensively on the question of whether the church should celebrate the Resurrection on the floating date of Passover or on the Sunday after the spring equinox. While writing at length about this question, he mentions the origin story for the name of the holiday: a goddess named *Eostre*, who represents spring and fertility. Pagans had celebrated *Eostre* in spring, so people new to Christianity started celebrating the Resurrection at the same time with the same name. It is quite possible that *Ostara* or *Eástre* comes from the word Ishtar. This has not been decided conclusively on a linguistic basis. Nevertheless, I am persuaded that they are the same.

As the cult of Inanna-Ishtar / Ashtoreth / Astarte / Aphrodite spread into the world and went to the British Isles, the Anglo-Saxon goddess of spring and rebirth may have taken on the name of Ishtar with the adapted pronunciation: *Eástre or Ostara*. Ishtar was venerated not only in Britain, but in Germany and other Germanic speaking lands as *Ostara, Eostre or Eastre*, the goddess of the sunrise. We know that Venus was also the goddess of sunrise and of the spring. As we look for clues, we see similarities with ancient Inanna / Ishtar and the more modern *Ostara* or *Eástre*. For example, we know that Inanna / Ishtar went down into the underworld where she was compelled to remain for half the year, which is symbolic of the fall and winter. When she emerged from the underworld, the earth put on green leaves and blossomed with rebirth. The goddesses' stories are the same; their names sound similar. We see remarkably similar epithets for this particular goddess suggesting they are the same.[482] (See Appendix 3 Inanna).

For early Americans, the Easter festival was celebrated by Catholics, but was rejected by Protestants because of its pagan influences. The Protestants also shunned the celebration because it was historically a day of heavy drinking and carousing. Over time and through immigration, America adopted wild hares and colored eggs, obvious symbols of fertility, into the traditions of the Resurrection holiday.

Ancient rites of the spring equinox celebrated the emergence of Inanna from the underworld as one resurrected or re-born. Other cultures celebrated annual spring rituals honoring the annual rebirth of the dying sun god, *Sol Invictus*, or Egyptian Horus, or Greek Dionysus, or Phrygian Attis. As spring blossomed and the warm sun tarried longer in the sky, people celebrated the sun. Modern "sunrise services" clearly hearken back to pagan solar celebrations at this time of year.

Currently, the fun focus of the day is the "Easter Bunny" and hunting eggs. The hare (rabbit) and eggs are the symbolic representation of the goddess *Eostre* (See Figure 65). A rabbit is known for fertility, giving birth multiple times per year with only a 30-day gestation period. The goddess of fertility was celebrated on the vernal equinox in March through April. When Christianity spread to the Anglo-Saxons, many traditions from the festival to *Eostre* were incorporated into the celebration of the Resurrection. The blending of goddess-honoring traditions with the Resurrection ceremony pleased pagans and encouraged many to convert. The celebration was even called *Eostre* (Easter) which was easy on the convert's ear. To make the church more palatable to pagans, it brought in ancient practices in order to score converts.

Do we have the authority to blend pagan practices with our worship of God? When the children of Israel built the golden calf, they said their feast was in honor of the true God. Do you recall how God reacted to worship that was mixed with pagan practices?

Three thousand people died. When they entered the Promised Land, Israel was told: "When you come into the land which the LORD your God is giving you, you shall not learn to follow the abominations of those nations" (Duet 18:9). God does not allow us to mix pagan elements into our worship; He will not accept it.

> Take heed to yourself that you are not ensnared to follow them, after they are destroyed from before you, and that you do not inquire after their gods, saying, 'How did these nations serve their gods? I also will do likewise.' You shall not worship the LORD your God in that way; for every abomination to the LORD which He hates they have done to their gods; for they burn even their sons and daughters in the fire to their gods (Duet 12:30–31) (Emphasis mine).

But you say, "God knows my heart. The easter bunnies are just for the kids to have fun. I'm not engaged in pagan practices when I color eggs or go to a sunrise service." We have seen in this book that even our prayers can be an abomination if we are walking in disobedience. There are practices that belong to the goddess, and these practices cannot be Christianized. We must not say we are celebrating Jesus' resurrection when we are really "baking cakes to the queen of heaven." We must not worship God in pagan ways and tell Him that He better like it. God is light and He has no darkness mixed in. In the same way, our worship must be pure with no pagan elements mixed in.

In sum, we have a religious holiday named after a pagan goddess with non-biblical practices—we knew an egg-laying rabbit was a strange holiday mascot! Perhaps we should abandon the bunnies and just observe the feast days that Jesus and the Apostles celebrated.

Appendix 5: Balaam Used Ishtar to Make Israel Commit Treason

Just as Satan enticed Adam and Eve to curse themselves, in the same manner, he uses the sensual goddess Ishtar to ensnare mankind and even God's own people. The gods Moses encountered when entering Canaan were Baal and Ashtoreth, or as they were also called, Dumuzid and the queen of heaven, Inanna. When Israel came to the border of Moab, King Balak hired the prophet Balaam to curse Israel. After several failed attempts, it became clear that Israel was blessed, and no one could bring a curse against her; that is, a frontal attack would not work. God turned the intended curse into a blessing. This means that when people intend to curse Israel, God can turn it into a blessing.

Balaam could not curse them, but he was greedy and thus found a way to have the people curse themselves. They sent in the young ladies of Moab to entice the Israelite men by saying, "Hey boys, you want to see how we 'worship' Baal of Peor (Numb 25).

> Now Israel remained in Acacia Grove, and the people began to commit harlotry with the women of Moab. They invited the people to the sacrifices of their gods, and the people ate and bowed down to their gods. So Israel was joined to Baal of Peor, and the anger of the LORD was aroused against Israel (Num 25:1–3).

Satan has continued to use this old trick because it works like a charm. Nevertheless, the "women caused the children of Israel, through the counsel of Balaam, to trespass against the LORD in the incident of Peor, and there was a plague among the congregation of the LORD" (Num 31:16).

Baal of Peor was a savage god who demanded a terrible price from his devotees. Yet as we have seen, Baal, Marduk and Ninurta are variations of the Nimrod-the-Rebel-who-became-a-*gibbor* theme.

And of course, behind Nimrod was Satan. The root of this rebellion started with Nimrod in the land of Shinar (Sumer).

Shortly before his death, Moses warned Israel that when God brought them into Canaan to dispossess the nations, they must not follow after the false gods (See Deut 12:31).

By getting Israel to worship Satan and his consort, Ashtoreth, the queen of heaven, they brought themselves under the curse of YHWH. Satan did the same thing with Adam and Eve. He did not try to kill Adam. He got Adam to do it himself. In fact, he did not go directly to Adam. He went through Eve, and then Adam followed suit. He incited Adam and Eve to covet something that was not theirs; and they lusted after counterfeit pleasure, gave in to temptation and transgressed. God has already promised us delights in His kingdom, but Satan promises us immediate, counterfeits in his kingdom.

Figure 66 Inanna and Dumuzid reproduction of a Sumerian sculpture
from http://www.reweaving.org/inanna3.html

Ezekiel says that God: "brought me in visions ... to Jerusalem, to the door of the temple ... where the seat of the image of jealousy was" [This is referring to an image of one of these gods or goddesses], which provokes jealousy (Ezek 8:3). "Son of man, do you see what they are doing, the great abominations that the house of Israel commits here, to make Me go far away from My sanctuary" (Ezek 8:6). ... "and there–every sort of creeping thing, abominable beasts, and all the idols of the house of Israel, portrayed all around on the walls" (Ezek 8:10). ... "and to my dismay, women were sitting there weeping for Tammuz" [Dumuzid] (Ezek 8:14) (See Figure 66).

They were in God's house, but they were not worshiping God. They were worshipping other things. Notice what God says in the book of Jeremiah:

Jeremiah confronted a group of Judeans who decided to pack up and go to Egypt, by saying, "Don't leave, worship God", and their response—"No!"

> "But we will certainly do whatever has gone out of our own mouth, to burn incense to the queen of heaven and pour out drink offerings to her, as we have done, we and our fathers, our kings and our princes, in the cities of Judah and in the streets of Jerusalem. For then we had plenty of food, were well-off, and saw no trouble (Jer 44:17).

In other words, "Don't tell us to come back to God, Jeremiah, because when we worshiped the queen of heaven, life was good for us. Things were good when we did that." That is the lie—that by worshipping these false gods, the people become convinced that the gods are looking out for their good, but they are not; the ultimate end is disaster. The gods may promote their well-being for a short time, but it is a house of cards that comes crashing down. And what is worse, their infidelity in whoring after foreign gods alienates them from their Creator and His love and provision.

Appendix 6: What are the Abominations of Babylon?

By lavishing perverted pleasures on mankind, the goddess has the world under her thumb. She is the one who reigns over the kings of the Earth, who reigns over the TV and radio stations—who reigns over social media and all things on the internet. She enslaves people with the allure of pleasure, but not God's pleasures.

She is ... THE MOTHER OF HARLOTS AND OF THE ABOMINATIONS OF THE EARTH (Rev 17:5). "Come out of her, my people, lest you share in her sins and ... receive of her plagues" (Rev 18:4).

What are the things that God hates? We do not have to guess; we can look in His Word and be informed. Let us take a look in the Bible and hold it as a mirror to check ourselves. In Leviticus 11: 'And every creeping thing that creeps on the earth shall be an abomination (Lev 11:41). There are certain animals that God said do not eat. When God said, "Look, that animal is not food for you; it's an abomination to you," then you should listen and not eat it; just stop and repent.

'You shall not lie with a male as with a woman. It is an abomination (Lev 18:22). Homosexuality, in God's opinion, is an abomination. In Appendix 3, I said, "Wait, we shouldn't throw stones at them." What I am saying is we need to be honest with ourselves, because what happens is that people feel justified to throw stones at this abomination, but not at the abominations that they hold dear. Let us go on in our list.

> They provoked Him to jealousy with foreign gods; With abominations they provoked Him to anger They sacrificed to demons, not to God, To gods they did not know, To new gods, new arrivals That your fathers did not fear (Deut 32:16-17).

359

We see that Solomon built a high place for Chemosh, the abomination of Moab (See 1 Kgs 11:7), the god who required child sacrifice, or as we would say with a modern word "abortion?" Why does abortion happen? —Because people have sexual relations outside of a committed relationship of marriage. They have pregnancies they do not want and choose to get rid of the baby. That is an abomination in God's sight. All right, that one is easy to throw stones at because I do not do that, I am a good Christian.

What else? Dishonest scales are an abomination to the LORD, But a just weight is His delight (Prov 11:1).

Dishonest scales. Well, I am not a merchant; I am not selling things so I cannot be guilty of that. However, maybe I am not being honest in my business dealings, even if I do not use a scale to weigh things, but are you giving good value? Are you stacking the scales to your favor and not being honest with how you sell things? Or how you buy things? Or how you do commerce? How do you negotiate and conduct business with others? Are you an upright businessman or businesswoman? Are you an upright customer? Do you point out your coworker's shortcomings and failures, but you hide and cover your own to protect your image? Are there rules that you want applied to other people (things they shouldn't be allowed to say, ways they ought to behave, things they shouldn't be allowed to get away with, etc.) but you exempt yourself from those same standards?

Another abomination: "One who turns away his ear from hearing the law, Even his prayer is an abomination" (Prov 28:9).

What? My prayers can be an abomination? If I will not hear and obey His instructions, my prayer can be an abomination. God said, "Don't do that," and if I do it, and then I pray—it is an abomination.

> These six things the LORD hates, Yes, seven are an abomination to Him: A proud look ... (Prov 6:19).

A proud look is at the top of the list. God hates a proud look. Why does He hate a proud look? Because if we were to really understand who we are in comparison to Him, we would see that we are lower than the ants—the ants that are under my feet and I walk on them without even thinking about it. We are less than that; we are a worm.

We are nothing, and yet we think that we are amazing and that people should take notice of who we are. If I think that I am better than my neighbor, and I have this haughty look, this is being proud. If I look down on my neighbor because I can do something a little better, or have a slightly higher IQ, that is an abomination to God.

> ... A lying tongue [is an abomination to God], Hands that shed innocent blood [that is an abomination] (Prov 6:17), A heart that devises wicked plans, Feet that are swift in running to evil (Prov 6:18), A false witness who speaks lies, And one who sows discord among brethren (Prov 6:19).

All these are abominations. We should look deep into this list. Proverbs 6:16–19 is our checklist; you should go study it, meditate on it and say, "Lord, search me, see if there's any wicked way in me, that I may repent and turn from that character trait that God abhors." Before we stand before our Creator and while there is time to change, we should do a self-inventory and ask, "Am I guilty of any of these? Do I have a proud look? Do I have a lying tongue, hands that shed innocent blood, a heart that devises wicked plans, feet that are swift in running into evil? Am I a false witness that speaks lies? Am I the one who sows discord among brethren?"

If any of these describe you, those actions are an abomination—As much as a man lying with another man is an abomination in God's sight. They offend God as much as someone getting an abortion. These acts are an abomination in God's sight just as much as this Mystery Babylon the great, who is the mother of harlots and abominations. When we commit these other abominations, we are worshipping her.

> Everyone proud in heart is an abomination to the LORD. In mercy and truth Atonement is provided for iniquity; And by the fear of the LORD one departs from evil (Prov 16:5–6).

If you saw yourself in these descriptions, there is hope. This is the antidote—the fear of the Lord. The cure is to understand who I really am compared to Him. When I have that right perspective on God, then I will have the right perspective with you, my brothers and sisters. I hope you will have the right perspective with me. We must fear God and humble ourselves in order to repent.

This takes us up to the "abomination of desolation" (Mark 13:14).

The abomination of desolation is all these things put together. One day someone known as the "Son of Perdition" will be the embodiment of all this sin, the man of sin. He will have a lying tongue that speaks outrageous lies and sows discord among brethren. His heart will devise wicked plans and his feet will run to evil. He will shed innocent blood. This haughty renaissance man will embody the abominations that we have reviewed. In the height of his arrogance, he will go and do the ultimate sacrilege.

Appendix 7: No Leaven: Symbol of a Pure Life

To celebrate the feast of Unleavened Bread, we change the recipe for our bread and do not use leavening agents, or we simply buy *matzah* that does not have leaven. In preparation for the feast, we review the Bible passage that tells us, "On the first day you shall remove leaven from your houses" (Exod 12:15), and we remember that yeast and leavening agents are symbolic of sin. Just as yeast puffs up bread, we see that selfishness and arrogance puff up a person to be haughty and sinful. As part of the celebration of the feast of Unleavened Bread, we look through our homes to try to find any leaven that might be there, such as bread crumbs, cookie crumbles and bits of baked goods. Then we get rid of it. We search in the corners and crevices because our goal is to have the house free of leaven, while at the same time, we search our spiritual house with the goal that it will be free of sin.

Paul says in First Corinthians 3:

> Do you not know that you are the temple of God and that the Spirit of God dwells in you? If anyone defiles the temple of God, God will destroy him. For the temple of God is holy, which temple you are (1 Cor 3:16–17).

But then he goes on in First Corinthians chapter 5, saying:

> It is actually reported that there is sexual immorality among you, and such sexual immorality as is not even named among the Gentiles–that a man has his father's wife! And you are puffed up, and have not rather mourned, that he who has done this deed might be taken away from among you. In the name of our Lord Jesus Christ, when you are gathered together, along with my spirit, with the power of our Lord Jesus Christ,

deliver such a one to Satan for the destruction of the
flesh, that his spirit may be saved in the day of the Lord
Jesus (1 Cor 5:1–5)

Paul is saying, "You need to stop fellowshipping with this guy."
Now, 'deliver him to Satan' means to let him pursue the evil he has
chosen, and it will run its course, and hopefully the bad results will
cause the person to return to God in repentance so that he will be
saved when Jesus comes back. God says that we must not let him
remain as part of the congregation thinking that he's okay. Isn't that
what Jesus said to the seven churches? You are doing this right and
this right, but I have this thing against you. He then instructs them
to change and warns them of the consequences of remaining in sin.
"Your glorying is not good. Do you not know that a little leaven
leavens the whole lump?" (1 Cor 5:6).

Because with this little bit of leaven (this immorality and this
arrogance), the problem is that it spreads. It is completely
incompatible with the kingdom of God, which is going to be
revealed at Jesus' second coming. Arrogance, immorality and
perversion have no place in God's kingdom. We need to start
practicing a life free of arrogance, immorality and perversion
now, not just wait until Jesus returns. If we wait until then, it is
too late. We have to practice it today. We are told to purge out the
old leaven because Christ, our Passover, was sacrificed for us.

> "You shall keep the Feast of Unleavened Bread; you
> shall eat unleavened bread seven days, as I commanded
> you, at the time appointed in the month of Abib (Exod
> 23:15).

And then Jesus took the bread. He took *matzah*, unleavened
bread, and He blessed it, and He broke it and said, "Take, eat;
this is My body" (Matt 26:26). That unleavened bread, the
matzah, is this picture—Jesus says, "This is me." There is no sin,
there is no impurity in His body; we are to take and eat that
matzah in remembrance of Him.

Then Paul says in First Corinthians:

> Therefore, purge out the old leaven, that you may be a new lump, since you truly are unleavened. For indeed Christ, our Passover, was sacrificed for us (1 Cor 5:7). Therefore let us keep the feast, not with old leaven, nor with the leaven of malice and wickedness, but with the unleavened bread of sincerity and truth (1 Cor 5:8). … But now I have written to you not to keep company with anyone named a brother, who is sexually immoral, or covetous, or an idolater, or a reviler, or a drunkard, or an extortioner–not even to eat with such a person (1 Cor 5:11).

We are to look at the plank in our own eye before we point out the speck in our brother's eye. That is what we do first. But after we have taken an inventory of our heart in great humility, then we want to be careful not to keep the wrong company.

It was Christ, who took His life in His hands; and He went to the cross as the sacrifice. He was the blood that was put on the door lintel of Passover. If we are under the blood, and we are saved, then God passes over us and we are protected from the judgment. But we must first get out the old leaven.

Paul is clear about the requirement for believers to live right; in fact, the entire Bible plainly states that followers of Jesus will live righteously. He says:

> Do you not know that the unrighteous will not inherit the kingdom of God? Do not be deceived. Neither fornicators, nor idolaters, nor adulterers, nor homosexuals, nor sodomites (1 Cor 6:9), nor thieves, nor covetous, nor drunkards, nor revilers, nor extortioners will inherit the kingdom of God (1 Cor 6:10). Flee sexual immorality. Every sin that a man does is outside the body, but he who commits sexual immorality sins against His own body (1 Cor 6:18). Or do you not know

that your body is the temple of the Holy Spirit who is in you, whom you have from God, and you are not your own? (1 Cor 6:19).

These are sobering words—"The unrighteous will not inherit the kingdom of God." Fellow believer, I want to challenge you, encourage you and exhort you during this time that God has given us an opportunity to look at our own lives; Too often we point our finger and say, "Well, it is because of the homosexuals, it's all their fault. If it were not for them, we would have a wonderful country."

They have their issues, we know that. However, did we look at the list of God's top ten? Do we see homosexuals and fornicators on the list? We absolutely do. Yet look deeper— covetousness —that 10th commandment, "You shall not covet." Nobody can see you coveting, except one. He can see you coveting. If we covet, we will not inherit the kingdom of God because it is incompatible with God's character.

How can you have fellowship with God if you are coveting? How can you have fellowship with God if you are committing any one of these behaviors that God calls abominations? This is an opportunity for us to look deep at our own hearts and say, "Lord! Forgive me, I have been coveting."

Some years ago, I was going through the 10 commandments and just doing an internal check of how I am doing. I started with the first, "Have no other gods before me, I am the Lord your God that brought you out of Egypt, You shall have no gods before me," and of course I repented, "Lord, I'm sorry." "You should not make any graven images," I do not know where I was on that; I think I had a pretty good score on that one. Then, "Don't take His name in vain," "Keep the Sabbath..." and I went through the commandments.

I got to number 10, and I realized that I had been coveting. I had been coveting my neighbor's house. I had been coveting my neighbor's wife. I had been coveting my neighbor's car and my neighbor's bank account. I had to repent. As I came to the realization that I had broken the command: "Do not covet," I then also realized that through coveting, I was actually having other gods in my life.

By breaking number 10, I was breaking number 1. "You shall have no other God before me." I was setting up idols in my heart. What I was really saying was, "God, I don't trust you; I don't believe you; I don't think you're sufficient for me." Therefore, I have to look to things outside of what I own and possess, and say, "Oh! If only I could have that thing, then I would be happy." When God has promised to be sufficient, to give more than enough. I was guilty of violating the 10th commandment. I was guilty of covetousness, which is idolatry. I was worshiping the harlot.

Idolaters are saying, "I don't think God is enough, the God of heaven, who made heaven and Earth is not enough for me; I want something else." That is what Mystery Babylon is all about. This is the kingdom that reigns over the entire Earth, and we all can fall prey to the lure of unrestrained desires that will ultimately enslave us in this kingdom. "… Babylon has fallen, fallen! All the idols of her gods lie shattered on the ground!" (Isa 21:9). It is idolatry to live an unchecked pattern of covetousness. God has instructed us to be humble and content, yet we refuse to be satisfied. We fall prey to the green-eyed monster and become envious and greedy, then plummet into covetousness. It is the one sin that nobody can see. I cannot see you coveting; You cannot see me coveting (unless you put chocolate too close to my face). But that is what is happening. We say, "Oh! If only I could have that." Coveting involves lusting for something you cannot have, whether it is of a sexual nature, finances, power, or fame, it is still lust, which is coveting. The further danger of covetousness is that it leads you to violate more of the 10 commandments. It always happens; It is guaranteed.

We read about the doctrine of Balaam in Revelation, chapter 2. Jesus said, "Look, you're doing okay here, but '… you have those who hold to the doctrine of Balaam, who taught Balak to put a stumbling block before the children of Israel, to eat things sacrificed to idols, and to commit sexual immorality (Rev 2:14). … Repent, or else I will come to you quickly and will fight against them with the sword of My mouth'" (Rev 2:16). We read about this incident in Numbers 25 when:

> "Israel … began to commit harlotry with the women of Moab (Num 25:1). … and the anger of the LORD was aroused against Israel" (Num 25:3).

> They provoked Him to anger with their deeds, And the plague broke out among them (Ps 106:29).

We profess to know the King of Kings and the Lord of Lords, who sent His son Jesus to die on the cross; yet we have idolatry in our hearts. We need to sober up. Let us not be deceived. What a man sows that he will also reap. If you sow to idolatry, you are going to reap idolatry. Paul tells us that those who practice such things will not inherit the kingdom of God. This is the time for us to repent, "Oh! God, forgive me."

Paul says the same thing in Galatians:

> But if you are led by the Spirit, you are not under the law. Now the works of the flesh are evident, which are: adultery, fornication, uncleanness, lewdness, idolatry, sorcery, hatred, contentions, jealousies, outbursts of wrath, selfish ambitions, dissensions, heresies, envy, murders, drunkenness, revelries, and the like; of which I tell you beforehand, just as I also told you in time past, that those who practice such things will not inherit the kingdom of God (Gal 5:18–21).

Maybe you have prayed to receive Christ as your Savior. Hallelujah! I am glad that you did. I would encourage you if you haven't, to pray, "Father, forgive me. Cleanse me of my sins. I make You my King." That is always a good thing. If you have not done that, do that. If you have done that, and you see yourself on this list, pray again, "Father, forgive me."

Peter says:

> "As obedient children, not conforming yourselves to the former lusts, as in your ignorance (1 Pet 1:14); ... knowing that you were not redeemed with corruptible things, like silver or gold, from your aimless conduct received by tradition from your fathers (1 Pet 1:18), but with the precious blood of Christ, as of a lamb without blemish and without spot (1 Pet 1:19). ... Since you have purified your souls in obeying the truth through the Spirit in sincere love of the brethren, love one another fervently with a pure heart (1 Pet 1:22).

Our God has found a way to forgive us for lusting after the harlot. He sent Jesus, Yeshua, our Mashiach or Messiah. It does not matter if you say it in Hebrew, it really does not. If you have not given your life to Him, if you have not repented of your sins, today is the day.

Are you lusting in ways that people cannot see but you know, and God knows? You say, "Well, you know what? I don't look at pornography." Great! That is good. But are you coveting other things? You might look at the list and say, "Well, none of those apply to me, none of them." Are you that perfect? Look at this list, these different lists that Paul gives us (See Appendix 5 Balaam). He says that if we practice these things, we will not inherit the kingdom of God. God is going to destroy the harlot. We need to purge out the leaven in our lives, or we will be purged when He comes back.

Appendix 8: Joel's Army

Joel received a similar message concerning what is coming and explained the incredible fear people will experience. "Before them the people writhe in pain; All faces are drained of color" (Joel 2:6). Jesus told us that the end will involve "men's hearts failing them from fear and the expectation of those things which are coming on the earth, for the powers of the heavens will be shaken" (Luke 21:26). Joel's prophecy, in fact, pins the timing of the hearts failing and "faces drained of color" to the arrival of the creatures from the Abyss. Joel says:

> Blow the trumpet in Zion, And sound an alarm in My holy mountain! Let all the inhabitants of the land tremble; For the day of the LORD is coming, For it is at hand: A day of darkness and gloominess, A day of clouds and thick darkness, Like the morning clouds spread over the mountains. A people come, great and strong, The like of whom has never been; Nor will there ever be any such after them, Even for many successive generations. A fire devours before them, And behind them a flame burns; The land is like the Garden of Eden before them, And behind them a desolate wilderness; Surely nothing shall escape them (Joel 2:1–3).

At the end of the chapter, he speaks of an army of locusts: "… the swarming locust has eaten... my great army[483] which I sent among you." (Joel 2:25). We know that this army is related to locusts, which reminds us of the army related to locusts in Revelation 9. These armies are composed of locusts, but they are not locusts. How does that work?

Joel calls them locusts but describes them as horses, just like John did in Revelation 9. "Their appearance is like the appearance of horses, and like war horses they run" (Joel 2:4). They are apparently locusts that do not look like locusts, but like horses.

The noise they make is like the "rumbling of chariots" (Joel 2:5). These creatures can "leap on the tops of the mountains" (Joel 2:5). That means that they have the capacity to fly or at least to jump exceedingly high—to the tops of mountains! It is a leap so big that it is equivalent to flying.

They evoke the image and sound of a fire, "like the crackling of a flame of fire devouring the stubble, like a powerful army drawn up for battle" (Joel 2:5). Their movement is like a spark jumping out of the fire; they leap like bits of a combusting log ablaze in flames They are very powerful. As they spread out over the earth, "Before them peoples are in anguish; all faces grow pale (Joel 2:6). These creatures are like nothing the world has ever seen before:

> Like warriors they charge; like soldiers they scale the wall. They march each on his way; they do not swerve from their paths. They do not jostle one another; each marches in his path; they burst through the weapons and are not halted. They leap upon the city, they run upon the walls, they climb up into the houses, they enter through the windows like a thief (Joel 2:7–9).

If they can leap to the top of a mountain, then naturally, they can scale walls. Man's weapons have no effect on them; they just burst through the weapons and are not halted! That means that people are presumably trying to stop the beings in this army, and they are not able to slow the creatures. These beings are able to just burst through the defensive weapons.

> The earth quakes before them; the heavens tremble. The sun and the moon are darkened, and the stars withdraw their shining (Joel 2:10).

This is an important clue regarding the timing, and it is going to help us see that the events in Revelation, chapter 9 are the same events being described in Joel.

And he opened the bottomless pit, and smoke arose out of the pit like the smoke of a great furnace. So the sun and the air were darkened because of the smoke of the pit (Rev 9:2).

We want to find two or three witnesses to a particular event in order to understand it better. When we find several references to the same event, we need to match up the information, in what I call biblical triangulation. It is similar to using cell towers to track a phone's location by measuring the time delay that a signal takes to return back to the towers from the phone. This delay is then calculated into distance and gives a fairly accurate location of the phone. We can use the information about the sun and the moon and the stars growing dark from Joel and Revelation and even, Isaiah 13:10 speaks of the event. When we triangulate using the parallel information, we get clues about the details and timing of the event.

Something pretty radical is happening. Let us just do a quick comparison. I summarized the information from Joel, chapter 2 and Revelation, chapter 9 in an outline (Next page).

Joel 2	Revelation 9
Timing Markers & Great Army, the same in both passages	
• Earthquake, Sun, Moon, stars do not shine • Powerful army	• Sun, moon, stars diminished by smoke • Army of 200 million
Joel's Description of creatures	John's Description of creatures
• look like horses running to war • loud like chariots / fire • capacity to fly / jump exceedingly high • people's hearts failing them • able to go over walls • march in formation, do not deviate • weapons have no effect	• Like a horse running to battle • Lion's head • Man's face • Something like crowns • Woman's hair • Lion's teeth • Something like breastplates of iron • Noisy wings • Scorpion's tail with stingers • Serpent-head tails • Fiery red, hyacinth blue, and sulfur yellow iron-like breastplate • Fire and brimstone from mouth

Table 9 Comparison of Joel Ch. 2 & Revelation Ch, 9

In Joel's description, we get a long-distance view of the scene which focuses on the coordinated movements of the horse-like creatures pressing forward in troops. Joel describes the people's collective reactions to the invasion. He focuses on the disciplined movements of the army of beasts that blasts quickly and forcefully upon a whole city. Joel notes how the beasts are not limited by gravity or deterred by walls or weaponry.

In Revelation, John describes the same horse-like creatures who are running to battle, but John gives a closer camera view. John describes the colors of the breastplates of the beasts. He gives a close-up sketch of individual beasts by describing the faces, crown, hair and even the teeth. He notes that the beasts can expel fire from their mouths. John and Joel are describing the same creatures, but Joel is viewing them at a distance, while John is up close.

The precursor to the explosion of charging beasts in both accounts, is the diminished or darkened moon and sun. John explains that the cause of the darkening is the smoke from the pit. The Abyss is opened with voluminous smoke which darkens the sky by blocking the luminaries. Both Joel and John agree that this is the time that the horse-like creatures appear and go to battle. Here, we have two witnesses to the event which agree that it begins with the opening of the Abyss and culminates with the launch of these muscular creatures invading and terrorizing people.

Bibliography

"Ancient Mesopotamian Gods and Goddesses," ORACC Museum, based on data prepared by the UK HEA-funded AMGG project, May 2011, http://oracc.museum.upenn.edu/ amgg/index.html.

Akkadian Dictionary, s.v. "Cherub," "Ug." Accessed through Association Assyrophile de France, http://www.assyrianlanguages.org/akkadian/.

Albenda, Pauline. "The "Queen of the Night" Plaque: A Revisit." *Journal of the American Oriental Society* 125, no. 2 (2005): 171-90. http://www.jstor.org/stable/20064325.

Altosalento. "Ceglie Messapica." http://www.altosalentorivieradeitrulli.it/nuova_pagina _17.htm.

Annus, Amar, 1999. "Ninurta and the Son of Man." In Melammu Symposia 2: R. M. Whiting (ed.), 'Mythology and Mythologies. Methodological Approaches to Intercultural Influences.' In *Proceedings of the Second Annual Symposium of the Assyrian and Babylonian Intellectual Heritage Project, Paris, October 4-7, 1999, Pg. 7-17.* Helsinki: The Neo-Assyrian Text Corpus Project, 2001. http://www.helsinki.fi/science/saa/ and http://www.aakkl. helsinki.fi/ melammu/.

Annus, Amar. *The God Ninurta in the Mythology and Royal Ideology of Ancient Mesopotamia.* State Archives of Assyria Studies, Volume 14. Helsinki: Neo-Assyrian Text Corpus Project, 2002.

BabelStone. *Burney Relief.* June 24, 2010. British Museum, London. Photograph. https://upload. wikimedia.org/wikipedia/commons/2/22/British_Museum_Queen_of_the_ Night.jpg.

Barton, George A. "On the Pantheon of Tyre." *Journal of the American Oriental Society*, 1901, Vol. 22 (1901), 115-17. http://www.jstor.com/stable/592422.

BBC News. "Gilgamesh tomb believed found." Last updated April 29, 2003. http://news.bbc.co. uk/2/hi/science/nature/2982891.stm.

Beaulieu, S., after Cornelius 2004. *Qudshu Plaque from a tomb in Akko, Israel, dated ca. 1550-1200 BCE.* Lost (stolen). Drawing: Plate 5.21.

Beaulieu, S., after Leick 1998. *Impression of Neo-Assyrian Seal dated ca. 750-650 BCE.* British Museum, London. Drawing: Plate 38.

Biblical Studies Foundation. *New English Translation Bible.* Richardson: Biblical Studies Press, L.L.C., 1996. Accessed at https://netbible.org/.

Black, J.A., G. Cunningham, E. Fluckiger-Hawker, E. Robson, and G. Zólyomi. *The Electronic Text Corpus of Sumerian Literature, "The Exploits of Ninurta." Oriental Institute of the University of Oxford. Accessed through ETCSL Project,* http://etcsl.orinst.ox.ac.uk/section1/tr162.htm.

Black, Jeremy and Anthony Green. *Gods, Demons and Symbols of Ancient Mesopotamia An Illustrated Dictionary*, Illustrator: Tessa Rickards. London: British Museum Press, 1992.

Black, Jeremy, and Green, Anthony. *Gods, Demons, and Symbols of Ancient Mesopotamia: An Illustrated Dictionary.* Austin: University of Texas Press, 1992.

Breitenberger, Barbara M. *Aphrodite and Eros The Development of Greek Erotic Mythology in Early Greek Poetry and Cult.* New York City and Oxfordshire: Routledge, Taylor & Francis Group, 2007.

Brisch, Nicole. *Ancient Mesopotamian Gods and Goddesses.* "Pablisag." 2013. Accessed through ORACC, http://oracc.museum.upenn.edu/amgg/listofdeities/pabilsag/index.html.

Bromiley, G. W. *The International Standard Bible Encyclopedia.* Grand Rapids: W. B. Eerdsmans, 1979. Accessed through TheWord Bible Software.

Brown, Francis, S. R. Driver and Charles A. Briggs. *A Hebrew and English Lexicon of the Old Testament.* Oxford: The Clarendon Press, 1907.

Brown, J. P. and E. M. Meyers. "Batanaia." https://pleiades.stoa.org/places/678054/batanaia.

Burkert, Walter. *The Orientalizing Revolution, Near Eastern Influence on Greek Culture in the Early Archaic Age,* 50. Cambridge and London: Harvard University Press, 1995. https://www. google.com/books/edition/_/cliUL7dWqNIC?hl=en&gbpv=0.

Buswell, J. Oliver. *Systematic Theology of the Christian Religion*, 264–65, Grand Rapids: Zondervan, 1962.

Campbell, Mike. "Sumerian Mythology Names," s.v. "Gilgamesh." Behind the Name. https://www.behindthename.com/names/usage/sumerian-mythology.

Carnahan, Wolf, ed. *The Epic of Gilgamesh, Tablet VI.* Translated by Maureen Gallery Kovacs. Accessed on Academy for Ancient Texts, http://www.ancienttexts.org/library/Mesopotamian /gilgamesh/tab6.htm.

Cartwright, Mark. *World History Encyclopedia, s.v.* "Melqart." https://www.ancient.eu/ Melqart/.

Charles, R. H., ed. *The Book of Enoch*, 63. Oxford: The Clarendon Press, 1893.

Charlesworth, James H. "Revealing the Genius of Biblical Authors: Symbology, Archaeology, and Theology." *Communio Viatorum* 46, Nr. 2, (2004): 124-40.

Chisolm, Hugh, ed. *Encyclopædia Britannica.* 11th ed., c.v. "Messapian Language." Cambridge: Cambridge University Press. 1911. Accessed through Dictionary Sensagent, http://dictionary. sensagent.com/Messapian%20language/en-en/.

Clarissa. "Asherah, Part III: The Lion Lady." *Queen of Heaven* (blog). Nov. 16, 2010. https://thequeenofheaven.wordpress.com/2010/11/16/asherah-part-iii-the-lion-lady/.

Clay, Albert T. "The Origin and Real Name of NIN-IB." *Journal of the American Oriental Society* 28 (1907): 135-44. https://doi.org/10.2307/592765.

Cole, S. W. "Nippur IV: The Early Neo-Babylonian Governor's Archive from Nippur." *OIP* 114, no. 4 (1996).

Definitions.net. "Chernobyl." https://www.definitions.net/definition/Chernobyl.

Dittenberger, W., ed. *Orientis Graeci Inscriptiones Selectae.* Leipsiae: S Hirzel, 1903.

Doniger, Wendy. *Merriam-Webster's Encyclopedia of World Religions,* 120, 140. Springfield: Merriam-Webster, Inc., 1990.

Edzard, D.O. "Mesopotamien. Die Mythologie der Sumerer und Akkader." *Götter und Mythen im Vorderen Orient Wörterbuch der Mythologie,* H.W. Haussig, and E. Schmalzriedt, eds. 17-140. Stuttgart: Klett-Cotta Verlag, 1965.

Electronic Text Corpus of Sumerian Literature. "Enlil in the E-kur (Enlil A): translation." Dec. 18, 2002. http://etcsl.orinst.ox.ac.uk/section4/tr4051.htm.

Elliott, Josh K. "'I'm emotional': Man bakes sourdough from 4,500-year-old Egyptian yeast." Global News, August 7, 2019. "https://globalnews.ca/news/5736305/yeast-egyptian-sourdough-4500-years-old/.

Elwell, Walter A. *Baker's Evangelical Dictionary of Biblical Theology*, s.v. "Evil." Ada: Baker Publishing Group, 1996.

Etheridge, J.W. *The Targum of Onkelos and Jonathan Ben Uzziel on the Pentateuch.* Piscataway: Gorgias Press, Sept. 2, 2005.

Even-Shosan, Avraham (אַבְרָהָם אֶבֶן־שׁוֹשָׁן). *The New Dictionary* (ha-milón he-khadásh הַמִּלוֹן הֶחָדָשׁ), 1 ed., s.v. "Hebrew Terms Derived from Sumerian." Jerusalem: Kiryat-Sefer Ltd. (קְרִיַת־סֵפֶר בַּע"ם), 1984. https://en.wiktionary.org/wiki/Category: Hebrew_terms_derived_from_Sumerian.

Faulk, L. and A. Scott. *Tales of the Patriarchs (*originally titled *Genesis Apocryphon).* Paraphrase of Dead Sea Scrolls Fragment 2: Column 2, Prepared for Into. to Hebrew: St. Joseph's University, Dec. 7, 1998. https://www. https://www.documentacatholicaomnia.eu/03d/sine-data,_Absens,_Dead_Sea_Scrolls_[Texts_And_Translations],_EN.pdf.

Fenet, Annick. *Les Dieux Olympiens Et La Mer*, 83-138. Rome: Ecole Française, 2016. https://books.openedition.org/efr/5584#illustrations.

Fenet, Annick. *The Olympian Gods and the Sea.* Fig 5. Rome: French School of Rome, 2016. Photograph by author. Accessed on Open Edition Books, https://books.openedition.org/efr/ 5584#illustrations.

Fleming, Donald C. *Bridgeway Bible Dictionary*, s.v. "Demons." Brisbane: Bridgeway Publications, 2004.

Fox, Robin Lane. *Traveling Heroes in the Epic Age of Homer*, 217. New York: Vintage Books, March 2010. Accessed http://ancientheroes.net/blog/alexander-the-great-zeus-ammon.

Foxvog, Daniel A. "Introduction to Sumerian Grammar," Jan. 4, 2016. In *Cuneiform Digital Library Preprints*, 2.0. Bertrand Lafont, ed. http://cdli.ucla.edu/?q=cuneiform-digital-library-preprints.

Frankfort, Henri. "House of the Mountain, Mountain of the Storm, and Bond Between Heaven and Earth," 21. In *The Art and Architecture of the Ancient Orient.* New Haven: Yale University Press, 1996.

Gallagher, W.R. "On the Identity of Hêlēl Ben Sahar of Is. 14:12-15," *UF* 26 (1994): 131-146.

Gentry, R. V. "Radioactive Halos." *Annual Review of Nuclear Science* 23 (1973): 347.

Gentry, Robert V. "Fingerprints of Creation." Accessed through Earth Science Associates, http://www.halos.com/index.htm.

George, A. R. *Enûma Eliš, The Babylonian Epic of Creation*. Tablet VI, 63:301–2. Babylonian Typographical Texts, 1992.

George, Andrew. *Archiv für Orientforschung*, 75–95. "The Tower of Babel: Archaeology, history and cuneiform texts," Jan. 2005. https://www.researchgate.net/publication /303824383_The_Tower_of_Babel_Archaeology_history_and_cuneiform_t exts.

George, Andrew. *Babylon: Focus mesopotamischer Geschichte, Wiege früher Gelehrsamkeit, Mythos in der Moderne, 67-86.* "E-sangil and E-temen-anki: the archetypal cult-centre," 1999. Accessed through School of Oriental and African Studies (SOAS), University of London, https:// eprints.soas.ac.uk/id/eprint/1598.

Gesenius, H.W.F. *Hebrew and Chaldee Lexicon to the Old Testament Scriptures*, translated by Samuel Prideaux Tregelles, 7th ed., s.v. "Og," "Rachal." Ada: Baker Publishing Group, 1990.

Gill, John. *Exposition of the Old Testament*, s.v. "Galatians 4:26." Sioux Falls: Graceworks Multimedia, 2011.

Gruner, L. *Monuments of Nineveh, Second Series, plate 5*, Austen Henry Layard, ed. 1853, Drawing. https://commons.wikimedia.org/w/index.php?curid=18217886.

Halloram, John A. *Sumerian Language Page*, s.v. "gug₅." https://www.sumerian.org/sumcvc. htm.

Hamp, Douglas. *Discovering the Language of Jesus*. Santa Ana: Calvary Chapel Publishing, 2005.

Hansen, William. *Handbook of Classical Mythology*, 177. Santa Barbara: ABC-CLIO, 2003.

Harris, Laird R., Gleason L. Archer, Jr. and Bruce K. Waltke. *Theological Wordbook of the Old Testament.* Chicago: Moody Publishers, 1980.

Hays, Christopher B. "Enlil, Isaiah, and the Origins of the ʾĕlilim: A Reassessment." *ZAW* 132, no. 2 (June 5, 2020). https://doi.org/10.1515/zaw-2020-2002.

Heidel, A. *The Gilgamesh Epic and Old Testament Parallels,* 17-18, 2nd ed. Chicago: University of Chicago Press, 1963.

Heiser, Michael. (Mysteries of Mt. Hermon) Interview with Douglas Hamp. *The Awakening Report*, podcast video. August 25, 2020. https://youtu.be/yjiZHLnhIRQ.

Heiser, Michael. (Mysteries of Mt. Hermon) Interview with Douglas Hamp. *The Awakening Report*, podcast video. August 25, 2020. https://youtu.be/yjiZHLnhIRQ.

Hesiod. *The Homeric Hymns and Homerica.* Translated by Hugh G. Evelyn-White, s.v. "The Theogony," 185. Cambridge: Harvard University Press; London: William Heinemann Ltd., 1914. Accessed through Perseus Digital Library with support by Annenberg CPB/Project, http://data.perseus. org/texts/urn:cts:greekLit:tlg0020.tlg001.

Hirsch, Emil G., M. Seligsohn and Wilhelm Bacher, eds. *Jewish Encyclopedia,* s.v. "Nimrod." 1906. Accessed through Jewish Encyclopedia.com, http://jewishencyclopedia.com/ articles/11548-nimrod.

Horn, Thomas R. "Biblical Example of Nephilim Resurrection?" Nov. 17, 2010. https://newswithviews.com/Horn/thomas155.htm.

Horn, Thomas R. "Could Modern Science Play a Role in the Coming Of Apollo?" Sept. 8, 2009. http://www.newswithviews.com/Horn/thomas121.htm.

Israel Ministry of Tourism. "Caesarea Philippi." Accessed through Land of the Bible, https://www.land-of-the-bible.com/Caesarea_Philippi.

Jacobsen, Thorkild. "The líl of dEn-líl." In *DUMU-É-DUB-BA-A: Studies in Honor of Åke W. Sjöberg*, H. Behrens, D. M. Loding and M. T. Roth, eds., 270. Philadelphia: UP Museum of Archeology and Anthropology, 1989.

Jacobsen, Thorkild. *The Harps that Once... Sumerian Poetry in Translation.* New Haven and London: Yale University Press, 1987.

Jeremias, Alfred. *Handbuch der altorientalischen Geisteskultur*, 74. Leipzig: JC Hinrichs'sche Buchhandlung, 1913.

Kaulins, Andis. *Lexiline: History of Civilization.* https://www.lexiline.com/lexiline/lexi37.htm.

Kittel, Gerhard, ed. *Theological Dictionary of the New Testament*, s.v. "demons." Translated by G. W. Bromiley. Grand Rapids: W. B. Eerdsmans, 1964.

Kramer, Samuel Noah. "The epic of Enmerkar and the Lord of Aratta," translation from *The Babel of Tongues: A Sumerian Version.* Journal of the American Oriental Society 88 (1968):108-11.

Kramer, Samuel Noah. *History Begins at Sumer.* Garden City: Doubleday, 1959.

Kramer, Samuel Noah. *The Sumerians.* Chicago: The University of Chicago Press, 1963.

Lamboley, Jean-Luc. *Les cultes de l'Adriatique méridionale à l'époque républicaine,* 133-41. Pessac: Ausonius Editions, 2000. https://doi.org/10.4000/books.ausonius.6837.

Lamboley, Jean-Luc. *The cults of the southern Adriatic during the republic era.* Pessac: Ausonius Editions, 2000. Accessed on Open Edition Books, https://books.openedition.org/ausonius/6837.

Legal Information Institute, Cornell Law School. "Adverse Possession." https://www.law. cornell.edu/wex/adverse_possession.

Leick, Gwendolyn *A Dictionary of Ancient Near Eastern Mythology,* 86. New York City: Routledge, 1998.

Liddell, H. G. and R. Scott. *A Greek-English Lexicon,* s.v. "Beta: B." Oxford: Clarendon Press, 1996. Accessed through Greek Alphabet, http://www.greekalphabeta.com/learn-about-beta-b-2.html, definitions culled from LSJ.

Liddell, H. G., Robert Scott and Henry Stuart Jones, eds. *Lexicon of Classical Greek,* 9th ed., Oxford: Oxford University Press, 1925..

Lindsey, Hal. *The Late Great Planet Earth.* Grand Rapids: Zondervan Academic, 1970.

Loftus, William, *Travels and Researches in Chaldea and Sinai.* New York: Robert Carter & Brothers, 1857. Accessed translation of Inscription by Nebuchadnezzar II, through Schoyen Collection, https://www.schoyencollection.com/history-collection-introduction/babylonian-history-collection/tower-babel-stele-ms-2063.

Lomas, Kathryn. "Crossing Boundaries: The Inscribed Votives of Southeast Italy." *Pallas,* no. 86 (2011): 311-29. http://www.jstor.org/stable/43606696.

Lomas, Kathryn. "Crossing Boundaries: The inscribed votives of Southeast Italy." Oct. 30, 2011. https://doi.org/10.4000/pallas.2208.

Luginbill, Robert. *The Satanic Rebellion: Background to the Tribulation,* "Part 1: Satan's Rebellion and Fall." http://ichthys.com.

Marcovich, Miroslav. "From Ishtar to Aphrodite." *Journal of Aesthetic Education,* 39. 2 (1996): 43–59, doi:10.2307/3333191, JSTOR 3333191.

Marcus, Joel. "The Gates of Hades and the Keys of the Kingdom (Matt 16:18-19)." *The Catholic Biblical Quarterly* 50, no. 3 (1988): 443-55. http://www.jstor.org/stable/43717704.

Mark, Joshua J. *World History Encyclopedia, s.v.* "Enlil." https://www.ancient.eu/Enlil/.

Mark, Joshua J. *World History Encyclopedia, s.v.* "Inanna." https://www.ancient.eu/Inanna/.

Marlowe, Creig. "A New Take on the Tower: 'The Sin of Shinar' (Gen 11:4)." *The Evangelical Journal of Theology* XX:1 (2011): 29-39.

Mattfeld, Walter R. "Pictures of the Serpent." Last revised Oct. 4, 2010. http://www. bibleorigins.net/Serpentningishzida.html.

McDonald, Fiona. "Scientists Just Unraveled the First-Ever Photo of Quantum Entanglement." *Sciencealert*. July 13, 2019. https://www.sciencealert.com/scientists-just-unveiled-the-first-ever-photo-of-quantum-entanglement.

MesopotamianGods.com. "Inanna / Ishtar." http://www.mesopotamiangods.com/inanna/.

Milik, J. T. *Aramaic Fragments of Qumran Cave 4,* 167. Oxford: Clarendon Press, 1976.

Millburn, Naomi. "The Weight & Height of Lions." https://animals.mom.com/weight-height-lions-2378.html.

Morgan, Cheryl. "Evidence for Trans Lives in Sumer." May 2, 2017. Accessed on Notches, Ancient World, http://notchesblog.com/2017/05/02/evidence-for-trans-lives-in-sumer/.

Murphy, Heather. "Man who had transplant finds out months later his DNA has changed to that of donor 5,000 miles away." *New York Times*. Accessed through *The Independent*, pub. Dec. 9, 2019. https://www.independent.co.uk/news/world/americas/dna-bone-marrow-transplant-man-chimera-chris-long-forensic-science-police-a9238636.html.

Murray, Stephen O. *Islamic Homosexualities: Culture, History, and Literature*, 66. Will Roscoe, ed. New York: NYU Press, 1997.

Myers, E. A. *The Ituraeans and the Roman Near East: Reassessing the Sources,* 65. Cambridge: University Press, 2012.

Nickelsburg, George. *1 Enoch 1. A Commentary on the Book of 1 Enoch*, 1–36; 81–108. Minneapolis: Fortress, 2001.

NOVA. "E = mc² Explained." http://www.pbs.org/wgbh/nova/einstein/lrk-hand-emc2expl.html.

Online Etymology Dictionary, s.v. "giant," "Nashville," "penis." https://www.etymonline.com

Palestine Exploration Fund, *Palestine Exploration Quarterly Statement 1869-71*. London: Palestine Exploration Fund, 1896-1936. Digitized by Univ. of Minn. https://hdl.handle.net /2027/umn.31951p010211321.

Papazian, Sjur. "The snake and the serpopard." (blog) July 29, 2014. https://aratta.wordpress. com/2014/07/29/the-snake-and-the-serpopard/.

Parpola, Asko. "Studia Orientalia." *Finnish Oriental Society*, 84 (1998).

Parrot, André. *The Tower of Babel, Studies in Biblical Archaeology 2,* 64. New York: The Philosophical Library Inc., 1955.

Pinchas, Artzi. *Encyclopedia.com.* "Sikkuth and Chiun." Feb. 20, 2021. https://www.encyclopedia.com/religion/encyclopedias-almanacs-transcripts-and-maps/sikkuth-and-chiun.

Pitcher, Molly. *New World Encyclopedia,* s.v. "Moloch." https://www.newworldencyclopedia. org/entry/Moloch.

Planck, Max, "Das Wesen der Materie [The Nature of Matter]." Speech at Florence, Italy, 1944. Accessed from Archiv zur Geschichte der Max-Planck-Gesellschaft, Abt. Va, RePg. 11 Planck, Nr. 1797.

Preus, Mary C. *Eloquence and Ignorance in Augustine's On the Nature and Origin of the Soul,* 56. Decatur: Scholars Press, 1985.

Provan, Charles D. *The Church Is Israel Now: The Transfer of Conditional Privilege.* Vallecito: Ross House Books, 2004.

Rama. *Wikimedia.* "Stele of Qadesh." Oct. 24, 2007. Louvre Museum, Paris. Photograph. https://commons.wikimedia.org/wiki/File:Stele_of_Qadesh_upper-frame.jpg

Rawlinson, George. *Egypt and Babylon From Sacred and Profane Sources.* New York: Charles Schribner's Sons, 1885. Accessed through Internet Archive, http://www.archive.org/stream /egyptbabylonfrom00rawl/egyptbabylonfrom00rawl_djvu.txt.

Rice, Bill, *Wikipedia.* "Caesarea Philippi." Jan. 21, 2011. Photograph. https://commons. wikimedia.org/w/index.php?curid=35423945.

Robertson, Archibald Thomas. *Robertson's Word Pictures*. Ada: Baker Publishing Group, 1923.

Rochberg, Francesca. *The Heavenly Writing.* Cambridge: Cambridge University Press, 2004.

Rodkinson, Michael L. *Babylonian Talmud.* "Tract Taanith (Fasting)", Book 4: Tracts Pesachim, Yomah and Hagiga, 1918, Accessed through Sacred-texts.com, http://www.sacred-texts.com/jud/t04/taa06.htm.

Rohl, David. *The Lost Testament: From Eden to Exile the Five-Thousand-Year History of the People of The Bible.* London: Century, 2002.

Rose, Geordie. (Quantum computing: Artificial Intelligence is Here). *Ideacity,* video. Aug. 25, 2015. https://youtu.be/PqN_2jDVbOU?t=277.

Salentoacolory. "Zeus of Ugento." Archiological Museum of Taranto. Photographs. https:// www.salentoacolory.it/museo-archeologico-taranto/.

Sauber, Wolfgang. *Aphrodite und Adonis.* https://commons.wikimedia.org/w/index.php?curid =3962125.

Siegfried, Tom. "A new 'Einstein' equation suggests wormholes hold the key to quantum gravity." *Science News*, Aug. 18, 2016. https://www.insider.com/a-new-einstein-equation-suggests-wormholes-hold-the-key-to-quantum-gravity-2016-8.

Smith, George. *The Chaldean Account of Genesis.* London: Henry Colburn, 1880.

Smith, William, ed. *Smith's Bible Dictionary 1863*. London: John Murray, 1863.

Smith, William. *Dictionary of Greek and Roman Geography,* s.v. "Batanaea." London: Walton and Maberly, 1854, Accessed through Perseus Digital Library with support by Annenberg CPB/Project, http://www.perseus.tufts.edu/hopper/text?doc=Perseus%3Atext%3A1999.04.0064%3Aalphabetic+letter%3DB%3Aentry+group%3D3%3Aentry%3Dbatanaea-geo.

Soncino Zohar, Shemoth. *Pseudepigrapha Lost Books of Eden.* Chapter LI: 2, 5-7.

Sourdough Companion. "The oldest starter?" Message Forum, July 3, 2009. https://sourdough. com/forum/oldest-starter.

Spooner, Henry G. *American Journal of Urology and Sexology*, Vol. 14. Morris Park West: Urologic Publishing Association, 1918.

Subramaniyan, Sethu. *Derga Temple, Aihole.* April 3, 2010. https://commons.wikimedia. org/w/index.php?curid=21764494.

Tate, Karl. "How Quantum Entanglement Works." *LiveScience,* April 8, 2013. https://www. livescience.com/28550-how-quantum-entanglement-works-infographic.html.

The Pennsylvania Sumerian Dictionary, s.v. "gug." Last updated June 26, 2006. http://psd. museum.upenn.edu/epsd/e1897.html.

Theosophical University Press. *Sunrise*, Feb. 7, 2012. http://www.theosociety.org/ pasadena/sunrise/52-02-3/s2oneh2.jpg.

Trustees of the British Museum. *Kudurru, Museum No. 90829.* British Museum, London. Photograph. https://www.britishmuseum.org/collection/object/W_1882-0522-1798.

Trustees of the British Museum. *Pillar in the Collection of Ancient Greek Inscriptions.* British Museum, London. Photograph. https://www.britishmuseum.org/collection/object/G_1903-0422-1.

Trustees of the British Museum. *World History Encyclopedia, s.v.* "Cylinder Seal with Ninurta." Feb. 1, 2017. British Museum, London. Photograph. https://www.ancient.eu/image/6317/ cylinder-seal-with-ninurta/.

UNED. "Melqart, God of Tyre, King of the Underworld." https://www2.uned.es/geo-1-historia-antigua-universal/RELIGION-FENICIA/melqart.htm.

United States Conference of Catholic Bishops. *Amos, Chapter 5.* http://usccb.org/bible/amos /5/.

Utley, Bob. *You Can Understand the Bible*. Marshall: Bible Lessons International, March 2013. Retrieved from TheWord Bible Software.

Vallée, Jacques. *Dimensions: A Casebook of Alien Contact*. New York: Ballantine Books, 1988.

Vallée, Jacques. *The Invisible College*, 233. Boston: Dutton, 1975.

Van der Toorn, Karel, Bob Becking and Pieter W. van der Horst, eds. *Dictionary of Deities and Demons in the Bible.* Grand Rapids: Wm. B. Eerdmans Publishing Co., 1999.

Von Soden, W. "Die Unterweltsvision eines assyrischen Kronprinzen," ZA 43 [1936] 17:56; Angim III 38. For the Annunaki and Igigi gods, cf. W. von

Soden, "Zur wiederherstellung der marduk-gebete bms 11 und 12," Iraq 31 (1969), 85:32; M. Civil, "Commentaries from Nippur," JNES 33 (1974), 336:13.

Waerzeggers, C. and M. Groß, et al., *Prosobab: Prosopography of Babylonia.* "Prosobab logogram list." https://prosobab.leidenuniv.nl.https://prosobab.leidenuniv.nl/pdfs /logogram.pdf.

Walter Bauer. *A Greek-English Lexicon of the New Testament and Other Early Christian Literature*, Frederick W. Danker, ed. Chicago: University of Chicago Press, 2000. Accessed through TheWord Bible Software, v.9.

Walton, John H. "Is there archaeological evidence of the Tower of Babel?" reprinted by permission from Bulletin for Biblical Research 5 [1995]: 155-75. List compiled H.C. Rawlinson, H.C. 1861 The Cuneiform Inscription s of Western Asia, v. 2. London: R.E. Bowler: 50: 1-23 a, b; Accessed at http://christiananswers.net/q-abr/abr-a021.html.

Werner, Gitt. *In the Beginning Was Information*. Translated by Jaap Kies. Bielefeld: Christliche Literatur-Verbreitung, 2000.

White, Gavin. "The Winter Solstice Period." Nov. 2009. Accessed through Skyscript, http://www .skyscript.co.uk/babylonian_sagittarius.pdf.

Wiggermann, F. A. M. *Mesopotamian Protective Spirits: The Ritual Texts,* 166-67. Groningen: Styx & PP Publications, 1992.

Wiggermann, F. A. M. *Nergal, Reallexikon der Assyriologie,* 215-26. Berlin: De Gruyter, 1999.

Wiggermann, F. A. M., D. O. Edzard, ed. Reallexikon der Assyriologie. Berlin: De Gruyter, 1995.

Wiggermann, F. A. M., *Sumerian Gods and their Representations.* "Transtigridian Snake Gods," 33-35. Groningen: Styx Publications, 1997.

Wikipedia. "An (cuneiform)." https://en.wikipedia.org/wiki/An_(cuneiform).

Wikipedia. "Bad (cuneiform)." https://en.wikipedia.org/wiki/Bad_(cuneiform)#:~:text= The%20cuneiform%20bad%2C%20bat%2C%20be,(capital%20letter%20(ma juscule)).

Wikipedia. "EPR paradox." https://en.wikipedia.org/wiki/EPR_paradox.

William, Whiston, ed. and transl. *Flavius Josephus, Antiquities of the Jews*. Auburn and Buffalo: John E. Beardsley, 1895.

Wolkstein, Diane & Samuel N. Kramer. *Inanna, Queen of Heaven and Earth: Her Stories and Hymns from Sumer*. New York: Harper & Row, 1983. Accessed through Internet Archive, https://archive.org/stream/input-compressed-2015mar28a29/done-compressed-2015mar28a29_djvu.txt.

Xianhua Wang, *Metamorphosis of Enlil in Early Mesopotamia,* 152. Munster: Ugarit-Verlag, 2011.

YashaNet. "Skins of Light and Flesh." http://www.yashanet.com/studies/judaism101/ sidebars/ohr.htm.

Yoder, Tyler R. "Ezekiel 29:3 and Its Ancient Near Eastern Context." *Vetus Testamentum*. Vol. 63, Issue 3 (Jan. 1, 2013).

Yonge, Charles Duke, ed. *The Works Of Philo Judaeus, Complete And Unabridged*. Peabody: Hendrickson Publishers, 1993.

Endnotes

[1] In Akkadian, a close cousin to Hebrew, šina (pronounced Shina) means "two" and nāru means "river." "two; ditto" Akk. *Šina;* "river, watercourse, canal" Akk. *Nāru* http://psd.museum.upenn.edu/nepsd-frame.html Shinar in Hebrew is "shnei neharot", or "two rivers." BDB: Brown, D. D., S. R. Driver, and C. A. Briggs. 1907. A Hebrew and English lexicon. Boston, Massachusetts and New York, New York: Houghton Mifflin Company.

[2] His name in the Hebrew is Heilel which should not be confused with *Halal* meaning praise.

[3] W.R. Gallagher, On the Identity of Hêlēl Ben Sahar of Is 14:12-15 UF 26 (1994) pp 131-146.

[4] Jacobsen 1989, The líl of dEn-líl. *DUMU-É-DUB-BA-A: Studies in Honor of Åke W. Sjöberg* (Behrens, H., D. M. Loding and M. T. Roth). Pg. 270.

[5] Jeremias, Alfred 1913. Handbuch der altorientalischen Geisteskultur. Leipzig. Pg. 74.

[6] Kramer, Samuel Noah *The Sumerians* The University of Chicago Press, Chicago, 1963. Pg. 37-42.

[7] Albert T. Clay, "Ellil, the God of Nippur" AJSL 23 (1907) 277.

[8] Christopher B. Hays, Enlil, Isaiah, and the Origins of the ʾĕlilim: A Reassessment, ZAW 2020; 132(2): 224–235, https://doi.org/10.1515/zaw-2020-2002

[9] Ibid.

[10] "It is generally admitted that the figure of Melqart and the forms of his cult are reflected in Ezekiel's oracle against the king of Tyre (Ezek 28: 1-19). This passage consists of two different sections (vv 1-10 and 11-19) both referring to the same personage." Melqart The Dictionary Of Deities And Demons In The Bible, Eds. K. Van Der Toorn, Bob Becking nd Pieter W. Van Der Horst (Boston, 1999). Pg. 564-566

[11] https://www.ancient.eu/Melqart/

[12] Melqart The Dictionary Of Deities And Demons In The Bible, Eds. K. Van Der Toorn, Bob Becking And Pieter W. Van Der Horst (Boston, 1999). Pg. 564-566

[13] On the Pantheon of Tyre Author(s): George A. Barton Source: Journal of the American Oriental Society , 1901, Vol. 22 (1901), Pg. 115-117 Published by: American Oriental Society Stable URL: http://www.jstor.com/stable/592422 This content downloaded from 184.96.236.153 on Fri, 28 Aug 2020 05:40:31 UTC

[14] https://www2.uned.es/geo-1-historia-antigua-universal/RELIGION-FENICIA/melqart.htm

[15] Heracles The Dictionary Of Deities And Demons In The Bible, Eds. K. Van Der Toorn, Bob Becking And Pieter W. Van Der Horst (Boston, 1999). 402-404

[16] Melqart The Dictionary Of Deities And Demons In The Bible, Eds. K. Van Der Toorn, Bob Becking And Pieter W. Van Der Horst (Boston, 1999). Pg. 564-566

[17] Ibid.

[18] The Dictionary Of Deities And Demons In The Bible, Eds. K. Van Der Toorn, Bob Becking And Pieter W. Van Der Horst (Boston, 1999). MELQART

[19] https://www.ancient.eu/Melqart/

[20] Melqart The Dictionary Of Deities And Demons In The Bible, Eds. K. Van Der Toorn, Bob Becking And Pieter W. Van Der Horst (Boston, 1999). Pg. 564-566

[21] Ibid.

[22] Heracles The Dictionary Of Deities And Demons In The Bible, Eds. K. Van Der Toorn, Bob Becking And Pieter W. Van Der Horst (Boston, 1999). 402-404

[23] TWOT Tophet.

[24] Ibid.

[25] Amar Annus, The God Ninurta in the Mythology and Royal Ideology of Ancient Mesopotamia, State Archives of Assyria Studies, Volume XIV Helsinki 2002. Pg. 142.

[26] Heracles The Dictionary Of Deities And Demons In The Bible, Eds. K. Van Der Toorn, Bob Becking And Pieter W. Van Der Horst (Boston, 1999). 402-404

[27] Ibid.

[28] Heracles The Dictionary Of Deities And Demons In The Bible, Eds. K. Van Der Toorn, Bob Becking And Pieter W. Van Der Horst (Boston, 1999). Pg. 402-404

[29] Ibid.

[30] F. A. M. Wiggermann, Mesopotamian Protective Spirits The Ritual Texts - Styx & PP Publications Groningen 1992. Pg. 161

[31] He later identifies these as cherubim: "This *is* the living creature I saw under the God of Israel by the River Chebar, and I knew they *were* cherubim," (Ezek 10:20).

[32] Wiggermann posits the base meaning for UŠUM as "Prime Venomous Snake" Tyler R. Yoder, "Ezekiel 29:3 and Its Ancient Near Eastern Context" Vetus Testamentum 63 (2013) 486-96

[33] Tyler R. Yoder, "Ezekiel 29:3 and Its Ancient Near Eastern Context" Vetus Testamentum 63 (2013) Pg. 486-96

[34] Ibid.

[35] Ibid.

[36] Ibid.

[37] "It is first attested by a 22nd-century BC cylinder inscription at Gudea." F. A. M. Wiggermann, *Mesopotamian Protective Spirits*, Pg. 167.

[38] Icon By editor Austen Henry Layard, drawing by L. Gruner - 'Monuments of Nineveh, Second Series' plate 5, London, J. Murray, 1853, Public Domain, https://commons.wikimedia.org/w/index.php?curid=18217886

[39] Tyler R. Yoder, "Ezekiel 29:3 and Its Ancient Near Eastern Context" Vetus Testamentum 63 (2013) Pg. 486-96

[40] Ibid.6

[41] Yoder has shown how God, in Ezekiel, used the term "great dragon" to describe who Pharaoh thought he was. "Behold, I am against you, O Pharaoh king of Egypt, O great monster." The Greek Septuagint "great monster" as τον δρακοντα τον μεγαν "great dragon" (Ezek 29:3). Yoder explains "The prophet could easily have drawn from an existing cache of unambiguous expressions to portray Pharaoh, but instead chose a term suffused with mythological overtones." Tyler R. Yoder,

"Ezekiel 29:3 and Its Ancient Near Eastern Context" Vetus Testamentum 63 (2013) 486-96.

[42] Wiggermann, F. A. M. (1992). *Mesopotamian Protective Spirits: The Ritual Texts*. Brill Publishers. Pg. 156.

[43] Frans Wiggermann, Reallexikon der Assyriologie (RlA) 8 1995 Pg. 455, 456.

[44] "The word nāḥāsh is almost identical to the word for "bronze" or "copper," Hebrew nĕḥōshet (q.v.). Some scholars think the words are related because of a common color of snakes (cf. our "copperhead"), but others think that they are only coincidentally similar." TWOT nāḥāsh

[45] Wiggermann, F. A. M. (1992). *Mesopotamian Protective Spirits: The Ritual Texts*. Brill Publishers. Pg. 156.

[45] Frans Wiggermann, Reallexikon der Assyriologie (RlA) 8 1995 Pg. 455, 456

[46] J. O. Buswell. *Systematic Theology of the Christian Religion*, I, Zondervan, 1962, Pg. 264–65.

[47] Revealing The Genius Of Biblical Authors: Symbology, Archaeology, And Theology *James H. Charlesworth, Princeton*

[48] Amar Annus "Ninurta and the Son of Man" Published in Melammu Symposia 2: R. M. Whiting (ed.), Mythology and Mythologies. Methodological Approaches to Intercultural Influences. Proceedings of the Second Annual Symposium of the Assyrian and Babylonian Intellectual Heritage Project. Held in Paris, France, October 4-7, 1999 (Helsinki: The Neo-Assyrian Text Corpus Project 2001), Pg. 7-17. Publisher: http://www.helsinki.fi/science/saa/

[49] Ibid.

[50] Jacobsen, Th. 1987 *The Harps that Once… Sumerian Poetry in Translation*. New Haven and London: Yale University Press. PG. 235.

[51] In his study, he notes the "Lion-headed Eagle (M. 14; third millennium A n z u d / Anzû), and Lion-Dragon … Second and first millennium Anzû." F. A. M. Wiggermann, Mesopotamian Protective Spirits The Ritual Texts – Siyx & Pp Publications Groningen 1992. Pg. 161

[52] F. A. M. Wiggermann, Mesopotamian Protective Spirits The Ritual Texts – Siyx & Pp Publications Groningen 1992. Pg. 161

[53] Wiggermann notes "bašmu, 'Venomous Snake'. The history of the bašmu is not yet completely clear. Positively bašmu's are the snake of the Kleinplastik (without horns and forepaws, VII. C. 2b), and the snake-monster with forepaws (and wings) from the palace of Esarhaddon." Ibid. Pg. 189.

[54] F. A. M. Wiggermann Mesopotamian Protective Spirits The Ritual Texts - Styx & PP Publications Groningen 1992. Pg. 166-167

[55] Ibid.

[56] Ibid.

[57] Ibid.

[58] http://www.assyrianlanguages.org/akkadian/dosearch.php?searchkey=4876&language=id

[59] God, Demons, and Symbols of Ancient Mesopotamia: Bašmu

[60] Transtigridian Snake Gods Wiggermann Pg. 35.

[61] Edzard, D.O. 1965. "Mesopotamien. Die Mythologie der Sumerer und Akkader." In H.W. Haussig (ed.), Götter und Mythen im Vorderen Orient. Wörterbuch der Mythologie, erste Abteilung, Bd. I, Pg. 17-140. Stuttgart: Ernst Klett Verlag.

[62] TWOT 985 כָּלַל(kālal) I, *perfect, make perfect.* (ASV, RSV similar.)

[63] Ezek 28:12-13; Isa 14:11

[64] TWOT: Cherub. See also http://www.assyrianlanguages.org/akkadian/ to bless; to praise; to dedicate (an offering), to thank, to congratulate; cherub.

[65] ISBE "Precious Stones" That the Hebrew texts used for the Septuagint, Vulgate (Jerome's Latin Bible, 390-405 A.D.) and English Versions of the Bible were not identical in all the verses in which there is mention of precious stones is especially clear from an analysis of the respective descriptions of the ornaments of the king of Tyre (Eze 28:13). In the Septuagint, 12 stones are mentioned; as already stated, they have precisely the same names and are mentioned in precisely the same order as the stones of the breastplate described in that version, the only difference being that gold and silver are inserted in the middle of the list. On the other hand, in Vulgate (Jerome's Latin Bible, 390-405 A.D.) and English Versions of the Bible descriptions of the ornaments, only 9 of the 12 stones of the breastplate are mentioned; they are not in the same order as the corresponding stones in the breastplate as described in those VSS, silver is not mentioned at all, while gold is placed, not in the middle, but at the end of the list.

[66] "To anoint an individual or an object indicated an authorized separation for God's service. Moses anointed Aaron "to sanctify him" (lĕqaddĕshô, Lev 8:12; cf. Ex 29:36 for the altar). Note the expression "anointed to the Lord" (I). māshaḥ, while representing a position of honor, also represents increased responsibility… though the agent might be the priest or prophet, writers speak of anointed ones as those whom the Lord anointed (e.g. I Sam 10:1; II Sam 12:7). Such language underscores that it is God who is the authorizing agent; that the anointed is inviolable (I Sam 24:8ff.); and that the anointed one is to be held in special regard (cf. I Sam 26:9ff.)…one may infer that divine enablement was understood as accompanying māshaḥ. TWOT

[67] [גָּנַן] (gānan) defend. (ASV and RSV also render "put a shield about," and "protect." גַּן (gan) enclosure, garden. גַּנָּה (gannâ) garden.מָגֵן (māgēn) shield. TWOT Harris, Laird R.; Archer, Gleason L.; Waltke, Bruce K.; Moody Publishers, Chicago: 1980. Entry 1580

[68] TWOT, Miqdāsh

[69] When Satan fell is a question often influenced by a person's view of the creation event itself. This chapter is intended to provide a simple explanation based on all of the biblical and relevant creation science available not to advocate for the Gap Theory, Old Earth Creation or Young Earth Creation view.

[70] TWOT ădāmâ: describes the connection between soil and Adam: "ădāmâ. *Ground, land, planet.* Originally this word signified the red arable soil".

[71] Exod 19:5; Deut 10:14; Ps 24:1, 50:12, 89:11

[72] John 12:31, 14:30, 16:11; Heb 2:15

[73] The word "agape" means fully committed to something, wholly devoted and dedicated.

[74] The Electronic Text Corpus of Sumerian Literature (http://etcsl.orinst.ox.ac.uk/section4/tr4051.htm)

[75] Amar Annus, The God Ninurta in the Mythology and Royal Ideology of Ancient Mesopotamia, State Archives of Assyria Studies, Volume XIV Helsinki 2002. Pg. 183

[76] Being like God is a good thing: we shall be in His likeness (Psalm 17:15), "partakers of the divine nature" (2 Peter 1:4) "we shall be like Him," (1 John 3:2) You shall be holy, for I the LORD your God *am* holy, (Lev 19:2, see also Lev 11:44-45; 20:7, 26; 1Pet 1:16). Disobeying God was bad.

[77] God created them with capacity to love but could not force them. Love must be freely chosen to be authentic. Likewise, He could create them with the ability to choose but could not force them. Choice, by definition, must be self-determined.

[78] In order to choose, there must be a real, authentic negative option, thus "evil." God said they could freely eat from any tree in the garden. Yet Adam eating from merely choosing to eat from an apple tree versus a pear tree would not constitute a self-governing choice because those trees had God's blessing. Adam needed a real negative option that he would choose to NOT take. Thus, to eat or NOT to eat from the tree of the Knowledge of Good and Evil provided them the opportunity of self-determination, of self-governance; to choose – freely, without any compulsion on God's part.

[79] TWOT Harris, Laird R.; Archer, Gleason L; Waltke, Bruce K.; Moody Publishers, Chicago: 1980. Entry 1580

[80] TWOT *avlata*

[81] This word rekhulatkha, (translated as "trading") has caused confusion about Satan's history. A popular theory, is the Gap theory which asserts Satan was in charge of an unrecorded, pre-Adamic empire eons ago found in the gap between Genesis 1:1 and 1:2. Advocates suggest verse two be translated "And the earth *became* formless and void..." According to Hebrew Grammar, "ve'ha'aretz hayta" indicates a parenthetical statement due to the word "and" followed by the subject followed by the verb, which is not the standard biblical Hebrew order. Hebrew והארץ היתה *vehaaretz hayta* is known grammatically as a copulative clause. (See Kautzsch and Cowley 1910:484) The *vav* (or *waw*) attached to the noun (the earth) acts as a type of parenthetical statement (See: Joüon, PG., & T. Muraoka 2005) thus: "... God created...the earth. (*Now* the earth was without form, and void.)" Earth in Gen 1:1 included all unorganized raw material God had created in no particular shape or form: "The earth was without *form, and void* (תהו ובהו *tohu vavohu*)" (Gen 1:2a) These words do not suggest that the earth was a wasteland waiting to be recreated. According to TWOT tohu vavohu, "Refers not to the result of a supposed catastrophe...but to the formlessness of the earth before God's creative hand began the majestic acts." (TWOT *Tohu*, See also: Fields 1978:58).

[82] [רכל] BDB 1. to go about (meaning dubious)

[83] Gesenius' Hebrew and Chaldee Lexicon to the Old Testament Scriptures

[84] LSJ Classical Greek Lexicon, διάβολος.

[85] Ibid. See also Thayer's: διαβάλλω: 1. to throw over or across, to send over; 2. to traduce, calumniate, slander, accuse, defame. BDAG διάβολος, to engagement in slander, *slanderous,* one who engages in slander

[86] Robert Luginbill, *The Satanic Rebellion: Background to the Tribulation, Part 1: Satan's Rebellion and Fall.* http://ichthys.com offers the following translation: "In your extensive conspiring, you were filled with wickedness, and you sinned." (Ezek 28:16)

[87] Gen 6:6, Gen 2:17

[88] Gen 3:17-19

[89] Rom 8:19-21

[90] Gen 3:24

[91] Isa 34:4; Rev 6:14

[92] Luke 3:38; John 1:18, 6:46; 1John 3:2

[93] 2Kgs 6:17

[94] Gen 3:15

[95] The Xianhua Wang Metamorphosis of Enlil in Early Mesopotamia Pg. 152

[96] Kramer, Samuel Noah The Sumerians The University of Chicago Press, Chicago, 1963. Pg. 37-41.

[97] Krebernik transcribed Obv. Col. 2 lines 5-9 of IAS 113 as, "UDKIŠ.NUN GAL nunám-NAGAR GAL du11-TUKU DU6-GAG-GAG UD UNU-ta LAGAB ki UD-ta LAGAB, as dEn-líl en nu-nam-nir en du11-ga nu-gi4-gi4 an ki-ta bad ki an-ta bad" Xianhua Wang The Metamorphosis of Enlil in Early Mesopotamia. Pg. 100.

[98] TWOT ʿăbûr is a preposition and conjunction always used with the prefix bĕ to express causal, purposive, and resultative relationships in agreement with the meanings of the root term ʿābar "movement from one to another," as from purpose (or cause) to accomplishment (or result).

[99] TWOT Adama

[100] Gen 2:19

[101] Isa 30:33; Ezek 1:26-27; Dan 7:9, 10

[102] R. V. Gentry, Annual Review of Nuclear Science 23 (1973), Pg.347.

[103] www.halos.com/index.htm.

[104] Ibid.

[105] Ex 19:18; Deut 4:11; Ps 97:3-5, 104:32, 144:5; Dan 7:9-11.

[106] https://conceptartempire.com/cel-animation/

[107] Isa 34:4; Rev 6:14

[108] Luke 3:38; John 1:18, 6:46; 1John 3:2

[109] 2Kgs 6:17

[110] John 8:44

[111] Isa 30:33; Ezek 1:26-27; Dan 7:9, 10

[112] 2Pet 3:9

[113] Ex 19:18; Deut 4:11; Ps 97:3-5, 104:32, 144:5; Dan 7:9-11

[114] Exod 19:5; Deut 10:14; Ps 24:1, 50:12, 89:11

[115] Exod 19:18; Ps 97:5, 104:32; Dan 7:9-10; Ezek 1:27

[116] Matt 4:8-9; John 12:31; 14:30; 16:11; Acts 26:18; 2Cor 4:4; Col 1:13; Heb 2:15; 1John 4:4; 1John 5:19

[117] Ezek 28:18

[118] 1Pet 5:8

[119] Prov 27:20, 30:15-16; Hab 2:4, 5; Luke 11:24

[120] Lev 17:7, 10-14; Ps 106:36-38

[121] Lev 17:11

[122] Deut 18:10

[123] Deut 12:31; 18:10; 2Kgs 16:3, 17:17, 21:6

[124] Isa 57:5; Ezek 23:37, 16:21.

[125] Prov 27:20, 30:15-16; Hab 2:4, 5; Luke 11:24, Lev 17:7; 1Cor 10:20

[126] Robin Lane Fox, *Traveling Heroes in the Epic Age of Homer,* Pg. 217; retrieved from: http://ancientheroes.net/blog/alexander-the-great-zeus-ammon

[127] Prov 27:20; 30:15-16; Hab 2:5; Luke 11:24

[128] See Michael S. Heiser, "Deuteronomy 32:8 and the Sons of God," BSac 158 (2001): 52-74.

[129] Philo, Questions and Answers on Genesis part 4, note 92.

[130] J.T. Milik, Aramaic Fragments of Qumran Cave 4 [Oxford: Clarendon Press, 1976], Pg. 167

[131] M Preus Eloquence and Ignorance in Augustine's On the Nature and Origin of the Soul, 56

[132] https://sourdough.com/forum/oldest-starter

[133] Underhill, Peter A. "Y Chromosome. " Genetics, 2003. Retrieved September 29, 2010 from Encyclopedia.com: http://www.encyclopedia.com/doc/1G2-3406500290.html.

[134] Retrieved September 30, 2010 from: http://www.ucl.ac.uk/tcga/ScienceSpectra-pages/SciSpect-14-98.html Science Spectra Magazine Number 14, 1998.

[135] Neil Bradman and Mark Thomas *Why Y? The Y Chromosome in the Study of Human Evolution, Migration and Prehistory*. See also http://www.ramsdale.org/dna13.htm.

[136] Though Enoch may have written portions of 1Enoch, as a whole, it lacks the divine stamp of divine to be Holy Scripture.

[137] Upon Ardis. Or, "in the days of Jared" R.H. Charles, ed. and trans., *The Book of Enoch* [Oxford: Clarendon Press, 1893], Pg. 63.

[138] TWOT 744 חָרַם (ḥāram) "ban, devote, destroy utterly." Also related to an Ethiopic root, meaning "to forbid, prohibit, lay under a curse."

[139] *The* Dictionary of Deities and Demons in the Bible, eds. K. van der Toorn, Bob Becking and Pieter W. van der Horst (Boston, 1999). Pg. 161-162

[140] E. A. Myers (11 February 2010). The Ituraeans and the Roman Near East: Reassessing the Sources. Cambridge University Press. Pg. 66–. ISBN 978-0-521-51887-1.

[141] Palestine Exploration Fund, 1869-1936. London, Pg. 426
https://babel.hathitrust.org/cgi/pt?id=umn.31951p010211321&view=1up&seq=41
8

[142] https://www.britishmuseum.org/collection/object/G_1903-0422-1

[143] WARREN PEFQS I [1869/1870] 210-215) and an inscription is dedicated tou
theou megistou k(ai) hagiou, "to the greatest and holy god". Dictionary of Deities
and Demons in the Bible, eds. K. van der Toorn, Bob Becking and Pieter W. van der
Horst (Boston, 1999). : Hermon

[144] E. A. Myers (11 February 2010). The Ituraeans and the Roman Near East:
Reassessing the Sources. Cambridge University Press. Pg. 66–. ISBN 978-0-521-
51887-1.

[145] Ibid.

[146] Nickelsburg, 1 Enoch 1. A Commentary on the Book of 1 Enoch, 1–36; 81–108,
Minneapolis: Fortress, 2001.

[147] *E. A. Myers (11 February 2010). The Ituraeans and the Roman Near East:
Reassessing the Sources. Cambridge University Press. Pg. 65–. ISBN 978-0-521-
51887-1. Retrieved 18 September 2012.*

[148] κατὰ κέλευσιν θεοῦ *OGI = Orientis Graeci Inscriptiones Selectae,* ed. W.
Dittenberger, Leipzig 1903-5. (Liddel Scott Jones)

[149] BDAG Μεγιστώ

[150] BDAG: ὀμνύω

[151] ἐντεῦθεν adv. pert. to extension from a source near the speaker, *from here* (En
22:13; Jos., Bell. 6, 299; 7, 22) Lk 4:9; 13:31; J 7:3; 14:31; 1 Cl 53:2 (Ex 32:7). ἄρατε
ταῦτα ἐ. *take these things away from here* J 2:16. κατάβηθι ἐ. *go home from here*
GJs 4:2. ἐντεῦθεν (for ἔνθεν) ἐκεῖ *fr. here to there* Mt 17:20 v.l. ἐντεῦθεν καὶ
ἐντεῦθεν *fr. here and fr. there = on each side* (c Num 22:24) J 19:18. For this
ἐντεῦθεν κ. ἐκεῖθεν Rv 22:2; ἡ βασιλεία ἡ ἐμὴ οὐκ ἔστιν ἐ. *my kingdom is not from
here*=ἐκ. τ. κόσμου τούτου J 18:36.

[152] http://www.greekalphabeta.com/learn-about-beta-b-2.html, definitions culled
from LSJ.

[153] Dictionary of Deities and Demons in the Bible, eds. K. van der Toorn, Bob
Becking and Pieter W. van der Horst (Boston, 1999): Bashan.

[154] *Molech, New World
Encyclopedia* https://www.newworldencyclopedia.org/entry/Moloch

[155] http://www.altosalentorivieradeitrulli.it/nuova_pagina_17.htm

[156] http://dictionary.sensagent.com/Messapian%20language/en-en/

[157] http://www.altosalentorivieradeitrulli.it/nuova_pagina_17.htm

[158] https://journals.openedition.org/pallas/2208

[159] Splendor of the Magna Graecia art, the Zeus of Ugento … from the great
Messapian city of Ozan (today's Ugento)…530 BC. …the cult for Zis Batàs,
https://www.salentoacolory.it/museo-archeologico-taranto/

[160] Ce sanctuaire, fréquenté depuis la fin du VIIIᵉ s. a.C. jusqu'au début du IIIᵉ s. P.C.,
est consacré à *Zis Batas,* divinité indigène appelée Zeus *Batios* par les Grecs, puis
Juppiter Optimus Maximus Batius (ou *Vatius*) par les Romains. Les cultes de

l'Adriatique méridionale à l'époque républicaine Jean-Luc Lamboley. Pg. 133-141, https://books.openedition.org/ausonius/6837.

[161] https://books.openedition.org/efr/5584#illustrations; see also https://books.openedition.org/ausonius/6837

[162] Les Dieux Olympiens Et La Mer Annick Fenet pg. 83-138. https://books.openedition.org/efr/5584#illustrations

[163] Lomas, Kathryn. "Crossing Boundaries: The Inscribed Votives of Southeast Italy." Pallas, no. 86 (2011): 311-29. Accessed October 19, 2020. http://www.jstor.org/stable/43606696.

[164] Ibid.

[165] Original French: La double dénomination de *Palaistiné* et d'*Ourania* souligne le caractère sémitique et oriental." https://books.openedition.org/efr/5584#illustrations

[166] Paolo M Gensini University of Perugia, Italy , Physics, Emeritus, Personal correspondence, Aug 16th, 2020.

[167] Private email communication with Professor Amar Annus Mon, Sep 28, 2020. See also https://en.wikipedia.org/wiki/An_(cuneiform)

[168] Frans Wiggermann, Nergal, Reallexikon der Assyriologie (RIA) 9 1999 Pg. 215-226.

[169] The cuneiform bad, bat, be, etc. sign is a common multi-use sign in the mid-14th-century BC Amarna letters, and the Epic of Gilgamesh. In the Epic it also has 5 Sumerogram uses (capital letter (majuscule)). From Giorgio Buccellati (Buccellati 1979) 'comparative graphemic analysis' (about 360 cuneiform signs, nos. 1 through no. 598E), of 5 categories of letters, the usage numbers of the bad sign are as follows: Old Babylonian Royal letters (71), OB non-Royal letters (392), Mari letters (2108), Amarna letters (334), Ugarit letters (39). The following linguistic elements are used for the bad sign in the 12 chapter (Tablets I-Tablet XII) Epic of Gilgamesh: Sumerograms: BE, IDIM, TIL, ÚŠ, ZIZ https://en.wikipedia.org/wiki/Bad_(cuneiform)#:~:text=The%20cuneiform%20bad%2C%20bat%2C%20be,(capital%20letter%20(majuscule)).

[170] Frans Wiggermann, Nergal, Reallexikon der Assyriologie (RIA) 9 1999 Pg. 215-226.

[171] Amar Annus, The God Ninurta in the Mythology and Royal Ideology of Ancient Mesopotamia, State Archives of Assyria Studies, Volume XIV Helsinki 2002. Pg. 178

[172] Ibid.

[173] https://aratta.wordpress.com/2014/07/29/the-snake-and-the-serpopard/

[174] Cole, S. W. (1996). The Early Neo-Babylonian Governor's Archive from Nippur. Oriental Institute of the University of Chicago.

[175] Burkert notes: "In oral instruction, however, something such as HAR was most unlikely to have been pronounced ... But even here a curious coincidence cannot be ruled out ... Skeptics could draw the conclusion that the whole thing was nonsense; the historian, however, finds the clearest evidence of cultural diffusion precisely in correspondences of details that seem most absurd and unnatural, hence least likely to be arrived at independently. The Etruscan disciplina ... has

preserved more of its eastern origins. The similarities are nevertheless indicative of a common source, of some historical connection which binds all the individual forms together." The Orientalizing Revolution, Near Eastern Influence on Greek Culture in the Early Archaic Age By Walter Burkert · 1995, Pg. Pg. 50. https://www.google.com/books/edition/_/cliUL7dWqNIC?hl=en&gbpv=0

[176] Private email communication with Professor Amar Annus October 5, 2020.

[177] https://www.britishmuseum.org/collection/object/G_1903-0422-1

[178] "It stretched from the border of Gilead in the South to the slopes of Hermon in the North." ISBE. See also (Deut 3:8)

[179] Charlesworth

[180] For example [כִּתִּים] Kittim is rendered κιτιοι (Kitioi) and Dodanim [דֹדָנִים] is rendered ροδιοι (interestingly the scribe most likely mistook the Hebrew dalet [ד] for a resh [ר] and hence it is rodioi. (Gen 10:4)

[181] Clay, Albert T. "The Origin and Real Name of NIN-IB." Journal of the American Oriental Society 28 (1907): 135-44. Accessed September 11, 2020.

[182] "BATANAEA (Βαταναία), a district to the NE. of Palestine... It was added to the kingdom of Herod the Great by Augustus." http://www.perseus.tufts.edu/hopper/text?doc=Perseus%3Atext%3A1999.04.0064%3Aalphabetic+letter%3DB%3Aentry+group%3D3%3Aentry%3Dbatanaea-geo

[183] https://pleiades.stoa.org/places/678054/batanaia

[184] 1 Enoch 15:8-16:1.

[185] Annus also notes the hero title of Ninurta / Ningirsu: "In Pre-Sargonic Lagaš the most popular divine epithet was that of Ningirsu, who was called very frequently ur-sag-dEn-líl-(lá), "the hero of Enlil." Amar Annus, The God Ninurta in the Mythology and Royal Ideology of Ancient Mesopotamia, State Archives of Assyria Studies, Volume XIV Helsinki 2002. Pg. 138

[186] BDAG

[187] http://jewishencyclopedia.com/articles/11548-nimrod; cf. Pes. 94b; comp. Targ. of pseudo-Jonathan and Targ. Yer. to Gen. x. 9., and Midrash Haggadah.

[188] The Targums of Onkelos and Jonathan Ben Uzziel On the Pentateuch With The Fragments of the Jerusalem Targum From the Chaldee By J. W. Etheridge, M.A. First Published 1862

[189] The place name "Tophet" and the false god "Molech" both have the vowels from "boshet" meaning "shameful."

[190] Amar Annus, The God Ninurta in the Mythology and Royal Ideology of Ancient Mesopotamia, State Archives of Assyria Studies, Volume XIV Helsinki 2002. Pg. 106

[191] Ibid.

[192] Ibid.

[193] David Rohl, he says: The Lost Testament: From Eden to Exile the Five-Thousand-Year History of the People of The Bible – 17 Oct. 2002.

[194] The Jewish Encyclopedia notes: "The difficulty of reconciling the Biblical Nimrod, the son of Cush, with Marduk, the son of Ea, may be overcome by interpreting the Biblical words as meaning that Nimrod was a descendant of Cush." http://jewishencyclopedia.com/articles/11548-nimrod

[195] Amar Annus, The God Ninurta in the Mythology and Royal Ideology of Ancient Mesopotamia, State Archives of Assyria Studies, Volume XIV Helsinki 2002. Pg. 122

[196] Ibid. Pg. 83-pg 88

[197] Ibid.

[198] Ibid. Pg. 14.

[199] While Heilel in Isaiah 14 is undoubtedly the Sumerian Enlil, an absolute identification of Anu with the biblical creator should be tentative.

[200] Amar Annus, The God Ninurta in the Mythology and Royal Ideology of Ancient Mesopotamia, State Archives of Assyria Studies, Volume XIV Helsinki 2002. Pg. 59

[201] Ibid. Pg. 67

[202] Ibid.

[203] OECT 11 69+70, Cf Amar Annus, The God Ninurta in the Mythology and Royal Ideology of Ancient Mesopotamia, State Archives of Assyria Studies, Volume XIV Helsinki 2002. Pg. 78

[204] Ibid.

[205] https://www.ancient.eu/Enlil/ Mark, Joshua J. "Enlil." Ancient History Encyclopedia. Last modified January 24, 2017. https://www.ancient.eu/Enlil/.

[206] https://www.independent.co.uk/news/world/americas/dna-bone-marrow-transplant-man-chimera-chris-long-forensic-science-police-a9238636.html

[207] The future implications of this research are far reaching and tie in directly to the Mark of the Beast. For our currently study, we will focus on what happened in the past.

[208] Special thanks to Tom Horn for first bringing this idea to my attention. https://newswithviews.com/Horn/thomas155.htm

[209] GIBBORIM The Dictionary Of Deities And Demons In The Bible, Eds. K. Van Der Toorn, Bob Becking And Pieter W. Van Der Horst (Boston, 1999).

[210] Ibid.

[211] Ibid.

[212] https://www.etymonline.com/search?q=giant

[213] Hansen notes "Hesiod describes them as being "great," referring perhaps to their stature, but the Giants are not always represented as being huge. Although the word giants derives ultimately from the Greek Gigantes, the most persistent traits of the Gigantes are strength and hubristic aggression." Hansen, William, Handbook of Classical Mythology, ABC-CLIO, 2004. Pg. 177.

[214] https://www.etymonline.com/search?q=giant

[215] Hesiod, Theogony, in The Homeric Hymns and Homerica with an English Translation by Hugh G. Evelyn-White, Cambridge, Massachusetts., Harvard University Press; London, William Heinemann Ltd. 1914. Pg. 185. Online version at the Perseus Digital Library.

[216] Philo addresses their number and stature: "they were very numerous indeed, and giants of exceeding tallness with absolutely gigantic bodies, both as to their magnitude and their strength," The Works Of Philo Judaeus, Complete And

Unabridged New Updated Edition Translated By Charles Duke Yonge, London, H. G. Bohn, 1854-1890.

[217] Amar Annus, The God Ninurta in the Mythology and Royal Ideology of Ancient Mesopotamia, State Archives of Assyria Studies, Volume XIV Helsinki 2002. Pg. 11

[218] Amar Annus, The God Ninurta in the Mythology and Royal Ideology of Ancient Mesopotamia, State Archives of Assyria Studies, Volume XIV Helsinki 2002. Pg. 19

[219] Josephus *Ant.* I: iv: 2.

[220] https://www.ancient.eu/image/6317/cylinder-seal-with-ninurta/

[221] Amar Annus, The God Ninurta in the Mythology and Royal Ideology of Ancient Mesopotamia, State Archives of Assyria Studies, Volume XIV Helsinki 2002. Pg. 102

[222] Ibid.

[223] Ibid.

[224] https://www.behindthename.com/names/usage/sumerian-mythology. See also: http://psd.museum.upenn.edu/nepsd-frame.html bilga [FRUIT] (4x: Ur III, Old Babylonian) wr. bil_2-ga "fresh fruit; male ancestor" - mes [HERO] ..."hero; (to be) manly; young man" ... $meš_3$=hero.

[225] Amar Annus, The God Ninurta in the Mythology and Royal Ideology of Ancient Mesopotamia, State Archives of Assyria Studies, Volume XIV Helsinki 2002. Pg. 158

[226] According to how genealogies work, A god + a god = 100% god. A god + human = 50% god AKA a demigod. A god + demigod = 100%+50%= 75% god +25% human. Lastly, A god + ¼ demigod = 62.5% which is roughly 2/3 god 1/3 human, which is Gilgamesh.

[227] Heidel, A. 1963 *The Gilgamesh Epic and Old Testament Parallels.* Chicago: University Press. Pgs. 17-18

[228] GIBBORIM The Dictionary Of Deities And Demons In The Bible, Eds. K. Van Der Toorn, Bob Becking And Pieter W. Van Der Horst (Boston, 1999).

[229] For example, resolving the eras in which they lived is one of the hurdles in proving they are the same person.

[230] Ibid.

[231] http://jewishencyclopedia.com/articles/11548-nimrod

[232] Kramer, S. N., ed. 1959 History Begins at Sumer. Garden City NY: Doubleday. Pg. 117

[233] Heidel, A. 1963 *The Gilgamesh Epic and Old Testament Parallels.* Chicago: University Press. Pgs. 17-18

[234] Josephus Antiquities of the Jews Book 5:2:3.

[235] *(Baruch 3:26).*

[236] Kramer, S. N., ed. 1959 History Begins at Sumer. Garden City NY: Doubleday. Pg. 117

[237] https://animals.mom.com/weight-height-lions-2378.html

[238] http://news.bbc.co.uk/2/hi/science/nature/2982891.stm

[239] (George 1992: 318-19, Edzard 1987). George, Andrew. (2005). The Tower of Babel: Archaeology, history, and cuneiform texts.

[240] John H. Walton, "Is there archaeological evidence of the Tower of Babel?" reprinted by permission from Bulletin for Biblical Research 5 [1995]: 155-75. List compiled H.C. Rawlinson, H.C. 1861 The Cuneiform Inscription s of Western Asia, v. 2. London: R.E. Bowler: 50: 1-23 a, b; accessed athttp://christiananswers.net/q-abr/abr-a021.html CF:*http://truthwatchers.com/tower*-of-babel-part-3-what-was-the-tower/

[241] André Parrot, *The Tower of Babel*, Studies in Biblical Archaeology 2 (New York: The Philosophical Library Inc., 1955), 64.

[242] TRACT TAANITH (FASTING) Babylonian Talmud, Book 4: Tracts Pesachim, Yomah and Hagiga, tr. by Michael L. Rodkinson, [1918], at sacred-texts.com. http://www.sacred-texts.com/jud/t04/taa06.htm

[243] CF Per John Gill 4:26: T. Bab. Taanith, fol. 5. 1. Gloss. in T. Bab. Sanhedrin, fol. 97. 2. Caphtor, fol. 14. 2. & 25. 2. & 65. 1. & 68. 2. & 71. 2. & 118. 2. Raziel, fol. 13. 1. & 27. 1. Tzeror Hammor, fol. 61. 3. & 150. 3. Nishmat Chayim, fol. 26. 2. Kimchi in Hos. xi. 19.

[244] On the other hand, Gesenius suggests, "in many of these supposed duals either a dual sense cannot be detected at all, or it does not agree at any rate with the nature of the Semitic dual, as found elsewhere." Gesenius Hebrew Grammar § 88. Of the Dual.

[245] See also: "House of the Mountain, Mountain of the Storm, and Bond Between Heaven and Earth." Frankfort, Henri. The Art and Architecture of the Ancient Orient. (New Haven, Connecticut: Yale University Press, 1996), Pg. 21

[246] Amar Annus, The God Ninurta in the Mythology and Royal Ideology of Ancient Mesopotamia, State Archives of Assyria Studies, Volume XIV Helsinki 2002.Pg. 9

[247] Creig Marlowe, A New Take on the Tower: "The Sin of Shinar (Gen 11:4)." The Evangelical Journal of Theology XX:1 (2011): 29-39.

[248] OECT 11 69+70, Amar Annus, The God Ninurta in the Mythology and Royal Ideology of Ancient Mesopotamia, State Archives of Assyria Studies, Volume XIV Helsinki 2002. Pg. 78

[249] https://en.wikipedia.org/wiki/EPR_paradox

[250] "A laser beam fired through a certain type of crystal can cause individual photons to be split into pairs of entangled photons. The photons can be separated by a large distance, hundreds of miles or even more. When observed, Photon A takes on an up-spin state. Entangled Photon B, though now far away, takes up a state relative to that of Photon A (in this case, a down-spin state). The transfer of state between Photon A and Photon B takes place at a speed of at least 10,000 times the speed of light, possibly even instantaneously, regardless of distance." https://www.livescience.com/28550-how-quantum-entanglement-works-infographic.html

[251]https://www.sciencealert.com/scientists-just-unveiled-the-first-ever-photo-of-quantum-entanglement

[252] https://www.insider.com/a-new-einstein-equation-suggests-wormholes-hold-the-key-to-quantum-gravity-2016-8

[253]Geordie Rose - Quantum Computing: Artificial Intelligence Is Here, Aug 25, 2015

https://www.utpjournals.press/doi/full/10.3138/uram.36.3-4.127 see also:
https://youtu.be/PqN_2jDVbOU?t=277 – his quote starts around minute 13:02.

[254]Geordie Rose - Quantum Computing: Artificial Intelligence Is Here, Aug 25, 2015
https://www.utpjournals.press/doi/full/10.3138/uram.36.3-4.127 see also:
https://youtu.be/PqN_2jDVbOU?t=277 – his quote starts around minute 13:02.

[255] http://jewishencyclopedia.com/articles/11548-nimrod.

[256] In a similar way to how "Ninurta," as "Lord of the Earth," has been distorted by
the biblical text as "Nimrod," or "Let's rebel."

[257] https://www.definitions.net/definition/Chernobyl

[258] George Smith, Chaldean Account of Genesis, 1880, Pg. 29

[259] George Rawlinson
http://www.archive.org/stream/egyptbabylonfrom00rawl/egyptbabylonfrom00ra
wl_djvu.txt

[260] "The epic of Enmerkar and the Lord of Aratta," translation from "The Babel of
Tongues: A Sumerian Version" by Kramer, S.N.; Journal of the American Oriental
Society 88:108-11, 1968

[261] Enûma Eliš· VI 63: George 1992: 301–2

[262] George, Andrew (2007) "The Tower of Babel: Archaeology, history and
cuneiform texts" Archiv für Orientforschung, 51 (2005/2006). Pg. 75–95. pdf
document.

[263] Nabopolassar – 2 Foundation cylinders with inscriptions from Nabopolassar
(Nebuchadnezzar's Father) – found 1880

[264] Ibid.

[265] Ibid.

[266] Inscription on Borsippa, by Nebuchadnezzar II, translated by William Loftus
Translated in 1857 for the book Travels and Researches in Chaldea and Sinai.
https://www.schoyencollection.com/history-collection-introduction/babylonian-
history-collection/tower-babel-stele-ms-2063

[267] Ibid.

[268] We see God's city, His Holy Mountain, Mount Zion, and the New Jerusalem
considered as one throughout the Bible: "Jerusalem shall be called the City of
Truth, The Mountain of the LORD of hosts, The Holy Mountain." (Zech 8:3) Also: "I
[am] the LORD your God, Dwelling in Zion My holy mountain. Then Jerusalem shall
be holy..." (Joel 3:17)

[269] http://etcsl.orinst.ox.ac.uk/section1/tr162.htm

[270] Amar Annus, The God Ninurta in the Mythology and Royal Ideology of Ancient
Mesopotamia, State Archives of Assyria Studies, Volume XIV Helsinki 2002.Pg. 81.

[271] E-sangil And E-temen-anki, The Archetypal Cult-centre – Andrew George

[272] Ibid.

[273] Ibid.

[274] Ibid.

[275] Rain Goddess. Cylinder seal. Mesopotamia. Akkad period, c. 2334-2154 B.C.
Shell. 33.5 X 19.5 mm. New York, Pierpont Morgan Library, Corpus 220. Retrieved

from: Wolkstein, Diane & Samuel N. Kramer 1983. *Inanna, Queen of Heaven and Earth: Her Stories and Hymns from Sumer*. New York: Harper & Row. https://archive.org/stream/input-compressed-2015mar28a29/done-compressed-2015mar28a29_djvu.txt

[276] CHAPTER THREE – NINURTA MYTHOLOGY AND THE MYTHS OF KINGSHIP Pg. 172 quoting (Wiggermann 1992: 161.)

[277] [Doniger, Wendy (1990), Merriam-Webster's Encyclopedia of World Religions, Springfield, Massachusetts: Merriam-Webster, Incorporated, ISBN 0-87779-044-2 (pgs. 120, 440)]

[278] Rev 17:16

[279] NET Notes to Zech 5:11

[280] *Spooner, Henry G. (1918). American Journal of Urology and Sexology. Urologic Publishing Association.*

[281] *Stele of Houy-C 86 14th Cent BC on display* Department of Egyptian Antiquities of the Louvre
Room 642, display case 1 Photo by Rama, Wikimedia Commons. https://commons.wikimedia.org/wiki/File:Stele_of_Qadesh_upper-frame.jpg

[282] The Dictionary Of Deities And Demons In The Bible, Eds. K. Van Der Toorn, Bob Becking And Pieter W. Van Der Horst (Boston, 1999). 454

[283] *http://www.bibleorigins.net/Serpentningishzida.html, p.11.*

[284] Leick, Gwendolyn (1998) [1991], A Dictionary of Ancient Near Eastern Mythology, New York City, New York: Routledge, Pg. 86.

[285] *https://www.ancient.eu/Inanna/*

[286] The "Burney Relief," which is believed to represent either Ishtar or her older sister Ereshkigal (c. 19th or 18th century BC) By Babel Stone (Own work), CC0, https://commons.wikimedia.org/w/index.php?curid=10862243

[287] Ancient Akkadian cylinder seal depicting the goddess Inanna resting her foot on the back of a lion... c. 2334-2154 BC http://www.theosociety.org/pasadena/sunrise/52-02-3/s2oneh2.jpg

[288] The Dictionary Of Deities And Demons In The Bible, Eds. K. Van Der Toorn, Bob Becking And Pieter W. Van Der Horst (Boston, 1999). 453

[289] Ibid. Ishtar 452-453.

[290] Ibid.

[291] The forms *Ašratu(m), Aširatu, Asirtu* (here 'Ashratu') appear infrequently in Akkadian and Hittite documents, and give only the sketchiest information concerning the goddess. The fact that she appears as the consort of Amurru (above) is evidence of Ashratu(m)'s Amorite (thus, West Semitic) origin. The Dictionary Of Deities And Demons In The Bible, Eds. K. Van Der Toorn, Bob Becking And Pieter W. Van Der Horst (Boston, 1999). Pg. 100.

[292] Dated ca. 1550-1200 BCE. Lost (stolen). Drawing © S. Beaulieu, after Cornelius 2004: Plate 5.21

[293] The Yale terracotta plaque portrays Inanna wielding a bow and being carried by lions. Albenda, Pauline. "The "Queen of the Night" Plaque: A Revisit." *Journal of the*

American Oriental Society 125, no. 2 (2005): 171-90. Accessed August 23, 2020. http://www.jstor.org/stable/20064325.

[294] Impression of a Neo-Assyrian seal dated ca. 750-650 BCE. British Museum. Drawing © 2008 S. Beaulieu, after Leick 1998: Plate 38.

[295] Marcovich, Miroslav (1996), "From Ishtar to Aphrodite", *Journal of Aesthetic Education*, 39 (2): 43–59, doi:10.2307/3333191, JSTOR 3333191

[296] Breitenberger, Barbara (2007), *Aphrodite and Eros: The Development of Greek Erotic Mythology*, New York City, New York and London, England.

[297] https://thequeenofheaven.wordpress.com/2010/11/16/asherah-part-iii-the-lion-lady/

[298] https://commons.wikimedia.org/w/index.php?curid=3962125

[299] The Dictionary Of Deities And Demons In The Bible, Eds. K. Van Der Toorn, Bob Becking And Pieter W. Van Der Horst (Boston, 1999). Pg. 66

[300] Parpola, Asko (1998), *Studia Orientalia*, 84, Finnish Oriental Society, ISBN 9789519380384

[301] https://commons.wikimedia.org/w/index.php?curid=21764494

[302] E-SANGIL AND E-TEMEN-ANKI, THE ARCHETYPAL CULT-CENTRE – Andrew George

[303] Rochberg, Francesca, *The Heavenly Writing* (Cambridge: Cambridge University Press, 2004)

[304] http://www.mesopotamiangods.com/inanna/

[305] The Dictionary Of Deities And Demons In The Bible, Eds. K. Van Der Toorn, Bob Becking And Pieter W. Van Der Horst (Boston, 1999). Ishtar 453

[306] [WESTERNER] (2454x: ED IIIb, Old Akkadian, Ur III, Early Old Babylonian, Old Babylonian) wr. mar-tu "westerner; west wind" Akk. Amurru. http://psd.museum.upenn.edu/nepsd-frame.html

[307] Clay, Albert T. "The Origin and Real Name of NIN-IB." Journal of the American Oriental Society 28 (1907): 135-44. Accessed September 11, 2020. doi:10.2307/592765.

[308] http://etcsl.orinst.ox.ac.uk/section1/tr162.htm

[309] Clay, Albert T. "The Origin and Real Name of NIN-IB." Journal of the American Oriental Society 28 (1907): 135-44. Accessed September 11, 2020. doi:10.2307/592765.

[310] *The* Dictionary of Deities and Demons in the Bible, eds. K. van der Toorn, Bob Becking and Pieter W. van der Horst (Boston, 1999). Amurru

[311] Ibid. REPHAIM 692-700

[312] "A snake is a frequent symbol of the healing gods. For religious-historical reasons, Ninurta became equated with the "Transtigridian snake god" as Tišpak, Ninazu and Elamite Inšušinak"– Amar Annus, The God Ninurta in the Mythology and Royal Ideology of Ancient Mesopotamia, State Archives of Assyria Studies, Volume XIV Helsinki 2002. Pg. 140.

[313] Transtigridian Snake Gods Wiggermann Pg. 35.

[314] The Dictionary Of Deities And Demons In The Bible, Eds. K. Van Der Toorn, Bob Becking And Pieter W. Van Der Horst (Boston, 1999). REPHAIM 692-700

[315] Ibid.

[316] Ibid.

[317] Amar Annus, The God Ninurta in the Mythology and Royal Ideology of Ancient Mesopotamia, State Archives of Assyria Studies, Volume XIV Helsinki 2002. Pg. 140.

[318] *The* Dictionary of Deities and Demons in the Bible, eds. K. van der Toorn, Bob Becking and Pieter W. van der Horst (Boston, 1999). Pg. 161-162. See: (KTU 1.108:1-3)

[319] *The* Dictionary of Deities and Demons in the Bible, eds. K. van der Toorn, Bob Becking and Pieter W. van der Horst (Boston, 1999). , Pg. 161-162 quotes BARTLET 1970:266-268.

[320] *KTU 1.100:41; 1.1 07: 17: and RS 86:2'235: 17*

[321] Ibid.

[322] *The* Dictionary of Deities and Demons in the Bible, eds. K. van der Toorn, Bob Becking and Pieter W. van der Horst (Boston, 1999). Pg. 161-162, quotes POPE 1977: 171: MOLLER ZA 65 [1975] 122.

[323] In the Bible, Bashan has two simultaneous meanings: " Bāŝān fertile, 'Stoneless piece of ground'," e.g. "rams of the breed of Bashan" (Deut 32:14), and snake-dragon: "Bāŝān II 'serpent', which is etymologically cognate with Ug btn 'serpent' (Akk bašmu; Ar batan; DAY 1985: 113-119: sec also Heb peten). A relation between I and II was proposed by Albright (BASOR 110 [1948J 17, n. 53; HUCA 23 [195D-1951J 27-28; cf. FENSIIAM, JNES 19 [1960J 292293; DAHOOD 1981:145-146)

[324] *The* Dictionary of Deities and Demons in the Bible, eds. K. van der Toorn, Bob Becking and Pieter W. van der Horst (Boston, 1999). , Pg. 161-162

[325] *The* Dictionary of Deities and Demons in the Bible, eds. K. van der Toorn, Bob Becking and Pieter W. van der Horst (Boston, 1999). , Pg. 161-162

[326] *The* Dictionary of Deities and Demons in the Bible, eds. K. van der Toorn, Bob Becking and Pieter W. van der Horst (Boston, 1999), Pg. 161-162

[327] Charlesworth, James H., "Revealing the Genius of Biblical Authors: Symbology, Archaeology, and Theology." Communio Viatorum 46 (2004): 124-40

[328] https://www.etymonline.com/search?q=nashville

[329] Gesenius: Og

[330] The Dictionary Of Deities And Demons In The Bible, Eds. K. Van Der Toorn, Bob Becking And Pieter W. Van Der Horst (Boston, 1999). Og. They also note: "also Ug PN bn 'gy, KTU 4.611:19)".

[331] ur-saĝ ug5-ga ì-me-ša-ke4-éš {i+me+(e)š+a+ak+eš} - Because they were slain heroes. (Gudea Cyl A 26:15). Pg. 47
en-na ba-ug5-ge-a {ba+ug5+e+Ø+a} -Until he shall die (Enki & Ninhursag 221 OB). Pg. 122
u4-da u4 ug5-ge-ĝu10 nu-un-zu {ug5+e+ĝu10+Ø} - If she does not know my dying day. (Dumuzi's Death 12 OB). Pg. 139.
Cuneiform Digital Library Preprints. http://cdli.ucla.edu/?q=cuneiform-digital-library-preprints Hosted by the Cuneiform Digital Library Initiative

http://cdli.ucla.edu Editor: Bertrand Lafont (CNRS, Nanterre) Number 2. Title: "Introduction to Sumerian Grammar" Author: Daniel A. Foxvog. Posted to web: 4 January 2016

[332] ug [DIE] (259x: ED IIIb, Old Akkadian, Ur III, Old Babylonian) wr. ug7; ug5; ugx (|BAD.BAD|) "plural and imperfect singular stem of uš [to die]" Akk. *mâtu*. http://psd.museum.upenn.edu/nepsd-frame.html [See also] mītu [ÚŠ :] (adj.) dead , deceased , departed ; Cf. *mâtu, mītūtān* http://www.assyrianlanguages.org/akkadian/dosearch.php

[333] https://prosobab.leidenuniv.nl/pdfs/logogram.pdf

[334] "Ninurta and the Son of Man" Published in Melammu Symposia 2: R. M. Whiting (ed.), Mythology and Mythologies. Methodological Approaches to Intercultural Influences. Proceedings of the Second Annual Symposium of the Assyrian and Babylonian Intellectual Heritage Project. Held in Paris, France, October 4-7, 1999 (Helsinki: The Neo-Assyrian Text Corpus. Project 2001), Pg. 7-17. Publisher: http://www.helsinki.fi/science/saa/. http://www.aakkl.helsinki.fi/melammu/. Pg. 8

[335] Ibid.

[336] http://psd.museum.upenn.edu/nepsd-frame.html

[337] Abraham Even-Shoshan (אַבְרָהָם אֶבֶן־שׁוֹשָׁן) et al., הַמִּלּוֹן הֶחָדָשׁ (ha-milón he-khadásh, "The New Dictionary"), Kiryat-Sefer Ltd. (קִרְיַת־סֵפֶר בְּעַ״ם) (1984), volume 1 of 3 (א to כ), page 531. CF. https://en.wiktionary.org/wiki/Category:Hebrew_terms_derived_from_Sumerian

[338] Ibid.

[339] *The* Dictionary of Deities and Demons in the Bible, eds. K. van der Toorn, Bob Becking and Pieter W. van der Horst (Boston, 1999). , Pg. 161-162. See: (KTU 1.108:1-3)

[340] "ug(2): lion; anger, fury; storm. ug4,5,7,8: n., death; dead person. v., to kill; to die (singular and plural marû stem; plural hamtu, which is sometimes reduplicated; cf., úš). ug6, u6[IGI.É]: n., amazement; gaze, glance (['EYE' + 'HOUSE']). v., to look at; to stare at, gaze; to be impressed. adj., astonishing." https://www.sumerian.org/sumcvc.htm

[341] http://psd.museum.upenn.edu/epsd/e1897.html

[342] 162 DDDB Bashan

[343] Deities and Demons in the Bible Nisroch

[344] Amos 5:2 NASB note: "Or Sakkuth (Saturn) or shrine of your Moloch"

[345] Amar Annus, The God Ninurta in the Mythology and Royal Ideology of Ancient Mesopotamia, State Archives of Assyria Studies, Volume XIV Helsinki 2002.

[346] "Sikkuth is identified with Sag/k.kud/t (transliterated in a Mesopotamian god list as Sa-ak-ku-ut!), an astral deity known also from the "An" god list found at Ugarit ...where it appears as [d]sag/k.k[ud]/t = [d]s[a]g/k.kud/t (Ugaritica, 5 (1969), 214, line 44)." https://www.encyclopedia.com/religion/encyclopedias-almanacs-transcripts-and-maps/sikkuth-and-chiun

[347] Amar Annus, The God Ninurta in the Mythology and Royal Ideology of Ancient Mesopotamia, State Archives of Assyria Studies, Volume XIV Helsinki 2002.

348 saĝ "head; person; capital" Akk. *qaqqadu*; *rēšu*
http://psd.museum.upenn.edu/nepsd-frame.html
349 ug [DIE] (259x: ED IIIb, Old Akkadian, Ur III, Old Babylonian) wr. ug$_7$; ug$_5$; ug$_x$
(|BAD.BAD|) "plural and imperfect singular stem of uš [to die]" Akk. *mâtu*.
http://psd.museum.upenn.edu/nepsd-frame.html
[See also] mītu [ÚŠ :] (adj.) dead , deceased , departed ; Cf. mâtu, mītūtān
http://www.assyrianlanguages.org/akkadian/dosearch.php
350 Amar Annus, The God Ninurta in the Mythology and Royal Ideology of Ancient
Mesopotamia, State Archives of Assyria Studies, Volume XIV Helsinki 2002. Pg. 19
351 Ibid.
352 1911 Encyclopædia Britannica, Volume 23: Variations include as Ῥομφά,
Ῥεμφάν, Ῥεμφάμ, Ῥαιφάν, Ῥεφάν [Rompha, Remphan, Rempham, Remphan]
353 "The arrow (šukudu) mentioned by Tiglath-pileser I is astronomically Ninurta's
star Sirius (see CAD s.v.), and the Arrow might be a metaphor for Ninurta himself.
In SAA Anzu III 10-11, both the same word for 'arrow'"... Amar Annus, The God
Ninurta in the Mythology and Royal Ideology of Ancient Mesopotamia, State
Archives of Assyria Studies, Volume XIV Helsinki 2002. Pg. 102
354 http://usccb.org/bible/amos/5/
355 Amar Annus, The God Ninurta in the Mythology and Royal Ideology of Ancient
Mesopotamia, State Archives of Assyria Studies, Volume XIV Helsinki 2002. Pg. 104
356 Ibid. Pg. 133-135
357 Amar Annus, The God Ninurta in the Mythology and Royal Ideology of Ancient
Mesopotamia, State Archives of Assyria Studies, Volume XIV Helsinki 2002. Pg. 104
358 Amar Annus, The God Ninurta in the Mythology and Royal Ideology of Ancient
Mesopotamia, State Archives of Assyria Studies, Volume XIV Helsinki 2002. Pg. 104
359 W. von Soden, "Die Unterweltsvision eines assyrischen Kronprinzen," ZA 43
[1936] 17:56; Angim III 38. For the Annunaki and Igigi gods, cf. W. von Soden, "Zur
wiederherstellung der marduk-gebete bms 11 und 12," *Iraq* 31 (1969), 85:32; M.
Civil, "Commentaries from Nippur," *JNES* 33 (1974), 336:13. Cited in: Pre-
publication version: Tyler R. Yoder, "Ezekiel 29:3 and Its Ancient Near Eastern
Context" Vetus Testamentum 63 (2013) 486-96.
360 Ibid. Nergal's title is [*ú-šum*]-*gal-lu şīru tābik imti elišunu*, cf (*CAD* U/W, Pg. 330)
361 Amar Annus, The God Ninurta in the Mythology and Royal Ideology of Ancient
Mesopotamia, State Archives of Assyria Studies, Volume XIV Helsinki 2002. book 3
Pg. 135-138
362 Pg. 104
363 Frans Wiggermann, Nergal, Reallexikon der Assyriologie (RIA) 9 1999 Pg. 215-
226.
364 Ibid.
365 bilga [FRUIT] (4x: Ur III, Old Babylonian) wr. bil$_2$-ga "fresh fruit; male ancestor"
Akk. *inbu*
pabilga [RELATION] (14x: Old Babylonian) wr. pa-bil$_2$-ga; pa-bil$_3$-ga; pa$_4$-bil$_2$-ga; pa-
bil-ga; pa$_4$-bil-ga; pa$_4$-bi-ga "a kinship term" Akk. *Abu*. saĝ [HEAD] (3582x: ED IIIa,
ED IIIb, Old Akkadian, Lagash II, Ur III, Early Old Babylonian, Old Babylonian,

unknown) wr. saĝ "head; person; capital" Akk. *qaqqadu*; *rēšu*
http://psd.museum.upenn.edu/nepsd-frame.html

[366] http://oracc.museum.upenn.edu/amgg/listofdeities/pabilsag/index.html

[367] http://www.skyscript.co.uk/babylonian_sagittarius.pdf

[368] The Dictionary Of Deities And Demons In The Bible, Eds. K. Van Der Toorn, Bob Becking And Pieter W. Van Der Horst (Boston, 1999). Ninurta

[369] (Richter 2004: 264). http://www.skyscript.co.uk/babylonian_sagittarius.pdf

[370] It measured 51 cm tall, 24 x 25 centimeters wide and weighed 61.50 kilograms (135 lbs).

[371] Museum number: British Museum # 90829. Registration number: 1882,0522.1798 The stone was written in cuneiform in Akkadian . The text contains a deed of gift recording a grant of fifty 'gur' of corn-land in the province of Bit-Pir'-Amurri by Meli-Shipak to Khasardu, the son of Sume."https://www.britishmuseum.org/collection/object/W_1882-0522-1798

[372] Pabilsag's association with the netherworld could be due to his syncretism with the underworld deity Nergal. oracc.museum.upenn.edu/amgg/listofdeities/pabilsag/index.html

[373] Museum number: British Museum # 90829. Registration number: 1882,0522.1798 https://www.britishmuseum.org/collection/object/W_1882-0522-1798

[374] (Richter 2004: 264). http://www.skyscript.co.uk/babylonian_sagittarius.pdf Gavin White www.skyscript.co.uk/white.html Nov 2009.

[375] Ancient Mesopotamian Gods and Goddesses

[376] Amar Annus, The God Ninurta in the Mythology and Royal Ideology of Ancient Mesopotamia, State Archives of Assyria Studies, Volume XIV Helsinki 2002.

[377] BDAG Ἀπολλύων: "Apollyon, the Destroyer, tr. of Ἀβαδδών (q.v., which itself is a tr. of אֲבַדּוֹן) Rev 9:11. (Whether the writer of Rev implied a connection with the deity Apollo cannot be determined)."

[378] Note the composite features of this creature: 1) Like a horse running to battle, 2) Lion's head, 3) Man's face, 4) Something like crowns, 5) Woman's hair, 6) Lion's teeth, 7) Something like breastplates of iron, 8) Noisy wings, 9) Scorpion's tail with stingers, 10) Serpent-head tails, 11) Fiery red, hyacinth blue, and sulfur yellow iron-like breastplate, 12) Fire and brimstone from mouth.

[379] The Greek text does not specifically state that people were sitting on the horses. It just says in the vision something was sitting on the horses with a chest, (thorax) area of red, blue, and yellow.

[380] The number of the army [στρατευμάτων strateumaton] of the horsemen [ιππικού] was two hundred million" (Rev 9:16).

[381] Hal Lindsey created a myth of a 200-million-man Chinese army. He says, "China is the beginning of the formation of this great power called "the kings of the east" by the apostle John ... a recent television documentary ... quoted the boast of the Chinese themselves that they could field a "people's army" of 200 million militiamen. In their own boast they named the same number as the Biblical prediction. Coincidence?" (Hal Lindsey, The Late Great Planet Earth (Grand Rapids,

MI: Zondervan, 1970. Pg. 86.) We should point out that China's "people's army" means two-hundred-million citizens wielding guns not a trained, standing army. Furthermore, the shape of the locusts was like horses running into battle, not like Chinese citizens holding guns. That interpretation is ethnocentric with the Chinese being the bad guys and the Americans being the good guys.

[382] Liddell-Scott-Jones Classical Greek Lexicon ιππικου: 1. "of a horse or horses." 2. "of horsemen or chariots." 3. "of riding or horsemanship, equestrian."

[383] Frans Wiggermann, Nergal, Reallexikon der Assyriologie (RlA) 9 1999 Pg. 215-226.

[384] θωρακας ως θωρακας σιδηρους these creatures have a chest area (thorax) like iron, not necessarily armor.

[385] Etymonline "Latin pēnis 'penis,' earlier 'tail,' ..."the meaning of pēnītus ['furnished with a tail']...suggest...'tail' is original, and 'penis' metaphorically derived from it... https://www.etymonline.com/search?q=penis

[386] Gavin White points this out in his paper.

[387] Amar Annus, The God Ninurta in the Mythology and Royal Ideology of Ancient Mesopotamia, State Archives of Assyria Studies, Volume XIV Helsinki 2002. Pg. 183

[388] Gods, Demons and Symbols of Ancient Mesopotamia An Illustrated Dictionary, Jeremy Black and Anthony Green Illustrations by Tessa Rickards THE BRITISH MUSEUM PRESS 1992.

[389] Robertson's Word Pictures, Matt 4:3.

[390] See the Awakening Report: Mysteries of Mt. Hermon, https://youtu.be/yjiZHLnhIRQ August 25, 2020.

[391] Again, thanks to Dr. Heiser for bringing out the nuances of this scene.

[392] https://www.law.cornell.edu/wex/adverse_possession

[393] Amar Annus, The God Ninurta in the Mythology and Royal Ideology of Ancient Mesopotamia, State Archives of Assyria Studies, Volume XIV Helsinki 2002. Pg. 14.

[394] Ibid. Pg. 83-pg 88

[395] ISBE, Gadara, (Ant., XIII, iii, 3)

[396] BDAG επετιμησε

[397] *The* Dictionary of Deities and Demons in the Bible, eds. K. van der Toorn, Bob Becking and Pieter W. van der Horst (Boston, 1999). Pg. 161-162

[398] By Bill Rice from Flat Rock, MI, USA - Caesarea Philippi, CC BY 2.0, https://commons.wikimedia.org/w/index.php?curid=35423945

[399] Josephus, Wars of the Jews 1:21:3

[400] https://www.land-of-the-bible.com/Caesarea_Philippi

[401] Bashan: Dictionary of Deities and Demons in the Bible, eds. K. van der Toorn, Bob Becking and Pieter W. van der Horst (Boston, 1999). . Pgs. 162-163.

[402] Bashan: Dictionary of Deities and Demons in the Bible, eds. K. van der Toorn, Bob Becking and Pieter W. van der Horst (Boston, 1999). . Pgs. 162-163. See: (KTU 1.1 08:2-3...)

[403] http://www.assyrianlanguages.org/akkadian/

[404] MARCUS, JOEL. "The Gates of Hades and the Keys of the Kingdom (Matt 16:18-19)." The Catholic Biblical Quarterly 50, no. 3 (1988): 443-55. Accessed September 30, 2020. http://www.jstor.org/stable/43717704.

[405] BDAG κατισχυσουσιν

[406] MARCUS, JOEL. "The Gates of Hades and the Keys of the Kingdom (Matt 16:18-19)." The Catholic Biblical Quarterly 50, no. 3 (1988): 443-55. Accessed September 30, 2020. http://www.jstor.org/stable/43717704.

[407] Ibid.

[408] Ibid.

[409] Marcus notes: "As the phrase "gates of Hades" is used in Matt 16:18, it seems to include not just the city of the dead itself but also its inhabitants, especially its demonic rulers. Such a connotation for "gates" is in line with what we see in the LXX version of Ps 24:7, which has altered the MT apostrophe of the gates of the city to an apostrophe of the rulers of the city." MARCUS, JOEL. "The Gates of Hades and the Keys of the Kingdom (Matt 16:18-19)." The Catholic Biblical Quarterly 50, no. 3 (1988): 443-55. Accessed September 30, 2020. http://www.jstor.org/stable/43717704.

[410] Ibid.

[411] "This mountain is called *Baal-Hermon*, Jdg 3:3; 1 Ch 5:23, possibly because Baal was there worshipped. (It is more than probable that some part of Hermon was the scene of the transfiguration, as it stands near Caesarea Philippi, where we know Christ was just before that event...)" *Smith's Bible Dictionary: Hermon.*

[412] Charlesworth notes: "No help is provided by studying the ancient translations of Psalm 68. The translator of the Septuagint in Ps 68[67]:23[22] was confused. After about the seventh century CE, in later minuscules, the text is presented with a capitalized "from" and a transliterated Bashan, (εκ βασαν). The text is ancient, since it has influenced the Vulgate: "Dixit Dominus: 'Ex Basan convertam, /convertam in profundum maris; ..." The translator of the passage in the Peshitta has rendered מבשן with the interesting *dmn byt sn.*, "who (are) from the house of teeth," or better idiomatically "who (are) from the edge of a steep rock." The Peshitta text probably resulted from a Syriac scribe's guess concerning the meaning of the Hebrew. That translation presents a meaningful rendering of Ps 68[67 in the LXX, but 68 in the Peshitta]. A lucid, even meaningful, rendering, however, should not be confused with an accurate translation of the original Hebrew." Charlesworth, J.H., Revealing The Genius Of Biblical Authors: Symbology, Archaeology, And Theology. Pg. 136

[413] *Easton, M.G., ed. (1897), Illustrated Bible Dictionary... (also known as Easton's Bible Dictionary) (3rd ed.),* London: T. Nelson & Sons: Hermon.

[414] Charlesworth, J.H., Revealing The Genius Of Biblical Authors: Symbology, Archaeology, And Theology. Pg. 137

[415] *The* Dictionary of Deities and Demons in the Bible, eds. K. van der Toorn, Bob Becking and Pieter W. van der Horst (Boston, 1999). Pg. 161-162

[416] Ibid.

[417] Ibid.

[418] Ibid.

[419] Discovering the Language of Jesus - Hamp

[420] TWOT: Abir

[421] Ibid.

[422] Against Heresies, Book 4, Chap. 27, Para. 2

[423] BDAG κηρύσσω

[424] Bob Utley, "You Can Understand the Bible," Bible Lessons International, March 2013. Retrieved from the Word Bible Software.

[425] Blasphemy, according to BDAG, is often known in relation to transcendent or associated entities slander, revile, defame, speak irreverently/impiously/disrespectfully of or about βλασφημία.

[426] John 12:31; 14:30; 16:11; Dan 10:13, 20; Job 1:6, 7

[427] Heb 9:16, 17; Col 2:14-15

[428] Mat 2:16

[429] Mat 4:1-11

[430] John 12:31; 14:30; 16:11

[431] Exod 33:11; Lev 26:12; Num 12:8; Matt 5:8, 18:10; Rom 8:19-22; 1Cor 13:12; 1John 3:2; Rev 6:14, 7:14, 21:3, 22:4, 2Pet 3:10, Isa 34:4

[432] Dan 7:18; Isa 60:14

[433] Isa 65:9

[434] Isa 65:22

[435] Job 1:12, 2:6, 1:10

[436] Dan 12:1

[437] Jude 1:9

[438] Rom 11:19, Eph 2:19

[439] 1Chr 16:13; Ps 33:12, 105:6, 43, 135:4; Isa 45:4, 65:9, 22; Deut 14:2

[440] Exod 15:15, 19:5, 34:9; Deut 4:20 7:6, 9:26

[441] Eph 1:4 See my latest paper Why God Did Not Elect Calvinists Part Two

[442] Eph 3:6-10; 2:12, 13, 19; 3:11

[443] Gen 12:1-2

[444] Rom 11:29; Gen 15

[445] Num 22:12, 18, 35; 24:10-13; Deut 23:5

[446] Num 24:14, 31:16; Mic 6:5; Rev 2:14

[447] Rom 2, Eph 2:12

[448] Rom 11:1-2, 16-24

[449] Dan 7:18; Duet 28:13; Isa 62:7

[450] He was proven accurate through the doctrine of Chrysostom Augustine and others who taught that the Hebrews had forfeited God's election and the nations, which had been brought into the commonwealth of Israel, had replaced the Hebrews! In time the nations persecuted God's people in the name of the very one who had come to restore them. The Bible is replete with passages where God said that he would never abandon his people, Israel, (1Sam 12:22; Ps 94:14; Jer 31:35-

37) whom he had elected and foreknown. (Rom 11:1-2; 1Pet 1:2) There is also a plethora of evidence outside of the Bible which demonstrate how Lucifer was able to subtly convince the nations which professed a relationship to Jesus that they had replaced the Hebrews. Consider *The Church Is Israel Now: The Transfer of Conditional Privilege* by Calvin Charles D. Provan. ISBN 978-1-879998-39-1.

[451] Dan 10:13

[452] John 1:11

[453] Heb 9:16, 17

[454] Rom 11:18

[455] 1Sam 12:22; Ps 94:14; Jer 31:35-37; Rom 11:1-2

[456] Rom 11:13-18

[457] Mat 22:1-14

[458] See Why God Did Not Elect Calvinists at douglashamp.com

[459] Origen tells us that the Church had no clearly defined teaching on their genesis; his view was that the Devil, after becoming apostate, induced many of the angels to fall away with him; these fallen angels were the demons *(De Prine.* pref. 6; Tatian, *Adv. Gr.* 20; cf. Rev 12:4). CF The Dictionary Of Deities And Demons In The Bible, Eds. K. Van Der Toorn, Bob Becking And Pieter W. Van Der Horst (Boston, 1999). Demons Pg. 238

[460] Theological Dictionary of the New Testament - Abridged Edition – demons

[461] BDAG: δαιμον

[462] Philo, *On the Giants*, II, 6

[463] Bridgeway Dict: Demons

[464] The Dictionary Of Deities And Demons In The Bible, Eds. K. Van Der Toorn, Bob Becking And Pieter W. Van Der Horst (Boston, 1999). Demons Pg. 238

[465] The Electronic Text Corpus of Sumerian Literature (http://etcsl.orinst.ox.ac.uk/section4/tr4051.htm)

[466] The Dictionary Of Deities And Demons In The Bible, Eds. K. Van Der Toorn, Bob Becking And Pieter W. Van Der Horst (Boston, 1999). Demons Pg. 238

[467] Theological Workbook of the Old Testament Shed. We know shedu is a deity because of the DINGIR symbol. See: University of Pennsylvania Sumerian lexicon: "šedu [SPIRIT] … [[dšedu2]]…Akk. šēdu "protective deity." http://psd.museum.upenn.edu/nepsd-frame.html

[468] Amar Annus, The God Ninurta in the Mythology and Royal Ideology of Ancient Mesopotamia, State Archives of Assyria Studies, Volume XIV Helsinki 2002. book 3 Pg. 142.

[469] The Dictionary Of Deities And Demons In The Bible, Eds. K. Van Der Toorn, Bob Becking And Pieter W. Van Der Horst (Boston, 1999). Demons Pg. 238

[470] The Dictionary Of Deities And Demons In The Bible, Eds. K. Van Der Toorn, Bob Becking And Pieter W. Van Der Horst (Boston, 1999). Demons Pg. 238 notes "According to Justin Martyr, 'the angels …' 'were captivated by love of women and engendered children who are called demons' (2 *Apol. 5;* cf. Gen 6: 1-4; I Enoch 6-21: Job. 4:22; 5: lff.; Jude 6)." Justin Martyr apparently thought such spirits

(demons) were a new class of beings, yet such a doctrine is incongruent with God's character.

[471] Rob Bryanton, Imagining the Tenth Dimension: A New Way of Thinking About Time and Space Paperback, 2007

[472] Das Wesen der Materie [The Nature of Matter], speech at Florence, Italy (1944) (from Archiv zur Geschichte der Max-Planck-Gesellschaft, Abt. Va, RePg. 11 Planck, Nr. 1797)

[473] http://www.pbs.org/wgbh/nova/einstein/lrk-hand-emc2expl.html. Not surprisingly, the Bible is millennia ahead of both Planck and Einstein. In Genesis 1:2 the Spirit of God is fluttering (*merachefet* מרחפת) over the face of the waters. The Hebrew term is the same action as a bird brooding, fluttering, or hovering over its nest.

[474] http://www.pbs.org/wgbh/nova/einstein/lrk-hand-emc2expl.html

[475] The Theological Wordbook of the Old Testament (TWOT) notes the noun "evil" is defined as "being that condition or action which in his (God's) sight is unacceptable (Jer 52:2; Mal 2:17; cf. Neh 9:28)," (TWOT עַל ra).

[476] Baker's Evangelical Dictionary of Biblical Theology defines evil in the following manner: "what is right was what was ordained by God, and what is wrong was what was proscribed by him, deviation from this paradigm constitutes what is evil." Baker's Evangelical Dictionary of Biblical Theology (1996): Evil.

[477] Roscoe, Will; Murray, Stephen O. (1997), Islamic Homosexualities: Culture, History, and Literature, New York City, New York: New York University Press, ISBN 978-0-8147-7467-0. Pg. 66.

[478] *http://notchesblog.com/2017/05/02/evidence-for-trans-lives-in-sumer/*

[479] The Dictionary Of Deities And Demons In The Bible, Eds. K. Van Der Toorn, Bob Becking And Pieter W. Van Der Horst (Boston, 1999).Pg. 454

[480] https://www.telegraph.co.uk/technology/facebook/10930654/Facebooks-71-gender-options-come-to-UK-users.html

[481] https://cnsnews.com/news/article/michael-w-chapman/johns-hopkins-psychiatrist-transgender-mental-disorder-sex-change

[482] The challenge we are faced with, due to Tyndale's unfortunate choice of using the word *Eástre,* is there is a lot of confusion as to what people mean when they say, "Happy Easter." Some are convinced that everybody who celebrates *Eástre* is participating in a pagan activity. Certainly, Easter bunnies and hunting for eggs are pagan activities. However, most followers of Christ who say, "Happy Easter", are celebrating the resurrection of Jesus and are not celebrating this goddess. Ideally, we ought to call it *First Fruits* because that's when Jesus rose from the dead.

[483] If it is a bad army, how can God call it his army? If it is His, it ought to be good. Right? God called Nebuchadnezzar, his servant when he was destroying Jerusalem. God can use people who are unrighteous, for a righteous purpose. For example, God used Nebuchadnezzar, who had his own selfish, evil desires to judge and destroy Jerusalem before he had his conversion experience. Ultimately, it will be God's army that He will use to accomplish a greater purpose.

www.ingramcontent.com/pod-product-compliance
Lightning Source LLC
La Vergne TN
LVHW040812010325
804864LV00007B/44